Communication in Cognitive Behavioral Therapy

Michela Rimondini
Editor

Communication in Cognitive Behavioral Therapy

 Springer

Editor
Michela Rimondini
Department of Public Health and Community Medicine
University of Verona
Piazzale L.A. Scuro 10
37134 Verona
Italy
michela.rimondini@univr.it

ISBN 978-1-4419-6806-7   e-ISBN 978-1-4419-6807-4
DOI 10.1007/978-1-4419-6807-4
Springer New York Dordrecht Heidelberg London

Printed on acid-free paper

Springer is part of Springer Science+Business Media (www.springer.com)

Preface

There are certainly several books that address the topic of interpersonal communication in the healing context, from a theoretical as well as pragmatic perspective. The peculiarity of the present manual is that it deepens the process of communication in the specific setting of Cognitive Behavioral Therapy (CBT). In psychotherapy the ability to explore and share meanings through a masterful use of communication skills is the main tool in the hands of the clinician. Specific therapeutic strategies such as *debating* or *cognitive restructuring* are effective insofar as the clinician shows proficiency in illustrating and applying them through a proper patient centered language.

The main aim of this handbook is to provide to the reader a comprehensive overview of the core issues regarding patient–therapist communication in CBT, moving from the basic assumption of inter-correlation between research, teaching and clinical activity. Indeed, for several reasons that widen from economical to ethical aspects, an evidence based clinical practice is strongly advocated by patients and healthcare providers. This brings to the need to overcome the methodological difficulties that historically discouraged research of communication in psychotherapy and to promote the development of methods capable to capture the complexity of this multifaceted process. Nevertheless the available clinical evidences and the knowledge collected up to know, have to be spread out to experienced and inexperienced healthcare providers, applying updated teaching methods based on adult learning models.

For this reason this book has been written by many different hands, since I have brought together a number of experts in psychotherapy, teaching and research coming from various backgrounds. Therefore the reader will be asked to navigate through the heterogeneity of styles that characterizes each chapter, in order to grasp the common denominator that integrate and collapse all contributions together. Nonetheless each chapter is intended as a stand-alone, not necessarily connected with the previous or the following, for the purpose of prompting answers to highly targeted and specific questions, without implying the reading of the whole book. Hopefully according to this aspect, the volume will be useful to a variety of users, ranging from statisticians or researchers interested in methods of analysis of therapist–patient communication, to faculties involved in the teaching of psychotherapy as well as of course to all those approaching at different levels of expertise and title CBT (psychologists, psychiatrists, counselor, nurses, etc...).

The book is divided into three main sections, introduced by a general synopsis where the main background theories in interpersonal communication and a selection of the existing systems of analysis of communication in psychotherapy are presented. *Part 1* focuses on the core verbal and non verbal communication (Chap. 5) skills applied during the consultation with patients, according to the three main functions of a clinical encounter, which are data gathering (Chap. 2), relationship building (Chap. 3) and information giving (Chap. 4). *Part 2* shifts the focus from the general description of communication skills in clinical setting to the analysis of their application in the three main disorder areas: mood disorders (Chap. 6), anxiety disorders (Chap. 7) and psychosis (Chap. 8). Finally, *Part 3* collapse together teaching and research insights, offering an outline of the existing methods and evidences. Chapter 9 contains a detailed description of learner-centered techniques that can enhance teaching in psychotherapy. The last chapters treat the theme of how to analysis the communication process in CBT following two different approaches: quantitative (Chap. 10) and qualitative (Chap. 11).

Verona, Italy   Michela Rimondini

Contents

Contributors

Barbara Barcaccia
Associazione di Psicologia Cognitivia APC, Rome, Italy

Franco Baldini
Associazione di Psicologia Cognitiva, Verona, Italy

Svein Hugo Bergvik
Department of Clinical Psychiatry, University of Tromsø, Tromsø, Norway

Hanneke De Haes
Department of Medical Psychology, Academic Medical Centre, Amsterdam,
The Netherlands

Lidia Del Piccolo
Department of Public Health and Community Medicine, University of Verona,
Verona, Italy

Arnstein Finset
Department of Behavioural Science in Medicine, University of Oslo,
Oslo, Norway

Claudia Goss
Department of Public Health and Community Medicine, Section of
Psychiatry and Clinical Psychology Organisation, University of Verona,
Verona, Italy

Elizabeth Kuipers
Department of Psychology, Institute of Psychiatry, King's College London,
London, UK

Francesco Mancini
Associazione di Psicologia Cognitivia APC, Rome, Italy

Maria Angela Mazzi
Department of Public Health and Community Medicine, University of Verona, Verona, Italy

Francesca Moretti
Department of Public Health and Community Medicine, University of Verona, Verona, Italy

Juliana Onwumere
Department of Psychology, Institute of Psychiatry, King's College London, London, England

Michela Rimondini
Department of Public Health and Community Medicine, University of Verona, Verona, Italy

Alberto Rossi
Department of Public Health and Community Medicine, University of Verona, Verona, Italy

Angelo Maria Saliani
Associazione di Psicologia Cognitivia APC, Rome, Italy

Jonathan Silverman
School of Clinical Medicine, Addenbrooke's Hospital, Cambridge, UK

Rolf Wynn
Institute of Clinical Medicine (FT), University of Tromsø, Tromsø, Norway

Christa Zimmermann
Department of Public Health and Community Medicine, University of Verona, Verona, Italy

Chapter 1
Background Theories and Main Systems of Analysis of Communication in Cognitive-Behavioral Therapy

Michela Rimondini

1.1 Introduction

The etymology of the term "communication" comes from the Latin expression *communicatio,* which identifies the action of sharing things. The concept of reciprocity seems therefore to be fondant in the original meaning of this word and definitely is in the connotation assumed in the present book. Indeed, in psychotherapy the healing process is mainly based on the combinations of words that allow the sharing of values, beliefs, feelings, and perceptions between two or more people. Through his narratives, the patient offers the description and significance of the presenting problems according to his perspective; the therapist has to return it enriched with a reformulation that contains elements of support and utility for the patient.

Communication has been largely studied over the centuries; a plentitude of theories and models have been produced. This topic is approached by many different disciplines, including anthropology, sociology, economy, psychology, philosophy, engineering, and many others. According to the different perspectives that can be assumed, a wide range of possible definitions is available, each identifying a specific aspect of the process.

As the object of this book is communication in cognitive-behavioral therapy, I will focus just on a specific area of *communication theory* (intended as the whole of the existing models on communication): interpersonal communication. After a brief introduction to the main concepts and theories on interpersonal communication, I will move to describe the dyadic interaction that happens in the healing context between the healthcare provider and the client. Particularly, I will focus on the clinician's application of communication skills during the consultation, describing some of the existing evidence on the effectiveness of a patient-centered approach in terms of clinical outcomes. The last section will propose an overview

M. Rimondini (✉)
Department of Public Health and Community Medicine,
University of Verona, Piazzale L.A. Scuro 10, 37134 Verona, Italy
e-mail: michela.rimondini@univr.it

M. Rimondini (ed.), *Communication in Cognitive Behavioral Therapy,*
DOI 10.1007/978-1-4419-6807-4_1, © Springer Science+Business Media, LLC 2011

of some of the existing instruments purposely developed for the analysis of clinician–patient communication.

1.2 Interpersonal Communication: Models, Definitions, and Key Notes

Hartley (1999) defines as interpersonal communication those interactions where *two individuals, face to face,* relate to each other, and the *form* and *content* of this interaction reflect *personal characteristics, social role,* and *type of relationship.* In this definition all uses of a medium of communication that stand between the sender and the receiver (papers, video, telephone) are excluded. Mentioning the *role* of the two speakers implies a heterogeneous range of possible relationships, which widen from the family context (e.g., mother–son), to the education setting (teacher–learner), and of course to the therapeutic context as well (doctor/psychotherapist–patient).

The role played by the speakers is one of the situational factors that, together with personal characteristics, provide a contextual backdrop of communication. Acting conjointly, they determine how people conduct themselves during social interactions (Hargie et al. 2000). According to Argyle et al. (1981), in any situation individuals act in accordance with more or less clearly recognized sets of expectations placed upon their role and social status. In addition to this element, the author indicates other free sources of influence: goal structure, rules, repertoire of elements, sequences of behavior, situational concepts, language and speech, and physical environment.

In the definition of interpersonal communication, a historically controversial topic is whether or not it is inevitable. Theories (Watzlawick et al. 1967; Scheflen 1974; Carson 1969) hypothesizing that "one cannot not communicate" rely on the assumption that to the extent that one person's behavior is contingent on that of another's, we will regard communication as having taken place between them. On the other hand, a few authors (Ekman and Friesen 1969; Wiener et al. 1972) have stressed the importance of *intentionality,* meant as a deliberate intention to communicate, transmit, or make available information. Bara and Cutica (2002) include this element together with shared attention, shared belief, and theory of the mind among the four core components of the ability to communicate. In psychotherapy, for example, intentionality is represented by the distinction between a patient's passive manifestation of the symptoms and his or her selection and production of words or nonverbal behaviors calculated to inform the therapist. The distinction between informative and communicative behavior is tricky, and in reality it is quite difficult to draw a line that divides one from the other. It is essential to remember that in clinical psychology and psychotherapy, both have strong implications in the assessment and intervention sessions.

Few models stress the hypothesis of a *goal-driven* interpersonal communication (Tracy and Coupland 1990; Kellermann 1992). In other words, an individual's inclination to relate one to each other may be fostered by the presence of an explicit or implicit aim. Berger and Calabrese (1975) suggested that what motivates communication acts is the attempt to collect information in order to reduce the uncertainty of relationships, which means to make more predictable and explainable present and future interactions with other people. Over the years, this theory has been further developed (Planalp and Honeycutt 1985). In particular, Douglas (1990) has shown that by asking questions, individuals reduce their uncertainty and consequently increase self-disclosure. Heath and Bryant (2000) have reformulated Bergers' model, advocating for a balance between stability and change, since according to the results of their studies, high levels of certainty also positively correlate with relationship-building inhibition. Recently, cognitive sciences have approached the study of the existing interdependency of goals and belief in cognitive agents (Castelfranchi and Paglieri 2007), and its implication for the psychotherapy setting in terms of belief changes and goal dynamics has been explored (Miceli and Castelfranchi 2005).

Interpersonal communication represents an *ongoing process*, an unfolding flow of single events chained to each other (Craig 1999). Communication requires that at least two contribute to the dynamic sequence of events in which each affects and is affected by the other in a system of reciprocal determination (Hargie and Dickson 2004). This widespread belief that the most appropriate way of studying interpersonal communication is considering it as a process seems not to be consistent in the research. Philosophically, one might argue that process is something that by definition can't be captured and each time we try to identify a unit of analysis, we no longer have the "process" (Knapp and Daly 2002). During the last decades, this has been partially overcome by the introduction of a new approach of interaction analysis, which observes specific sequences of verbal or nonverbal behaviors across a given time span (turn, specific conversation, whole psychotherapy, etc.) (Zimmermann et al. 2003; Goss et al. 2005; Del Piccolo et al. 2007). For further deepening of the topic, see Chapter 10.

1.3 From Interpersonal Communication to Communication Skills

During the 1990s, a variety of approaches investigating what actually happens during interpersonal communication flourished and an increasing interest toward the identification of communication skills and specific communication patters of analysis led to the development of quantitative and qualitative methods for human interaction examination. New issues emerged in various contexts, such as workplace, cultures, mass media, education, and health care as well.

In the clinical setting, the study of *formal* aspects of communication, meant as the way a message is sent, includes both patients' and healthcare providers' units of speech. For example, patients' expressions can be analyzed in terms of syntactic correctness/richness and use of bizarre, evocative, or repetitive sentences. Provider utterances can be processed in order to check which skills (i.e., open questions, summarizing, emphatic comments) are used, or what communication patterns seem to be more effective during interactions with patients.

What drove the efforts of researchers, clinicians, and educators to deepen and expand the study of communication skills is their positive impact on important clinical variables such as prognosis, adherence to treatment, or personal satisfaction. The next section will present some of the main research performed in this field; these data are partially reprised in other chapters of the book (i.e., Chapters 2–5), when stressing the importance of founding one's own professionalism (whenever it is possible) on an evidence-based model.

1.3.1   Communication Skills and Clinical Outcomes: Why Effective Communication Enhances the Quality of Care

As an Italian writer, to explain the importance of communication skills for good clinical practice, I will use a metaphor where a good clinician with poor communication skills is compared to an excellent bottle of Barolo without a corkscrew. The bottle may be produced by selecting the best grapes from the best vineyards, aged in barrels made of fine wood, and preserved according to the ideal temperature and humidity conditions, but if it cannot be opened, no one will have the opportunity to appreciate its smell or taste. Similarly, a clinician with an excellent theoretical background from the best schools of medicine, psychology, or psychotherapy, passionate about her job, and with years of experience in the field will waste all her talent if is she is not able to disclose these competencies and make them available for the patient. Reversibly, having a corkscrew in the hand enables us to open the bottle of wine, but does not guarantee that we will make the best use of it, like using it for cooking or for getting drunk. Likewise, the appropriateness in micro-skill application comes from the theoretical background, clinical experiences, personal attitudes, and self-awareness of the clinician, which means that the professionalism relies on the co-presence of all these elements blended together.

Regarding the impact of communication style on patient satisfaction and collaboration, it has been noted that directive communication, typical of the biomedical approach, is appreciated only by a few special categories of patients: those with acute organ problems, those in a state of emergency (Buller and Buller 1987), or those with a high level of anxiety (Graugaard et al. 2003), while, in general, patient-centered communication techniques are related to higher patient satisfaction (Hall and Dornan 1988; Putnam et al. 1985; Stewart 1995; Maly et al. 1999; Taira et al. 1997; Kinnersley et al. 1999). In particular, a holistic approach to the person, considering the entire lifeworld (Barry et al. 2001), raises patient satisfaction. Brown et al. (1996) indicate as effective the ability to group and integrate together, in a shared description, the "raw" information that comes from the patient and the provider's interpretations of the problem based on his or her competence. In particular, the ability to recognize and elicit verbal and nonverbal cues and concerns, through the use of back-channel responses or open questioning, increases the probability of obtaining new information and makes clients feel listened to and taken into consideration.

Even the possibility to express personal expectation and theories on the presenting disease is positively correlated with higher levels of satisfaction and improves patients' attitude toward their condition (Jackson et al. 2001; Lazare et al. 1975).

An indirect implication of raising patient satisfaction, as well as improving the relationship with their healthcare provider, is the prevention of complaints of malpractice (Kaplan et al. 1994) and drop-out (Rossi et al. 2002).

Other external indices for the evaluation of the interview, such as adherence to treatment, prognosis, and client's collaboration in the therapeutic process, have shown to be positively affected by the use of patient-centered communication skills (Svensson et al. 2000; Mead and Bower 2002; Bodenheimer et al. 2002).

Last but not least, in terms of the effect played on the psychotherapeutic process, a proper use of emotion-handling communication techniques, such as empathic comments and legitimating, has been shown to create and strengthen the therapeutic relationship. It is known that during a first psychiatric visit, patients might feel worried because they do not know exactly what to expect (Michaels and Sevitt 1978). The negative effect anxiety plays on cognitive functioning is widely recognized; for example, subjects tend to overestimate the probability of negative events (Ley et al. 1976; Butler and Mathews 1983) or process information following a selection bias that leads the patient to perceive situations as more threatening (Eysenck et al. 1987).

1.4 Communication Skills in the Medical Setting

Over the last two decades, medicine has witnessed a growing interest in the topic of communication. Moving from Rogers' (1946) client-centered therapy, to the philosophical contributions of Jaspers (1913), and to the biopsychosocial model of Engel (1977), a new way of approaching patients during the medical interview has been developed that now is largely known as the patient-centered approach (Tate 1994; Cohen-Cole 1991; Novack et al. 1997; Lipkin et al. 1995).

The clinical functions that the doctor has to achieve according to this approach expand those previously identified by the traditional biomedical model and can be summarized by referring to the model proposed by Cohen-Cole (1991) (see also Chapters 2, 3, and 4): (1) relationship building (therapeutic alliance) and elicitation and management of patient's emotions and feelings; (2) data gathering and exchange of information with the patient in order to understand the reason for his visit from a holistic point of view, which takes into account, besides symptoms or health-related issues, also the psychosocial context; (3) giving information and sharing treatment plans with the patient.

The transition to this new approach raised the complexity of doctor–patient interactions, revealing a lack of competency in those areas where previously doctors were not used to proceeding. To investigate the emotional experience of a patient, his expectations of recovery, his support network, or to motivate him to change a disruptive habit turned out to be a very difficult task for doctors. This has led to the necessity to integrate the anatomical and physiological background knowledge traditionally taught in the university medical curriculum with skills aimed at implementing doctors' communicational/relational style.

Consequently, a growing interest in the study of communication processes and the identification of effective communication techniques has flourished during the last decades. Doctor–patient communication has gradually become a quite popular topic that each year produces a greater number of publications that consider various aspects, such as the effectiveness of the theoretical model (Smith 1996; Zimmermann and Tansella 1996), the validation of medical interview classification systems (Brown 1995; Cape 1996; Roter 1993; Ong et al. 1995), or training in the use of communication techniques (Goldberg et al. 1993; Gask 1992; Smith et al. 1998).

1.4.1   Translating Communication Skills and Patient-Centered Approach from the Medical Setting to Psychotherapy

The consolidation of evidence-based medicine over the years has implied that even in psychotherapy, many efforts have been made in order to experimentally validate the effectiveness of the interventions proposed. Without any doubt, CBT has been one of the most fertile in the production of trials and efficacy studies. However, the detailed analysis of the communicative exchange, regardless of the psychotherapeutic techniques applied, has remained a relatively unexplored field of investigation. Little is known about how psychotherapists communicate with patients during the encounter and even less on which communication skills are more effective in the patient's eyes.

In order to partially bridge this gap, the impressive body of evidence collected until now in medicine could be partially applied to the field of psychotherapy. But to what extent is this possible? Which cautions should we follow when comparing these two settings? The present sections will outline divergences and similarities in the meaning assumed by some of the key concepts commonly used both in medicine and psychotherapy.

1.4.1.1   The Biopsychosocial Model in Psychotherapy

Engel proposed in 1977 the biopsychosocial approach and a few years later published a paper where he further elaborated the model to demonstrate its practical application in patient care. The exemplified case of Mr. Glover offers a deepened and bright description of the psychological elements generating, modulating, and maintaining a medical condition (acute myocardial infarction) (Engel 1980).

All patients, independent of the setting, present as basic expectations the desire to be listened to, understood, helped, and possibly healed. In general medicine, these expectations are generally related to somatic symptoms and disorders. The psychosocial context of symptoms or emotional distress is often a marginal part of the physician's nonpriority agenda or partially "hidden" in the agenda of patients. Reversely, in psychotherapy both agendas focus on the psychological and social functioning of the patient. Excluding some particularities, like psychosomatic disorders, medical aspects in psychotherapy emerge prevalently as traumatic events (i.e., cancer, chemotherapy, abortion) that may threaten patients' psychological wellness or as physiological correlates of emotional or mental states (i.e., tachycardia, sleep disorders). On the other hand, the psychological dimension here is enriched and articulated in different domains: affective (emotions, feelings, moods, thoughts related to affection), cognitive (memory, perception, thought, attention), and behavioral (phobic avoidance, obsessive rituals, abnormal behaviors related to sexuality, nutrition, or other functions).

Generally, in medicine an increase in the exploration of the psychosocial domains, which often remain neglected or not properly explored, is strongly advocated. Conversely, in psychotherapy an occasional underestimation of the biological area might be expected, while the widespread belief is that by definition, this can't apply to the other two domains. But this is not necessarily true. For instance, a psychotherapy too focused on cognitive/affective components of the disorder, which in other words takes into account prevalently the psychological area, may risk underestimating key elements that come from the analysis of the social dimension, such as activating/traumatic events that occurred in a patient's past that generated dysfunctional beliefs or reinforcement given by attachment figures that maintain disruptive behaviors.

But also, the psychological area can be partially neglected in a clinical approach that is too focused on the presenting symptoms, where, for example, secondary emotive reactions to the main symptom—"the problem on the problem" described also in Chapter 6—might be ignored during the consultation (i.e., investigating and targeting the intervention just on patients' anxiety feelings when exposed to some critical situations, without verifying the presence of depressive or hostile reactions related to the impact of the primary emotion).

1.4.1.2 Therapist-Centered vs. Person-Centered Approach

Person-centered therapy was developed by Carl Rogers in the 1940s and 1950s (Rogers 1946, 1959), subsequently inspiring also in medicine the accomplishment of a more holistic clinical approach to the patient. In a medical setting, generally the application of a doctor-centered approach overlaps with the adoption of a biomedical model centered on the disease presented by the patient, while a patient-centered style corresponds to the adoption of a biopsychosocial model of illness. This means that doctors who put their medical background (experience and knowledge) at the center of the healing process tend to underestimate the potential contribution offered by the patients and reiterate a quite stereotyped and rigid communication/relational style independently from the person that they are visiting.In psychotherapy, of course, this criterion can't be followed in order to analyze to what extent the clinician is centered on his or her own agenda, because as previously said, medical aspects are often marginal. Talking about psychological or social aspects is not a guarantee of being centered on a patient's agenda; this depends on the way these are explored and described. Let's assume that the therapist decides to do some debating with the patient on a dysfunctional belief previously identified. A therapist-centered way for doing this may be to start without previously preparing/motivating the patient for the exercise (does she agree about the need to change her way of thinking? Does she feel comfortable in trying to do that? How is her sense of mastery?). Another example may be represented by the therapist's attitude to lead the Socratic dialog instead of promoting a patient's internal brainstorming based on his own ideas. In this case, the expression of an underlying therapist-centered approach is in the attempt of the clinician to make the patient feel familiar with ideas that he hasn't generated, instead of helping him to personally generate ideas, in some way extracted from his agenda, that consequently will be perceived as part of himself.

1.4.1.3   Shared Decision-Making Model

In medicine sharing a decision on a treatment plan usually implies for the patient a choice of two or more options, generally evidence-based, given by the doctor according to her objective evaluation of the elements observed and brought by the patient. In psychotherapy the objectiveness can't be an axiom by definition. Part of the information conveyed by the clinician refers to his own interpretations or attributions of meaning to events and symptoms. In this field it is more complicated to generate etiological hypotheses or choose universally validated and accepted treatment plans, independent of the psychotherapy approach followed. Even more delicate and subtle becomes the distance that the therapist must be able to play in assisting the patient to life changes oriented to his or her psychological well-being. Moving in the field of existential choices (changes in work, relationships, personal values, lifestyle), where the line between functional and dysfunctional is often fleeting and changeable depending on the perspective taken, is quite a tricky task for the therapist, who is called upon to play the role of neutral facilitator of the patient's internal decision-making process.

At the same time, it could appear somewhat contradictory that besides this nondirective approach, which characterizes the relationship with the patient in this setting, at the same time mental health care is the unique field where an obligatory medical treatment (meant as forced hospitalization/medication) is allowed. Indeed, in these cases protecting the patient's health becomes a priority over his involvement and agreement in the decision made (see also Chapter 4).

1.5 Communication Skills in Psychotherapy

The ability to effectively communicate with patients has been recognized as one of the core competencies of healthcare providers (ACGME 2000). Psychotherapists in particular largely base their intervention on the verbal interaction with their clients. Through words it's possible to access, understand, legitimate, and enhance patients' internal world. Communication is therefore one of the core instruments in the hands of the therapist, and actually it can compromise or enhance the effectiveness of an intervention.

Since the middle of the last century, a few authors have approached the analysis of communication in the psychotherapeutic setting not just from a theoretical perspective but also following a pragmatic vision, aimed at identifying specific communication patterns (Rogers 1946; Dominick 1958; Riess 1957) or effective therapist behaviors. Few authors have shown the importance of a clinician's personal qualities such as genuineness, warmth, and understanding (Truax and Carkhuss 1967; Mitchell et al. 1977) and directiveness (Shapiro and Budman 1973) in psychotherapy. Ackerman and Hilsenroth (2003), in a review that examined the above-described therapist's personal attributes and also in-session activities that positively influence the therapeutic relationship, have shown that techniques such as exploration, reflection, noting past therapy success, accurate interpretation, facilitating the expression of affect, and attending to the patient's experience, were found to contribute positively to the alliance.

The structure of speech within the interview setting is another topic that has attracted researchers' interest because of the obvious implications it has on the exploration of the interactive process between psychotherapist and patient. The study of this process can be approached differently, examining, for example, the meaning of speech content or analyzing the formal proprieties. Beck and Perry (2008a, b) have recently proposed a set of seven quantitative measures that operationalize interview structure (i.e., mean word length of interviewers' interventions, or total number of interviewer utterances) based on their literature revision, and their validity has been assessed in psychiatry and psychotherapy.

The first attempts to assess the use in psychotherapy of the ones that now might be defined as patient-centered interviewing skills are partially ascribable to some studies based on a clinical model for psychiatrists and psychotherapists, named the *Conversational Model* (Hobson 1977). The effects of structured training courses based on it have been assessed through quantitative analyses of word-by-word doctor speech during the consultation (Maguire et al. 1984; Goldberg et al. 1984; Margison and Shapiro 1986; Lieberman and Cobb 1987). Findings suggested that training in interview skills increased desirable interviewing behaviors, although some skills were more amenable to learning than others. For example, checking and summarizing increased, while acknowledging and responding to patients' emotions did not; this last aspect in particular has been recently confirmed (Rimondini et al. 2010).

Psychiatrists are reported to be more empathic than other physicians (Hojat et al. 2002) and to have better relational skills (Sierles et al. 2004). However, according to the few studies available in the literature, these abilities can't always be taken for granted (Maguire and Rutter 1976; Fairbairn et al. 1983). For example, at the beginning of their career, young psychiatrists seem to be good passive listeners, and they let patients talk freely, without interrupting, but the use of more complex skills such as active listening or emotion-focusing interventions appear to be more critical (Rimondini et al. 2006). A study conducted on a small sample of psychiatrists (Goss et al. 2008), applying the OPTION Scale—an instrument that measures patient involvement in the consultation—shown a low level of involvement, suggesting that psychiatrists may not be completely aware of the potential benefits of sharing treatment decisions or information regarding the prognosis or diagnosis. In psychotherapy the disclosure of the diagnosis implies different clinical and ethical issues and is felt in some cases, such as psychosis, to be highly problematic. A few studies have indicated that although advocated by patients (Macpherson et al. 2003; Paccaloni et al. 2004), rarely do psychiatrists communicate the real diagnosis of schizophrenia or psychosis (McCabe et al. 2002; Paccaloni et al. 2008) and the most frequent justifications for this choice are cited as cognitive impairment, possible negative impact on treatment adherence, or the patient's emotions (Paccaloni et al. 2005). This set of discrepancies might be partially explained by the deficiency in medical curriculum and psychiatric residency of courses on doctor–patient communication. Likewise, the teaching of these skills, when present, is often based on traditional methods such as lectures and seminars, despite the fact that it has been shown that interactive trainings that include structured feedback on personal communication style effectively improve the learners' performance (Naji et al. 1986; Krasner et al. 1998; Rimondini et al. 2010).

It could be argued that this does not necessarily apply to the setting of psychotherapy, where clinicians come from different backgrounds, like psychology, and during their training a much greater effort is spent improving their interpersonal abilities. Unfortunately, studies systematically assessing clinicians' use of communication skills are quite rare in a psychotherapy setting. A study conducted on a sample of 23 residents (all psychologists) in cognitive-behavioral psychotherapy has shown a good use of passive and active listening skills, while the application of interventions that structure the interview such as summarizing is not as frequent as it should be (Rimondini 2008).

Much more evidence has to be collected in this field in order to have a realistic perception of the actual state of the art and of the gray areas that need to be deepened and improved. By systematically quantifying the influence psychotherapists' and their patients' communicative behaviors have on specific treatment variables, it will be possible to identify communicative behaviors that are essential to efficient and effective care. According to Cruz and Pincus (2002), the research strategy should include three types of research: descriptive, etiological, and interventional. Descriptive studies may be the basis for developing or adapting measures that capture the essence of the communication process and translate it into categories or dimensions. The interaction analysis systems associated with other measures could then be used to undertake etiological investigations, and the results obtained should then drive the development of interventions aimed at improving psychotherapists' communication skills. Therefore, the next section will review and briefly describe some of the existing instruments implemented for the analysis of clinician–patient communication. It might be a prompt for promoting research in this area, where several clinical questions are still waiting to be answered. For further exploration of quantitative and qualitative methods of analysis, see Chapters 10 and 11.

1.5.1 Systems of Analysis of Therapist–Patient Communication

The present section offers an overview of some of the existing tools somewhat dedicated to the analysis of the verbal interaction between psychotherapist and patient. Most of these tools are rating scales, which have the advantage of being quite easily applicable, but compared to classification systems, they offer just a global perception of the interview's quality, while a punctual analysis of each expression produced by the therapist is not provided.

The criterion that guided my selection was to indentify instruments that give priority to the possible to communication skills instead of focusing just on particular psychotherapy strategies (i.e., building a functional analysis, debating), although this difference is often quite artificial. Basically, this was done in order to offer a range of classification systems or rating scales differently related to the psychotherapeutic approach followed; so in some cases the underlying psychotherapeutic approach will be very blurred, while in others the classification categories will appear as evident expressions of the theoretical model adopted. In these last cases, I obviously privileged the description of rating scales based on a cognitive-behavioral approach, selecting those more representative among the ones available in the literature, such as *The Academy of Cognitive Therapy Case Formulation Rating*, or *The Comprehensive Psychotherapeutic Interventions Rating Scale* (Trijsburg et al. 2002). Of course, the literature also offers several instruments referring to other psychotherapy approaches, such as psychodynamic or psychoanalytic (Fuqua et al. 1986; Alberts and Edelstein 1990; Krasner et al. 1998).

1.5.1.1 Rutter's System of Analysis of Therapist's Communication

Rutter and colleagues developed in the 1980s a set of measures for assessing a therapist's interviewing style and his or her use of communication skills (Rutter and Cox 1981). The measures, according to different specific parameters, assessed five therapist's dimensions: talkativeness, directiveness, type of questions and statements, interventions designed to elicit or respond to feelings. and interviewer's nonverbal behavior (see Fig. 1.1).

TALKATIVENESS	• Number of words spoken per unit time • Number of separate floor-holdings • Number of words per floor-holdings
DIRECTIVENESS	• Number of questions raising a new topic/area • Number of probes per subject area • Direct request for detailed description • Interviewer interruptions • Informer interruptions
TYPE OF QUESTIONS AND STATEMENTS	• Double questions • Multiple choice questions • Open questions • Closed questions • Checks
INTERVENTIONS DESIGNED TO ELICIT OR TO RESPOND TO FEELINGS	• Request for feeling • Interpretations • Expressions of sympathy • Cues responded to • Responses to expressed feelings
INTERVIEWERS' NON-VERBAL BEHAVIOUR	• Hand gestures while talking • Listening responses • Head nods while listening • Reciprocal smiles by interviewer • Reciprocal smiles by informant • Missed looks by interviewer • warmth • sympathy

Fig. 1.1 Set of measures proposed by Rutter and Cox (1981) to assess therapist communication style

This set of instruments, which was originally developed for the assessment of communication skills used during the first visit with parents of children hospitalized in a psychiatric ward, has been applied in several studies in order to determine the clinician's ability in eliciting factual information (Cox et al. 1981b) or the patient's emotions (Cox et al. 1981a). The validity of the described measures proved to be acceptable, but training is needed for proper application.

1.5.1.2 Verona Coding Definitions of Emotional Sequences to Code Health Providers' Responses

Developed over the years by a European group of experts in research and teaching of communication skills in health care, this instrument is specifically oriented to the assessment of provider responses to cues and concerns expressed by the patient during the consultation (Del Piccolo et al. in press). Cues and concerns represent important hubs that can influence the subsequent evolution of clinician–patient communication during the interview; so handling these critical points properly is considered one of the core provider's competences.

The first step in the coding procedure is to identify cues and concerns according to some rules specified in a accompanying manual. The provider's expression—verbal or nonverbal—immediately following a cue or concern is then coded

NON EXPLICIT	PROVIDE SPACE	• Ignore • Shutting down • Information advise
	REDUCE SPACE	• Silence • Back channel • Acknowledge • Active invitation • Implicit empathy
EXPLICIT	PROVIDE SPACE	• Switching • Post-poning • Information advise • Active blocking
	REDUCE SPACE	• Acknowledgment content • Exploration content • Acknowledgment affective • Exploration affective • Empathy

Fig. 1.2 The grouping of the Verona coding definitions of emotional sequences to code health providers' responses to patients' cues and concerns

according to two major conceptual factors or axes: *explicitness* and *space provision* for further disclosure of the cue or concern. Finer details on the specific function of the response are then captured by a second-level group of subcategories (see Fig. 1.2). Reliability indices showed that the agreement between raters is substantial.

An example of individual category coding might be, "Would you like to tell me more?" (active invitation), "I would like to talk with you of this in a minute" (postponing), and "I understand this must be really hard for you, especially as you are so scared about this operation" (empathy). The instrument has already been used in many different medical settings, including podiatry, internal medicine, general practice, and psychiatry. The authors are developing some additional coding rules for application in particular populations of patients (i.e., cultural/ ethnicity).

1.5.1.3   Verona Psychiatric Interview Classification System

The VR-PICS is a modified version of the Verona Medical Interview Classification System (Del Piccolo et al. 2004, 2005), adapted to the psychiatric setting (Rimondini et al. 2004). It possesses satisfactory inter-rater reliability, with percentage agreements between 80 and 86% and Cohen's k between 0.88 and 0.87 (Rimondini et al. 2006). The VR-PICS consists of 39 mutually exclusive categories, 23 for psychiatrist and 16 for patient speech. The clinician categories can be generally divided into three groups: patient-centered expressions, doctor-centered expressions, and neutral expressions (see Fig. 1.3).

In particular, the first group of expressions includes active listening such as reflections and open-ended or patient agenda completing questions ("... something else?"), orienting transitions ("I need more information on this topic before

PATIENT CENTRED	Passive listening	• Facilitation • Reflecting
	Active listening Sign posting	• Open question • Explaining transition • Clarifying, checking,summarizing • Asking for opinion • Completing agenda
	Detecting and Handling of emotions	• Appraisal(legitimizing, empathy, participation,respect) • Open question on emotion
DOCTOR CENTRED		• Information giving • Giving Instructions • All closed questions • Brief answer • Disapproval
NEUTRAL		• Reassurance • Agreement • Conversation • Bid for repetition • Asking for understanding • Simple transition • Silence

Fig. 1.3 The grouping of the Verona Psychiatric Interview Classification System categories provided for psychiatrist speech

going on ..."), sign-posting expressions of clarifying ("what do you mean by 'occasional drinker'?"), checking and summarizing, expressions of seeking and handling emotions ("How do you feel about this? You must feel quite upset over this news ..."), and asking patients' point of view. On the other hand, examples of doctor-centered expressions comprise instructions and suggestions (e.g., "You should be more self-confident"), disapproval (e.g., "This was not a good thing to do"), or closed-ended questions. Finally, all the other utterances that can't be labeled by definition as patient- or doctor-centered are included in neutral expressions—i.e., simple reassurance ("Don't worry!") or undemanding behavior such as simple facilitations ("Hmm," Aah...). This instrument has been used to assess how psychiatrists respond to patients' cues and concerns (Rimondini 2006) and also to verify the effectiveness of a training course in communication skills for residents in psychiatry (Rimondini 2010) (see also Chapter 10).

1.5.1.4   Goldberg's Classification System

This system was used in a series of studies (Maguire et al. 1984; Goldberg et al. 1984) to test the application and effects of a psychotherapeutic model—the "Conversational Model" (Hobson 1977)—in samples of psychotherapists and psychiatrists. This psychotherapy model essentially consists of a process of interpersonal learning by means of a focused "conversation," the assumption being that exploring and seeking solutions to a patient's feelings and interpersonal problems during the

CUE RECOGNITION	Whether the statement made by the therapist is in response to a verbal or nonverbal cue released by the patient
THERAPIST INVOLVMENT	Whether the therapist talking to the patient expresses himself using the first person singular or plural
NEGOTIATION	Whether the therapist expressed an openness to correction
FUNCTION	Whether the therapist's statement was formulated as a question, information, advice, framework-giving comment, understanding or linking hypothesis
CONTENT	Whether the therapist's statement was referred to psychiatric symptoms, feelings, relationship with others, doctor-patient relationship
TIME FOCUS	Whether the therapist's statement was referred to past, current time, here-and-now, future

Fig. 1.4 Goldberg et al.'s (1984) main categories for assessing therapists' verbal expressions

therapeutic sessions enables the patient to then generalize them outside the room, in his or her daily life.

The system requires that all clinician verbal units are transcribed and then divided into statements, and each statement is then rated according to six categories (see Fig. 1.4). Within each code there are "model" or desirable behaviors (i.e., *express purpose of the interview, linking hypothesis, use of negotiation*) vs. "non-model" behaviors (i.e., *closed questions, giving advice*).

1.5.1.5 The Three Interactograms of Cobb and Lieberman

This system of analysis has been proposed by Lieberman and Cobb (1987), who originally developed these three *Interactograms* in order to verify the effectiveness of their method, the *Grammar of Psychotherapy*, of teaching communication and psychotherapy (Cobb and Lieberman 1987). The authors created three self-assessment forms meant to examine the interaction between therapist and patient, hence the name *Interactograms*. The first one was designed to examine each actual intervention made by the clinician while interviewing the patient, the second is based on the *Six-Category Intervention Analysis* by Heron and focuses on the intention manifested by the therapist during the interview, while the last interactogram is an analysis of the relationship process, where the focus is on macro-skills used throughout the entire interview (see Fig. 1.5).

Micro-skills included in the *Interactogram I* in the category *encouraging* are expressions such as "please tell me more" or "go ahead," while in *empathic* we might find statements like, "Yes, you feel you've just about had enough today." An example of therapist intention, coded in the *Interactogram II* as *Informative*, might be a statement aimed to teach, inform, and impart new information to the patient. Finally, *Interactogram III* includes more complex therapist interventions, such as a series of educated guesses or ideas that would be the basis for further

INTERACTOGRAM I	QUESTIONS	• Non-leading open • Non-leading closed • Leading open or closed
	FACILITATIONS	• Noise • Silence
	STATEMENTS	• Orientation/introducing • Reassuring • Encouraging/empathic • Summarizing • Checking/seeking clarification • Focusing/scanning/prompting • Self-revelation • other
INTERACTOGRAM II	AUTHORITATIVE CATEGORIES	• Prescriptive • Informative • Confronting
	FACILITATIVE CATEGORIES	• Cathartic • Catalytic • Supportive
INTERACTOGRAM III	See original paper (Liberman and Cobb, 1987)	

Fig. 1.5 The three Interactogram categories by Lieberman and Cobb (1987)

discussion: "I know your father died over two years ago, but I wonder if in a sense you are still haunted by him."

The application of this method implies the availability of a video- or audiotaped psychotherapy session. In particular, *Interactogram I* leant itself to the purpose of the present chapter, which is offering instruments for analyzing clinician communication skills. The global use of the three forms represents a structured self-assessment method that can be adopted in individual or small group supervision.

1.5.1.6 Sheffield Psychotherapy Rating Scale

This tool is derived from the Collaborative Study Psychotherapy Rating Scale (Hill et al. 1992), Form-6, and was developed in order to compare different therapeutic approaches (cognitivebehavioral vs. exploratory therapy) in the treatment of depression (Shapiro and Firth 1987). The tool is composed of 59 items assessing the application of quite general communication skills (e.g., *summarizing, exploration of feelings*) beside very specific techniques of cognitivebehavioral therapy (e.g., *recording thoughts, planning/practicing alternative behaviors*) (see Fig. 1.6). Raters vote on a seven-point Likert scale for each item on the basis of their general impression and according to some coding rules for rating. For example, the highest score in the assessment of the item *Encouraging independence* might be attributed to an intervention where the therapist explicitly stated to the patient that the therapeutic goal is to make the patient able to do things on his or her own (e.g.,"As we work together, I'd like you to become less and less reliant on my input").

- Setting and following the Agenda
- Homework reviewed
- Supportive Encouragement
- Convey Expertise
- Therapist's Communication Style
- Involvement
- Warmth
- Rapport
- Empathy
- Formality
- Collaboration
- Encourages Independence
- Negotiating Style
- Language of Mutuality
- Specific Examples
- Exploratory Therapy Rationale
- Relating Interpersonal Change to Therapy
- Patterns of Relationships
- Cue Basis
- Metaphor
- Focusing
- Confrontation

- Disclosure
- Limitations
- Understanding Hypotheses
- Linking Hypothesis
- Explanatory Hypothesis
- Sequences of Interventions
- Structuring the Session
- Exploration of Feelings
- Acknowledgment of Affect
- Acceptance of affect
- Relationship of Thoughts and Feelings
- Rationale for Cognitive Procedures
- Relate Improvement to Cognitive Change
- Reporting Cognitions
- Exploring Personal Meaningfgf
- Recognizing Cognitive Errors
- Exploring Underlying Assumptions
- Distancing of Beliefs
- Examine Available Evidence

- Testing Beliefs Prospectively
- Searching for Alternative Explanations
- Realistic Consequences
- Adaptive/Functional Value of Beliefs
- Maintaining Gains
- Rationale for Behavioural Procedures
- Practicing "Rationale Responses"
- Planning Practicing Alternative Behaviors
- Skills Training
- Homework Assigned
- Increasing Pleasure and Mastery
- Scheduling/Structuring Activities
- Self-Monitoring
- Recording Thoughts
- Manipulating Behaviors via Cues and Consequences
- Negotiating Therapy Content
- Explanation of Therapist's Direction
- Summarizing

Fig. 1.6 Items comprising the Sheffield Psychotherapy Rating Scale

1.5.1.7   The Cognitive Therapy Scale Revised

Originally developed by Young and Beck (1980) and recently reviewed (Blackburn et al. 2001,) this scale, like the one previously described, is one of the most related to the cognitive-behavioral theory and part of the skills assessed here is a clear expression of the application of a CB protocol during the therapy session. It is composed of 12 items (see Fig. 1.7) and for each one a few key features are listed in order to aid with the rating (0–6 Likert scale). The items widen from the assessment of very specific aspects of therapy, such as *Homework Setting,* where the therapist receives the highest score when he shows *excellent homework negotiation, or sets highly appropriate homework in the face of difficulties,* to items that assess aspects more inherent to the global process occurring during the psychotherapy encounter. For example, item 10 evaluates the degree of *Conceptual Integration,* meaning the therapist's ability to make the patient understand how his or her perceptions and interpretations, beliefs, attitudes, and rules relate to his or her problem.

AGENDA SETTING & ADHERENCE	• presence/absence of an agenda which is explicit, agreed and prioritized, and feasible in the time available • appropriateness of the contents of the agenda • appropriate adherence to the agenda
FEEDBACK	• presence and frequency, or absence, of feedback • appropriateness of the contents of the feedback • manner of its delivery and elicitation
COLLABORATION	• verbal skills (e.g. non-hectoring) • non-verbal skills (e.g. attention and use of joint activities) • sharing of written summaries
PACING AND EFFICIENT USE OF TIME	• the degree to which the session flows smoothly through the discrete phases • the appropriateness of the pacing throughout the session • the degree of fit to the learning speed of the patient
INTERPERSONAL EFFECTIVENESS	• empathy - the therapist is able to understand and enter the patient's feelings imaginatively and uses this understanding to promote change • genuineness - the therapist has established a trusting working relationship • warmth-the patient seems to feel liked and accepted by the therapist
ELICITING OF APPROPRIATE EMOTIONAL EXPRESSION	• facilitation of access to a range of emotions • appropriate use and containment of emotional expression • facilitation of emotional expression, encouraging appropriate access and differentiation of emotions
ELICITING KEY COGNITIONS	• eliciting cognitions that are associated with distressing emotions • the skillfulness and breadth of the methods used (i.e. Socratic questioning, etc.) • choosing the appropriate level of work for the stage of therapy (i.e. automatic thoughts)
ELICITING BEHAVIOURS	• eliciting behaviors that are associated with distressing emotions • the skillfulness and breadth of the methods used (i.e. imagery, role-plays, etc.)
GUIDED DISCOVERY	• the style of the therapist - this should be open and inquisitive • the effective use of questioning techniques (e.g. Socratic questions) should encourage the patient to discover useful information
CONCEPTUAL INTEGRATION	• the presence/absence of an appropriate conceptualization which is in line with goals of therapy • the manner in which the conceptualization is used (e.g. homework etc.).
APPLICATION OF CHANGE METHODS	• the appropriateness and range of both cognitive methods (e.g. cognitive change diaries, etc.) and behavioral methods (e.g. response prevention, etc.) • the skill in the application of the methods • the suitability of the methods for the needs of the patient
HOMEWORK SETTING	• presence/absence of a homework task in which clear and precise goals have been set; • the task should be derived from material discussed in the session • the homework task should be set jointly, and sufficient time should be allowed for it to be explained clearly

Fig. 1.7 Items comprising the Cognitive Therapy Scale Revised, with features that need to be considered when scoring

1.6 Conclusion

The present chapter offers some reflections on the dyadic interaction that occurs between people in the healing contexts, particularly in psychotherapy. Communication is one of the main tools on which the therapist bases his or her clinical practice, and the effectiveness of an intervention largely relies on this element. The success of a communication exchange between patient and therapist depends on the co-presence of different elements blended together: the robustness of the theoretical background, previous clinical experiences in the field, the degree of practitioner self-awareness of his or her own emotional/cognitive functioning, and the appropriateness in the use of communicative micro-skill.

Even if much more evidence has to be collected in this field, psychotherapists' proper use of communication skills has been demonstrated to have a positive impact on clinical outcomes, patient satisfaction, and collaboration. The literature offers several instruments dedicated to the analysis of verbal interaction between psychotherapist and patient, widening from rating scales to coding systems, which capture communication skills and patterns differently.

References

ACGME. (2000). ACGME: Outcome project. ACGME General Competencies Version 1.3. 9.28.99.

Ackerman, S., & Hilsenroth, M. (2003). A review of therapist characteristics and techniques negatively impacting the therapeutic alliance. *Psychotherapy, 38*, 171–185.

Alberts, G., & Edelstein, B. (1990). Therapist training: A critical review of skill training studies. *Clinical Psychology Review, 10*, 497–511.

Argyle, M., Furnham, A., & Graham, J. A. (1981). *Social situation*. New York: Cambridge University Press.

Bara, B., & Cutica, I. (2002). La comunicazione [In Italian]. In C. Castelfranchi, F. Mancini, & M.Miceli (Eds.), *Fondamenti di Cognitivismo Clinico*. Torino: Bollati Boringhieri.

Barry, C., Stevenson, F., Britten, N., Barber, N., & Bradley, C. (2001). Giving voice to the lifeworld. More humane, more effective medical care? A qualitative study of doctor–patient communication in general practice. *Social Science and Medicine, 53*, 487–505.

Beck, S., & Perry, C. (2008a). The definition and function of interview structure in psychiatric and psychotherapeutic interviews. *Psychiatry, 71*, 1–12.

Beck, S., & Perry, C. (2008b). The measurement of interview structure in five types of psychiatric and psychotherapeutic interviews. *Psychiatry, 71*, 219–233.

Berger, C., & Calabrese, R. (1975). Some explorations in initial interaction and beyond: Toward a developmental theory of interpersonal communication. *Human Communication Research, 1*, 99–112.

Blackburn, I., James, I., Milne, D., Baker, C., Standart, S., Garland, A., et al. (2001). The revised cognitive therapy scale (CTS-R): Psychometric properties. *Behavioural and Cognitive Psychotherapy, 29*, 431–446.

Bodenheimer, T., Lorig, K., Holman, H., & Grumbach, K. (2002). Patient self-management of chronic disease in primary care. *Journal of the American Medical Association, 288*, 2469–2475.

Brown, J. (1995). *Assessing communication between patients and doctors, a manual for scoring patient-centred communication*. Montreal: CSFM Working Papers Series.

Brown, B., Nolan, P., Crawford, P., & Lewis, A. (1996). Interaction, language and the "narrative turn" in psychotherapy and psychiatry. *Social Science and Medicine, 43*, 1569–1578.

Buller, M., & Buller, D. (1987). Physicians' communication style and patient satisfaction. *Journal of Health and Social Behaviour, 28*, 375–388.

Butler, G., & Mathews, A. (1983). Cognitive processes in anxiety. *Advances in Behavioural Therapy, 5*, 51–62.

Cape, J. (1996). Psychological treatment of emotional problems by general practitioners. *British Journal of Medical Psychology, 69*, 85–99.

Carson, R. (1969). A theory of communication in psychotherapy. *Psychotherapy: Theory, Research, and Practice, 3*, 7–13.

Castelfranchi, C., & Paglieri, F. (2007). The role of beliefs in goal dynamics: Prolegomena to a constructive theory of intentions. *Synthese, 155*, 237–263.

Cobb, J., & Lieberman, S. (1987). The grammar of psychotherapy. A descriptive account. *British Journal of Psychiatry, 151*, 589–594.

Cohen-Cole, S. (1991). *The medical interview: The three-function approach.* St. Louis: Mosby-Year.

Cox, A., Holbrook, D., & Rutter, M. (1981a). Psychiatric interviewing techniques. VI. Experimental study: Eliciting feelings. *British Journal of Psychiatry, 139*, 144–152.

Cox, A., Rutter, M., & Holbrook, D. (1981b). Psychiatric interviewing techniques V. Experimental study: Eliciting factual information. *British Journal of Psychiatry, 139*, 29–37.

Craig, R. (1999). Communication theory as a field. *Communication Theory, 9*, 119–161.

Cruz, M., & Pincus, H. (2002). Research on the influence that communication in psychiatric encounters has on treatment. *Psychiatric Services, 53*, 1253–1265.

Del Piccolo, L., Putnam, S.M., Mazzi, M.A., Zimmermann, C. (2004). The biopsychosocial domains and the functions of the medical interview in primary care: construct validity of the Verona Medical Interview Classification System. *Patient Educ Couns. 53*(1): 47–56.

Del Piccolo, L., Mead, N., Gask, L., Mazzi, M. A., Goss, C., Rimondini, M., et al. (2005). The English version of the Verona medical interview classification system (VR-MICS). An assessment of its reliability and a comparative cross-cultural test of its validity. *Patient Education and Counseling, 58*, 252–264.

Del Piccolo, L., Mazzi, M. A., Dunn, G., Sandri, M., & Zimmermann, C. (2007). Sequence analysis in multilevel models. A study on different sources of patient cues in medical consultations. *Social Science and Medicine, 65*, 2357–2370.

Del Piccolo, L., de Haes, H., Heaven, C., Jansen, J., Verheul, W., Bensing, J., Bergvik S., Deveugele M., Eide H., Fletcher I., Goss C., Humphris G., Kim YM., Langewitz W., Mazzi MA., Mjaaland T., Moretti F., Nübling M., Rimondini M., Salmon P., Sibbern T., Skre I., van Dulmen S., Wissow L., Young B., Zandbelt L., Zimmermann C., & Finset, A. (2010). http://www.ncbi.nlm.nih.gov/pubmed/20346609 Development of the Verona coding definitions of emotional sequences to code health providers' responses (VR-CoDES-P) to patient cues and concerns. *Patient Education and Counseling 25*. [Epub ahead of print].

Dominick, B. (1958). Communication in psychotherapy. *American Journal of Psychotherapy, 12*, 253–263.

Douglas, W. (1990). Uncertainty, information-seeking, and liking during initial interaction. *Western Journal of Speech Communication, 54*, 66–81.

Ekman, P., & Friesen, W. (1969). The repertoire of nonverbal behavior: Categories, origins, usage, and coding. *Semiotica, 1*, 49–97.

Engel, G. (1977). The need for a new medical model: A challenge for biomedicine. *Science, 196*, 129–136.

Engel, G. (1980). The clinical application of the biopsychosocial model. *American Journal of Psychiatry, 137*, 535–544.

Eysenck, M., MacLeod, C., & Mathews, A. (1987). Cognitive functioning and anxiety. *Psychological Research, 49*, 189–195.

Fairbairn, S., Maguire, P., Chambers, H., & Sanson-Fisher, R. (1983). The teaching of interviewing skills: Comparison of experienced and novice trainers. *Medical Education, 17*, 296–299.

Fuqua, D., Newman, J., Scott, T., & Gade, E. (1986). Variability across sources of performance ratings: Further evidence. *Journal of Counseling Psychology, 33*, 353–356.

Gask, L. (1992). Training general practitioners to detect and manage emotional disorders. *International Reviews of Psychiatry, 4*, 293–300.

Goldberg, D., Hobson, R., Maguire, P., Margison, R., O'Dowd, T., Osborn, M., et al. (1984). The clarification and assessment of a method of psychotherapy. *British Journal of Psychiatry, 144*, 567–575.

Goldberg, D., Jenkins, L., Millar, T., & Faragher, E. (1993). The ability of trainee general practitioners to identify psychological distress among their patients. *Psychological Medicine, 23*, 185–193.

Goss, C., Mazzi, M. A., Del Piccolo, L., Rimondini, M., & Zimmermann, C. (2005). Information-giving sequences in general practice consultations. *Journal of Evaluation in Clinical Practice, 11*, 39–49.

Goss, C., Moretti, F., Mazzi, M., Del Piccolo, L., Rimondini, M., & Zimmermann, C. (2008). Involving patients in decisions during psychiatric consultations. *British Journal of Psychiatry, 193*, 416–421.

Graugaard, P. K., Eide, H., & Finset, A. (2003). Interaction analysis of physician–patient communication: The influence of trait anxiety on communication and outcome. *Patient Education and Counseling, 49*, 149–56.

Hall, J., & Dornan, M. (1988). What patients like about their medical care and how often they are asked: A meta-analysis of the satisfaction literature. *Social Science and Medicine, 27*, 935–939.

Hargie, O., & Dickson, D. (2004). *Skilled interpersonal communication: Research, theory and practice*. London: Routledge.

Hargie, O., Saunders, C., & Dickson, D. (2000). *Social skills in interpersonal communication* (2nd ed.). London: Routledge.

Hartley, P. (1999). *Interpersonal communication* (2nd ed.). London: Routledge.

Heath, R., & Bryant, J. (2000). *Human communication theory and research* (2nd ed.). Mahwah, NJ: Lawrence Erlbaum Associates.

Hill, C., O'Grady, K., & Elkin, I. (1992). Applying the Collaborative Study Psychotherapy Rating Scale to rate therapist adherence in cognitive-behavior therapy, interpersonal therapy, and clinical management. *Journal of Consultant Clinical Psychology, 60*, 73–9.

Hobson R. (1977). A conversational model of psychotherapy. *AUTP Newsletter* Jan, 14–18.

Hojat, M., Gonnella, J., Nasca, T., Mangione, S., Vergare, M., & Magee, M. (2002). Physician empathy: Definition, components, measurement, and relationship to gender and specialty. *American Journal of Psychiatry, 159*, 1563–1569.

Jackson, J., Chamberlin, J., & Kroenke, K. (2001). Predictors of patient satisfaction. *Social Science and Medicine, 52*, 609–620.

Jaspers, K. (1913). *Allgemeine psychopathologie [In German]*. Berlin: Springer.

Kaplan, H., Sadock, B., & Grebb, J. (1994). *Kaplan and Sadock's synopsis of psychiatry: Behavioral sciences, clinical psychiatry* (7th ed.). Baltimore: Lippincott William & Wilkins.

Kellermann, K. (1992). Communication: Inherently strategic and primarily automatic. *Journal of Communication Monographs, 59*, 288–300.

Kinnersley, P., Stott, N., Peters, T., & Harvey, I. (1999). The patient-centredness of consultations and outcome in primary care. *British Journal of General Practice, 49*, 711–716.

Knapp, M., & Daly, J. (2002). *Handbook of interpersonal communication*. Thousand Oaks, CA: Sage Publications.

Krasner, R., Howard, K., & Brown, A. (1998). The acquisition of psychotherapeutic skill: An empirical study. *Journal of Clinical Psychology, 54*, 895–903.

Lazare, A., Eisenthal, S., & Wasserman, L. (1975). The customer approach to patienthood. Attending to patient requests in a walk-in clinic. *Archives of General Practice, 32*, 553–558.

Ley, P., Whitworth, M., Skilbeck, C., Woodward, R., Pinsent, R., Pike, L., et al. (1976). Improving doctor–patient communication in general practice. *Journal of Royal College of General Practitioners, 26*, 720–724.

Lieberman, S., & Cobb, J. (1987). The grammar of psychotherapy. Interactograms: Three self-monitoring instruments for audiotape feedback. *British Journal of Psychiatry, 151*, 594–601.

Lipkin, M., Putnam, S., & Lazare, A. (1995). *The medical interview clinical care, education, and research* (p. XXII). New York: Springer. Frontiers of primary care.

Macpherson, R., Varah, M., Summerfield, L., Foy, C., & Slade, M. (2003). Staff and patient assessments of need in an epidemiologically representative sample of patients with psychosis – Staff and patient assessments of need. *Social Psychiatry and Psychiatric Epidemiology, 38*, 662–667.

Maguire, G., Goldberg, D., Hobson, R., Margison, F., Moss, S., & O'Dowd, T. (1984). Evaluating the teaching of a method of psychotherapy. *British Journal of Psychiatry, 144*, 575–580.

Maguire, G., & Rutter, D. (1976). History-taking for medical students. I-Deficiencies in performance. *Lancet 2*, 556–558.

Maly, R., Bourque, L., & Engelhardt, R. (1999). A randomized controlled trial of facilitating information giving to patients with chronic medical conditions: Effects on outcomes of care. *Journal of Family Practice, 48*, 356–363.

Margison, F., & Shapiro, D. (1986). Hobson's conversational model of psychotherapy – Training and evaluation: Discussion paper. *Journal of the Royal Society of Medicine, 79*, 468–472.

McCabe, R., Heath, C., Burns, T., & Priebe, S. (2002). Engagement of patients with psychosis in the consultation: Conversation analytic study. *British Medical Journal, 325*, 1148–1151.

Mead, N., & Bower, P. (2002). Patient-centred consultations and outcome in primary care: A review of the literature. *Patient Education and Counseling, 48*, 51–61.

Miceli, M., & Castelfranchi, C. (2005). Anxiety as an "epistemic" emotion: An uncertainty theory of anxiety. *Anxiety, Stress, and Coping, 18*, 291–319.

Michaels, R., & Sevitt, M. (1978). The patient and the first psychiatric interview. *British Journal of Psychiatry, 132*, 288–292.

Mitchell, K., Bozarth, J., & Krauft, C. (1977). A reappraisal of the therapeutic effectiveness of accurate empathy, non-possessive warmth and genuineness. In S. Gurman & A. Razin (Eds.), *Effective psychotherapy: A handbook of research*. Oxford: Pergamon Press.

Naji, S., Maguire, G., Fairbairn, S., Goldberg, D., & Faragher, E. (1986). Training clinical teachers in psychiatry to teach interviewing skills to medical students. *Medical Education, 20*, 140–147.

Novack, D., Suchman, A., Clark, W., Epstein, R., Najberg, E., & Kaplan, C. (1997). Calibrating the physician. Personal awareness and effective patient care. *Journal of the American Medical Association, 278*, 502–509.

Ong, L., de Haes, J., Hoos, A., & Lammes, F. (1995). Doctor–patient communication, a review of the literature. *Social Science and Medicine, 40*, 903–918.

Paccaloni, M., Moretti, F., & Zimmermann, C. (2005). Giving information and involving in treatment: What do psychiatrists think? A review. *Epidemiologia e Psichiatria Sociale, 14*, 198–216.

Paccaloni, M., Pozzan, T., & Zimmermann, C. (2004). Being informed and involved in treatment: What do psychiatric patients think? A review. *Epidemiologia e Psichiatria Sociale, 13*, 270–83.

Paccaloni, M., Rimondini, M., Pozzan, T., & Zimmermann, C. (2008). The communication of the diagnosis of schizophrenia. Focus group findings on psychiatrists' point of view. *Epidemiologia e Psichiatria Sociale, 17*, 65–76.

Planalp, S., & Honeycutt, J. (1985). Events that increase uncertainty in personal relationships. *Human Communication Research, 11*, 593–604.

Putnam, S., Stiles, W., Jacob, M., & James, S. (1985). Patient exposition and physician explanation in initial medical interviews and outcomes of clinic visits. *Medical Care, 23*, 74–83.

Riess, B. (1957). Communication in psychotherapy. *American Journal of Psychotherapy, 11*, 774–789.

Rimondini, M. (2008). *L'uso di tecniche comunicative in psicoterapia*. Unpublished manuscript, Associazione Psicologia Cognitiva, Verona.

Rimondini, M., Del Piccolo, L., Goss, C., Mazzi, M., Paccaloni, M., Zimmermann, M. (2006). Communication skills in psychiatry residents. How do they handle patient concerns? *Psychotherapy and Psychosomatics, 75*, 161–169.

Rimondini, M., Del Piccolo, L., Goss, C., Mazzi, M., Paccaloni, M., Zimmermann, C. (2010). The evaluation of training in patient-centred interviewing skills for psychiatric residents. *Psychological Medicine, 40*, 467–476.

Rimondini, M., Goss, C., & Zimmermann, C. (2004). La formazione in competenze comunicative in Psichiatria. Il VR-COPSYT. *Rivista di Psichiatria, 39*, 244–250.

Rogers, C. (1946). The non-directive method as a technique for social research. *American Journal of Sociology, 50*, 279–283.

Rogers, C. (1959). A theory of therapy, personality and interpersonal relationships as developed in the client-centered framework. In S. Koch (Ed.), *Psychology: A study of a science* (Formulations of the person and the social context 3rd ed.). New York: McGraw-Hill.

Rossi, A., Amaddeo, F., Bisoffi, G., Ruggeri, M., Thornicroft, G., & Tansella, M. (2002). Dropping out of care: Inappropriate terminations of contact with community-based psychiatric services. *British Journal of Psychiatry, 181*, 331–338.

Roter, D. L. (1993). *The Roter method of interaction process analysis.* Baltimore: Johns Hopkins University Press.

Rutter, M., & Cox, A. (1981). Psychiatric interviewing techniques: I. Methods and measures. *British Journal of Psychiatry, 138*, 273–282.

Scheflen, E. (1974). *How behavior means.* New York: Anchor Press.

Shapiro, R., & Budman, S. (1973). Defection, termination and continuation in family and individual therapy. *Family Process, 12*, 55–67.

Shapiro, D., & Firth, J. (1987). Prescriptive v. exploratory psychotherapy. Outcomes of the Sheffield Psychotherapy Project. *British Journal of Psychiatry, 151*, 790–799.

Sierles, F., Vergare, M., Hojat, M., & Gonnella, J. (2004). Academic performance of psychiatrists compared to other specialists before, during, and after medical school. *American Journal of Psychiatry, 161*, 1477–1482.

Smith, R. (1996). *The patients' story. An integrated approach to doctor–patient interviewing.* New York: Brown and Company.

Smith, R., Lyles, J., Mettler, J., Stoffelmayr, B., Van Egeren, L., Marshall, A., et al. (1998). The effectiveness of intensive training for residents in interviewing. A randomized, controlled study. *Annals of Internal Medicine, 128*, 118–26.

Stewart, M. (1995). Effective physician-patient communication and health outcomes: A review. *Canadian Medical Association Journal, 152*, 1423–1433.

Sudak, D., Beck, J., & Wright, J. (2003). Cognitive behavioral therapy: A blueprint for attaining and assessing psychiatry resident competency. *Academic Psychiatry, 27*, 154–159.

Svensson, S., Kjellgren, K. I., Ahlner, J., & Saljo, R. (2000). Reasons for adherence with antihypertensive medication. *International Journal of Cardiology, 76*, 157–163.

Taira, D., Safran, D., Seto, T., Rogers, W., & Tarlov, A. (1997). The relationship between patient income and physician discussion of health risk behaviors. *Journal of the American Medical Association, 278*, 1412–1417.

Tate, P. (1994). *The doctor's communication handbook.* New York: Radcliffe Medical Press.

Tracy, K., & Coupland, N. (1990). Multiple goals in discourse: An overview of issues. *Journal of Language and Social Psychology, 9*, 1–13.

Trijsburg, R., Frederiks, G., Gorlee, M., Klouwer, E., den Hollander, A., & Duivenvoorden, H. (2002). Development of the Comprehensive Psychotherapeutic Interventions Rating Scale (CPIRS). *Psychotherapy Research, 12*, 287–317.

Truax, C., & Carkhuss, R. (1967). *Toward effective counseling and psychotherapy: Training and practice.* Chicago: Aldine.

Watzlawick, P., Beavin, J., & Jackson, D. (1967). *Pragmatica della Comunicazione Umana [In Italian].* Rome: Astrolabio.

Wiener, M., Devoe, S., Rubinow, S., & Geller, J. (1972). Non verbal behaviour and non verbal communication. *Psychological Review, 79*, 185–214.

Young, J. & Beck, A. (1980). *Cognitive therapy scale: Rating manual.* Unpublished manuscript, University of Pennsylvania, Philadelphia, PA.

Zimmermann, C., Del Piccolo, L., & Mazzi, M. (2003). Patient cues and medical interviewing in general practice: Examples of the application of sequential analysis. *Epidemiologia e Psichiatria Sociale, 12*, 115–123.

Zimmermann, C., & Tansella, M. (1996). Psychosocial factors and physical illness in primary care: Promoting the biopsychosocial model in medical practice. *Journal of Psychosomatic Research, 40*, 351–358.

Chapter 2
Assessment Stage: Data Gathering and Structuring the Interview

Claudia Goss, Alberto Rossi, and Francesca Moretti

2.1 Introduction

The aims of the assessment in cognitive-behavioral therapy (CBT) are to derive a detailed and shared formulation of the person's presenting problems and, together, to develop an individualized treatment plan. As in the traditional psychological assessment, the main goals of cognitive-behavioral assessment are to diagnose disorders, discuss with the patient the goals of the treatment, plan the treatment, and try to facilitate positive changes in the patient starting from the first encounters with the therapist. An essential part of the assessment is the process of data gathering. Without collecting good information, it will not be possible to understand the patient's problem(s), and consequently his or her collaboration and trust may be compromised. Communication is therefore a key element in this stage of the therapy and represents the bridge between the patient's perspective and the therapist's theoretical framework.

Using communication skills appropriately allows the therapist to obtain more information on the presented problem, increases the reliability of the collected information, signals an interest in the patient's views and experiences, stimulates the patient's participation and collaboration, and, finally, makes the consultation more effective. The communication style (both verbal and nonverbal behaviors) can be viewed as a sort of therapist's visiting card, probably one of the stronger criteria through which patients judge the therapist's attitude to listen and understand their problems and test the therapist's ability to provide help and support. Communication skills are also important tools to help patients to better understand their problem(s) and cope with them.

This chapter aims to provide information on the communication skills that can be helpful to clinicians in assessing patients in psychotherapy. As previous studies

C. Goss (✉)
Department of Public Health and Community Medicine, Section of Psychiatry and Clinical Psychology, University of Verona, Policlinico G.B. Rossi, Piazzale L.A. Scuro 10, 37134 Verona, Italy
e-mail: claudia.goss@univr.it

M. Rimondini (ed.), *Communication in Cognitive Behavioral Therapy*, DOI 10.1007/978-1-4419-6807-4_2, © Springer Science+Business Media, LLC 2011

on this matter have been conducted predominantly in medical settings, we will first describe some theoretical background and findings from research on communication in this field. Second, we will try to give some practical suggestions and examples that can make interactions with patients more effective and efficient. More in detail, the chapter is organized in three main sections. In Sect. 2.2 we will describe the main theoretical models of doctor–patient communication and mention some research studies in a medical context (see also Chapter 1). In Sects. 2.3 and 2.4 we will describe and discuss communication skills useful for gathering information in the assessment stage and for structuring the interview, respectively.

2.2 Knowledge and Evidence on Doctor–Patient Communication in Medical Settings

2.2.1 Theoretical Background

In the last 30 years, a great amount of literature has been written on doctor–patient communication in medical settings, leading to several theoretical frameworks that have progressively defined the essential elements of an effective medical interview. Specifically, the following models can be considered as key issues that have contributed to change the traditional paternalistic approach: (a) the biopsychosocial model (Engel 1977); (b) the process model of stress and coping (Lazarus and Folkman 1984); and (c) the patient-centered approach and the integrated model (Smith et al. 2002). We will give a brief description of them here.

(a) *The biopsychosocial model.* This model was developed by Engel, who theorized that biological, psychological (e.g., beliefs, relationships, stress), and social factors all play a significant role in the onset, progression, and outcome of illness. This model includes the person with the disease (e.g., emotions, theories, impact on everyday life) as well as the disease itself, because it integrates the psychosocial and social dimensions with the biomedical aspects. This concept emphasizes that body and mind are not separable and that the modern health provider can best understand the patient only as a whole person. This position was in contrast with the traditional biomedical model, according to which a good health status simply depends on the absence of any specific illness. The patient is considered as an integrated joining of biological, psychological, and social components and he or she undertakes an essential role in his or her own care as a precious source of relevant information able to complete clinicians' knowledge. Doctors' competence and patients' experiences integrate each other, equally contributing to achieve an accurate diagnosis, greater health outcomes, and humane care. The primary aim has shifted from "cure" to "take care of" the patient, the patient's point of view is actively explored, and he or she is more engaged in the therapeutic process (see also Chapter 1).

(b) *The process model of stress and coping.* Illness can be considered a stressful life event with psychosocial consequences (crisis) to cope with. Richard Lazarus and Susan Folkman suggested a framework for evaluating the processes of coping with stressful events. According to the model, the impact of stressful experiences depends on the transaction between people and the environment (Transactional Model). Specifically, the ability to manage stressful events depends on how each person evaluates the stressor (e.g., positive, controllable, challenging, irrelevant) and on individual awareness and assessment of all the available resources to deal with the event. Therefore, the level of stress following an event may be attenuated by changing individuals' perceptions of stressors and by improving their confidence in their ability to implement a successful coping strategy. Considering illness as a stressful event, the model of stress and coping can constitute a valuable basis for describing patient responses in critical care.

(c) *The patient-centered approach and the integrated model.* Several articles have been published on the patient-centered approach as opposed to the traditional doctor-centered (paternalistic) approach (Lesser 1985; Pendleton and Hasler 1983; Smith 1997; Stewart et al. 1995; Smith et al. 2002). Good patient care and cure require that the physician explores at the same time both the biomedical and psychosocial dimensions of illness. Psychosocial variables may influence the onset and course of a disease as well as biological variables and therefore become essential factors in order to define a therapeutic plan that is specific for each single patient and that is supported by his or her motivation (Rimondini et al. 2003; Weston et al. 1989). According to this, the patient-centered and medical-centered approaches are complementary and should be integrated in the interviewing process to elicit both personal and symptom data (Smith et al. 2002). In such an approach, open-ended questions are largely used as well as acknowledgment of patients' feelings, emotions, beliefs, and opinions, and active patient participation is strongly encouraged (Smith et al. 2002).

In order to better understand this approach, it is fundamental to become familiar with the concept of *agenda* (Tate 1994). When approaching a medical encounter, each patient has in mind specific issues he or she would like to discuss, but also expectations, beliefs, ideas, fears, and worries related to these issues. Other important information includes life events and the impact of symptoms on quality of life. All these essential pieces of information represent the *agenda of the patient.* Peltenburg et al. (2004) introduced the term *emerging agenda* in order to define all the "concerns or issues not expected to be on the agenda by either the patient or the physician before the consultation." Eliciting these unexpected themes becomes essential in order to contextualize the problems presented by each patient and develop a personalized and effective therapeutic plan. Patients often introduce their agenda by expressing cues and concerns. Concerns are a clear and unambiguous expression of an unpleasant current or recent emotion, with or without related issues (e.g., "I feel frightened" or "I am worried about my high blood pressure"). Cues are verbal or nonverbal hints that suggest an underlying unpleasant emotion and therefore would need to be clarified or explored by the health provider. Understanding and eliciting patients' agenda is essential to implementing the patient-centered approach and requires that physicians use several communication skills.

Starting from these theoretical backgrounds, Cohen-Cole (1991) developed the *three-function model of the medical interview* (see also Chapters 1, 3, and 4). The model has been designed in order to supply a tool able to translate into clinical practice the previously described theoretical models. The author identifies three fundamental components of the interview:

1. building the relationship and responding appropriately to the patient's emotions (relational skills);
2. collecting all relevant data to understand the patient's problem (data-gathering skills);
3. educating the patient about her illness and motivating her to adhere to treatment (information-giving skills, negotiating and motivating strategies).

Biological as well as psychological, emotional, and relational aspects need to be considered all together as different parts of the same problem and need to be fully explored, understood, and appropriately managed (function 2). In spite of the paternalistic model, where the patient was just a passive recipient of a doctor's prescription, the patient-centered approach allows the patient to play an active role in his own care, providing him with all the information/instruments necessary to take part in the therapeutic decisions (function 3). While functions 2 and 3 represent different stages of the medical encounter, function 1 passes through the whole interview since each step of the medical interview should be based on an efficacious therapeutic alliance built up with a series of relational skills (see Chapter 3). According to the offered theoretical background, it is possible to identify the criteria of an efficacious doctor–patient interaction. The patient is guided by the doctor to offer in a precise and reliable way, and in an adequate timeframe, the maximum amount of relevant information necessary to understand his health and life problems. The patient and the healthcare provider work as partners in order to find an agreement and get a shared idea on what the main problem is. The patient is offered the opportunity to have an active role in her own care and is stimulated by the physician to be involved, to participate and collaborate in treatment decisions. In this way, the patient feels understood and sustained by the healthcare provider and feels free to express emotions.

2.2.2   Research Findings on Doctor–Patient Communication

An accurate and detailed information-gathering process, together with the implementation of a collaborative relationship, is essential to achieve greater health outcomes. Specifically, improved health outcomes occur when patients feel free to express topics of perceived immediate importance, and when physicians pay appropriate attention to what the patient wants or needs to convey (Smith 2002; Stewart et al. 1995). The patient-centered approach is a valid tool to get such an open dialogue between the doctor and patient. Several studies have shown the benefits of the patient-centered approach on outcomes of patient care. These advantages are higher patient satisfaction (Williams et al. 1998; Safran et al. 1998; Kinnersley et al. 1999), better recall and understanding of information (Roter et al. 1987; Hall et al. 1988), improved adherence to treatment (Butler et al. 1996; Safran et al. 1998; Svensson et al. 2000), more efficient coping strategies with disease, improvement of the health status (Ryff and Singer 2000; Ong et al. 1995; Stewart 1995; Maly et al. 1999; Mead and Bower 2002; Eijk and Haan 1998; Bodenheimer et al. 2002), and a decrease in referrals to other specialists (Stewart et al. 2000; Little et al. 2001). A growing body of evidence supports the importance of health provider–patient communication in the interview and its role on both biomedical and psychological outcomes of care. The need to improve the doctor–patient communication has been widely recognized also for psychiatric patients, and communication skills have been proposed as "core skills" in the curriculum of psychiatrists (Scheiber et al. 2003; Walton and Gelder 1999). Studies on communication skills in psychiatry have remained rare despite the observations that psychiatrists needed training in interviewing skills (Maguire 1982; Goldberg et al. 1984; McCready and Waring 1986; Rimondini et al. 2006). Some studies evaluating the effects of training (Maguire et al. 1984; Lieberman et al. 1989; Harrison and Goldberg 1993) found that training in interview skills is indeed useful for psychiatrists even if individual outcomes differed, not all psychiatrists improved, and some undesirable behaviors, such as close-ended questioning, proved resistant to change. Such findings present a challenge to communication research in psychiatry, which only recently has been taken up again (Nuzzarello and Birndorf 2004; Rimondini et al. 2010).

All these findings suggest that specific communication skills are also important in psychotherapy and that they can play an essential role in improving patient–therapist relationship and outcomes.

2.3 The Data-Gathering Process

Data gathering is an essential part of the cognitive-behavioral assessment, which generally occurs during the first phase of psychotherapy. Some authors debate the existence of a clear-cut distinction between the assessment and the therapeutic stage: where the planned intervention "officially" starts and the therapist, through the use of cognitive-behavioral–specific techniques, focuses on the management/treatment of the emerged problems.

In this section we will focus mostly on the first assessment encounters, even though information gathering can also occur later on during the therapy, and the clinician should be able to go back and restart the data gathering at any time.

2.3.1 Setting and Barriers

To facilitate the data-gathering phase and the relationship building, therapists should also consider the setting in which the interview is conducted. Therapists should be aware of the potential communicative barriers that can have a negative impact on the interaction (such as noise, lack of confidentiality, elements in the room that may suggest a hierarchy between the therapist and the patient) and they should make an effort to remove or minimize all obstacles, the clear ones as well as those that are less evident. The interview should be conducted in a silent and private room, with both the patient and the therapist comfortably seated in chairs of equal height, without being separated by a desk or table. If a desk or a table is needed in the room, it could be placed against the wall with the therapist and the patient sitting to the side. The therapist and patient can also sit at the corners of the table so that they can look at each other without obstacles in the middle. Moreover, if it is possible, they should not sit exactly opposite, with an adequate distance between the two parties, so that the patient can choose either to look directly at the therapist or to look at something else without feeling too uncomfortable. If the therapist needs to take notes, he or she should be aware of the potential negative impacts of this on the relationship (e.g., the patient may feel not listened to) and should be able to manage it (for example, by taking just the essential notes or by not losing eye contact during important emotional moments).

Language and cultural barriers are others important obstacles that may interfere with the data-gathering process, leading to incomplete or an inaccurate amount of information. The therapist should avoid jargon and should try to make the patient feel at ease, for example, by making empathic comments when a patient seems to be worried about his ability to clearly explain the problem(s) (e.g., "It might be not easy to talk freely about our feelings. Every word coming up in your mind may be useful and important to try to better understand what you are feeling in this situation"). Differences in socioeconomic and cultural background are also obstacles that might be difficult to overcome since age, gender, education, economic position, religion, and so forth are unchangeable. The therapist should create a nonjudging atmosphere where these differences can be made explicit and accepted. A useful strategy to overcome these unremovable and unchangeable barriers is commenting on them while using an empathic, not critical, and open attitude (e.g., "I'm wondering whether our age difference may be a problem for you"). For a further description of nonverbal components potentially affecting doctor–patient interaction, see Chapter 5.

2.3.2 The Data-Gathering Process: Aims and Contents

The role of the therapist in this stage is to listen carefully and, if necessary, to guide patients through their story-telling. The process of gathering information therefore has the following aims:

- understanding the patient's problems from the patient's point of view (exploring the patient's agenda);
- understanding the patient's problems from the therapist's point of view and inserting them in the cognitive-behavioral framework (formulation);
- considering in which direction the interpersonal style of the patient (if in the direction of an attachment deficit in personal relationships, or toward a deficit of autonomy, of personal efficacy) is evolving and building the therapeutic relationship;
- listening attentively, allowing the patient to complete statements without interruptions and leaving her space to think before answering or going on after pausing;
- checking if information gathered about both views (the patient's and the therapist's) is accurate, complete, and mutually understood;
- promoting the patient's trust and collaboration also by picking up cues and concerns (see Chapter 3);
- structuring the interview to ensure efficient information gathering;
- using concise, easily understandable language.

As in a medical context, in psychotherapy the patient's agenda may differ substantially from the therapist's agenda (Fig. 2.1).

The contents of the *patient's agenda* to be explored are similar to those in the medical context, even if they are more focused on psychosocial aspects. It is important to check with the patients for their ideas on the possible cause of their problem (*patient's theory*) and the reasons why the problem has been maintained during time. It is a common and natural tendency to give a meaning to what happened to us in our life both to events and to distressful experiences. People tend to search for meaning even when no causal events have occurred. The patient's theory can also be a good starting point to explore his cognitive functions. The way in which clients explain the nature and possible causes of their problem provides the therapist with good information for the cognitive-behavioral formulation. It is possible to discover naive theories, particularly if there are severe symptoms that compromise the reality testing. Sometimes patients can attribute their illness to particular events, resulting in misleading attribution. Again, for the cognitive-behavioral therapist, this is important information that can help her to better adjust and structure the psychotherapy. Another content area to be explored is the *patient's expectations*. Whether it is the first contact with a mental health provider or he has already had previous experiences, the client may approach the interview with several preconceived notions or questions about psychotherapy. Media can also influence the image of mental health providers, such as psychologists and psychiatrists. Cognitive-behavioral therapy prescribes an open and directive style of the interview, and patients might be surprised by that. For the clinician it is therefore useful to take into account these beliefs and expectations that may influence the patient's responses. In those cases where there is a pharmacological treatment or previous treatment/therapy experiences, it is necessary to explore the effects and duration of the past treatments and to discover if patients are

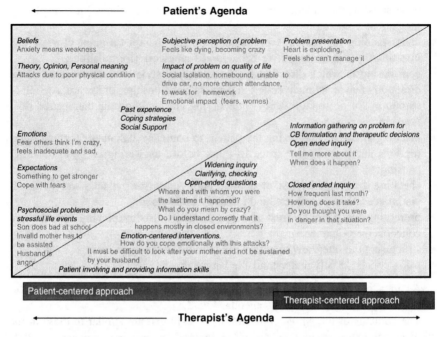

Fig. 2.1 Patient's and therapist's agendas with examples (modified from Tate 1994)

experiencing any side effects that may represent distressful symptoms (e.g., nausea, drowsiness, anxiety, sexual dysfunction).

The therapist should ask also about the *impact* of patients' problems on daily life, for example, in their ability to work, to cope with day-to-day chores, to pursue their hobbies, leisure, and social activities. In particular, the impact on relationships and social context should be carefully assessed (e.g., friends, family). The therapist can discover that problems are acute (for example, a low mood that compromises social activities) or that they are related to a more stable personality trait that has created difficulties at times and they are now more evident. Another important aspect to explore is patients' perception of practical and emotional *support* received from important key persons, such as relatives, friends, and others. Family and social context reactions can vary from being too protective to completely disinterested or even intolerant. Once again, these aspects are very useful information, to know both patients' coping strategies and their possible problematic relationships. In conclusion, collecting the patient's agenda is helpful for several reasons: It provides a more precise idea of his problem from his her perspective; it contributes to relationship building; and it also provides useful information to complete the therapist's agenda and to conceptualize the case from a cognitive-behavioral perspective.

On the other hand, the aim for the first sessions of the psychotherapy in the *therapist's agenda* is to build on a general assessment of the background, current circumstances, and mental state of the patient. The links among feelings, thoughts, and behaviors have to be tested out. Symptoms should be explored following a dimensional approach that examines the degree and nature of distress (if any) and the frequency, amount of preoccupation, and effect on the individual's functioning. Understanding the content of the dysfunctional beliefs is necessary to discuss and debate them later. Yet, in the early stage of the assessment, it is necessary to extract particular issues to focus upon, using a cognitive ABC formulation (Ellis 1962) to understand activating events (e.g., "My boss might yelling at me"), beliefs (e.g., "It would be terrible if ..."), and consequences (e.g., fear and guilt with behavioral avoidance), and subsequently challenge them. The ABC formulation should be considered, however, as a general mental scheme that the therapist bears in mind in the entire data gathering. It can also be used in the conduction of the functional behavioral assessment, where it is important to describe in detail the problematic behavior (behavioral unit: B), in which situations this behavior occurs (antecedents: A), and what happens after its occurrence (consequences: C). Also, the goals of the treatment should be openly discussed and agreed with the patient at the beginning of the treatment, just at the end of the assessment process. An empirical study (Rossi et al. 2008) has demonstrated that this prescription has a value for the technique itself, but also to limit the drop-out phenomenon, which could be considered a key outcome indicator in psychotherapy.

2.3.3   Data-Gathering Process: Communication Skills

At the beginning of the interview, it is more useful to adopt an open inquiry so the therapist can let the patient's narrative express freely. The therapist should be careful not to interrupt the patient too soon, as the first problem described may not be the most important one. Going too deeply too soon can lead to the risks of both losing information and compromising the relationship. On the other hand, the order in which events, memories, concerns, and other psychological themes are verbalized is never accidental. Mathematicians have known for a long time that it is impossible for any person to generate prolonged sequences of random numbers, as they soon fall on significant schemas. The mind prefers order to chaos, and the same happens to the patient's narrative.

Several communication skills are useful for the information-gathering process. We will provide a brief description with some general examples of the following: listening, facilitations, reflections, clarifications, open- and close-ended questions, checking, summarizing, and reformulations. Therapists can feel more natural and spontaneous using certain skills, whereas for others they need more practice order to feel comfortable with their use. Extending the foundation of know and abilities can result in a significant improvement in therapist–patient c cation. Chapters 6 and 7 offer many examples of the application of th psychotherapy sessions.

2.3.3.1 Listening

Listening abilities are the basic skills for information gathering but also for building and reinforcing the therapeutic alliance. The effective use of listening skills allows, on one hand, the patient time to think and to contribute more without being interrupted and, on the other hand, the therapist to have time to listen, think, and respond with more flexibility. Without the listening skills that signal the therapist's interest in the patient, the patient may remain uncertain about his or her real attitude toward the patient's problems. For these reasons, listening is more important than speaking when we try to give voice to things that have been previously locked up. Through silence, the therapist invites the patient to fill in the emptiness, and makes the patient feel that she has permission to do it, not according to an external rule or someone's else desire, but following her more intimate nature (Bara and Cutica 2002). The goal of listening is also to respond to what the patient is saying, through actions such as eye contact or brief vocal utterances, which clearly indicate that the therapist is attentive to the patient's story. Listening abilities include giving space to the patient and following his pace. Because of this, listening can be more passive or more active.

Passive Listening

Passive listening includes the appropriate use of silence and use of nonverbal and verbal facilitation (see later in the section). Waiting time, brief silence, and pauses can very easily and naturally facilitate the speaker to tell more. Longer silences are also appropriate with expression difficulties or if it seems that the patient is about to be overwhelmed by deep emotions. The aim here is to assist the patient to express thoughts or feelings that are occurring inside her mind at that time. Sometimes silence can be a source of anxiety for both the patient and the therapist. If this occurs, it is up to the clinician to interrupt it and create a more comfortable situation.

Much of our attitude toward listening is signaled through our *nonverbal behavior* (see Chapter 5), which immediately gives the patient strong cues to our level of interest in him and his problem(s). Nonverbal behaviors include posture, movement, proximity, direction of gaze, eye contact, gestures, effect, vocal aspects (e.g., tone, volume, and rates), facial expression, touch, physical appearance, and environmental aspects. We can convey listening to, and therefore interest for, the patient's story through all these nonverbal behaviors, but particularly important is eye contact. The way the therapist looks at the patient while listening can be something that encourages the patient to talk freely, but it can also be misinterpreted. Misinterpretation can be due both to the therapist's attitude or to patient pathology (e.g., suspiciousness) and can inhibit therapist–patient communication and compromise their alliance. Another important thing to keep in mind is that it is necessary to give congruency between the verbal and nonverbal messages. We cannot express interest in another person while looking out the window.

Moreover, we know that in psychotherapy the first impression is important and can contribute to generate dysfunctional interpersonal processes, which the therapist should be able to recognize and appropriately manage (Safran and Segal 1990).

Active Listening

Active listening can be defined as an approach that requires intense concentration on the patient's verbal and nonverbal expression and is aimed at understanding and responding to the patient's feelings and fears and at understanding the links between the illness and the patient's life. It is as much an attitude of mind as a specific interviewing technique (Ford et al. 2000). Active listening signals interest in the patient, to listen carefully to her story, to prevent the therapist from making a premature hypothesis, to observe the patient for verbal and nonverbal cues (see Chapter 5). Active listening is therefore the result of all the therapist's efforts and of the atmosphere he is able to create with patients in order to understand them.

Examples

The patient experiences thoughts racing through her head. The therapist may observe flight of ideas and find it difficult to follow what the patient is saying or to interrupt her because of the swiftness and quantity of speech.

Pt: I have so many other things to tell you ...

Th: I see. ...You are thinking too many different things, all at once. Maybe we can try to focus our attention on one of them, perhaps the most important one to you at the moment.

2.3.3.2 Facilitations

These skills encourage patients to say more about the topic, indicate that the therapist is interested in what they are saying, and let them continue freely in their narrative. Using these skills at the beginning of the interview allows the patient's agenda to emerge. Facilitation can also be used to recognize and pick up cues to feelings and emotions and to make the patient feel understood and sustained. Facilitations are simple and neutral expressions such as, "Hmm," "ah," "I see," "yes" to go with body movements and facial expressions, such as nodding and smiling. Even something as simple as a slight eye movement can be effective if used properly. All these simple expressions following the patient's speech facilitate his narrative and make him feel listened to, understood, and supported. Through these brief actions patients can see and feel that the therapist is listening, following, and understanding their narrative.

Examples

Pt: I feel a little bit down.

Th: Hmm (looking at the patient and nodding).

Pt: I have been feeling down since my husband lost his job.

Th: Please go on.

2.3.3.3 Reflections

These statements are used to signal listening, to help patients continue in a particular direction, and to facilitate them in their narrative. The goal is to let them know the therapist is listening, by reflecting back what they have just said. Reflections encourage patients to clarify further or expand the information and allow the therapist to check that he has accurately understood what has been said. Listening to the therapist repeats what she just said gives the patient the chance to reconsider things, assess if the information is accurate, reflect on feelings and thoughts, and become more aware of her inner psychological process. As facilitations, reflections can also be used for recognizing and picking up cues to feelings and to make the patient feel understood and sustained (see Chapter 3). Reflections can be simple repetitions of words or a longer part of what the patient has said (echoing). This echoing skill can be very efficient in letting patients go on in their narrative, but can also be used to direct them to a particular topic of interest. The therapist can actually decide what phrase, word, or part of the speech he wants to repeat, underlining particular content and/or emotion. Reflections confirm that the therapist is listening and attentive and are more well constructed than the simple facilitation. In addition, reflections convey to patients that their role in the data-gathering process is important and valued. As this skill gives a direction to the patient's narrative, it can be considered slightly more directive than simple facilitation or silence. We also label reflection skills when the therapist completes the patient's sentence. This kind of mind reading can be very effective for building a relationship, as well as to facilitate the patient's narrative.

Examples

Pt: I have some problems with my partner and I feel very guilty.
Th: feel guilty (echoing). *In this case we expect that the patient will continue to talk about her feelings and emotions regarding her partner.*
Th: some problems (echoing). *In this other case, we expect the patient will continue to talk about the sort of problems she has with her partner.*
Pt: I don't know what to do in this situation. *(The patient stops talking and gazes intensively at the therapist.)*
Th: You look a little bit worried... *(Rreflection of a possible emotion-educated guess)*
Pt: In this particular situation I feel like I'm ...
Th: in a cage... *(completing patient's statement)*
Pt: Exactly, it is a very hard situation and I don't know how to deal with it.

2.3.3.4 Clarification

The patient's choice of words, or expression, can often have different meanings, and it is important to ascertain which one is intended. Clarification is therefore useful to check statements that are vague or need amplification. Used when the patient has chosen words with a confusing, vague, or unclear meaning, clarification prompts the patient for more precision, clarity, or completeness.

Examples

Pt: I'm feeling upside down.
Th: What do you mean by "feeling upside down"?
Pt: My husband is ignoring me.
Th: What do you mean by "ignoring" . . .?

2.3.3.5   Open-Ended Questions

In the first part of the interview, the use of open questions may have more advantages compared with closed questions. Open-ended questions are those beginning with "what, who, when, why," etc., which allow the patient to answer in an open way. They therefore encourage patients to freely their story more freely and give the therapist time and space to listen and to think about the patient's problem and story rather than thinking of what to ask or explore next. Open-ended questions help the exploration of problems from both the patient's and the cognitive-behavioral therapist's point of view. In the early stage of the assessment, it is worthwhile to ask patient-centered open questions in order to priority to the client's perspective and let her direct the narrative. Sometimes this may lead to an initial lack of specific information necessary for a well-defined cognitive-behavioral formulation (preceding scenario of an unpleasant emotion, avoidance behaviors, thoughts and feelings during unpleasant moments). The collection of these data will be necessarily postponed in the phase of the assessment that is more centered on the clinician's agenda (see Sect. 2.4.1), where closed and open questions will be used in order to complete missing or too generic descriptions.

Moreover, these skills represent the first step for patient involvement, as they foster his collaboration and participation. Open-ended questions are therefore important, to open the interview, to facilitate free patient expression, to help in defining problematic areas, and to explore new topics introduced by the patient. As the interview proceeds, the therapist may need to become more directive in exploring certain areas in more detail; she can say, for example, "Tell me more about this feeling guilty." Open-ended questions allow more details but also discourage irrelevant elaborations by patients. By using these interventions, the therapist can complete the patient's agenda. For several reasons, patients may not have in mind all their problems or they may not consider it important to mention some particular aspects. It is therefore important that the therapist checks whether there are other problems that have not yet been mentioned. These issues can be noted but not immediately explored. The clinician can first carry on with questions about further problems until the patient indicates that there are no more and leave the problem's exploration until later on in the interview. Open questions not only invite patients to open up but also show that the therapist values and respects their observations and encourages input and participation (see also Chapter 4), promoting an active patient role, which is essential in cognitive-behavioral psychotherapy. A more active role in therapy can contribute to increasing patients' sense of control over the interaction, which often leads to a better outcome.

Questions for the cognitive-behavioral therapist are used both in the information-gathering stage and in the more therapeutic stage as a cognitive-behavioral–specifictechnique, such as in, for example, the Socratic dialogue (Freeman et al. 2005), or to educate patients to pay more attention to their emotions and thoughts and on their consequences in everyday life.

Examples

Th: Would you tell me in your own words what has brought you here today? *(Starting the interview)*
Th: What else about your feelings in this situation? *(Completing the patient's agenda)*
Th: What kind of problem have you experienced with this medicine? *(Exploring patient's agenda: treatment)*
Th: How is your low mood affecting your life at the moment? *(Exploring patient's agenda: impact)*
Th: How do you feel about the support you are receiving in this situation by your family? *(Exploring patient's agenda: social support)*
Th: What do you think was the starting point of your problems? *(Exploring patient's agenda: patient theory)*
Th: When you came in today, you probably had some idea of how I could help you. *(Exploring patient's agenda: expectation)*
Th: What has been your experience with this problem over the last year? *(Exploring patient's agenda: coping strategies)*
Th: How would you describe your relationship with others? *(Exploring therapist's agenda)*
Pt: During lunch my husband was talking to a friend on the phone and ignored me completely.
Th: What did that mean for you? *(Exploring therapist's agenda)*
Pt: Probably that I am not an interesting person to talk to.

2.3.3.6 Closed Questions

Closed questions are those that imply a yes or no answer or a forced choice between two or more options. They are therefore specific and focused, and they discourage the patient from talking. As the interview proceeds, it is important for the therapist to become gradually more focused on his agenda. This can be done initially by using more topic-oriented open questions in order to direct the interview to a specific area of interest (e.g., interference of symptoms with the quality of life). In a second step, the clinician needs to move to closed questions to elicit fine details and to better understand the problem from the cognitive-behavioral perspective. Moving from open questions to more closed questions can be done by using transitions and summarizing (see Sect. 2.3.1). For example, the therapist can say, "Now I'm going to ask you several questions that can help us to focus better on your problem." Closed questions are therefore necessary to investigate specific areas and to analyze symptoms in detail. Closed questions can be very useful if skillfully used. They can give quick and narrowly focused information that can be tremendously important at some stages of the assessment. These interventions are generally used after the patient-centered data collection to complete the patient's problem(s) in more detail. They also allow hypothesis testing, and by restraining the patient's spontaneous information flow, they therefore reduce patient participation. A possible risk of using too many closed questions is to force the patient into prepackaged answers. It is possible that during hypothesis formulation, the therapist thinks too fast and wants to test a premature hypothesis. For example, the therapist can assume that in a certain circumstance the patient feels an unpleasant emotion. Instead of asking, "How do you feel?" he may ask, "Do you feel inadequate in that situation?" If the answer is "no," the therapist might think that there are no unpleasant emotions linked to that particular situation. Attention should particularly be paid to depressed patients, who are generally very passive or with patients who want to please the therapist, such as those with dependent personality traits. If closed questions are used too early in the interview, patients can become passive and reluctant to share information and the therapist runs the risk of appearing authoritarian, controlling, and superior, with little interest in having a partnership with the patient. Too many closed questions moreover can give the impression that the therapist is rushing through the interview, being disinterested in the patient's story. Therefore, closed questions should be well balanced and used in the interview only after the patient's agenda has been widely explored and a good relationship established.

2.3.3.7 Checking

The aim of this communication skill is to check, test, or verify the accuracy of the therapist's subjective understanding of the patient's narrative. Specifically, the clinician makes a statement that represents her inner understanding of a patient's concept, expression, or phrase and asks the patient for feedback or correction. This skill allows a bidirectional exchange of information (from the patient's initial statement, through the therapist's comprehension, to the patient's correction) that avoids misunderstandings and helps the therapist when in doubt, confused, or too overwhelmed by the patient's narrative. Misunderstandings can have a negative impact on the therapeutic alliance and on the motivation to psychotherapy and need to be identified and corrected as soon as possible. A misunderstanding may lead the clinician to misinterpret the patient's problems and provide a formulation not adapted to the patient, with negative consequences on the entire therapeutic process.

There are other reasons that make this skill essential for the good outcome of psychotherapy. First of all, a patient who feels that the therapist is doing his best to understand the patient's problems, emotions, and opinions will have more trust and be more willing to continue the psychotherapy. Moreover, describing problematic situations or unpleasant feelings can be a difficult task for patients. They might be worried they are not able to clearly express what they feel and/or think. Meeting a therapist who gives the opportunity to reword a concept in order to get a shared comprehension on it may be very helpful for them to achieve this challenging task. Finally, checking makes the patient feel that his perspective on the problem is taken into great consideration and actively searched, which makes him feel involved in the therapeutic process and increases his commitment to psychotherapy.

According to what we have said, when checking, it is important to pay attention to both the form and the content of the statement. Efficacious checking needs to be short and concise, but at the same time exhaustive and emphatic. It may be useful staring with an introduction like, "What you are telling me is that . . ." using a pleasant tone of voice and giving the statement the intonation of a question, not a judgment. These expedients will help the patient feel free to correct the therapist. Moreover, the clinician should be able to decide which content needs to be checked and focused on.

Examples

> Th: You told me that you experienced anxiety in the supermarket. Is this correct?
> Th: Help me to be clearer on this. You said . . .
> Th: You are sure . . . you never experienced this before?
> Th: Just to see if I've got this right, you went to that conference in Boston and started to feel confused in front of the people sitting there.
> Pt: I feel so depressed. . . . I've never felt like this. . . . And I fear that things could get worse. . . . But psychotherapy is such a big commitment. . . . I don't know. . . .
> Th: You are telling me that despite the fact you are feeling pretty bad, you are not sure about psychotherapy?

2.3.3.8 Summarizing

Summarizing is the deliberate step of making an explicit verbal summary of the information gathered so far. We know that there are several sources of possible distortions in communication that can occur. They can be related to the patient, to the setting, or to the therapist. In any case, summarizing can facilitate the comprehension and improve patient–therapist communication. Clinicians cannot take for granted their understanding without checking the accuracy of the gathered information, and direct feedback from the patient is the best guarantee. The therapist should therefore be able to summarize the patient's problems, by using the patient's words when possible, to verify her own understanding of what has been said and to invite patients to correct the interpretation or provide further information. Summarizing, if used frequently throughout the interview, is a good method of ensuring the accuracy and completeness of information gathered. It also signals listening to the patients and facilitates them to go further with explanations of their problems, but at the same time it brings them back to the point and prevents them from becoming lost. Summarizing is a useful skill because it increases the clarity and completeness of the information, provides space to think about review, and helps to formulate hypotheses. It allows the ordering of thoughts and clarifies in the therapist's mind what aspects he wants to explore in more detail. Moreover, it allows the patient's perspective (or agenda) to be integrated with the cognitive-behavioral framework (or the therapist's agenda). It is therefore important to summarize all the information gathered from both the patient's and the therapist's points of view. The patient can agree on his summarized vision and start to become familiar with the new framework, laying the foundation for patient involvement in the therapeutic process.

Summarizing can also be used to structure the interview, as described in more detail below.

Examples

Th: You told me your wife began to change some years ago. You suspected she had a love affair with a friend of yours. Since then, you've started to feel down, with this persistent thought in your mind about your wife. Now she is pregnant and you still have a lot of doubts about the real father.

Th: I'd like to sum up with you what you said so far: The panic attacks started three months ago when your husband was rushed to the hospital for respiratory problems. This event made you think about the possibility of losing your husband and raising your children alone. Moreover, you are going through a difficult financial situation. These thoughts have become more and more serious and are still present even though your husband has recovered well.

2.3.3.9 Reformulation

Reformulation lies between data gathering and information giving. It can be considered a more specific cognitive-behavioral technique rather than a simple communication skill. Reformulation means to restate with the therapist's own words the content or emotion expressed by the patient; therefore, it is mostly related to the content expressed. In this paraphrasing the therapist can add some educational or therapeutic messages, for example, showing the linkage between events and emotions. Reformulation differs from simple summarizing, because the clinician adds something new, potentially helpful for the therapeutic process. Reformulation combines elements of clarification, facilitation, summarizing, and reflections. The patient's explanation is redefined in terms of a measurable construct that will be incorporated in a cognitive-behavioral model of treatment.

Examples

Pt: I don't know what would happen if my wife really needed my help. ... She is so demanding ...
Th: In other words, it sounds as if you are worried that you might be overwhelmed by the situation.
Pt: I feel stupid. ... I shouldn't have said all those bad things to him. ... I should have waited before answering. ... Now he does not want to talk to me anymore. ... I always act like that ... faster than my thoughts ...
Th: What you are telling me is that you have the impression that your impulsiveness sometimes impairs your relationships ...

2.4 Structuring the Interview in Psychotherapy

The goal of the assessment interview in cognitive-behavioral therapy is to collect all the relevant information in order to achieve a better understanding of patient's problem(s) and together with the patient to make some decisions on how to deal with the problem(s) (plan a therapeutic program). The therapist's abilities to provide the consultation with a clear organization and to orient the patients throughout the entire assessment phase become fundamental for the single interview and for the duration of the psychotherapy. These abilities become part of a process and are based on several different skills, such as the agenda setting, the use of orienting expressions, summarizing, transitions, and sign-posting. The assessment phase can be divided into four different stages with specific goals. In the first stage, the therapist helps the patient to explore, define, and clarify the problem(s) (exploring patient's agenda); in the second stage, the therapist explores the patient's problem from a cognitive-behavioral perspective, referring to theoretical models (exploring therapist's agenda); in the third stage, the therapist provides the patient with all the relevant information regarding his problem(s) and tries to incorporate the cognitive-behavioral theories and models with the patient's agenda (developing a new perspective-reformulation); finally, in the fourth stage, the therapist and the patient set reasonable therapeutic goals and decide how to achieve these goals (decision making). These stages seldom occur all together during the first consultation, and sometimes the therapist needs several encounters to assess the patient before starting the more specific and technical therapeutic phase. The clinician should always be aware of these different stages during the process of assessment. This awareness helps to give clarity to the interview and assists the therapist in organizing the sessions according to the specific aims that need to be achieved.

The interview structure should to be shared with the patient, too. First of all, the clinician should elicit the goal of the assessment phase (e.g., "Before deciding whether to start psychotherapy, I'll need some preliminary meetings to collect information about your current problem(s). Only in a second time we will decide together what we need to work on."). Moreover, the patient also should be made aware of the shift from one stage to another when it occurs within the same interview or between different sessions. The therapist can close an interview's stage with a brief summary followed by a transition to introduce the new stage (e.g., "Up to now we have agreed upon some goals you consider important for your welfare. Now and in the next session I would like to start to discuss with you what can be done to achieve these goals.").

Each session of the assessment phase therefore needs to be structured according to its specific aims. The following steps may help to ideally structure assessment appointments: (a) opening the interview, which includes greetings and elicitation of the goals of the consultation (if it is the first encounter, this will be to assess the reason for coming); (b) gathering information, with particular attention to the patient's agenda; (c) exploring the patient's problem(s) from the therapist's perspective; (d) sharing information and decisions; and (e) a closure phase (Fig. 2.2).

In our opinion, such a clear and ordered approach, with transitions and summaries, allows accurate and efficient data gathering and facilitates patient participation, also having a positive effect on the therapeutic alliance and on the patient's motivation for psychotherapy. Organizing the available time is also useful, especially with patients who tend to wander from one subject to another. Obviously, it is important that the therapist follows these steps only as a suggestive guide that does

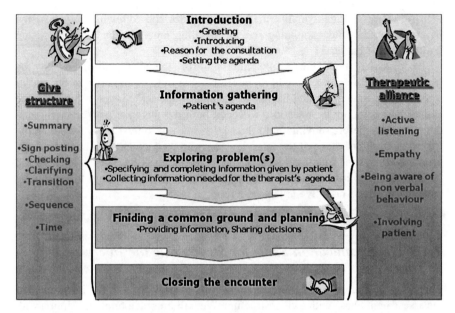

Fig. 2.2 The structure of the interview (modified from Silverman et al. 1998)

not need to be strictly applied, but they have to be changed if necessary and/or adapted to the specific needs of each patient (e.g., a patient who is too anxious may not be able to listen and understand the therapist's information in that particular moment; the therapist therefore should be able to recognize and handle the emotion and to postpone the information giving, even if it was previously agreed).

2.4.1 Structuring the Interview: The Goals

The goals of structuring are organizing the session(s), orienting the patient throughout the session, reviewing, recognizing possible missing data, and consistently ordering the gathered information (from both the patient's and the therapist's perspective). Providing structure to the interview and eliciting it with patients facilitates their overall comprehension and gives them a chance to become more active in the therapy. Structuring the interview therefore ensures efficient information gathering and enables the patient to feel involved in the therapeutic process.

Most people asking for psychological help can have preconceived ideas about psychologists, psychotherapists, and psychiatrists, and sometimes they may even ignore the differences among these professionals. Providing initial information about what is going to happen during the interview can help patients reduce unpleasant emotions related to their expectations and reduce their uncertainty. Moreover, structuring the interview together with asking patients' opinions can help to promote patient involvement, essential for the following stages of the psychotherapy; while combining it with handling emotion can aid relationship building (see Chapter 3).

To organize both the single interview or the different stages of the psychotherapy, therapists should therefore be able to (a) summarize at the end of a particular point (this could happen at the end of a specific issue or during/at the end/at the beginning of a session) to check both the therapist's and the patient's understanding before moving on to the next section or to next step of the therapy, (b) move from one stage of the interview (or from an encounter) to another, using agenda setting, time framing, transition, and sequencing skills. The therapist should be able to achieve these tasks while keeping attention on listening, following the patient's flow and narrative at the same time.

2.4.2 Communication Skills for Structuring the Interview

There are several helpful communication skills to provide both the interview and the assessment phase with a clear structure. We will present a brief description with some examples of the following: setting the agenda, time framing and sequencing, orienting expressions, and summarizing.

2.4.2.1 Setting the Agenda

Setting the agenda can be done just after the introduction phase and orients the patient about the duration and the aims of the session. Explaining what the therapist intends to do during the session is also essential for building the relationship. Stating the purpose of the interview aids the patient to prepare for the direction of the interview, for example, knowing the available time for the interview helps patients to better focus on the more distressful problems and to put all their effort into expressing their agenda by the end of the consultation. Setting the agenda makes it less likely that the patient will miss talking about important issues and reduces the risk of being overwhelmed by irrelevant aspects. It is important to check with the patient if the amount of time is enough for him. Sometimes patients think the time is too short, so the therapist can explain that although everything may not be completed in only one session, the patient can have more time during the following session to go into the problem(s) thoroughly. Setting the agenda contributes also to reinforcing the patient's trust through a clear expression of the therapist's intents. This can be useful also with suspicious patients, such as paranoid personality disorder. If therapists are used to audiotaping the interview or taking notes, these activities should also be explained from the very beginning. The therapist can explain the reason why she is doing this and remind the patient that all the material collected is personal and confidential. Most patients are reassured by seeing the therapist writing down notes, as they feel they are more taken into consideration. An exception can be represented by the suspicious patient, who may disagree with these procedures and ask the therapist not to do it. In this case the therapist can explore the reasons for asking this and take the chance to better explore these mistrustful feelings. This open attitude, shown from the beginning, improves patients' participation and collaboration.

Sometimes clients are referred by third parties (e.g., family doctor, psychiatrist, relatives, friends) to the therapist's attention. In these cases some personal information may already be available before the consultation, and so a good practice is to start the interview by summarizing these data briefly.

Setting the agenda in the second and subsequent sessions can start with summarizing problems raised during the last encounter and asking the patient which problem he would like to start talking about first.

Examples

Th: Generally, the first session will last about 45 minutes. In this available time I would like to have a general idea of your problem(s). So first of all, I will ask you some questions about the main reason for coming in today.

Th: During the last session you mentioned some distressful events that happened in the last year and some difficulties you have at work and with your husband too. I'd like to talk more about these topics today. Which of these would you like to tell me more about first?

Th: After you tell me more about these depressive feelings, I will share with you my ideas about how the therapy can be helpful.

2.4.2.2 Time Framing and Sequencing

Time framing refers to all the abilities helpful in arranging the patient's talk in order to give a logical and temporal sequence to the reported events. The therapist needs to know when each problem started, as some symptoms can be an expression of acute distress while others can reflect more personality traits. Moreover, it is important to find out whether there is a temporal sequence between events and emotions or distress and thoughts. This makes it possible to explain to the patient, even in the following stages, the possible link between these aspects from a cognitive-behavioral framework or the role of life events as triggers of illness. Patients can date events and problems accurately if they are encouraged and educated to do so. This can be helpful also in the subsequent stages, when the therapist will ask the patient to do homework (e.g., ABC exercises). The therapist may wish to inquire about time-sequence issues, by asking the patient what occurred immediately before or after a given event, with particular attention to emotions, thoughts, and behaviors. *Sequencing* means to structure the interview by developing a logical order, accepted also by the patient, and by providing a rationale for doing and saying particular things during the sessions. Sequencing also means to design appropriate turn-taking in speaking, pacing, and using the available time efficiently. The therapist should be able to tactfully limit peripheral and unproductive discussion and pace the session appropriately for the patient, allowing other slots of time to explore others aspects of care if necessary.

Examples

Th: What was happening while you were experiencing anxiety peak?
Pt: Nothing.
Th: I know this might be difficult, but try to remember ...
Pt: Hmm. . . . Maybe I was starting to think that my heart was beating too fast. I was worried I was having a heart attack.
Th: I was wondering if it could be possible that your anxiety is related to this sort of dangerous thoughts.

2.4.2.3 Orienting Expressions (Transitions and Sign-Posting)

These expressions are used to progress from one session of the interview to another and to explain the rationale to talk or ask about a particular issue. Orienting expressions are explanations of the reasons why the therapist has decided to move toward another topic, to return to a previous one, or to change stage during the interview. Transitions can also be used to move from the patient's agenda to the therapist's agenda. This skill also orients the interview, and facilitates the collaboration, encouraging the patient's involvement in the therapeutic process and his active role-taking. Orienting expressions facilitate the patient's understanding about the aims of the interview and about the reason behind certain therapist interventions. In this way the patient can feel that she is playing an important part in the therapeutic process, which can foster the therapeutic alliance.

Transitions can also be used to move from one content item to another. Transitions can be simple, brief orienting words or phrases or motivated explanations for changes in interview content.

Examples

Th: Now I need to ask you about ...
Th: I want to go back to ...
Th: I want to ask you more about your feelings in that specific situation you told me about.
Th: You mentioned the important role of your family during your childhood ...
Th: We have 10 minutes left before the end of this session.

2.4.2.4 Summarizing

Summarizing has already been described in the previous chapter for its important role in structuring the interview. It helps the therapist to feel more comfortable with the gathered information, and not to become lost, particularly with patients who give confused descriptions or give incoherent and unintegrated narratives. Summarizing is essential to put all the information together, to make order, and to give a logical sense to the data collected. It aids the therapist in bringing patients back to their point, increasing the quality of the gathered information, and better structuring patients' narrative. This intervention supports both the patient and the therapist in improving the quality of their communication and provides an opportunity for them to work cooperatively in achieving a better understanding of the patient's problems and trying to solve them. It is helpful also because it allows the therapist to realize what areas need further exploration and to consider in which direction she wants to go next. Summarizing can facilitate the identification of the most important problem for the patient. When too many issues have been raised for just one session, the therapist and patient negotiate and agree on what will be addressed in the next sessions and when they will consider the deferred issue (see Chapter 4).

Examples

Th: You told me you were scared in that situation because you thought that others could harm you. I would like to ask you more about what happened.
Th: I have written down the goals you would like to achieve with this therapy; they are to improve your self-esteem, to increase your public relations skills, and to become less shy.
Th: Today we have talked about your current problem. In the next session I will ask you more about your social background and your family.

2.5 Conclusion

In a cognitive-behavioral perspective, an essential part of the assessment phase is the process of data gathering. Without collecting good information, it will not be possible to understand the patient's problem(s), and consequently her collaboration and trust may be compromised. Communication is therefore a key element in this stage of the therapy and represents the bridge.

Using communication skills appropriately allows the therapist to obtain more information about the presented problem, increases the reliability of collected information, signals interest in the patient's views and experiences, stimulates the patient's participation and collaboration, and, finally, makes the consultation more effective. An accurate and detailed information-gathering process, together with the implementation of a collaborative relationship, is essential to achieve greater health outcomes.

At the beginning of the interview, it is more useful to adopt an open inquiry so the therapist can let the patient's narrative be expressed freely. The role of the therapist in this stage is to listen carefully and, if necessary, to guide patients through their story-telling. Moreover, providing structure to the interview and eliciting it with the patients facilitates their overall comprehension and gives them a chance to become more active in the therapy. Structuring the interview therefore ensures efficient information gathering and enables the patient to feel involved in the therapeutic process.

Several communication skills are useful for the information-gathering process and for structuring the interview. We have provided a brief description with some general examples of the following: listening, facilitations, reflections, clarifications, open- and close-ended questions, checking, summarizing, reformulating, setting the agenda, time framing and sequencing, and orienting expressions. Therapists can feel more natural and spontaneous using certain skills, whereas for others they need more practice in order to feel comfortable with their use. Extending the foundation of knowledge and abilities can result in a significant improvement in therapist–patient communication.

References

Alaszewski, A., & Horlick-Jones, T. (2003). How can doctors communicate information about risk more effectively? *British Medical Journal, 327*, 728–731.

Bara, B. G., & Cutica, I. (2002). La comunicazione [In Italian]. In C. Castelfranchi, F. Mancini, & M. Miceli (Eds.), *Fondamenti di cognitivismo clinico* (pp. 258–280). Torino: Bollati Boringhieri.

Bodenheimer, T., Lorig, K., Holman, H., & Grumbach, K. (2002). Patient self-management of chronic disease in primary care. *Journal of the American Medical Association, 288*, 2469–2475.

Braddock, C. H., Edwards, K. A., Hasenberg, N. M., Laidley, T. L., & Levinson, W. (1999). Informed decision making in outpatient practice: Time to get back to basics. *Journal of the American Medical Association, 282*, 2313–2320.

Butler, C., Rollnick, S., & Stott, N. (1996). The practitioner, the patient and resistance to change: Recent ideas on compliance. *Canadian Medical Association Journal, 154*, 1357–1362.

Charles, C., Gafni, A., & Whelan, T. (2000). How to improve communication between doctors and patients. Learning more about the decision making context is important. *British Medical Journal, 320*, 1220–1221.

Cohen-Cole, S. A. (1991). *The medical interview: The three-function approach*. St. Louis: Mosby-Year.

Desmond, J., & Copeland, L. R. (2000). *Communication with today's patients*. San Francisco: Jossey-Bass.

Edwards, A., Elwyn, G., & Mulley, A. (2002). Explaining risks: Turning numerical data into meaningful pictures. *British Medical Journal, 324*, 827–830.

Eijk, J. T., & Haan, M. (1998). Care for the chronically ill: The future role of health care professionals and their patients. *Patient Education and Counseling, 35*(3), 233–240.

Ellis, A. (1962). *Reason and emotion in psychotherapy*. New York: Lyle Stuart.

Elwyn, G., Edwards, A., & Britten, N. (2003). What information do patients need about medicines? "Doing prescribing": How doctors can be more effective. *British Medical Journal, 327*, 864–867.

Elwyn, G., Edwards, A., Kinnersley, P., & Grol, R. (2000). Shared decision making and the concept of equipoise: The competencies of involving patients in healthcare choices. *British Journal of General Practice, 50*, 892–899.

Engel, G. L. (1977). The need for a new medical model. A challenge for biomedicine. *Science, 196*, 129–136.

Ford, S., Hall, A., Ratcliffe, D., & Fallowfield, L. (2000). The Medical Interaction Process System (MIPS): An instrument for analysing interviews of oncologists and patients with cancer. *Social Science and Medicine, 50*, 553–566.

Freeman, F., Felgoise, S. H., Nezu, C. M., Nezu, A. M., & Reinecke, M. A. (2005). *Encyclopedia of cognitive behavior therapy*. New York: Springer.

Gask, L., & Usherwood, T. (2002). ABC of psychological medicine. The consultation. *British Medical Journal, 324*, 1567–1569.

Goldberg, D. P., Hobson, R. F., Maguire, G. P., Margison, F. R., O'Dowd, T., Osborn, M., et al. (1984). The clarification and assessment of a method of psychotherapy. *British Journal of Psychiatry, 144*, 567–575.

Hall, J. A., Roter, D. L., & Katz, N. R. (1988). Meta-analysis of correlates of provider behavior in medical encounters. *Medical Care, 26*, 657–675.

Harrison, J., & Goldberg, D. (1993). Improving the interview skills of psychiatry trainees. *European Journal of Psychiatry, 7*, 31–40.

Jefford, M., & Tattersall, M. H. (2002). Informing and involving cancer patients in their own care. *Lancet Oncology, 3*(10), 629–637.

Kennedy, J. G. (2003). What information do patients need about medicines? "Doc, tell me what I need to know" – A doctor's perspective. *British Medical Journal, 327*, 862–863.

Kinnersley, P., Scott, N., Peters, T. J., & Harvey, I. (1999). The patient-centredness of consultations and outcome in primary care. *British Journal of General Practice, 49*, 711–716.

Lazarus, R. S., & Folkman, S. (1984). *Stress, appraisal, and coping*. New York: Springer.

Lee, S. J., Back, A. L., Block, S. D., & Stewart, S. K. (2002). Enhancing physician-patient communication. *Hematology (American Society of Hematology. Education Program)*, 464–483.

Lesser, A. (1985). Problem-based interviewing in general practice: A model. *Medical Education, 19*, 299–304.

Lieberman, S., Cobb, J., & Jackson, C. H. (1989). Studying the "Grammar of Psychotherapy" Course using a student and control population. Some results, trends and disappointments. *British Journal of Psychiatry, 155*, 842–845.

Lipkin, M., Putnam, S. M., & Lazare, A. (1995). *The medical interview: Clinical care, education, and research*. New York: Springer.

Little, P., Everitt, H., Williamson, I., Warner, G., Moore, M., Gould, C., et al. (2001). Observational study of effect of patient centredness and positive approach on outcomes of general practice consultations. *British Medical Journal, 323*, 908–911.

Maguire, P. (1982). Psychiatrists also need interview training. *British Journal of Psychiatry, 141*, 423–424.

Maguire, P. (2000). *Communication skills for doctors. A guide to effective communication with patients and families*. London: Arnold.

Maguire, G. P., Goldberg, D. P., Hobson, R. F., Margison, F., Moss, S., & O'Dowd, T. (1984). Evaluating the teaching of a method of psychotherapy. *British Journal of Psychiatry, 144*, 575–580.

Makoul, G., Arntson, P., & Schofield, T. (1995). Health promotion in primary care: Physician–patient communication and decision making about prescription medications. *Social Science and Medicine, 41*(9), 1241–1254.

Maly, R. C., Bourque, L. B., & Engelhardt, R. F. (1999). A randomized controlled trial of facilitating information giving to patients with chronic medical conditions: Effects on outcomes of care. *Journal of Family Practice, 48*, 356–363.

McCready, J. R., & Waring, E. M. (1986). Interviewing skills in relation to psychiatric residency. *Canadian Journal of Psychiatry, 31*, 317–322.

Mead, N., & Bower, P. (2002). Patient-centred consultations and outcome in primary care: A review of the literature. *Patient Education and Counseling, 48*, 51–61.

Miller, W. R., & Rollnick, S. (1991). *Motivational interviewing: Preparing people to change addictive behavior*. New York: Guilford Press.

Moja, E. A., & Vegni, E. (1998). La medicina centrata sul paziente [In Italian]. *Annali Italiani di Medicina Interna, 13*(1), 56–64.

Moja, E. A., & Vegni, E. (2000). *La visita medica centrata sul paziente [In Italian]*. Milano: Raffaello Cortina Editore.

Nuzzarello, A., & Birndorf, C. (2004). An interviewing course for a psychiatry clerkship. *Academic Psychiatry, 28*, 66–70.

Ong, L. M., de Haes, J. C., Hoos, A. M., & Lammes, F. B. (1995). Doctor–patient communication: A review of the literature. *Social Science and Medicine, 40*, 903–918.

Peltenburg, M., Fischer, J. E., Bahrs, O., van Dulmen, S., & van den Brink-Muinen, A. (2004). The unexpected in primary care: A multicenter study on the emergence of unvoiced patient agenda. *Annals of Family Medicine, 2*(6), 534–540.

Pendleton, A., & Hasler, J. (1983). *Doctor–patient communication*. London: Academic Press.
Platt, F. W., & Gordon, G. H. (1999). *Field guide to the difficult patient interview*. Baltimore: Lippincott Williams & Wilkins.
Putnam, S. M., & Stiles, W. B. (1993). Verbal exchanges in medical interviews: Implications and innovations. *Social Science and Medicine, 36*(12), 1597–1604.
Rimondini, M., Del Piccolo, L., Goss, C., Mazzi, M., Paccaloni, M., & Zimmermann, C. (2006). Communication skills in psychiatry residents – How do they handle patient concerns? An application of sequence analysis to interviews with simulated patients. *Psychotherapy and Psychosomatics, 75*, 161–169.
Rimondini, M., Del Piccolo, L., Goss, C., Mazzi, M., Paccaloni, M., & Zimmermann, C. (2010). The evaluation of training in patient-centred interviewing skills for psychiatric residents. *Psychological Medicine, 40*, 467–476.
Rimondini, M., Goss, C., & Zimmermann, C. (2003). L'intervista psichiatrica come strumento di base per valutare l'esito delle cure. La valutazione dell'esito dei trattamenti in psichiatria [In Italian]. *Nòòs, 3*, 191–204.
Rollnick, S., Mason, P., & Butler, C. (1999). *Health behaviour change. A guide for practitioners*. Edinburgh, UK: Churchill Livingstone.
Rossi, A., Rimondini, M., Biscontin, T., Costella, O., Lelli, F., Mannucci, I., et al. (2008). Drop-out from cognitive-behaviour therapy: Findings from a case-control study. *Cognitivismo clinico, 5*(2), 156–173.
Roter, D. L., Hall, J. A., & Katz, N. R. (1987). Relations between physicians' behaviors and analogue patients' satisfaction, recall, and impressions. *Medical Care, 25*, 437–451.
Roter, D. L., Hall, J. A., & Katz, N. R. (1988). Patient–physician communication: A descriptive summary of the literature. *Patient Education and Counseling, 12*, 99–119.
Ryff, C. D., & Singer, B. H. (2000). Biopsychosocial challenges of the new millennium. *Psychotherapy and Psychosomatics, 69*, 170–177.
Safran, J. D., & Segal, L. S. (1990). *Interpersonal process in cognitive therapy*. New York: Basic Books.
Safran, D. G., Taira, D. A., Rogers, W. H., Kosinski, M., Ware, J. E., & Tarlov, A. R. (1998). Linking primary care performance to outcomes of care. *Journal of Family Practice, 47*, 213–220.
Scheiber, S. C., Kramer, T. A., & Adamowski, S. E. (2003). The implications of core competencies for psychiatric education and practice in the US. *Canadian Journal of Psychiatry, 48*, 215–221.
Semerari, A. (2002). *Storia, teorie e tecniche della psicoterapia cognitiva [In Italian]*. Milano: Laterza.
Silverman, J., Kurtz, S., & Draper, J. (1998). Explanation and planning. In J. Silverman, S. Kurtz, & J. Draper (Eds.), *Skills for communicating with patients*. Oxon, UK: Radcliffe Medical Press.
Slade, M., Leese, M., Ruggeri, M., Kuipers, E., Tansella, M., & Thornicroft, G. (2000). Does meeting needs improve quality of life? *Psychotherapy and Psychosomatics, 69*, 183–189.
Smith, R. C. (1997). *La Storia del Paziente. Un Approccio Integrato all'Intervista Medica [In Italian]*. Roma: Il Pensiero Scientifico Editore.
Smith, R. C. (2002). *Patient-centered interviewing. An evidence-based method*. Philadelphia: Lippincott Williams & Wilkins.
Stewart, M., Brown, J. B., Donner, A., McWhinney, I. R., Oates, J., Weston, W. W., et al. (2000). The impact of patient-centered care on outcomes. *Journal of Family Practice, 49*, 796–804.
Stewart, M., Brown, J. B., Weston, W. W., McWhinney, I. R., McWilliam, C. L., & Freeman, T. R. (1995). *Patient-centered medicine. Transforming the clinical method*. London: Sage Publications.
Stiles, W. B., & Putnam, S. M. (1992). Verbal exchanges in medical interviews: Concepts and measurement. *Social Science and Medicine, 35*, 347–355.
Street, R. L., Jr. (1991). Information-giving in medical consultations: The influence of patients' communicative styles and personal characteristics. *Social Science & Medicine, 32*, 541–548.

Svensson, S., Kjellgren, K. I., Ahlner, J., & Saljo, R. (2000). Reasons for adherence with antihypertensive medication. *International Journal of Cardiology, 76*, 157–163.

Tate, P. (1994). *The doctor's communication handbook.* New York: Radcliffe Medical Press.

Towle, A., & Godolphin, W. (1999). Framework for teaching and learning informed shared decision making. *British Medical Journal, 319*, 766–771.

Tuckett, D., Boulton, M., Olson, C., & Williams, A. (1985). *Meeting between experts: An approach to sharing ideas in medical consultations.* London: Tavistock Publications.

Walton, H., & Gelder, M. (1999). Core curriculum in psychiatry for medical students. *Medical Education, 33*, 204–211.

Weston, W. W., Brown, J. B., & Stewart, M. A. (1989). Patient-centred interviewing. Part I: Understanding patients' experiences. *Canadian Family Physician, 35*, 147–151.

Chapter 3
Building the Working Alliance in Brief Psychotherapies

Christa Zimmermann and Hanneke De Haes

3.1 Introduction

3.1.1 The Working Relationship and Other Communicative Functions

Psychotherapy is unconceivable without communication between the healthcare provider and the client. Thus, good communication is essential for effective treatment in mental health care. Yet, what actually happens during the psychotherapy encounter has been given limited attention in the literature to date.

Different functions were be distinguished in medical communication (de Haes and Bensing 2009). These seem to apply to mental health care equally well. First, relationship building, or *fostering the relationship,* is considered. Relevant elements such as respect, trust, and rapport are necessary components of such a therapeutic relationship. Second, therapists need to *gather information* from their patients about symptoms, experiences, and expectations for establishing a diagnosis and treatment plan (see Chapter 2). Third, *information is provided*: Patients need information to understand their illness and treatment, to make decisions, and to cope throughout the treatment trajectory. As a fourth function, we distinguished involving the patient in *decision making* (see Chapter 4). In both the shared and the informed decision-making models, communication is essential to reach decisions based on preferences and possibilities along with the patient (Charles et al. 1997). A fifth communicative function is the support or promotion of behavior related to the treatment: This may involve medication use, therapy attendance, or homework to be done. We have proposed the term *enabling disease and treatment-related behavior.* Finally, the sixth function, the need to *respond to emotions,* is obvious in

C. Zimmermann (✉)
Department of Public Health and Community Medicine, University of Verona,
Policlinico G.B. Rossi, Piazzale L.A. Scuro, 10, 37134 Verona, Italy
e-mail: christa.zimmermann@univr.it

M. Rimondini (ed.), *Communication in Cognitive Behavioral Therapy,*
DOI 10.1007/978-1-4419-6807-4_3, © Springer Science+Business Media, LLC 2011

the mental health context. Mental health problems are laden with emotion, and obviously clinicians cannot deny those. On the contrary, they are the essential elements, or may even be the core material, in the treatment of psychological distress. The six functions described have separate characteristics and go along with specific communicative behaviors. At the same time, they are not independent. A good relationship is most important. It is needed in the assessment of underlying problems, in conveying information and making the patient understand what is at stake, in making satisfactory decisions as well as in promoting treatment-related behavior, and finally, in giving the patient the room and confidence that emotions can be safely explored. In fact, without a good relationship, none of the other goals in the therapeutic encounter can be pursued optimally.

3.1.2   What Do We Mean by "Working Alliance"?

The question then is, what does a good relationship entail? In the literature the terms *relationship, therapeutic relationship, alliance, therapeutic alliance,* and *working alliance* seem to be used interchangeably (Kivlighan 2007). As will be explained in more detail later, we choose to use the term *working alliance,* as it fits in the influential conceptual framework forwarded by Bordin (1979) and can be well connected to the practice and principles of CBT:

"An alliance is an agreement between two or more parties, made in order to advance common goals and to secure common interests" (http://en.wikipedia.org/wiki/Alliance). This definition relates to the element of commonality of interests, to the attainment of goals, and to the agreement about these. It is also in line with prominent views in psychotherapy. Horvath and Luborsky (1993) have given a historic overview of the main conceptions regarding the relationship in psychotherapy. The authors relate, first, to the psychodynamic origin of the concept of alliance. Transference is obviously of central importance in the context of psychoanalytic or psychodynamic therapy. Yet, the alliance is, increasingly, considered by dynamic theorists not only as transference but also as a distinct reality-based part of the patient's self. They cite Freud's (1913) notion in *The Dynamics of Transference* that "... the analyst maintaining 'serious interest' in and 'sympathetic understanding' of the client permits the healthy part of the client's self to form a positive attachment to the analyst" (p. 561). As a result of this interest and understanding, the client could believe in the therapist's communications and explanations. Thus, the therapist makes it possible for the patient to undertake the task of healing.

One of the later, strongest advocates of the therapeutic relationship was undoubtedly Carl Rogers (1951). In fact, for Rogers, while describing client-centered therapy, the therapeutic relationship was the main if not the only vehicle for the success of treatment. The therapists' unconditional acceptance of the client was, in his humanistic view, a sufficient basis for therapeutic gain. The client can change when "... moving from an unworthy, unacceptable and unlovable person to the realization that he is accepted, respected and loved in this limited relationship with the therapist. .... As the client experiences the attitude of the acceptance which the therapist holds toward him, he is able to take and experience this same attitude towards himself" (pp. 159–160). Rogers' position concerning the working relationship is that people have a self-actualizing potential that can be actualized under appropriate conditions. These conditions imply a relationship nurtured by an unconditional positive regard and empathy that are genuinely felt by the therapist (Goldfried and Davila 2005).

These notions suggest that the role of the working alliance depends on the therapeutic modality chosen. Indeed, psychoanalysts and client-centered therapists had different views regarding its function. Even more extreme, strict behaviorists placed primary emphasis on the relevance of techniques in the treatment of mental problems, and put little or no weight on the relationship of therapist and client for the effectiveness of therapy. In his seminal paper, Bordin (1979) took an opposite standpoint. He departs from a "pan theoretical position." He asserts that "the working alliance between the person who seeks change and the one who offers to be a change agent is one of the keys to the change process. The working alliance can be defined and elaborated in terms which make it universally applicable" (p. 252). In other words, the importance as well as the nature of the working alliance are evident in whatever change process is at stake and, thus, in any psychotherapeutic approach. Bordin (1979) indeed takes the definition of the working alliance one step further. He distinguishes three aspects of the working alliance. He initially relates these to the psychodynamic therapy but makes them similarly applicable to other therapeutic traditions. First, he distinguishes the *agreement on goals*. The patients' goals and the mutual agreement between patient and therapist on these goals are to be the groundwork in psychotherapy. Psycho-analytic therapy is more likely to be directed toward the enduring core of thought, whereas behaviorally oriented therapies are likely to be oriented toward more specific segments of the individual's life. Second, Bordin speaks about *tasks*. The goals agreed upon will be translated into specific tasks. Collaboration between patient and therapist involves an agreed-upon contract that takes into account some concrete exchanges. Behavioral therapy involves, like others, the honest reporting of one's life and possibly requires self-observation or other homework tasks. "The effectiveness of such tasks," Bordin asserts, lies in "furthering movement toward the goal and the vividness with which the therapist can link the assigned task to the patient's sense of his difficulties and his wish to change" (p. 254). The third distinction Borden makes is that of *bonds*. The setting of goals and finding agreement on tasks are closely linked to and prosper depending on the nature of the relationship between therapist and patient. A basic level of trust and willingness to cooperate must be involved in all varieties of therapeutic relationships.

The model presented by Bordin has several strengths. First, it looks at the working alliance not just from the perspective of the underlying relationship and rapport. Likewise, constructive and explicit collaboration between patient and therapist is suggested to be of prime importance. This approach is therefore easily linked to the principles and practices of cognitive-behavioral therapy (CBT). CBT aims to solve problems through a goal-oriented approach. The emphasis is primarily on the here and now, problem solving, and utilizing rationality and behavioral activation (Leahy 2008). The therapeutic techniques may include concrete tasks such as keeping a diary; challenging events, feelings, thoughts, and behaviors; facing avoided activities; and experimenting with new behaviors and reactions. CBT is characterized by a clear operationalization of problems, an emphasis on measurable changes (i.e., tasks), and, thus, measurable goal-attainment. It uses a combination of nondirective and directive techniques. Thus, a positive bond between the patient and the therapist is needed for goals to be agreed upon and tasks to be accepted and accomplished. As Leahy (2008) states, in CBT: "It is important to think of the therapeutic relationship or alliance as an on-going process, rather than an achievement that is fixed at one point in time, since the relationship is interactive and iterative, reflecting the patient's response to the therapist's response to the patient. Furthermore, the current therapeutic relationship may be a window into prior or current other relationships, thereby providing an opportunity for the therapist and patient to have first-hand experience of how past relationships permeate current functioning" (p. 770).

3.2   Alliance and Outcome: Some Selected Empirical Findings

The conceptual framework proposed by Bordin has, among other things, stimulated the development of instruments to assess the strength of the working alliance. Martin and colleagues (2000) have reviewed in a meta-analysis 79 studies that relate alliance to treatment outcomes. Alongside, they investigated the psychometric qualities of the instruments most commonly used. The alliance ratings of patients, therapists, and observers were generally found to have adequate reliability. Most of the alliance scales were shown to be related to outcomes also. Among the scales that have undergone the most empirical scrutiny, they suggest that the Working Alliance Inventory (WAI) is likely to be the appropriate choice for most research projects. The WAI was developed by Horvath and colleagues (e.g., Horvath and Greenberg 1989) and is based on Bordin's pan-theoretical model of alliance. The scale covers overall alliance as well as the three aspects of alliance distinguished by Bordin: the bond, the agreement on goals, and the agreement on tasks. Goal-related items included subjects such as lack of good understanding, mutual agreement on goals, and differences in ideas. Task-related items cover issues such as agreement on steps taken, usefulness of activities, and correctness of the way of working. Bond-related items are addressing confidence, mutual liking, appreciation, and trust. Patient-, therapist-, and independent observer-rated versions are available. Also, short versions have now been developed (e.g., Andrusyna et al. 2001).

The 79 published and unpublished studies trough 1997 reviewed by Martin and colleagues (2000) all concerned the effect of alliance on outcomes of psychotherapy. The main conclusion was that, overall, the alliance-outcome correlation was 0.22–0.23. This finding was followed by a search for moderator variables in separate samples of homogeneous groupings. When the overall alliance-outcome correlation was disaggregated by type of outcome measure, type of alliance rater (patient, therapist, or observer), type of outcome rater (patient, therapist, or observer), time of alliance rating (early middle, late, or averaged across sessions), methodological quality, or type of psychotherapy, the model failed to account for additional variance. Only by the use of different alliance scales was additional variance explained. It is interesting to note that the effect of alliance seems to be independent of the type of therapy provided. The authors indeed conclude that the working alliance may be therapeutic in and of itself.

The working alliance has been investigated in a magnitude of settings covering numerous populations since then. Studies have addressed methodological aspects, the predictors of a positive or negative working alliance, the effects of the alliance, as well as the difference in alliance through various treatment phases.

For example, Tryon and colleagues (2008) have commented upon the relatively skewed scoring in working alliance assessment. The results of their meta-analysis of data from over 6,000 clients and therapists indicated that clients tend to use only the top 20% of the rating points and that the therapists tend to use only the top 30% of the ratings. Kivlighan (2007) stressed the importance of the interdependence of and agreement in the patient's and therapist's perspective on the therapeutic alliance. He found indeed that a large proportion of the variance in the working alliance (64%) could be attributed to the dyadic level. At the same time, Baldwin and colleagues (2007) have questioned the sheer absence of multi-level modeling in alliance research. They found among over 300 patients treated by 80 therapists, that therapist rather than patient variance predicted psychotherapy outcomes.

Relatively little attention is given to the development of the working alliance. Creed and Kendall (2005) reported that the working alliance of children with anxiety disorders receiving CBT was predicted positively by collaboration and negatively by pushing the child to talk. Costantino et al. (2005) found the alliance in CBT among depressive patients to be related to the patients' expectations for improvement, as well as their baseline symptom severity. Other authors have stressed the relevance of emotional engagement (Sexton et al. 1996) and early attachment for the establishment of a working alliance (Obegi 2008; Janzen et al. 2008).

Very different populations have been studied. For example, Taft and colleagues (2003) found the working alliance predicted lower levels of physical and psychological abuse among violent partners receiving group behavioral therapy. Loeb et al. (2005) found that early alliance predicted lower posttreatment purging frequency among bulimia nervosa patients receiving CBT. Change in perfectionism and depression were predicted on the basis of therapeutic alliance in patients receiving CBT with or without medication (Klein et al. 2003; Hawley et al. 2006). Strauss and coauthors (2006) reported that patients with an avoidant or an obsessive-compulsive personality disorder who rated their early alliance more strongly were more likely to benefit from CBT. Chiu et al. (2009) found that a stronger child–therapist alliance early in treatment predicted greater improvement in parent-reported outcomes at midtreatment but not posttreatment. However, improvement in the child–therapist alliance over the course of treatment predicted better posttreatment outcomes. Interestingly, Knaevelsrud and Maercker (2006) also found an effect of Internet-based CBT among patients having experienced a traumatic event.

The results reported by Chiu et al. (2009) point to the need to differentiate between alliance in different treatment phases. Similarly, Fitzpatrick and colleagues (2001) point out that at different levels, different therapists' interventions have shown to be effective.

All in all, there is now a rich literature concerning the working alliance. The effectiveness of the working alliance within CBT has been established in quite diverse populations. Yet methodological questions remain. Also, the background of what explains a good or a less positive alliance throughout different therapy phases may be elaborated further. As stated in the introduction, an important factor in this respect is likely to be the communicative behavior that helps or hinders the therapist in connecting to the patient and reaching an effective outcome in CBT. Indeed, only limited attempts have been made to identify the "micro-skills" underlying better working relationships (Leahy 2008). These "micro-skills," or communicative behaviors, will be addressed in the remainder of this chapter.

3.3   What Communicative Behavior Is Relevant for the Working Alliance?

Given that alliance, however measured, contributes to CBT outcomes and that therapy-specific techniques cannot be separated from the context of the emotional and collaborative relationship between patient and therapist, interventions focused on the development and maintenance of alliance, rather than being optional, are necessary conditions for a successful treatment. The quality of the alliance determines whether or not therapy-specific techniques can be effectively employed or will be accepted by the patient. In other words, it is not the technical aspect of therapy, but rather how, when, and when not the therapist applies each technical aspect of therapy (e.g., assigning homework) that will determine directly whether collaboration is reduced or enhanced (Gastonguay et al. 1996; Rector et al. 1999; Loeb et al. 2005). Effectively employed therapy techniques that promote change will in turn improve the alliance. Knowing therefore which communicative aspects are associated with alliance offers the clinician helpful tools to improve therapeutic practice.

The following sections consist of a straightforward description of verbal communicative techniques that in many studies were shown to be related to alliance building across different psychotherapeutic orientations. Exhaustive reviews of these methodologically and theoretically highly complex studies may be found in the literature (Ackerman and Hilsenroth 2001, 2003; Lejuez and Hopko 2006; Leahy 2008; Elvins and Green 2008). The importance of nonverbal behavior in contributing to the working alliance will not be addressed in the context of this chapter. Nonverbal communication aspects are discussed in Chapter 5.

3.3.1 Alliance Building in the Assessment Interview

Clearly, one of the initial goals of manual-based CBT sessions is to establish a positive alliance. However, in a recent review Hilsenroth and Cromer (2007) underline the importance of the pretherapy assessment session for the development and maintenance of the working alliance between patient and therapist (see also Chapter 2). They describe a therapeutic model of assessment, which summarizes therapist interventions of proven effectiveness in establishing patient-rated high-quality alliance already during assessment, easily to be maintained in subsequent therapy sessions if conducted by the same therapist.

The communicative approach proposed has to be seen as a general therapeutic stance to help patients increase motivation for change and to prepare them for psychotherapy in psycho-educational, relational, and collaborative terms. The model underscores the importance of therapists' active attempts to foster a positive working alliance as early as possible.

The model applies to a wide range of therapeutic orientations, with many relevant features for CBT assessment phases. It has the distinctive characteristics of a traditional assessment process: information gathering, feedback of assessment results, information on therapy, and definition of therapy goals and tasks. At the same time, it expands the focus by paying attention to the patient's agenda (beliefs regarding the cause of distress, expectations, experience, and concerns) as well as to the relational aspects between therapist and patient that emerge during the interview. The communicative approach is patient-centered, giving space to the patient to initiate discussion of salient themes ("What is most important for you?"), clarifying sources of distress ("When in particular do you feel upset?"), and exploring feelings ("What were your feelings in that situation?"). The aim is to create right from the beginning an empathic relationship and an effective collaboration in defining individualized treatment goals and tasks.

Paraphrasing some examples reported by the authors by which to approach or explore relational aspects in the information-gathering phase, the therapist may say:

"We discussed a lot of things, but is there something that we haven't touched yet that you think is important to knowing you as a person?" Or: "Today we talked a lot about your problem, and I wonder how that might play out in here between the two of us. Or: How do you feel right now sharing your problems with me?"

Similarly, the therapist may introduce at this stage therapeutic elements by commenting empathically on the patient's report of acute stressors: "This must be very hard for you."

Moving to the phase of reviewing the assessment findings, the model alerts the therapist to start with feedback elements that match the patient's own ideas and preconceptions, which may have emerged already in the information-gathering phase. Such a validation of the patient's experience and views strengthens the therapeutic bond and helps the patient to accept more discrepant information and to learn alternative ways of thinking about herself.

At the conclusion of the feedback phase, the therapist offers information about the treatment, discusses their reciprocal roles, checks the patient's understanding and view of the proposed form of treatment, and leaves space for expressing doubts and asking questions: for example, "There might be something I was not clear about, can you help me?" "How do you feel about this therapy approach?" "You look a bit doubtful! What are your questions?"

The stage is then set for the concluding discussion of the pretreatment interview(s) where patient and therapist work together to find agreement on treatment goals and procedural issues regarding time tables, frequency of therapy sessions, and costs.

Not surprisingly, similar therapist interventions have been identified in previous studies of pretherapy and first therapy sessions. For example, Bachelor (1995) asked patients what, in their opinion, improved the working alliance. He could identify three groups of therapists' interventions appreciated by patients: nurturing, collaborative, and insightful facilitating interventions.

These interventions have an uneven distribution over the different phases of the pretreatment session(s) as described by the model of Hilsenroth and Cromer (2007), reflecting the changing activity level of the therapist, from low in the information-gathering phase to high in the feedback and collaborative session.

The information-gathering phase, according to the model, might be said to be characterized by many nurturant therapist interventions, among which Bachelor includes facilitating behaviors and listening skills such as facilitations (e.g., "Tell me more!"), reflections (e.g., "You say you had a bad moment!") together with respectful and nonjudgmental statements (e.g., "You have tried hard to find a solution") and validating comments that make the patient feel understood and sustained (e.g., "Most people in such a situation as you are in would feel upset and distressed").

The feedback and therapeutic goal-defining phases might be said to be characterized by more collaborative and insight-oriented interventions such as discussing alternate ways to interpret situations, checking and clarifying doubts, exploring in-session affect, and keeping the patient focused on relevant topics. Particularly in this phase the therapist must be prepared to respond in a nondefensive way to possible skepticism or challenges regarding the relationship. The following paraphrased dialogue reported in Hilsenroth and Cromer (2007) offers a good example for a nondefensive response that actively promotes, without undue prompting, the expressions of what feelings are experienced by the patient in the sessions:

Th: Take your time. . . . It's normal to feel a bit nervous the first time speaking to someone new about such personal issues.
Pt: Nervous? I am not nervous. Maybe you are nervous!
Th: Well, you are right, that is part of what I feel when I meet people for the first time. . . . You might have picked up on that; what do you think? Do you feel some nervous energy in here?
Pt: Yeah . . . maybe I am a tiny bit nervous too. . . .

Rumpold and colleagues (2005), in another study on the development of alliance during the assessment phase, draw attention to the fact that the reduction in patient's strain imposed by suffering must not be one of the primary goals of this phase. The authors tried instead, as a motivation-enhancing intervention, to increase the patient's awareness of the negative consequences of the disorder. Surprisingly, this intervention was associated with patient reports of reduced suffering already in the subsequent encounter. This observation parallels previous findings that a relaxing, comfortable first session risks increasing subsequent patient drop-out (Tryon 1990) and is less appreciated by patients than a discussion of uncomfortable and painful topics (Ackerman et al. 2000). Indeed, patients expect to share difficult topics and might frown on too cheerful therapists.

This does not mean that patients in this early pretreatment stage would not need to have positive expectations regarding the efficacy of the proposed therapy. Patients' early positive expectations to improve their condition, for example, were found related to better alliance ratings at first and middle CBT sessions for bulimia nervosa when compared with patients who believed less in therapy (Costantino et al. 2005). To foster patient expectations in improvement, the authors suggest making explicit hope-inspiring statements, such as,

"It makes sense that you sought this type of help for your difficulties," or "Your problems are exactly the type for which this therapy can be of help" (p. 209).

To avoid the risks of a too "smooth" interview, and to alert patients that they are expected to have an active role within and outside the CBT sessions, therapists' hope-inducing statements, to be effective, should underline not only the therapists' engagement and potency, but also the patients' active engagement:

"You can be helped, but it requires hard work from both of us" (Mohl et al. 1991).

This example shows also how therapists may build mutuality by using the term *us*.

3.3.2 Communicative Interventions Contributing to Alliance over the Course of Psychotherapy

As Horvath (2005) pointed out, the building of a trusting relationship, the agreement on tasks and goals, and the focus on a collaborative stance (and consequently the communicative approach described so far) are "reasonable uniform requirements typical of the beginning phase of most therapies" (p. 5). Although these alliance elements (and corresponding communication techniques) might retain their relevance in the course of therapy, he hypothesizes that the mature phase of alliance might be characterized by different and more appropriate relational patterns. One way to test this hypothesis of changes in alliance quality is to relate communicative behaviors observed across different time points of psychotherapy to measures of alliance.

Sexton et al. (2005) used the depth of the patient–therapist relationship-or "connection"-as an alliance marker to study the process of alliance building in the first two therapy sessions. Connection during session was rated on a five-point scale ranging from 1 (no mutual agreement) to 5 (close connection, mutuality in conversation). A decrease in the depth of connection was observed when therapists were less engaged in listening, made statements devoid of emotional content, and provided information and advice. Patient silence, not talking about self, and low level of emotional engagement also decreased the connection. Accordingly, the connection increased with the therapist's information gathering and listening and when the central topic was about the patient. These last findings parallel some of the desirable interaction patterns proposed by Hilsenroth and Cromer (2007) for the first part of the pretherapy assessment session.

An earlier study by Sexton et al. (1996) gives a good idea of the different alliance-fostering interventions and interactions that operate over time, findings with empirical support for various other patient groups and different therapy approaches and reviewed in detail by Ackerman and Hilsenroth (2003).

The authors examined micro-interactions between therapist and patient occurring during the course of cognitively oriented psychotherapy. They explored micro-processes related to a patient-rated alliance and their change over the course of therapy. High-alliance sessions were defined as those with the highest 60% alliance ratings, whereas those with the lowest 40% alliance ratings were defined as low-alliance sessions. The videotaped sessions were rated for emotional (e.g., irritated, dejected, tense, neutral, positive) and verbal (e.g., listening, negative, neutral, positive) therapy content, activity type (e.g., question, advice and information, explanation, reflecting, superficial or deep therapeutic work), and topic (e.g., patient, other person, therapy).

High-alliance first sessions were characterized by a recurrent pattern of therapist engagement – patient tension – therapist engagement. Therapists listened, reflected less, gave less advice than low-alliance therapists, and expressed less uncertainty. Their patients talked more about their difficulty (negative verbal content) than low-alliance patients (neutral verbal content). High-alliance first sessions had fewer topic changes and therapists regularly redirected the topic from discussion of the therapy to the patient.

In the midphase, the activity level of high-alliance therapists increased while that of patients decreased, quite the opposite pattern compared with that of the first session: Therapists took charge and reflected and explained more, while patients listened more and expressed less discouragement. The unequal activity level of therapist and patient, reflecting a dominance–submission dynamic, however, coexisted with an intense mutual emotional exchange to which therapist and patient contributed equally. In contrast, in low-alliance mid-sessions, therapists were less active and less engaged. Patients listened less and responded mainly with negative contents, and therapists gave less positive replies to patients' negative statements.

In the end phase of therapy, high-alliance therapists continued to be active by affirming, giving advice, and listening less. Patients contributed with less therapeutic contents and maintained a low level of discouraged statements, suggesting a process of consolidation that would be expected in the conclusive phases of therapy. Low-alliance therapists instead, compared with mid-sessions and with their high-alliance counterparts, seemed now more involved in therapeutic work. They responded less negatively to patients, gave more verbal support, and both patients and therapists became more emotionally engaged.

First sessions of high-alliance therapies thus are characterized by an early patient-centered relationship achieved mainly by the use of listening skills and empathic communication. In the successive, much more structured and demanding middle and late CBT therapy sessions, therapists' interventions are increasingly directive and actively therapy-centric; the patient is open to advice and information and engages in therapeutic work. Mutuality in emotional exchange by supporting and positive statements and attention to relational issues keep patients on the therapeutic track. Consolidation of and mutual agreement on therapeutic achievements together with a continuing positive interpersonal exchange characterize the final therapy phase. Compared to high-alliance therapies, low-alliance therapies seem to lag behind and to proceed with a slower rhythm of therapeutic work, probably determined by greater concern with psycho-educational issues (information, advice) in the earlier therapy phases, at the expense of relationship-building interventions, considered universally the core interventions for alliance development.

Creed and Kendall (2005) examined therapists' behavior in the third and seventh sessions of CBT for children with anxiety disorder which were associated with high-alliance ratings obtained from the children. Three of eight therapist behaviors were significant predictors of children's perception of alliance at session 3. High alliance was obtained for therapists who presented treatment as a team effort, used words like *we* and *us*, let the child set up goals for therapy, and encouraged the child's participation and feedback, all behaviors focused on collaboration. Hope-inducing and emotion-focusing statements such as showing respect and understanding for the child's feeling showed no association with alliance, probably being more decisive and pertinent to alliance in the first sessions, which were not considered here.

Surprisingly, "finding common ground" – the therapist emphasizing issues that might be of common interest, such as responding with "me too" or trying to elicit "me too" from the child – was associated with low-alliance ratings. "You are good at hockey! I played hockey for years, too," or similar efforts to connect with the child may be felt as forced and overdone. When commonalities naturally emerged in later sessions, they were unrelated to alliance.

Pushing the child to talk about anxiety when the child clearly becomes uncomfortable was associated with poor alliance. This therapist behavior remained the only variable that predicted poor alliance at session 7. These findings suggest that the effect of therapist behaviors on alliance may be different for particular patient populations.

3.3.3 Alliance Ruptures and Critical Communication Incidents

Alliance may fluctuate and ruptures are an expected part of the therapy. Alliance ruptures are defined as deterioration in the relationship between therapist and patient (Safran and Muran 1996), difficulty in maintaining the alliance, or simply significant negative shifts in quality (Strauss et al. 2006). They are likely to occur when therapists neglect difficulties in the relationship or participate and reinforce dysfunctional interpersonal cycles, such as reacting defensively or with hostility to a hostile or critical patient statement. Ruptures, when resolved, are considered important opportunities for change and therapeutic progress. Ignored or addressed improperly, ruptures may increase patient resistance and obstruct change. For example, patients in cognitive therapy for avoidant and obsessive-compulsive personality disorders who reported unrepaired ruptures showed negligible symptom reduction on the SCID, whereas all patients who experienced a rupture repair reduced symptoms by 50% and more (Strauss et al. 2006).

Markers of rupture, together with repair interventions, were identified by obtaining alliance measures for different parts of the therapy session and relating observed drops in alliance and possible reestablishment of alliance to critical concomitant patients' and therapists' interactions observed by external judges (Gastonguay et al. 1996). For example, in a low-alliance part of the therapy session, the patient may say,

"I don't see how this task can help me," whereupon the therapist may say (repairing), "Okay, maybe you are right. Let's see why you think it will not work."

Alternatively, patients were asked after the session to identify any problem or tension that had occurred, to provide a short description of the critical event, and to indicate if and how it had been addressed. Alliance rupture based on patient reports of therapeutic misunderstandings (Rhodes et al. 1994) occurred when the therapist behaved in a way the patient did not like, such as giving unwanted advice, criticizing the patient, or omitting to do what the patient expected, for example, forgetting important facts. Resolution was reported when the therapist accommodated or changed behavior and the patient perceived the therapist's willingness to negotiate treatment goals and felt he would be able to continue working with the therapist.

Examples of patient-reported rupture events reported by Safran and Muran (1996) include,

"I did not quite understand where we were going,"
"I feel we've got off the track,"
"It seemed as nothing I said was right. I don't feel he is hearing what I say" (p. 452).

Other specific patient behaviors that observers identified as ruptures were withdrawal in the form of disengagement from therapist, therapy, or emotions; unresponsiveness to the therapists' intervention; or confrontation expressed as anger, resentment, dissatisfaction, or negative feelings regarding therapy (Safran and Muran 1996; Gastonguay et al. 1996).

Alliance ruptures experienced as communication failures may be reported also by the therapists themselves by describing a verbal exchange in which the patient said something that caused uneasiness and irritation in the therapist and was felt as a problem in the therapeutic relationship.

An example of an unrepaired rupture is the following:

Pt: I see few improvements with this therapy.
Th: Don't be that impatient; you will see that regular homework will have effects.

Pt: At the moment I have to work overtime, quite busy though.
Th: I see, but try to do your best.

Markers of alliance ruptures that signal negative emotions and strains in the patient–therapist relationship thus may be more or less subtle and range from nonverbal behavior (e.g., restlessness, avoiding eye contact, raising or lowering voice) to unequivocal therapy-interfering behaviors (disagreement with therapeutic tasks, coming late, skipping sessions, not doing assigned homework).

Such rupture markers introduced by patients are important cues to their emotional "agenda." If such cues are ignored and not recognized and acknowledged or remain unexplored, strains in the alliance may exacerbate and increase the risk of therapy drop-out. This is likely to be the case when therapists strictly adhere to CBT strategies and are unable to switch to a patient-centered approach to explore and validate patients' emotions "here and now."

Ruptures remain unrepaired also when therapists insist on trying to refocus patients' negative reports into the cognitive-behavioral model, despite patients' signaled or expressed need to disclose and discuss such emotions.

Gastonguay et al. (1996), in a qualitative analysis of unrepaired rupture episodes, highlighted the most frequent pitfalls of CB therapists when addressing ruptures in cognitive therapy sessions for depression. Therapists dealt with such alliance problems not by investigating the source of the patients' rupture-suggesting behavior (therapist, therapy, or stressful external event) and its emotional impact on interpersonal relationships with significant others (including the therapist), but treated it as manifestation of patients' distorted thoughts or dysfunctional beliefs. They tried to resolve the problem by increasing their adherence to the cognitive model and draw attention to the role of cognitions in causing negative emotions and on the importance of replacing these distorted thoughts. Such interventions, in turn, increased patients' reluctance and opposition to therapy and therapist. Other ineffective ways to address reluctance and disagreement on therapeutic tasks were attempts to underscore the positive consequences that patients would derive from doing them. Instead of exploring therapy aspects or own behaviors that could have been responsible for patients' reluctance, pressures to engage patients in activities they did not feel ready to do risk compromising the alliance problem even further.

It appears therefore that therapists fail to be empathic and supportive by a too strict and inflexible adherence to cognitive-behavioral techniques, a risk that is likely to increase when conducting manualized treatments. The observed (here unproductive) interventions are in line with Beck et al.'s view (1979) that difficulties with treatment tasks may be caused by patients' distorted view of cognitive therapy and consequently has to be challenged. However, in sessions with significant alliance drops, similar insistence and pressures are undue and clearly have to be avoided and substituted by shifting the attention to the relationship problems in the therapy room and their resolution.

The patient-centered skills found important for developing and maintaining alliance throughout the therapy sessions are equally useful for the repair of such communication failures. These skills may often be overlooked in training cognitive-behavioral therapists, since greater emphasis is placed on techniques and processes thought to be sufficient for change.

For example, how could the rupture reported in the above dialog be repaired?

Pt: I see few improvements with this therapy.
Th: Don't be that impatient; you will see that regular homework will have effects.
Pt: At the moment I have to work overtime, quite busy though.

In this example the therapist has several, equally effective, repair options: to explore the patient's view; to clarify sources of distress; to facilitate the expression of emotion; to be empathic and supportive.

"You have to work overtime..." *(Tries to clarify sources of distress by reflection)*
Or:
"You see no improvement..." *(Signals listening and facilitates patient by a reflecting statement to add further information to the issue)*
Or
"How is it for you not to see any improvement?" *(Facilitating the expression of negative feelings toward therapy or therapist by open-ended question)*
The patient might answer:
"I feel disappointed and discouraged!"
Or even become critical:
"I am rather annoyed because I feel that you expect too much from me !"

Therapist's replies to negative emotions:
"Each of us would be disappointed and frustrated not seeing any improvement." *(Legitimating and accepting patient's view)*
Or:
"It must be difficult for you to do your homework when you have to work over time".
Or: **"It must be frustrating to be in therapy and not seeing any improvement."** *(Empathic comments to make patient feel understood and sustained)*

Therapist's replies to criticisms or hostility:
"May be you are right, that I demand and push you too much." *(Non defensive validating of patient's view)*
Or:
"I appreciate that you are so frank with me. I should have noticed that I pushed you too hard." *(Non defensive respecting and apologizing)*
Or:
"From what you are saying, there must be something that did not work out well between us two, didn't it?" *(Acknowledging the breach in alliance)*

Similar repair interventions convey interest in the patient's views and feelings, caring, understanding, and respect as well as an empathic and nonjudgmental attitude, and focus on the "bonding" component in Bordin's definition of alliance. These interventions are the repair ingredients for the therapeutic change potential of rupture events.

3.4 Conclusion

Therapists are advised to constantly monitor the therapeutic relationship, to keep a watchful eye on rupture markers, and to attend to their own contribution to the alliance when in trouble. When they find their alliance persistently low, they might benefit from supervision and training.

There is some evidence that therapists can be trained to learn alliance-enhancing communication techniques. Hilsenroth et al. (2004) showed that a structured training in the Therapeutic Assessment Model not only improved early alliance but also predicted high-quality alliance also for the subsequent psychotherapy sessions. Similarly, Crits-Christoph et al.'s (2006) alliance training produced moderate to high increases in alliance. Providing therapists with feedback on their natural occurring errors and helping them to modify alliance-detracting behaviors enhanced outcome for potential treatment failures across patients (Harmon et al. 2007). Such findings suggest that CBT courses should consider the importance of highlighting specific alliance-promoting strategies in their clinical training, in particular regarding the earliest patient contacts and the occurrence of rupture events to be expected in the course of therapy. A positive alliance facilitates greater disclosure and active collaboration of patients in targeting, testing, and correcting dysfunctional beliefs and to accelerate patients' move to the stage of forming alternative beliefs. A diligent and competent application of CBT techniques therefore risks remaining ineffective without feeling responsible and in control for what is happening in the interpersonal and working relationship with the patient.

References

Ackerman, S. J., Hilsenroth, M. J., Baity, M. R., & Blagys, M. D. (2000). Interaction of therapeutic process and alliance during psychological assessment. *Journal of Personality Assessment, 75*, 82–109.

Ackerman, S. J., & Hilsenroth, M. J. (2001). A review of therapist characteristics and techniques negatively impacting the therapeutic alliance. *Psychotherapy, 38*, 171–185.

Ackerman, S. J., & Hilsenroth, M. J. (2003). A review of therapist characteristics and techniques positively impacting the therapeutic alliance. *Clinical Psychology Review, 23*, 1–33.

Andrusyna, T. P., Tang, T. Z., De Rubeis, R. J., & Luborsky, L. (2001). The factor structure of the working alliance inventory for cognitive behavioural therapy. *Journal of Psychotherapy Research and Practice, 10*, 173–178.

Bachelor, A. (1995). Clients' perception of the therapeutic alliance: A qualitative analysis. *Journal of Counseling Psychology, 42*, 323–337.

Baldwin, S. A., Wampold, B. E., & Imel, Z. E. (2007). Untangling the alliance–outcome correlation: Exploring the relative importance of therapist and patient variability in the alliance. *Journal of Consulting and Clinical Psychology, 75*, 842–852.

Beck, A. T., Rush, A. J., Shaw, B. F., & Emery, G. (1979). *Cognitive therapy of depression.* New York: Guilford Press.

Bordin, E. S. (1979). The generalizability of the psychoanalytic concept of the working alliance. *Psychotherapy: Theory, Research and Practice, 16*, 252–260.

Charles, C., Gafni, A., & Whelan, T. (1997). Shared decision making in the medical encounter: What does it mean? *Social Science and Medicine, 44*, 681–692.

Chiu, A. W., McLeod, B. D., Har, K., & Wood, J. J. (2009). Child–therapist alliance and clinical outcomes in cognitive behavioral therapy for child anxiety disorders. *Journal of Child Psychology and Psychiatry, 50*, 751–758.

Costantino, M. J., Arnow, B. A., Blasey, C., & Agras, W. S. (2005). The association between patient characteristics and the therapeutic alliance in cognitive-behavioral and interpersonal therapy for bulimia nervosa. *Journal of Consulting and Clinical Psychology, 73,* 203–211.

Creed, T. A., & Kendall, P. C. (2005). Therapist alliance-building behavior within a cognitive-behavioral treatment for anxiety in youth. *Journal of Consulting and Clinical Psychology, 73,* 498–505.

Crits-Christoph, P., Conolly Gibbons, M. B., Crits-Christoph, K., Narducci, J., Schamberger, M., & Gallop, R. (2006). Can therapists' be trained to improve their alliances? A preliminary study of alliance fostering psychotherapy. *Psychotherapy Research, 16,* 268–281.

De Haes, H., & Bensing, J. (2009). Endpoints in medical communication research, proposing a framework of functions and outcomes. *Patient Education and Counseling, 74,* 287–294.

Elvins, R., & Green, J. (2008). The conceptualization and measurement of therapeutic alliance. *Clinical Psychology Review, 28,* 1167–1187.

Fitzpatrick, M. R., Stalikas, A., & Iwakabe, S. (2001). Examining counselor interventions and client progress in the context of the therapeutic alliance. *Psychotherapy, 38,* 160–170.

Freud, S. (1913). On the beginning of treatment: Further recommendations on the technique of psychoanalysis. In J. Strachey (Ed. and Trans.), *The standard edition of the complete psychological works of Sigmund Freud* (pp. 122–144). London: Hogarth Press.

Gastonguay, L. G., Goldfried, M. R., Wiser, S., Raue, P. J., & Hayes, A. M. (1996). Predicting the effects of cognitive therapy for depression: A study of unique and common factors. *Journal of Consulting and Clinical Psychology, 64,* 497–504.

Goldfried, M. R., & Davila, J. (2005). The role of relationship and technique in therapeutic change. *Psychotherapy, 42,* 421–430.

Harmon, S. C., Lambert, M. J., Smart, D. M., Hawkins, E., Nielsen, S. L., Slade, K., et al. (2007). Enhancing outcome for potential treatment failures: Therapist–client feedback and clinical support tools. *Psychotherapy Research, 17,* 379–392.

Hawley, L. L., Ringo Ho, M. H., Zuroff, D. C., & Blatt, S. J. (2006). The relationship of perfectionism, depression, and therapeutic alliance during treatment for depression: Latent difference score analysis. *Journal of Consulting and Clinical Psychology, 74,* 930–942.

Hilsenroth, M. J., & Cromer, T. D. (2007). Clinical interventions related to alliance during the initial interview and psychological assessment. *Psychotherapy: Theory, Research, Practice, Training, 44,* 205–218.

Hilsenroth, M. J., Peters, E., & Ackerman, S. (2004). Effects of structured clinical training on patient and therapist perspectives of alliance in early psychotherapy. *Psychotherapy: Theory, Research, Practice, Training, 39,* 309–323.

Horvath, A. O. (2005). The therapeutic relationship: Research and theory. *Psychotherapy Research, 15,* 3–7.

Horvath, A. O., & Greenberg, L. S. (1989). Development and validation of the Working Alliance Inventory. *Journal of Counseling Psychology, 36,* 223–233.

Horvath, A. O., & Luborsky, L. (1993). The role of the therapeutic alliance in psychotherapy. *Journal of Consulting and Clinical Psychology, 61,* 561–573.

http://en.wikipedia.org/wiki/Alliance

Janzen, J., Fitzpatrick, M., & Drapeau, M. (2008). Processes involved in client-nominated relationship building incidents: Client attachment, attachment to therapist, and session impact. *Psychotherapy: Theory, Research, Practice, Training, 45,* 377–390.

Kivlighan, D. M. (2007). Where is the relationship in research on the alliance? *Journal of Counseling Psychology, 54,* 423–433.

Klein, D. N., Schwartz, J. E., Santiago, N. J., Vivian, D., Vocisano, C., Castonguay, L. G., et al. (2003). Therapeutic alliance in depression treatment: Controlling for prior change and patient characteristics. *Journal of Consulting and Clinical Psychology, 71,* 997–1006.

Knaevelsrud, C., & Maercker, A. (2006). Does the quality of the working alliance predict treatment outcome in online psychotherapy for traumatized patients? *Journal of Medical Internet Research, 8,* e31.

Leahy, R. L. (2008). The therapeutic relationship in cognitive behavioural therapy. *Behavioural and Cognitive Psychotherapy, 36*, 769–777.

Lejuez, C. W., & Hopko, D. R. (2006). The therapeutic alliance in behaviour therapy. *Psychotherapy: Theory, Research, Practice, Training, 42*, 456–468.

Loeb, K. L., Wilson, G. T., Labouvie, E., Pratt, E. M., Hayaki, J., Walsh, B. T., et al. (2005). Therapeutic alliance and treatment adherence in two interventions for bulimia nervosa: A study of process and outcome. *Journal of Consulting and Clinical Psychology, 73*, 1097–1107.

Martin, D. J., Garske, J. P., & Davis, M. K. (2000). Relation of the therapeutic alliance with outcome and other variables: A meta-analytic review. *Journal of Consulting and Clinical Psychology, 68*, 438–450.

Mohl, P. C., Martinez, D., Ticknor, C., Huang, M., & Cordell, L. (1991). Early drop outs from psychotherapy. *Journal of Nervous and Mental Diseases, 172*, 417–423.

Obegi, J. H. (2008). The development of the client-therapist bond through the lens of attachment theory. *Psychotherapy, 45*, 431–446.

Rector, N. A., Zuroff, D. C., & Segal, Z. V. (1999). Cognitive change and the therapeutic alliance: The role of technical and nontechnical factors in cognitive therapy. *Psychotherapy, 36*, 320–328.

Rhodes, R. H., Hill, C. E., Thompson, B. J., & Elliot, R. (1994). Client retrospective recall of resolved and unresolved misunderstanding events. *Journal of Consulting and Clinical Psychology, 41*, 473–483.

Rogers, C. R. (1951). *Client-centered therapy*. Cambridge, MA: Riverside Press.

Rumpold, G., Doering, S., Smrekar, U., Schubert, C., Koza, R., Schatz, D., et al. (2005). Changes in motivation and the therapeutic alliance during pre-therapy diagnostic and motivation-enhancing phase among psychotherapy outpatients. *Psychotherapy Research, 15*, 117–127.

Safran, J. D., & Muran, J. C. (1996). The resolution of ruptures in the therapeutic alliance. *Journal of Consulting and Clinical Psychology, 64*, 347–458.

Sexton, H. C., Hembre, K., & Kvarme, G. (1996). The interaction of the alliance and therapy microprocess: A sequential analysis. *Journal of Consulting and Clinical Psychology, 64*, 471–480.

Sexton, H., Littauer, H., Sexton, A., & Tommeras, E. (2005). Building an alliance: Early process and the client therapist connection. *Psychotherapy Research, 15*, 103–116.

Strauss, J. L., Hayes, A. M., Johnson, S. L., Newman, C. F., Brown, G. K., Barber, J. P., et al. (2006). Early alliance, alliance ruptures and symptom change in a nonrandomized trial of cognitive therapy for avoidant and obsessive-compulsive personality disorders. *Journal of Consulting and Clinical Psychology, 74*, 337–345.

Taft, C. T., Murphy, C. M., King, D. W., Musser, P. H., & DeDeyn, J. M. (2003). Process and treatment adherence factors in group cognitive-behavioral therapy for partner violent men. *Journal of Consulting and Clinical Psychology, 71*, 812–820.

Tryon, G. S. (1990). Session depth and smoothness in relation to the concept of engagement in counseling. *Journal of Consulting and Clinical Psychology, 37*, 248–263.

Tryon, G. S., Blackwell, S. C., & Hammel, E. F. (2008). The magnitude of client and therapist working alliance ratings. *Psychotherapy, 45*, 546–551.

Chapter 4
Providing Information and Involving the Patient in the Therapeutic Process

Claudia Goss and Francesca Moretti

4.1 Introduction

Specific conceptualization of each clinical case is crucial to provide a framework for understanding the patient's maladaptive behaviors and modifying dysfunctional attitudes. The therapist should formulate the case at an early stage, preferably during the evaluation process (or assessment stage); the formulation can be modified at any time whenever new information is collected. After the assessment phase, the therapist should be in a position to provide the patient with a preliminary formulation of the problem. This would include a brief description of the current problem, an explanation of how the problem has developed, and a summary of the contributing factors. As the treatment is based on this formulation, it is important that patients are asked for feedback on its accuracy and for their opinions about it. Sharing this conceptualization with the patient can also help the data-gathering process and the assessment stage since it provides a guide to the patient as to which aspects to focus on, and what interpretations and underlying beliefs to identify. After testing new material, the patient and therapist can then add it into the preliminary formulation. As new data are collected, the therapist can reformulate the case on the basis of these new data.

Defining therapeutic goals is another important part of cognitive-behavioral therapy and involves agreeing with the patients on detailed, specific goals for each of the problematic areas to be worked on, as well as setting up intermediate subgoals. There are many points in favor of setting goals at the assessment stage (Hawton et al. 1989). It helps to make explicit what the patient can expect from treatment. It can point out areas of miscommunication that, together with patients,

C. Goss (✉)
Department of Public Health and Community Medicine, Section of Psychiatry and Clinical Psychology, University of Verona, Policlinico G.B. Rossi, Piazzale L.A. Scuro 10, 37134 Verona, Italy
e-mail: claudia.goss@univr.it

M. Rimondini (ed.), *Communication in Cognitive Behavioral Therapy*, DOI 10.1007/978-1-4419-6807-4_4, © Springer Science+Business Media, LLC 2011

can be reconceptualized and reformulated. Goal setting emphasizes the possibility of change, and begins to focus the patient on future possibilities rather than simply on symptoms and problems. It also reinforces the active role of the patient in the therapeutic process. Moreover, defining goals helps to give structure to the treatment and provides the opportunity for an evaluation of outcome directly related to the individual's presented problems.

As most cognitive-behavioral treatments demand a high level of commitment on the patient's part, some treatment can actually fail because patients do not apply the agreed-upon procedures. It can be therefore helpful discussing with the patient some of the components that make up a desire for change, correcting any misconceptions, and making an informed and shared decision about whether it would be worthwhile continuing with the treatment. The therapist should be able to explore the patient's beliefs about the problem and psychotherapy before providing new information and working on the patient's motivation. Providing information and involving patients are therefore crucial tasks for the therapeutic process and aim to provide patients with a better understanding of their illness or problems. As cognitive-behavioral therapy is based on a collaborative approach, providing information during the first encounters or during the assessment phase is an essential aspect both for relationship building and proceeding with the psychotherapy itself.

Virtually, all of the most important communication skills can be learned and improved with practice. This chapter aims to provide the reader with some valuable information that can improve patient–therapist interaction in psychotherapy. In the first part of the chapter, we will describe findings from research on communication in the medical setting; in the second part, we will try to give some practical suggestions and examples that can make interactions with patients more effective and efficient. More in detail the chapter is therefore organized into two main sections. In the second section, we will discuss some main theoretical models (Sect. 4.2.1) and research studies available from both the medical (Sect. 4.2.2) and psychiatric fields (Sect. 4.2.3). In the third section, we will describe and discuss communication skills useful when the therapist informs and involves patients, with particular attention to the first encounters.

4.2 Knowledge and Evidence on Doctor–Patient Communication in the Medical Setting

In this chapter we will first examine the theoretical background that subtends the models and the skills we will discuss later on in this chapter. In particular, we have chosen to give a brief description of the following issues: the patient-centered interview and the three-function approach, the Shared Decision-Making (SDM) model, and the Motivational Interview (MI). Second, we will give a concise examination of main studies based on these theoretical concepts in both medical and psychiatric contexts.

4.2.1 Doctor–Patient Communication in the Medical Setting: Theoretical Background

In recent years, doctor–patient communication and doctors' training have become central issues for research. Several theoretical frameworks have been developed and specific communication skills have been identified according to the different purposes and phases of the medical interview. In order to better understand how the processes of information-giving and patient-involving have changed over time, we will refer to three key models: (1) the patient-centered interview and the three-function approach (Levenstein et al. 1986; Smith et al. 2002; Cohen-Cole 1991); (2) the Shared Decision-Making Model (Charles et al. 1999a, b); and (3) the Motivational Interview (Miller and Rollnick 1991; Rollnick and Miller 1995; Rollnick et al. 1999).

4.2.1.1 The Patient-Centered Interview and the Three-Function Model

Throughout the last 20 years, the doctor–patient relationship has strongly changed: The traditional paternalistic model, where the "doctor knows the best" and the patient is just a passive and silently compliant receiver of care, has been gradually changed into a more interactive model where the patient is considered as an active agent of its own care (Evans et al. 2003).

Physicians are the *experts on illness and disease in general*; they know the etiopathogenetic processes, the diagnostic procedures, and all the available therapeutic evidence-based options. On the other hand, patients have been personally experiencing their illness, its impact on their everyday life, its social context and meaning and can be considered as *experts of their disease*. Patients' perspective becomes an important source of information that can help to better understand the patient's problem and create a more personalized and effective treatment plan (Weston et al. 1989). The need to consider patients' experience and point of view has increasingly emphasized the importance of the "patient-centered approach" (Smith 2002; Mead and Bower 2000). Following this approach, physicians are called to collect not only the doctor's agenda but also the patient's agenda, trying to "enter the patients' world, to see the illness through the patients eyes" (see Chapter 2). The physician is therefore engaged in "active listening," in open-ended inquiry, in making empathic statements, and in facilitating patients' questions.

Both physicians and patients have become actively involved in the process of care, leading the shift from an asymmetrical and imbalanced interaction toward a more symmetric and collaborative relationship (Charles et al. 1997; Slingsby 2004). Giving and sharing information with the patient together with discussing and negotiating treatment plans have become fundamental aspects of a good medical interview (Cohen-Cole 1991; Lipkin et al. 1995).

According to the three-function model, an effective medical interview should accomplish (1) gathering data to understand patients' problems (collect both patient's and doctor's agenda), (2) developing a relationship and responding to patients' emotions (building up a therapeutic alliance), and (3) educating patients about their illness, negotiating a treatment plan, and motivating them (information giving and involving patients in the therapeutic process). The three functions require different techniques: communication skills and data-gathering techniques; interpersonal and emotional response skills; and adherence-management skills (such as education/information, negotiation, and motivation).

Specifically, the third function, which is the focus of this chapter, has the following objectives: (a) ensure the patient's understanding of the nature of the illness; (b) ensure the patient's understanding of suggested diagnosis procedures; (c) ensure the patient's understanding of treatment possibilities; (d) achieve consensus between physician and patient over the previous three objectives; (e) achieve informed consent; (f) improve coping mechanisms (including the ability to deal with uncertainty); (g) ensure lifestyle changes; (h) facilitate motivation to change health behaviors (Lipkin et al. 1995).

The growing interest toward the third function of the medical interview has led to the development of the *SDM model* (Braddock et al. 1999; Charles et al. 1999a), which encourages patients' active participation in medical decisions regarding their own care.

4.2.1.2   The Shared Decision-Making Model

The SDM model has been developed and explored in recent years (Charles et al. 1999a, 2000). The concept of "consumer involvement" is also becoming of great interest at the local or national policy level in different countries, and central governments have invested considerable financial resources to encourage initiatives to promote patient and public involvement (Harter and Loh 2007). According to the SDM model, both patients and physicians should be actively involved in the decision-making process so that a therapeutic option can be chosen according to all the relevant medical information as well as patients' preferences and values (Charles et al. 1997).

A similar concept to SDM, frequently used in different health settings, is "concordance." Concordance refers to a consultation process between a healthcare provider and a patient and it advocates a sharing of power in the clinician–patient interaction (Weiss and Britten 2003).

Some studies have analyzed the information-giving process as the first step to implementing an SDM approach. Lee and Garvin (2003) argued how giving information alone is inadequate to produce effective communication because it entails the concept of "transferring information" from an active communicator (the doctor) to a passive receiver (the patient). The authors underlined the importance of moving toward a more successful "two-way relationship" based on the notion of "information exchange" and implying an active dialog between two partners.

Moreover, according to the model, sharing information is just an initial step of the decision-making process: The doctor and the patient need to engage in an open dialogue where an agreement on a final decision can be discussed and negotiated (Charles et al. 1999b).

SDM concepts have been studied in different medical settings, particularly in general medicine, oncology, endocrinology (Sullivan et al. 2006; Montori et al. 2006; Merenstein et al. 2005; Murray et al. 2006; Towle et al. 2006; Shepherd et al. 2007; Coulter 1997; Elwyn et al. 2000), and more recently, also in psychiatry (McCabe et al. 2002; Hamann et al. 2003, 2004, 2005, 2009; Mendel et al. 2009). Involving patients in therapeutic decisions increases the patient's adherence to the planned treatment. However, more specific strategies to motivate patients to follow a therapeutic plan are extremely useful, especially when a therapeutic plan includes the need to change unhealthy behaviors.

4.2.1.3   The Motivational Interview

The Motivational Interview (MI) is a specialized method developed in the addiction field in order to help people to change disruptive behaviors. Motivational interviewing is a directive, client-centered counseling style for eliciting behavioral change by helping clients to explore and resolve ambivalence. Compared with nondirective counseling, it is more focused and goal-directed. The examination and resolution of ambivalence is its central purpose, and the counselor is intentionally directive in pursuing this goal (Miller and Rollnick 1991; Rollnick and Miller 1995). The MI approach rises from the observation that advice giving alone is not sufficient to induce change (Ashenden et al. 1997; Butler et al. 1999). According to the Prochaska and DiClemente model of change (Prochaska and DiClemente 1992, 1983, 1986), any change is not a single event but a dynamic process embracing six different stages (Precontemplation, Contemplation, Preparation, Action, and Maintenance). MI represents a valid instrument to understand patients along the entire process of change and help them to proceed to the next step (Miller and Rollnick 1991). MI utilizes a set of specific skills both to foster and to maintain the individual's desire to change and combines a patient-centered approach with a more directive approach. It was applied first in drug-addiction situations with good evidence of efficacy (Dunn et al. 2001; Burke et al. 2003; Britt et al. 2004). In a second step its efficacy has been explored in other health behavior areas (Martins and McNeil 2009) such as smoking behaviors (Butler et al. 1999; Williams and Deci 2001; Britt et al. 2004), promoting diet and exercise (Mhurchu et al. 1998; Harland et al. 1999; Burke et al. 2003; Befort et al. 2008), and in chronic conditions such as diabetes (Williams et al. 1998a; Kirk et al. 2001; Jones et al. 2004) and hypertension (Ogedegbe et al. 2008; Scala et al. 2008). Bodies of evidence in these fields are promising, but the quality of available trials is not yet of a good enough level to be strongly generalized (Knight et al. 2006).

4.2.2   From Theory to Practice: Findings from Research
on Doctor–Patient Communication in the Medical Setting

Another reason the interest in the informational-decisional stage of the medical interview has steadily increased over recent years is partly because the informational needs of patients have been more clearly stated.

Several studies have shown that patients desire more information and involvement in their own care. The majority of patients want to be informed about their diagnosis and the causes and the course of illness (Frederikson 1995), and many patients would like to take part in decisions regarding treatment options and in the management of the therapeutic plan (Guadagnoli and Ward 1998). Coulter and colleagues (1999) observed that patients ask for information in order to understand what is wrong, gain a realistic idea of the prognosis, understand the procedures and the expected outcomes of possible tests and treatments, learn about available services, receive help to entail efficacious coping strategies, have their suffering legitimized, learn how to prevent further problems, and identify self-help groups.

Others studies have shown the heterogeneity of patient needs. Patients may differ in the type and quantity of information they wish (Elwyn et al. 2003a, b) and in their preferred level of involvement (Benbassat et al. 1998; Müller-Engelmann et al. 2008). There are also patients who explicitly state they would prefer just a little and not too much detailed information and would like to delegate the decisions to the physician or their relatives (Rodriguez-Osorio and Dominguez-Cherit 2008; Deber et al. 2007). Physicians are called to recognize this heterogeneity in patients' desires in order to adapt the information-giving process and the level of involvement according to the needs and level of comprehension of each individual patient. Patients tend to identify the doctor as their main source of information, enforcing the physician's role in creating a collaborative relationship (Makoul et al. 1995). Accordingly, doctors should learn how to best perform this role and how to elicit and satisfy their patients' manifest needs for information. The patient-centered approach and SDM are therefore fundamental theoretical frameworks to guide the clinician in this difficult task.

The evidence shows that good patient-centered communication has a positive and important impact on several health outcomes (Little et al. 2001), such as patient general health status (Ong et al. 2000; Stewart 1995; Maly et al. 1999; Mead and Bower 2002), patient satisfaction (Williams et al. 1998b; Safran et al. 1998; Kinnersley et al. 1999), patient understanding of suggested treatment (Roter et al. 1987; Hall et al. 1988), and treatment adherence (Maly et al. 1999; Svensson et al. 2000). Specifically, the doctor–patient relationship seems to be an important variable in order to positively affect treatment adherence, and a key role is played by the extent to which the doctor knows the patient as a whole, as a person (Safran et al. 1998).

An active involvement of the patient in decision making is also associated with better outcomes (Joosten et al. 2008), including higher satisfaction with decisions (O'Connor et al. 2001) and better health psychological outcomes (Krones et al. 2010; Gattellari et al. 2001; Mead and Bower 2002). Moreover, satisfaction with retrieved information improves patients' coping strategies and consequently leads to a better quality of care (Maly et al. 1999). According to this evidence, succeeding in considering the patient as an expert partner with whom to worktogether becomes essential to performing an effective patient-centered and collaborative relationship and to get better treatment outcomes (Coulter 2002).

Thus, the way the physician communicates with the patient, particularly during the informational-decisional stage of the medical interview, gains greater importance. Some studies show that the level of the patients' participation depends directly on how the physician conducts the interview and on how he or she presents the information (Charles et al. 2000). Sequential analysis of a medical interview shows that physician speech has an immediate effect on what is said by the patient in the next verbal turn and has an impact on the quality of interactions in general (Mazzi et al. 2003; Zimmermann et al. 2003). With regards to patients' participation, the degree of patient involvement during a consultation is therefore strictly influenced by communicative choices made by health professionals (Drew et al. 2001). Questions that prompt patients to express their opinion and encourage their involvement are considered important patient-centered skills in the information/negotiation phase of the medical interview (Charles et al. 2000).

Despite doctors having a central role in performing a patient-centered and collaborative consultation, studies show that physicians still tend not to involve their patients (Goss et al. 2007a, b). Moreover, patients rarely have the opportunity to give opinions or ask questions while doctors are interviewing (Goss et al. 2005). These results suggest a limited degree of patient involvement in the consultation and confirm previous findings despite the evidence that doctor's knowledge of a patient's point of view improves the efficacy of the information-giving process (Braddock et al. 1997).

Recent studies have explored different types of interventions to promote patient involvement, first of all by directly stimulating patients' participation in consultations. Patients may be encouraged by their doctor to ask questions, eventually preparing a list before the visit (Kidd et al. 2004) or selecting the questions from a list of all possible queries available before meeting the doctor (prompt sheet) (Butow et al. 1994; Brown et al. 1999, 2001; Bruera et al. 2003; Glynne-Jones et al. 2006; Clayton et al. 2003, 2007). Moreover, Elwyn and colleagues (2004) showed the efficacy of an intervention specifically developed to teach clinicians the basic skills and abilities needed to implement a collaborative approach. Although not always concordant, the findings are promising and, according to the importance of this issue and its consequence on health outcomes, need to be further explored.

4.2.3   From Theory to Practice: Discussion on the Evidence from Psychiatric Literature

The evidence of the low level of treatment adherence reported for psychiatric patients (Nosé et al. 2003) and the finding that patient participation in decision making has a positive effect on outcomes and adherence to treatment, especially for chronic diseases (Joosten et al. 2008; Ong et al. 1995; Little et al. 2004), have contributed to attract researchers' attention to SDM concepts and patient involvement skills also in the field of psychiatry (Hamann et al. 2003; Adams and Drake 2006). Psychiatric patients themselves seem to prefer a more collaborative relationship with their psychiatrist and ask for active involvement in decisions regarding their own health care (Hamann et al. 2005; Paccaloni et al. 2004, 2006).

Despite the potential efficacy of patient-centered approach and SDM and the evidence that patients demand a more active role, recent studies in a psychiatric context (Goosenssen et al. 1997; Goss et al. 2008) have shown low levels of patient involvement, suggesting that the doctor-centered approach is still prominent in this setting (Kent and Read 1998; Colombo et al. 2003). These observations raise the question of whether psychiatrists are aware of the potential benefits of sharing treatment decisions with their patients. Health professionals seem to inaccurately guess their patient preferences (Strull et al. 1984) and behave according to their assumptions. Moreover, some studies show several barriers that still impede psychiatrists from implementing a collaborative approach into practice, such as the fear of stigmatizing patients or worsening their mental status, with the consequent fear of lowering patient motivation in following treatments (Paccaloni et al. 2005). Cognitive impairment has been claimed to be a major barrier in sharing information and decisions with psychiatric patients, especially for those suffering from schizophrenia (Paccaloni et al. 2005; Hope 2002; Hamann et al. 2009). At present, there is no strong evidence to confirm these concerns; even if a correlation seems to exist among the level of decisional ability and the presence of delusions, poor insight, and poor cognitive test results, the presence of cognitive impairment was not specifically related to any psychiatric diagnosis (Cairns et al. 2005; Jeste et al. 2006; Prentice et al. 2005; Palmer et al. 2004). Decisional capacity, moreover, can be maximized by developing individual ability (educational program) or/and simplifying the decisional task (Wong et al. 2000).

The question is to what extent barriers raised by psychiatrists represent a real obstacle to the implementation of a more collaborative approach. Maybe psychiatrists perceive informed patients as difficult to manage, and they tend to implement a more traditional and paternalistic approach thought to be more efficacious in monitoring their patients. Other explanations for the low level of patient involvement observed may be the lack of specific communication skills. The difference in the level of patient involvement observed among psychiatrists suggests the influence of a personal communication style (Goss et al. 2008). This evidence confirms previous findings that showed that without specific training in interviewing skills, psychiatrists display an idiosyncratic self-made approach in conducting consultations (Rimondini et al. 2006, 2009). Finally, most psychiatrists seem to support the conviction that SDM strategies in this specific field are of limited use (Paccaloni et al. 2005).

These findings raise important questions that invite more systematic future research. Implementation of the SDM model in psychiatry via the development of specific interventions (Rimondini et al. 2006; McCabe et al. 2002; Slingsby 2004) could provide an important step toward meeting patients' needs and improving adherence to treatment. Helpful interventions in encouraging greater patient participation can range from informative advice, feedback on psychiatrists' current performance, increase in consultation length, to more complex training courses in patient-involving communication skills.

Several studies have shown how the level of patient involvement tends to improve with the length of consultation (McCabe et al. 2002; Adams and Drake 2006; Goss et al. 2008). Moreover, there is evidence that a specific training course can increase SDM performance in general practice (Elwyn et al. 2004). This might apply also to psychiatry, although in this setting some skills may be more or less relevant.

In a recent review on intervention studies to improve treatment adherence in psychiatric patients, all included studies failed to consider the role of patient involvement communication skills (Nosé et al. 2003). Maybe such skills are taken for granted in psychiatry, with the risk of losing an important opportunity to improve health outcomes via patient satisfaction and adherence. Specific assessment tools to test the efficacy of planned interventions are also strongly advocated. An example could be the OPTION scale, which is a 12-item scale developed by Elwyn and colleagues to measure the extent to which clinicians (medical, nursing, or other relevant professionals) involve patients in decisions during consultations (Elwyn et al. 2003a, b). The Italian version of the scale has recently been validated in a general practice setting, showing satisfactory psychometric properties (Goss et al. 2007a, 2008).

The debate about how and when to encourage patients to participate in decisions about their care and about what are the most appropriate tools and outcome measures to evaluate the process is still open but with promising results to be spread to psychotherapy also.

4.3   Providing Information and Involving the Patient in Cognitive-Behavioral Therapy

As cognitive-behavioral therapy is based on a collaborative approach, information delivered during the first encounters or during the assessment phase is essential both for relationship building and for proceeding with the therapy. Involving the patient can be envisioned as a process that requires different abilities: (1) information-gathering and relationship-building skills; (2) providing information skills; and (3) specific

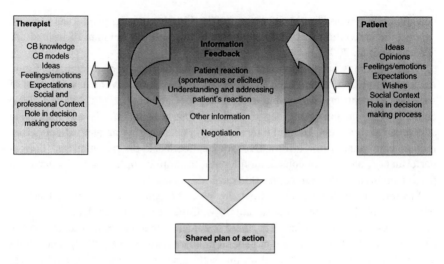

Fig. 4.1 Information-providing process

abilities to involve the patient in the SDM process. Providing information can be considered therefore a first step toward the patient's involvement (Fig. 4.1).

Providing information and involving the patient is a process in which two sides, patient and therapist, work together to reach a shared goal. Involving the patient in the therapeutic process means considering the patient as a partner and making the patient feel more responsible for his own care, with a desirable positive effect on the therapeutic alliance and on motivation to treatment.

As the clinical interview is an interactive process, it is influenced by the characteristics of both the patient and the therapist. The therapeutic encounter becomes a meeting between two different experts: the therapist, who is the expert on the general psychopathology, and the patient, who is the expert on her specific mental distress affecting her everyday life in several different and individual ways. In order to proceed with the psychotherapy, the clinician needs to respect the patient's position and create an efficient dialogue by actively involving the patient.

Patients should feel that their contributions are essential for the therapeutic process and that they are far from being just passive recipients of a therapy decided and undertaken by the therapist alone. Patient and therapist become partners in the psychotherapy, and every outcome (including the level of patient involvement) is the result of this fruitful interaction.

By providing information, the therapist helps patients to know, better understand. and accept their problems (disease) and to find strategies for coping and changing behaviors. In this section we will focus on providing information and patient-involving skills, whereas content of information (e.g., information about the nature of anxiety, vicious cycles, cognitive-behavioral models) is not the main target of this chapter. For more details regarding the content of provided information, we refer the reader to more specific cognitive-behavioral therapy guides and books (e.g., Bellack and Hersen 1998).

4.3.1 Setting

The setting where encounters take place is obviously fundamental in order to create a positive atmosphere and lay the basis for an effective collaboration between therapist and patient. A welcoming room where both patient and therapist can comfortably sit down like two members of a team, engaging in an open discussion (e.g., without emphasizing the asymmetry of roles), is essential to make the patient feel at ease and to create an atmosphere of reciprocal respect in which the process of sharing and receiving information can occur. All the barriers to listening should be avoided. The consultation room should be cozy but essential, without too much stuff that can divert the patient's attention. Quiet and silence are also fundamental and therapists should do their best to avoid interruptions, such as a ringing phone. Whenever a barrier cannot be removed (e.g., annoying noises from the outside), it is possible to discuss it with the patient so that its potential negative effect on the relationship can be minimized. To create a productive and collaborative atmosphere, another potential useful strategy is setting the agenda of the session and organizing the time well, for example, making the appointments in order to leave some space before the next patient. In this time the clinician can recap the key points of the session and prepare himself for the following visit. This helps both patient and therapist, who can feel they have enough space to talk and think about problems without experiencing time pressure.

4.3.2 Objectives and Tasks of Providing Information and Involving the Patient

General communication skills can be very useful at the beginning of the therapeutic process, particularly during the preliminary assessment encounters. After these first sessions, patients should leave the therapist's room with a cognitive-behavioral–based conceptualization of their presenting problem(s) and a basic idea of how the problem can be addressed in psychotherapy.

Providing information and involving patients in the therapeutic process aim for several important goals:

- Provide clear and tailored information regarding the patient's problem (e.g., symptoms, nature of problem, maintaining factors), workup, and psychotherapy. To achieve this goal, the therapist should give comprehensive and appropriate information, by assessing each individual patient's information need and providing the correct amount and type of information without being too restrictive or overloading. Moreover, information should be given in a way that is easy for the patient to remember and understand.
- Achieve a shared vision of the problem(s) and its management by incorporating the patient's perspective, exploring the patient's thoughts and feelings about the

received information, and encouraging a two-way interaction (a dialogue) rather than a one-way transmission.

- Negotiate possible differences. Different opinions between patient and therapist should be considered as normal and, rather than obstacles to the therapeutic process, they should become a fundamental starting point to a collaborative and productive dialogue. Once the difference between opinions is on the table, giving the patient the opportunity to discuss it without compromising the therapeutic relationship can increase both the therapeutic alliance itself and the likelihood of reaching a shared agreement that is strongly supported by both parties.
- Involve the patient in the therapeutic process and planning collaboratively. This allows patients to understand the therapeutic process and to be involved in decision making to the level they wish and increases patients' commitment to the therapeutic plan.
- Maintain relationship (see Chapter 3). Building relationship is a crosswise task throughout the session and in the psychotherapy itself. The therapist should be actively oriented to this objective throughout the consultation in order to reinforce the therapeutic alliance and maintain a collaborative atmosphere.
- Improve coping mechanisms (such as the ability to deal with uncertainty) and enhance perceived self-autonomy and self-efficacy. As these skills are more related to specific cognitive-behavioral techniques and to specific problems (e.g., depression), we refer the reader to more detailed literature (e.g., Hawton et al. 1989; Beck 1995).
- Motivate the patient to change. As above, also for these more specific motivational skills, we suggest referring to motivational interviewing techniques (Miller and Rollnick 1991).

4.3.3   Communication Skills

To implement a collaborative approach aimed at providing patients with all relevant information and keeping them involved in the therapeutic process, several communication skills can be used. These general skills are as follows: abilities to provide information, abilities to pick up patient's reactions (emotions, feelings, ideas, opinions, expectations, social context, patient's desired role in the therapeutic process), abilities to acknowledge and legitimate these reactions, abilities to work to reach shared plans and goals, abilities to negotiate and motivate, and finally the abilities to use all these skills considering that particular patient, her context, personality, and resources (Table 4.1).

In more detail, the informational-decisional stage of an interview entails several abilities: (a) drawing attention to the patient's problem(s) and structuring information; (b) exploring the patient's preferences, expectations, and past experiences; (c) providing information; (d) focusing the patient's attention; (e) checking the patient's understanding; (f) exploring the patient's reaction to received information;

Table 4.1 Objectives, Tasks, and Skills of Providing Information and Involving Patient

Objectives	Tasks	Skills
Therapist understands patient's model, including what the psychological problem(s) means to the patient personally (i.e., impact on life's meaning, ability to function, ability to relate to others)	• Ask questions and make facilitations • Repeat back the patient's model to check understanding • Look for and handle emotions	• Asks questions about the patient's ideas, asks for opinions • Uses reflections and checking • Uses understandable language • Asks for feedback • Responds to emotions, picks up cues
Therapist explains cognitive-behavioral models and therapy and provides information	• Personalize • Find out what patient wants to know • Find out what patient already knows • Provide information (therapist's model) • Find out how patient feels about information being presented • Check patient's understanding of therapist's model • Present alternatives • Explain risks/benefits	• Uses understandable language • Chunks • Asks for feedback • Responds to emotions, picks up cues • Personalizes by stating relationship between patient's symptoms and specific cognitive-behavioral frameworks (e.g., ABC) • Makes repetition of important information • Focuses attention on important information • Refers to written material • Asks what patent knows • Asks what patient wants to know • Explains logical process • Gives alternatives • Orients patient to interview process • Elicits emotions • Asks patient's opinion
Negotiation about: – Differences – Final choice	• Identify differences • Correct mis-information • Negotiate plan including priorities	• Asks patient's opinion about explicit differences • Points out differences • Points out similarities • Corrects mis-information • Points out pros and cons of patient's point of view • Points out pros and cons of therapist's point of view • Underlines patient responsibility for making decision and psychotherapy • Uses motivational skills See above

(continued)

Table 4.1 (continued)

Objectives	Tasks	Skills
Therapist gives additional information relevant to each content area (symptoms, diagnosis, workup, treatment)	• Personalize • Find out what patient wants to know • Find out what patient already knows • Give information (model) • Finds out how patient feels about information being presented • Check patient's understanding of therapist's model • Present alternatives • Explain risks/benefits	
Patient gives informed consent	Therapist specifically asks for consent, including signing consent form if necessary	
Patient improves coping mechanisms including self-motivation	Motivational interviewing tasks	Discuss patient's resources (asking, telling, reinforcing)

(g) offering opportunities to ask questions; (h) sharing the therapist's own thoughts, feelings, and experiences (self-disclosure); (i) negotiating skills; (j) exploring the patient's social resources and providing support; and (k) closing the encounter and planning future sessions.

It may seem that these listed abilities need to be sequentially applied. Actually, their use depends both on the relationship established with each patient and on the different possible conditions. The therapist needs to be flexible in order to adapt each technique to the specific and particular situation, considering each patient's need and expectations. The dialogue should be fluent, and it would be absolutely counterproductive to apply these techniques as part of a predetermined and rigid model of conducting the interview. The therapist can use more than one skill at the same time when necessary or decide to give priority to one aspect over the other. Sometimes in the descriptions readers might find repetitions, because providing information and involving the patient is a process that engages two parties bidirectionally and changes over time. It is therefore difficult describing communication skills being at the same time practical and flexible. In light of these observations, the skills and examples we are going to discuss serve only to constitute a useful starting point to better disentangle the complexity of providing information and patient involvement in the psychotherapeutic process. It is important to underline that the examples provided are intended to be general. The more the therapist is able to tailor the skill to each patient's situation, the more the skill is effective in promoting patient participation and collaboration.

4.3.3.1   Drawing Attention to Patient's Problem(s) and Structuring Information

Providing information and involving the patient require good abilities in structuring each session and the psychotherapy (see Chapter 2). Before starting the "real" psychotherapeutic work with the patient, there has to be clarity about which specific problem or problems the therapist and the patient will work on. The therapist can start by summarizing the patient's problem(s) and looking for an agreement about his formulation. Understanding the patient's disease from the therapist's perspective (cognitive-behavioral formulation) is not sufficient. For example, saying that a patient is suffering from depression [referring to Beck's cognitive theory of depression and the cognitive negative triad; (Beck et al. 1979; Beck 2008)] is of limited information since in order to work with the patient, we need to establish what depression means for that individual patient.

Empathy and relationship-building skills (see Chapter 3) are, of course, essential for understanding the patient's perspective. Without empathy, the patient remains just a list of symptoms, and every attempt to capture her view of the problem is doomed to failure. Using active listening (see Chapter 2) allows the therapist to better understand, interpret, and evaluate patients and their problem(s). This allows the therapist to collect a great deal of information and to reformulate patients' narrative in a way that can provide them with new meanings to be more deeply explored subsequently during the psychotherapy.

Drawing clients' attention to these personal meanings is the first step for the information-giving process and for involving patients in further work. Agreement on problem(s) and its management can be firstly explored from the patient's perspective and only at a second time can be offered a new vision that incorporates both the therapist's [e.g., model of anxiety as suggested by Clark (1986)] and the patient's vision ("I don't go out alone anymore; I fear I can have another panic attack"). The clinician should listen carefully to a patient's perspective, trying to empathize with his feelings, provide a based conceptualization (formulation) of the presenting problem, and transmit the feeling that this conceptualization is shared. This allows the patient to add eventual important details, leading to a more and more precise patient's definition of problematic issues. After being sure to have clearly understood the client's theory about his problem(s), the therapist can provide a more comprehensive view and give a basic description of how the problem can be addressed in therapy, trying to combine information and expectations from both parts.

Examples

Th: You told me you came to see me today because you have felt depressed since your wife left. I think we can try to better explore this depression.

Th: You told me you have felt insecure about your future since the stroke. You used to do a lot of sports, were very active at work, and a referral for your family before the stroke. I think this event may have forced you to reconsider your present life entirely. . . .

Th: You expect me to better explore your feelings, particular these anxiety episodes you have in specific places, and about how to cope with this new life situation.

4.3.3.2 Exploring Patient's Opinions, Preferences, Expectations, and Past Experiences

After recapping information on the patient's problem(s), integrating both the patient's and therapist's perspectives, and checking the patient's understanding, the clinician may want to find out what the patient already knows about psychotherapy and what information he wants to know about it. Open-ended questions are very useful to obtain relevant information about the patient's preferences and previous experience with the problem's management and therapies. Additionally, the therapist can also assess the preferred approach to receiving information, for example, the use of graphs, pictures, or drawings. As in cognitive-behavioral therapy, the patient's participation and active collaboration is crucial, and so the therapist should always pay attention to the patient's reaction to the delivered information (see Sect. 4.3.3.6). Concerns or feelings should be actively searched whenever appropriate, for example, by directly asking the patient how she feels or what she thinks. The therapist can also elicit the patient's preferred level of involvement in the therapeutic process, for example, by exploring the patient's view/feelings on the assignment of specific homework (see "Examples" below). The communication skills described in Chapter 2, particularly listening and summarizing, can be very useful for exploring the patient's needs.

Examples

Th: What do you want to know about psychotherapy? *(Assessing amount and quality of information the patient desires)*

Th: What kind of information do you want about the problem you have described? *(Assessing amount and quality of information the patient desires)*

Th: What do you know about cognitive-behavioral psychotherapy? Have you ever heard of it? *(Exploring the patient's knowledge)*

Th: How do you think therapy can help you with your problem? *(Exploring the patient's expectations/desires)*

Th: What is your idea about how to manage your problem? *(Exploring the patient's expectations/desires)*

Th: "You said you already tried psychotherapy in the past. How was it? *(Exploring past experiences)*

Th: Cognitive-behavioral therapy requires that you do some homework, for example, recording feelings and thoughts you experience during those particular moments you described. What are your thoughts on that? *(Exploring the patient's opinion/ideas)*

4.3.3.3 Providing Information

Before starting the information-giving process, the therapist has already collected reliable information from patients, has recapped this information with them, and has checked that he has correctly understood the presented problem(s) from the patient's perspective (see also Chapter 2).

The ability to give clear and effective information can be improved by taking time to listen to and identify the patient's questions. It is therefore important that the therapist take time to plan how to deliver information to the patient, as this can require more than one session.

Therapist should try to present information in a way that will maximize the patient's understanding and participation in the therapeutic process. Information should *be tailored* for that individual person and related to the framework of his or her problem. From a medical context, we know that providing tailored information is more effective in promoting changes rather than general advice-giving (Ashenden et al. 1997; Butler et al. 1998).

The therapist should *avoid jargon* and complicated words, name emotions, and feelings, and, when possible, use the patient's own words to describe the problem(s). If the therapist is in doubt about the actual patient's understanding, she can repeat the explanation using different and certainly simpler words. The patient's understanding cannot be taken for granted. The use of some psychological terms can be checked during the consultation, as fluency in native language can greatly change from patient to patient.

The therapist can explain specific psychological terms and translate jargon into language that the patient can easily understand. Examples of problematic terminology include "affect," "obsession," "reinforcement," "depression," "phobia," and "schema." Using common wordings instead of jargon or giving an explanation is not "dumbing down" the presentation of ideas in a way that insults the patient's intelligence. On the contrary, it is a way to promote active collaboration. Using common words may be difficult for the therapist who feels his professionalism in some way minimized. We think that professionalism depends quite on the capacity to implement an empathic and familiar attitude without, of course, being too friendly—in other words, being able to stay with patients and their world without feeling the own role jeopardized is an integral part of the therapist's professionalism.

Some words or phrases can set off anxious or angry *patient reactions*. For example, when sharing a diagnosis, a phrase like "your depressive feeling …," if not previously mentioned by the patient, can be misunderstood and the term "depression" may be interpreted according to previous experiences or popular beliefs. A patient could feel the term "depression" is a threat to her well-being and could become anxious regarding the future course of the disease (e.g., fear of becoming unable to work or incapable of maintaining her social role). Whenever we give feedback on a patient's feelings, it may be useful to describe emotions using *soft terms* (e.g., "You look a little bit anxious" rather than, "You look very anguished" or "It seems to me you are a little bit down" rather than, "It seems to me you are depressed"). This provision can help to avoid the misunderstanding of a therapist's overemphatic expressions that can be read by the patient as signs of a more severe clinical condition.

Educated guess can be a useful strategy to explore the patient's emotions, especially when faced for the first time during the therapy (e.g., "I am wondering whether you feel a little bit concerned by the idea of starting the psychotherapy"). This strategy leaves the patient with the opportunity to reject the hypothesis if it is not true or too difficult to admit at this stage of the therapeutic process. The therapeutic alliance does not risk being compromised, and the patient can feel more willing to accept even unpleasant feelings (such as fear, suspiciousness, and anger).

When therapists use phrases or terms that touch off emotional responses, patients tend to focus their attention more on these reactions, leaving no space to receive further information. If the therapist is not aware of these patient reactions, the information-giving process may be disturbed with negative consequences both on the therapeutic alliance and on patients' motivation to the therapy. Suggestions rather than directions help the patient to feel more involved in the therapeutic process. The therapist therefore should always present information with space left for a reply from the patient (see also Sect. 4.3.3.6).

Particular attention should be paid to *language construction* and coherence. The therapist can divide information into discrete sections and develop a logical sequence, in order to share with the patient the reason (rationale) for providing that specific information or to explain what therapy is supposed to do or how it works. Providing information step by step also allows the therapist to take time to explore the patient's reaction (see below). It is well known that listening to a monotonous speaker delivering a lengthy explanation can lead to a loss of concentration very quickly. A long and complex monologue risks compromising the patient's understanding, because too much information at once is difficult to remember. The therapist runs the risk that the patient remains behind, still thinking about the first part of the explanation, while she has already gone on to give more information. To improve the patient's understanding, therefore, information should be given in small pieces, at appropriate times, avoiding premature advice, information, or reassurance, and being careful not to transmit any kind of judgment or superior attitude. The therapist should pause and check for the patient's understanding before proceeding. Once patients have assimilated the first information, they are ready to receive more and new information. In this process, nonverbal behaviors such as eye contact, intonation, and volume and rate of speech are important to foster the patient's understanding. Silent, implied messages, via body language, can encourage patients to take an active role in the therapeutic process (see Chapter 5). Importance should be given to the context in which clinical encounters take place, as a comfortable setting is a good introduction for further patient collaboration and for building the therapeutic alliance.

On some occasions there can exist more than one way of managing patients' problems or structuring psychotherapy (e.g., performing weekly or longer sessions; adding psychopharmacological treatment; involving others relatives to collect additional important information). When different options exist, the therapist can *present alternatives* and discuss the pros and cons with patients in order to involve them in the therapeutic process and share decisions. *Examining the pros and cons* (using also a balance sheet) can also be applied when patients are in doubt about personal decisions and ask the therapist for advice. In order to involve patients in exploring all the options and help them to make a choice, the patient and therapist list all the available alternatives together, and subsequently the pros and cons of each option are analyzed and discussed, taking into account the patient's view and preferences. After this process patients should be in the position to better balance which is the best choice for them (for an example of a decisional sheet, see the Ottawa Personal Decision Guide; O'Connor and Jacobsen 2007).

Therapists can use *figures of speech* such as analogies and similes, which can be a graphic way to give explanations to patients in terms they can easily understand or visualize (Desmond and Copeland 2000). It is important, of course, that these or other figures of speech align clearly with the situation the therapist is trying to simplify. If used appropriately with the therapeutic message, analogies and similes can be very powerful aids to involve patients in the therapeutic process and motivate them to change. Metaphors can also be useful, particularly when brought into the dialogue by patients themselves. When using metaphors, the therapist should be careful that the patient has really understood the meaning and has not taken them too literally (examples of metaphors and their use can be found in Lyddon and Alford 2002).

In providing information, the therapist can also be helped by the use of leaflets and other *visual materials*, such as drawings, diagrams, models, schemes, and handouts. Through planned use of this written material, the therapist can promote greater client attention and understanding of their problems. For example, the therapist can draw during the consultation vicious cycles, anxiety models, or ABC models, which can help patient to better understand the link between emotions and thoughts. Using written material during the session and sharing it can also increase patient collaboration for future sessions and for homework assignments. The therapist, for example, can start drawing an ABC model during the session and then give the task to the patient to continue the exercise at home (homework). The therapist can use existing material or can create new handouts with the patient. In the first case, to personalize handouts, it is possible to write the patient's name on the top or underline information that is particularly pertinent for that individual person and his or her therapy. Customizing written material contributes to making the patient feel listened to and understood and enhances both the relationship and the patient's involvement. The therapist should be careful in some particular instances where confidentiality may be compromised. For example, some patients do not like to take written material home because they do not want their family members to know they are seeing a psychotherapist. Therefore, this possibility should be checked with the patient before giving written material (see Sect. 4.3.3.6).

Examples

Th: This feeling of "inadequacy" you were talking about seems part of a more complex picture, including depressive feelings and anxiety when you face certain situations. ... *(Providing integrated feedback including both patient's and therapist's perspective)*

Th: You told me about an 'obsessive' fear of contamination that obliges you to wash your hands several times in a day. Actually, an obsession is an uncontrollable and persistent thought that a person cannot help thinking even though it creates a lot of anxiety. *(Explaining specific psychological terms)*

Th: We can work on your depressive feelings with the psychotherapy alone or by adding a drug prescription. *(Listing available options)* Both options have pros and cons that we can explore together. What do you think about it?

Th: During a panic attack your brain goes haywire and starts sending messages of danger to your body *(Using similes or others figures of speech)*

Th: You said that at the supermarket on Monday you felt very anxious and in your mind the main thought was, "I am anxious and all the people here will notice that."

Pt: Right.

Th: Let's try to put this information on a piece of paper. I'll draw three columns. The first one is for the situation "being at the supermarket," the second one is for thoughts and beliefs and we can write "everyone will notice I am anxious," in the third one we'll write the emotion, which is anxiety. *(Using written material)* What are your thoughts?

4.3.3.4 Focusing Patient's Attention

By using focusing techniques, the therapist underlines important aspects by attracting the patient's attention to specific issues. This is particularly useful to improve the patient's understanding and involvement. Using focusing skills, the patient feels actively involved in the process, acting as a partner and not just as a passive recipient to be filled in by the therapist. Moreover, the therapist can provide patients with a sort of map that guides them through the informative process, facilitating their ability to follow the received information and their comprehension. The ability to highlight the essential aspects is an important feature for an effective explanation, particularly for long ones, where the patient may have difficulties in identifying from the presented information the key points to be remembered. The therapist therefore can focus the patient's attention on relevant topics and use repetitions and summarizing to reinforce important information.

Examples

Th: There are three important things that I would like to discuss with you.

Th: I would like to stop for a moment on these "depressive feelings" you told me, and try to give a description with your help of what happens when you feel down. I think it is an important point.

Th: Listen to me carefully. I'd like to explain better what can be done to try to solve these problems.

Th: I think it is important to spend some more time by sharing information about these feelings of anxiety you have just told me about.

4.3.3.5 Checking the Patient's Understanding (Feedback)

It is well known that the message sent is not always equivalent to the message received. We may remember a child game (called the "wireless phone" in Italy) in which the first player starts by whispering a message to the person next to him and so on in a chain until the last of the players has heard the message. The last player announces the message, and generally all participants roll with laughter at how much the original message has been distorted. Therapists therefore cannot rely on patients' understanding based only on nonverbal behavior, such as nodding, or simple verbal expressions of agreement such as "yes" or "right." On the other hand, checking comprehension in a more direct way could unintentionally make the patient feel inadequate. If information is not really clear for the patient, he or she may feel stupid if the therapist asks questions such as, "Did you understand?" or "Is everything okay?" Patients may feel forced to answer "yes" even if they have not really understood. The responsibility for any lack of understanding therefore should be borne by the therapist. It is useful avoiding closed questions for several reasons: One is related to the problem just mentioned above (patients can feel judged); others are that patients can be reluctant to admit confusion or can find it easier to answer "yes" instead of thinking seriously about what has been said. The therapist should therefore check the patient's understanding of the delivered information, using open questions or asking the patient to repeat what has been said. Checking the patient's understanding with open questions also promotes active participation. The therapist can invite the patient to summarize her understanding of presented information. A patient who has correctly understood received information will be able to repeat all the relevant parts. Patient restatement has a valuable and powerful effect, not only on his understanding but also from a therapeutic point of view as he begins to view the problem and its management from a different perspective, one that can promote change. The therapist, on the other hand, can also use the patient's response as a guide to know how to proceed.

Examples

Th: We have said several things so far. Could you please tell me what kind of information you remember best?

Th: I'm not sure whether I explained that very well. Could you please try to repeat what we have said so far?

Th: Sometimes I may give too much information at once. I am wondering what aspects you have retained

4.3.3.6 Exploring Patient's Reaction to Received Information

Every time therapists give information, they should expect a patient reaction. The reaction can be mainly emotional, cognitive, or both. Patients can clearly verbalize an emotional/cognitive reaction to the received information or can only give some hidden signals of its presence. In this last case, we should be able to pick those signals up, being particularly alert to verbal and nonverbal cues, and explore better an emotional reaction before responding or providing new information.

If the reaction is sufficiently clearly expressed, it can be managed by acknowledging it, addressing it where necessary, and handling emotions properly (see Chapter 3). Reactions not clearly expressed should be elicited by the clinician in terms of feelings, concerns, worries, beliefs, opinions, and ideas. The therapist checks the patient's opinion/concerns/feelings about received information or about how problems are to be managed. Ideas or concerns about received information can be difficult to assess.

The patient can find it difficult to answer questions such as, "How do you feel regarding the therapeutic proposal?" or "What do you think about your problem?" Besides using open questions, the therapist can explore the patient's reaction by suggesting common fears or thoughts, using pauses appropriately, and giving space to the patient's spontaneous expressions.

Some patients can be uncomfortable with a too involved and directive approach or may not be willing to engage in cognitive-behavioral treatment for different reasons. For example, they can find homework too difficult to comply with either because they do not have enough time or because of depressive symptoms or feelings of losing freedom and control. The therapist should be prepared to address these and other concerns that can arise when providing information on cognitive-behavioral psychotherapy. If necessary, the therapist can also use negotiating skills (see above), returning to explore the patient's view and trying to understand it before proceeding with new explanations.

Whenever an emotional reaction is too overwhelming, the information-giving process needs to be stopped and dealing with patients' feelings becomes the priority. The cognitive functioning of the client, in fact, can be compromised by intense emotional reactions, as they influence attention, concentration, and listening ability. This also means that the therapist should be prepared to provide any remaining relevant information in further sessions. As already said, a good relationship is fundamental to create the positive atmosphere in which patients can feel free to express their feelings and concerns.

Examples

Th: It seems you are not very comfortable with this information I've given you. Maybe you have other ideas about how to manage the situation. . . . *(Acknowledging patient's reaction)*

Th: You seem concerned about my proposal of planning weekly sessions. *(Empathic comment)*

Th: Your concerns about psychotherapy (therapist can specify what those are) are understandable. *(Legitimating)*

Th: What do you think about my proposal of planning weekly psychotherapy sessions? *(Asking for the patient's cognitive reaction)*

Th: During the time until the next session, what I suggest to do is trying to fill in this ABC exercise in a similar way to how we did it today. I'm wondering how you feel about this. *(Asking for the patient's emotional reaction)*

Th: Every change may cause contrasting feelings of both hope and apprehension. I'm wondering how you feel initiating psychotherapy. *(Asking for the patient's emotional reaction)*

Th: I have just described the cycle that occurs when you are in crowded places, such as the supermarket yesterday. What do you think about it? *(Asking for the patient's cognitive reaction)*

Th: Does this plan seem reasonable to you? *(Exploring the patient's opinion/idea)*

Th: I like to encourage my patients to share their thoughts with me in order to know whether we're on track. What do you think about the therapeutic plan? *(Exploring the patient's opinions/ideas)*

Th: I suggested also seeing a psychiatrist in this situation, but maybe you are thinking of something different. ... *(Asking for the patient's reaction by exploring expectations/ desires)*

4.3.3.7 Offering Opportunities to Ask Questions

To promote participation and collaboration, it is important to offer explicit opportunities to ask questions during the information-giving process, both in the single session and during the whole course of the psychotherapy. A productive and facilitating atmosphere can be created by active listening, which lets the patient feel free to ask questions (see Chapter 2). If the patient does not ask any questions spontaneously, the therapist should actively encourage her contributions by asking questions, seeking clarification, or expressing doubts. As stated before, using closed questions such as, "Do you have any questions?" or simply, "Anything to ask?" can be tricky. Closed questions can be leading questions that force patients to answer "no" depending on several different factors, such as the therapist's vocal intonation, the patient's feeling at that particular moment, the quality of the relationship, and the atmosphere created during the session. The patient, in fact, may say "no" only because he cannot feel free enough to answer "yes," particularly during the first session when the relationship may not be well established already.

Examples

Th: I've given you a lot of information regarding the therapy. I'm wondering if you have any questions to ask about it.

Th: In the first encounters patients generally can have questions or doubts about the psychotherapy. As this might be also your case, what kind of questions would you like to ask me?

Th: Sometimes I may be not clear enough. So please feel free to ask questions so we can clarify the situation or any doubts that we may come across.

4.3.3.8 Sharing Therapist's Own Thoughts Feelings and Experiences (Self-Disclosure)

We can broadly define self-disclosure as statements or expressions that reveal something personal about the therapist. Self-disclosure in psychotherapy has a controversial history and has seen different positions with arguments both for and against its practice, also in cognitive-behavioral approaches (Henretty and Levitt 2010; Barglow 2005). Some people affirm that self-disclosure may reduce the patient's perception of the therapist's competence, or may lead to negative feelings with the possible result of decreasing the motivation for therapy or the desire to change. Others state that self-disclosure provides social comparison data and makes the patient feel understood, increasing the patient's engagement in the psychotherapy. The debate is also about whether self-disclosure is a boundary violation, which unethically exploits patients, or a boundary crossing, which is the therapist's attempt to adapt an existing therapeutic alliance to foster the patient's capacity to work in therapy (Glass 2003).

It is not the point here to discuss these and other potential different positions and probe the question. We believe that sometimes self-disclosure has a potential benefit on the relationship and on patient involvement. Therapist self-disclosure must be used for the benefit of the patient, based therefore first and foremost on his or her welfare. It should be patient-centered, based on a genuine relationship, and clinically driven. From this point of view, the therapist can decide to share his or her expertise about the patient's problem (diagnosis) or disclose personal experience with the problem (or questions) presented by patients.

Examples

Pt: I get very scary watching that movie. I shouldn't be so afraid.

Th: I have seen that movie too. It is a really scary movie and I generally do not like those kinds of movies.

Pt: I do not know if you can really understand how I feel at this moment

Th: It is difficult, I cannot feel exactly what you feel, but as a matter of fact I went through something very similar when a friend of mine died in a car accident last year.

Pt: These voices are really distressing me. When I listen to music they go away a little bit. I really like classical music.

Th: I like it, too. I find it really relaxing and I think it can help you cope with these distressing voices.

4.3.3.9 Negotiating Skills

Negotiation can be defined as a process in which two or more parties try to make an agreement on what they can give and receive. In this view, negotiation is a sort of exchange with the main objective of reaching a shared plan or goals. Negotiation skills can be therefore useful in order to overcome eventual disagreement between patient and therapist.

During an argument in a social context, what generally happens is that each person tends to defend his or her own position and deny the validity of the other person's position. This situation may produce defensive reactions, increasing the distance between the two parties. In a psychotherapeutic process, trying to avoid such a counterproductive reaction is fundamental in order to create a collaborative atmosphere, and it lays the basis for productive work with the patient. Negotiating skills are potential instruments to resolve the conflict and reach such an important goal.

The first step toward effective negotiation is being aware of both parties' position. For example, if the different positions regard the therapeutic plan, the therapist should first explore the patient's view/opinion about how to manage the problem (see also Sect. 4.3.3.6). Asking patients about their expectations can help discover eventual unrealistic positions and shed light on patients' motivation throughout the therapy. Only after the patient's view has been explored in detail can the therapist reveal his or her position, providing only essential information and paying more attention to both hidden and evident disagreements raised by the patient. Emotional dissonance between verbal and nonverbal reactions expressed by the patient should be carefully noticed as well as signals of unexpected resistance, such as getting distracted, interrupting the therapist while speaking, trying to devalue the therapist's position, being inattentive, and so on. In order to facilitate the patient's expression of disagreement, the therapist should create an atmosphere of empathic and nonjudgmental listening (see Chapter 3). It is important that the therapist understands and accepts the patient's view, as this makes the patient feel that different opinions are accepted and legitimated.

Open questions or hypotheses that try to explain the nature of the disagreement can also be used to explore better and different positions. Making the disagreement explicit, together with underlining that the therapist and patient are working together to reach a shared goal, signals respect for the client and contributes to minimize the disagreement itself.

Once all the positions have been clearly stated and elicited, the therapist can try to negotiate a balance between them. He or she can also use in this case problem-solving techniques to involve the patient in the solution of the disagreement. Different options should be discussed, and whenever possible a proposal that combines both ideas should be proposed. The therapist can discuss with the patient the pros and cons of different alternatives, and if the therapist has previously explored the patient's ideas, this discussion can be better tailored by keeping in mind important issues for that individual patient. Involving the patient in this dissertation enhances the therapeutic alliance and increases the possibility of reaching a shared plan and/or goals. At this point the therapist may recognize that he has misunderstood something or made a mistake in building the patient's cognitive-behavioral model. If this happens, these thoughts and doubts can be shared with the patient, reinforcing the alliance and the patient's involvement in the therapeutic process.

As the final goal is reaching a shared plan, negation can be a process that takes time and requires more than one session to be completed. If the patient remains resistant, the clinician should be prepared to postpone discussion until the following session. Sometimes we can also consider the hypothesis of making a referral to a therapist whose approach to the presenting problem better fits with the patient's expectations. This can be considered as a shared decision as well as a patient's refusal of therapeutic proposal if accurately explored and discussed with the patient. Sometimes patients need more time to think about what has been said during the session. They may want to talk to their family or friends in order to compare their thoughts and opinions or collect other information (for example, searching the Internet), or they may need time to elaborate fears or concerns regarding psychotherapy (e.g., "If I need psychotherapy, I am really crazy" or "I am not able to mange my life with my limited energy. I am an unsuccessful person").

The therapist will therefore negotiate a following appointment where to explore better the disagreement and try to find together with the patient a solution that can combine both positions, or she could negotiate intermediate goals. For example, if writing down an ABC exercise as homework is too difficult for a patient, the therapist can propose to audiotape feelings and thoughts immediately after specific situations the therapist and patient have previously agreed on. The patient's opinion on this new proposal of course should then be checked. Another example can be represented by very depressed patients for whom every little commitment can be very hard to maintain. Instead of suggesting the patient do pleasant activities (e.g., listen to music, reading a book), the therapist can propose starting with very little things such as only writing down a list of these pleasant activities (e.g., "For the next session I would like you to think about pleasant activities you used to do and write down a list of such activities. What do you think?"). By doing this, the patient feels he is able to manage the problem and can feel satisfaction for the agreed goal achieved.

Examples

Th: You look thoughtful. . . . I'm wondering if there is something I've just said about how to manage your anxiety when you are at the supermarket that may have concerned you in some way. *(Acknowledging patient's reaction)*

Th: You said that writing down an ABC exercise is too big a commitment for you to follow. On the other hand, I think doing some exercises between our sessions is very important for feeling better. How can we do put together our different positions? What do you think? *(Making different opinions explicit)*

Th: I agree with you that weekly psychotherapy is a big time commitment, but at the same time I think it is important for you to take some time to better understand what has been happening in these last two months and cope with your depressive feelings. *(Making different opinions explicit)*

Th: I see you haven't made up your mind yet. On the one hand, you want to better explore these new feelings of anxiety you have and try to solve problems with your wife, and on the other hand, you think that if your wife discovered you are seeing a psychotherapist, it would worsen your relationship. It is a real dilemma. *(Making patient's inner discrepancy explicit)*

Th: You told me you are in a period in which you feel that the psychotherapy is not useful anymore and want to interrupt it. Can we spend this session talking about the pros and cons of leaving or continuing psychotherapy? *(Helping patients to think about different options)*

Th: You told me the psychiatrist suggested a drug treatment for your depression, but you are not convinced, as you fear that antidepressant may lead to weight gain and you said that your body image is really important for you.

Pt: Right.

Th: I think that drugs can help people feel better and at the same time allow us to work better in psychotherapy.

Pt: Yes, I know.

Th: What I can propose is helping you to monitor your body weight and take some time to talk about your feeling of low self-esteem, referring also to your body image. *(Making proposal on common ground)* What do you think?

4.3.3.10   Exploring Patient's Social Resources and Providing Support

In every moment of the therapeutic process it is important that the therapist provides support to patient without being judgmental. Therapists offer support and underline their availability to help patients even if they can have different opinions on the patient's problem and/or on its management. Exploring the patient's social context and previous experience on how the patient has managed a difficult situation can help the therapist to better understand the patient's available resources to deal with current problems. Moreover, by doing this, the therapist can also reach greater patient involvement. The therapist can provide encouragement by positively commenting on the way patients have coped with previous distressing situations and applauding their courage for seeking help or for having coped with the problem so far. It is important that the therapist leaves patients with a sense of optimism for the possibility that psychotherapy can help them relieve their problem(s). The therapist should encourage patients also to be involved in implementing plans, to take responsibility for their own life, and to be self-reliant. In this sense, providing support also means reassuring patients, and helping them in building and reinforcing self-esteem and self-efficacy [for these specific skills, see more specific cognitive-behavioral books (e.g., Bandura 1986, 1995, 1997)].

Examples

Th: From what you have just told me, I can see you have valid reasons to be scared by making such a decision. The decision is yours, and I cannot force you in one or the other direction. If you like, I can help you in exploring the pros and cons of each option in more detail. *(Underlining the patient's responsibility and freedom combined with underlining the therapist's support to the patient)*

Th: I see we have different opinions about how to manage this situation. I am on your side and I am willing to help you to find a solution. *(Underlining the therapist's support)*

Th: It is a difficult situation and I realize that the final decision it is up to you. What I can do is help you to better understand the different aspects of this choice and try to look at both sides of the coin. *(Underlining the therapist's support)*

Th: From your point of view, who or what can be helpful to cope with this situation? *(Assessing and mobilizing patient's inner and social resources and support for coping and changing behavior)*

Th: What do you think can help you in making such a difficult decision? *(Assessing and mobilizing patient's inner and social resources and support for coping and changing behavior)*

Th: What are your thoughts about how to manage this problem? *(Assessing and mobilizing patient's inner and social resources and support for coping and changing behavior)*

4.3.3.11   Closing the Encounter and Planning Future Sessions

Planning psychotherapy implies using skills for structuring the session (see Chapter 2) but also for planning future encounters. The therapist provides information about the duration and frequencies of psychotherapy sessions in order to achieved shared goals with the patient.

The closure of the session is another important aspect. Even if the therapist states right from the beginning the length of the interview, patients can sometimes feel the available time was too short or that the therapist is not really interested in his or her problem or does not give it the right importance. Closure is of particular importance during first encounters, as it is in this assessment stage where the therapist builds with the patient the program for the following encounters. It is therefore desirable that the therapist and patient agree that the closure process is beginning. The therapist should signal in an unhurried manner that the interview is coming to the end and should be prepared to take the risk that the patient may feel the time was too short. At a certain point during the session, the therapist can also indicate the need for a decision-making (or deferring) stage. Closure can be preceded by a brief summary of what has been said and discussed or agreed upon during the interview. This can also be another opportunity at this final stage for the patient to ask questions or add something. Finally, the therapist and patient agree and arrange further appointments or indicate the need to review the decision (or what else they have shared during the session and agreed on).

During subsequent sessions, the clinician should remember to review the previous agreement and check first how things have gone from the previous session until now. Afterward he can explore the patient's feelings and thoughts about what was said and agreed on during the previous session. The therapist should reinforce the patient's efforts and be prepared to accept that the patient did not accomplish what was agreed upon (e.g., homework). In this case the therapist restarts the process by exploring the patient's difficulties without making judgments in order to avoid feelings of inadequacy. They will work together to find a solution on how to achieve shared goals. Here, again, problem-solving techniques can also be helpful. Promoting patient's adherence to therapy therefore means always being patient-centered, reviewing agreements and goals with patients, being prepared to accept different opinions and views, and being open to understand their position and discuss with them what to do next. The therapist should also be prepared to change goals and plans with the patients if new information arises or situations change.

Examples

Th: We said you have an anxiety problem when you stay with people you don't know very well. We agreed to see each other to better explore the problem and find out how it can be managed. Is there anything else you want to say or ask before we close? *(Brief summary and agenda completion; see also Chapter 2)*

Th: We'll need to draw things to a close now. *(Expressing need for a closure)*

Th: A lot of interesting things arose during this first encounter. I think we can better explore some aspects you mentioned in the next session. What do you think? *(Planning the next encounter)*

Th: Until the next encounter, what would we like to do? *(Involving patient in planning the following encounter)*

Th: In the last session we identified some distressing situations and we decided you would write down the thoughts and feelings you generally experience in those situations. How are you getting on with this exercise? *(Reviewing what was agreed upon)*

References

Adams, J. R., & Drake, R. E. (2006). Shared decision-making and evidence-based practice. *Community Mental Health Journal, 42*, 87–105.

Ashenden, R., Silagy, C., & Wellere, D. (1997). A systematic review of the effectiveness of promoting lifestyle change in general practice. *Family Practice, 14*, 160–175.

Bandura, A. (1986). *Social foundations of thought and action: A social cognitive theory.* Englewood Cliffs, NJ: Prentice Hall.

Bandura, A. (Ed.). (1995). *Self-efficacy in changing societies.* New York: Cambridge University Press.

Bandura, A. (1997). *Self-efficacy: The exercise of control.* New York: Freeman.

Barglow, P. (2005). Self-disclosure in psychotherapy. *American Journal of Psychotherapy, 59*, 83–99.

Beck, J. S. (1995). *Cognitive therapy.* New York: Guilford Press.

Beck, A. T. (2008). The evolution of the cognitive model of depression and its neurobiological correlates. *American Journal of Psychiatry, 165*, 969–977.

Beck, A. T., Rush, A. J., Shaw, B. F., & Emery, G. (1979). *Cognitive therapy of depression.* New York: Guilford Press.

Befort, C. A., Nollen, N., Ellerbeck, E. F., Sullivan, D. K., Thomas, J. L., & Ahluwalia, J. S. (2008). Motivational interviewing fails to improve outcomes of a behavioral weight loss program for obese African American women: A pilot randomized trial. *Journal of Behavioral Medicine, 31*, 367–377.

Bellack, A. S., & Hersen, M. (1998). *Behavioral assessment: A practical handbook.* Boston: Allyn and Bacon.

Benbassat, J., Pilpel, D., & Tidhar, M. (1998). Patients' preferences for participation in clinical decision making: A review of published surveys. *Behavioral Medicine, 24*, 81–88.

Braddock, C. H., Edwards, K. A., Hasenberg, N. M., Laidley, T. L., & Levinson, W. (1999). Informed decision making in outpatient practice: Time to get back to basics. *Journal of the American Medical Association, 282*, 2313–2320.

Braddock, C. H., Fihn, S. D., Levinson, W., Jonsen, A. R., & Pearlman, R. A. (1997). How doctors and patients discuss routine clinical decisions. Informed decision making in the outpatient setting. *Journal of General Internal Medicine, 12*, 339–345.

Britt, E., Hudson, S. M., & Blampied, N. M. (2004). Motivational interviewing in health settings: A review. *Patient Education and Counseling, 53*, 147–155.

Brown, R., Butow, P. N., Boyer, M. J., & Tattersall, M. H. (1999). Promoting patient participation in the cancer consultation: Evaluation of a prompt sheet and coaching in question-asking. *British Journal of Cancer, 80*, 242–248.

Bruera, E., Sweeney, C., Willey, J., Palmer, J. L., Tolley, S., Rosales, M., et al. (2003). Breast cancer patient perception of the helpfulness of a prompt sheet versus a general information sheet during outpatient consultation: A randomized, controlled trial. *Journal of Pain and Symptom Management, 25*, 412–419.

Burke, B. L., Arkowitz, H., & Menchola, M. (2003). The efficacy of motivational interviewing: A meta-analysis of controlled clinical trials. *Journal of Consulting and Clinical Psychology, 71*, 843–861.

Butler, C. C., Pill, R., & Stott, N. C. (1998). Qualitative study of patients' perceptions of doctors' advice to quit smoking: Implications for opportunistic health promotion. *British Medical Journal, 316*, 1878–1881.

Butler, C., Rollnick, S., Cohen, D., Russel, I., Bachmann, M., & Stott, N. (1999). Motivational consulting versus brief advice for smokers in general practice: A randomized trial. *British Journal of General Practice, 49*, 611–616.

Butow, P. (2001). The importance of communication skills to effective cancer care and support. *New South Wales Public Health Bulletin, 12*, 272–274.

Butow, P. N., Dunn, S. M., Tattersall, M. H., & Jones, Q. J. (1994). Patient participation in the cancer consultation: Evaluation of a question prompt sheet. *Annals of Oncology, 5*, 199–204.

Cairns, R., Maddock, C., Buchanan, A., David, A. S., Hayward, P., Richardson, G., et al. (2005). Prevalence and predictors of mental incapacity in psychiatry in-patients. *British Journal of Psychiatry, 187*, 379–385.

Charles, C., Gafni, A., & Whelan, T. (1997). Shared decision-making in the medical encounter: What does it mean? (Or it takes at least two to tango). *Social Science and Medicine, 44*, 681–692.

Charles, C., Gafni, A., & Whelan, T. (1999). Decision-making in the physician-patient encounter: Revisiting the shared treatment decision-making model. *Social Science and Medicine, 49*, 651–661.

Charles, C., Gafni, A., & Whelan, T. (2000). How to improve communication between doctors and patients. Learning more about the decision making context is important. *British Medical Journal, 320*, 1220–1221.

Charles, C., Whelan, T., & Gafni, A. (1999). What do we mean by partnership in making decisions about treatment? *British Medical Journal, 319*, 780–782.

Clark, D. M. (1986). A cognitive model of panic. *Behaviour Research and Therapy, 24*, 461–470.

Clayton, J., Butow, P., Tattersall, M., Chye, R., Noel, M., Davis, J. M., et al. (2003). Asking questions can help: Development and preliminary evaluation of a question prompt list for palliative care patients. *British Journal of Cancer, 89*, 2069–2077.

Clayton, J. M., Butow, P. N., Tattersall, M. H., Devine, R. J., Simpson, J. M., Aggarwal, G., et al. (2007). Randomized controlled trial of a prompt list to help advanced cancer patients and their caregivers to ask questions about prognosis and end-of-life care. *Journal of Clinical Oncology, 25*, 715–723.

Cohen-Cole, S. A. (1991). *The medical interview: The three-function approach*. St. Louis: Mosby-Year.

Colombo, A., Bendelow, G., Fulford, B., & Williams, S. (2003). Evaluating the influence of implicit models of mental disorder on processes of shared decision making within community-based multi-disciplinary teams. *Social Science and Medicine, 56*, 1557–1570.

Coulter, A. (1997). Partnerships with patients: The pros and cons of shared clinical decision-making. *Journal of Health Service Research & Policy, 2*, 112–121.

Coulter, A. (2002). After Bristol: Putting patients at the centre. *British Medical Journal, 324*, 648–651.

Coulter, A., Entwistle, V., & Gilbert, D. (1999). Sharing decisions with patients: Is the information good enough? *British Medical Journal, 318*, 318–322.

Deber, R. B., Kraetschmer, N., Urowitz, S., & Sharpe, N. (2007). Do people want to be autonomous patients? Preferred roles in treatment decision-making in several patient populations. *Health Expectations, 10*, 248–258.

Desmond, J., & Copeland, L. R. (2000). *Communicating with today's patients*. San Francisco: Jossey-Bass.

Drew, P., Chatwin, J., & Collins, S. (2001). Conversation analysis: A method for research into interactions between patients and health-care professionals. *Health Expectations, 4*, 58–70.

Dunn, C., Deroo, L., & Rivara, F. P. (2001). The use of brief interventions adapted from motivational interviewing across behavioral domains: A systematic review. *Addiction, 96*, 1725–1742.

Elwyn, G., Edwards, A., & Britten, N. (2003). What information do patients need about medicines? "Doing prescribing": How doctors can be more effective. *British Medical Journal, 327*, 864–867.

Elwyn, G., Edwards, A., Hood, K., Robling, M., Atwell, C., Russell, I., et al. (2004). Achieving involvement: Process outcomes from a cluster randomized trial of shared decision making skill development and use of risk communication aids in general practice. *Family Practice, 21*, 337–346.

Elwyn, G., Edwards, A., Kinnersley, P., & Grol, R. (2000). Shared decision making and the concept of equipoise: The competencies of involving patients in healthcare choices. *British Journal of General Practice, 50*, 892–899.

Elwyn, G., Edwards, A., Wensing, M., Hood, K., Atwell, C., & Grol, R. (2003). Shared decision making: Developing the OPTION scale for measuring patient involvement. *Quality & Safety in Health Care, 12*, 93–99.

Evans, R., Edwards, A., & Elwyn, G. (2003). The future for primary care: Increased choice for patients. *Quality & Safety in Health Care, 12*, 83–84.

Frederikson, L. G. (1995). Exploring information-exchange in consultation: The patients' view of performance and outcomes. *Patient Education and Counseling, 25*, 237–246.

Gattellari, M., Butow, P. N., & Tattersall, M. H. (2001). Sharing decisions in cancer care. *Social Science and Medicine, 52*, 1865–1878.

Glass, L. (2003). The gray areas of boundary crossings and violations. *American Journal of Psychotherapy, 57*, 429–444.

Glynne-Jones, R., Ostler, P., Lumley-Graybow, S., Chait, I., Hughes, R., Grainger, J., et al. (2006). Can I look at my list? An evaluation of a "prompt sheet" within an oncology outpatient clinic. *Clinical Oncology (Royal College of Radiologists (Great Britain)), 18*, 395–400.

Goossensen, A., Zijlstra, P., & Koopmanschap, M. (2007). Measuring shared decision making process in psychiatry: Skills versus patient satisfaction. *Patient Education and Counseling, 67*, 50–56.

Goss, C., Fontanesi, S., Mazzi, M. A., Del Piccolo, L., & Rimondini, M. (2007a). The assessment of patient involvement across consultation. The Italian version of the OPTION scale [In Italian]. *Epidemiologia e Psichiatria Sociale, 16*, 339–349.

Goss, C., Fontanesi, S., Mazzi, M. A., Del Piccolo, L., Rimondini, M., & Zimmermann, C. (2007b). Shared decision making: The reliability of the OPTION scale in Italy. *Patient Education and Counseling, 66*, 296–302.

Goss, C., Mazzi, M. A., Del Piccolo, L., Rimondini, M., & Zimmermann, C. (2005). Information-giving sequences in general practice consultations. *Journal of Evaluation in Clinical Practice, 11*, 339–349.

Goss, C., Moretti, F., Mazzi, M. A., Del Piccolo, L., Rimondini, M., & Zimmermann, C. (2008). Involving patients in decisions during psychiatric consultations. *British Journal of Psychiatry, 193*, 416–421.

Guadagnoli, E., & Ward, P. (1998). Patient participation in decision-making. *Social Science and Medicine, 47*, 329–339.

Hall, J. A., Roter, D. L., & Katz, N. R. (1988). Meta-analysis of correlates of provider behavior in medical encounters. *Medical Care, 26*, 657–675.

Hamann, J., Langer, B., Leucht, S., Busch, R., & Kissling, W. (2004). Medical decision making in antipsychotic drug choice for schizophrenia. *American Journal of Psychiatry, 161*, 1301–1304.

Hamann, J., Leucht, S., & Kissling, W. (2003). Shared decision making in psychiatry. *Acta Psychiatrica Scandinavica, 107*, 403–409.

Hamann, J., Mendel, R., Cohen, R., Heres, S., Ziegler, M., Bühner, M., et al. (2009). Psychiatrists' use of shared decision making in the treatment of schizophrenia: Patient characteristics and decision topics. *Psychiatric Services, 60*, 1107–1112.

Hamann, J., Mischo, C., Langer, B., Leucht, S., & Kissling, W. (2005). Physicians' and patients' involvement in relapse prevention with antipsychotics in schizophrenia. *Psychiatric Services, 56*, 1448–1450.

Harland, J., White, M., Drinkwater, C., Chinn, D., Farr, L., & Howel, D. (1999). The Newcastle exercise project: A randomised controlled trial of methods to promote physical activity in primary care. *British Medical Journal, 319*, 823–832.

Harter, M., & Loh, A. (2007). Shared decision making in diverse health care system [special issue]. *Zeitschrift für ärztliche Fortbildung und Qualitätssicherung [German Journal for Evidence and Quality in Health Care], 101*, 203–281.

Hawton, K., Salkovskis, P. M., Kirk, J., & Clark, M. (1989). *Cognitive behavior therapy for psychiatric problems*. New York: Oxford University Press.

Henretty, J. R., & Levitt, H. M. (2010). The role of therapist self-disclosure in psychotherapy: A qualitative review. *Clinical Psychology Review, 30*, 63–77.

Hope, T. (2002). Evidence-based patient choice and psychiatry. *Evidence-Based Mental Health, 5*, 100–101.

Jeste, D. V., Depp, C. A., & Palmer, B. W. (2006). Magnitude of impairment in decisional capacity in people with schizophrenia compared to normal subjects: An overview. *Schizophrenia Bulletin, 32*, 121–128.

Jones, K. D., Burckhardt, C. S., & Bennett, J. A. (2004). Motivational interviewing may encourage exercise in persons with fibromyalgia by enhancing self-efficacy. *Arthritis and Rheumatism, 51*, 864–867.

Joosten, E. A., DeFuentes-Merillas, L., de Weert, G. H., Sensky, T., van der Staak, C. P., & de Jong, C. A. (2008). Systematic review of the effects of shared decision-making on patient satisfaction, treatment adherence and health status. *Psychotherapy and Psychosomatics, 77*, 219–226.

Kent, H., & Read, J. (1998). Measuring consumer participation in mental health services: Are attitudes related to professional orientation? *International Journal of Social Psychiatry, 44*, 295–310.

Kidd, J., Marteau, T. M., Robinson, S., Ukoumunne, O., & Tydeman, C. (2004). Promoting patient participation in consultations: A randomised controlled trial to evaluate the effectiveness of three patient-focused interventions. *Patient Education and Counseling, 52*, 107–112.

Kinnersley, P., Scott, N., Peters, T. J., & Harvey, I. (1999). The patient-centredness of consultations and outcome in primary care. *British Journal of General Practice, 49*, 711–716.

Kirk, A. F., Higgins, L. A., Hughes, A. R., Fisher, B. M., Mutrie, N., Hillis, S., et al. (2001). A randomized, controlled trial to study the effect of exercise consultation on the promotion of physical activity in people with type 2 diabetes: A pilot study. *Diabetic Medicine, 18*, 877–882.

Knight, K. M., McGowan, L., Dickens, C., & Bundy, C. (2006). A systematic review of motivational interviewing in physical health care settings. *British Journal of Health Psychology, 11*, 319–332.

Krones, T., Keller, H., Becker, A., Sönnichsen, A., Baum, E., & Donner-Banzhoff, N. (2010). The theory of planned behaviour in a randomized trial of a decision aid on cardiovascular risk prevention. *Patient Education and Counseling, 78*(2), 169–176.

Lee, R. G., & Garvin, T. (2003). Moving from information transfer to information exchange in health and health care. *Social Science and Medicine, 56*, 449–464.

Levenstein, J. H., McCracken, E. C., McWhinney, I. R., Stewart, M. A., & Brown, J. B. (1986). The patient-centred clinical method. 1. A model for the doctor–patient interaction in family medicine. *Family Practice, 3*, 24–30.

Lipkin, M., Putnam, S. M., & Lazare, A. (1995). *The medical interview. Clinical care, education, and research*. New York: Springer.

Little, P., Everitt, H., Williamson, I., Warner, G., Moore, M., Gould, C., et al. (2001). Observational study of effect of patient centredness and positive approach on outcomes of general practice consultations. *British Medical Journal, 323*, 908–911.

Little, P., Kelly, J., Barnett, J., Dorward, M., Margetts, B., & Warm, D. (2004). Randomised controlled factorial trial of dietary advice for patients with a single high blood pressure reading in primary care. *British Medical Journal, 328*, 1054–1058.

Makoul, G., Arntson, P., & Schofield, T. (1995). Health promotion in primary care: Physician–patient communication and decision making about prescription medications. *Social Science and Medicine, 41*, 1241–1254.

Maly, R. C., Bourque, L. B., & Engelhardt, R. F. (1999). A randomized controlled trial of facilitating information giving to patients with chronic medical conditions: Effects on outcomes of care. *Journal of Family Practice, 48*, 356–363.

Mazzi, M. A., Del Piccolo, L., & Zimmermann, C. (2003). Event-based categorical sequential analyses of the medical interview: A review. *Epidemiologia e Psichiatria Sociale, 12*, 81–85.

McCabe, R., Heath, C., Burns, T., & Priebe, S. (2002). Engagement of patients with psychosis in the consultation: Conversation analytic study. *British Medical Journal, 325*, 1148–1151.

Mead, N., & Bower, P. (2000). Patient-centredness: A conceptual framework and review of the empirical literature. *Social Science and Medicine, 51*, 1087–1110.

Mead, N., & Bower, P. (2002). Patient-centred consultations and outcomes in primary care: A review of the literature. *Patient Education and Counseling, 48*, 51–61.

Mendel, R., Hamann, J., Traut-Mattausch, E., Jonas, E., Heres, S., Frey, D., et al. (2009). How psychiatrists inform themselves and their patients about risks and benefits of antipsychotic treatment. *Acta Psychiatrica Scandinavica, 120*, 112–119.

Merenstein, D., Diener-West, M., Krist, A., Pinneger, M., & Cooper, L. A. (2005). An assessment of the shared-decision model in parents of children with acute otitis media. *Pediatrics, 116*, 1267–1275.

Mhurchu, C. N., Margetts, B. M., & Speller, V. (1998). Randomized clinical trial comparing the effectiveness of two dietary interventions for patients with hyperlipidaemia. *Clinical Science, 95*, 479–487.

Miller, W. R., & Rollnick, S. (1991). *Motivational interviewing: Preparing people to change addictive behavior*. New York: Guilford Press.

Montori, V. M., Gafni, A., & Charles, C. (2006). A shared treatment decision-making approach between patients with chronic conditions and their clinicians: The case of diabetes. *Health Expectations, 9*, 25–36.

Müller-Engelmann, M., Krones, T., Keller, H., & Donner-Banzhoff, N. (2008). Decision making preferences in the medical encounter – A factorial survey design. *BMC Health Services Research, 8*, 260.

Murray, E., Charles, C., & Gafni, A. (2006). Shared decision-making in primary care: Tailoring the Charles et al. model to fit the context of general practice. *Patient Education and Counseling, 62*, 205–211.

Nosé, M., Barbui, C., & Tansella, M. (2003). Clinical interventions for treatment non-adherence in psychosis: Meta-analysis. *British Journal of Psychiatry, 183*, 197–206.

O'Connor, A., & Jacobsen, S. (2007). *Ottawa personal decision guide*. Retrieved February 2010, from http://decisionaid.ohri.ca/decguide.html

O'Connor, A. M., Stacey, D., Rovner, D., Holmes-Rovner, M., Tetroe, J., Llewellyn-Thomas, H., Entwistle, V., Rostom, A., Fiset, V., Barry, M., & Jones, J. (2001). Decision aids for people facing health treatment or screening decisions. *Cochrane Database of Systematic Reviews*, (3), CD001431.

Ogedegbe, G., Chaplin, W., Schoenthaler, A., Statman, D., Berger, D., Richardson, T., et al. (2008). A practice-based trial of motivational interviewing and adherence in hypertensive African Americans. *American Journal of Hypertension, 21*, 1137–1143.

Ong, L. M., de Haes, J. C., Hoos, A. M., & Lammes, F. B. (1995). Doctor–patient communication: A review of the literature. *Social Science and Medicine, 40*, 903–918.

Paccaloni, M., Moretti, F., & Zimmermann, C. (2005). Giving information and involving in treatment: What do psychiatrists think? A review [In Italian]. *Epidemiologia e Psichiatria Sociale, 14*, 198–216.

Paccaloni, M., Pozzan, T., Rimondini, M., & Zimmermann, C. (2006). Knowledge and informative needs of patients with the diagnosis of schizophrenia, explored with focus group methods. *Epidemiologia e Psichiatria Sociale, 15*, 128–137.

Paccaloni, M., Pozzan, T., & Zimmermann, C. (2004). Being informed and involved in treatment: What do psychiatric patients think? A review. *Epidemiologia e Psichiatria Sociale, 13*, 270–283.

Palmer, B. W., Dunn, L. B., Appelbaum, P. S., & Jeste, D. V. (2004). Correlates of treatment-related decision-making capacity among middle-aged and older patients with schizophrenia. *Archives of General Psychiatry, 61*, 230–236.

Prentice, K. J., Gold, J. M., & Carpenter, W. T. (2005). Optimistic bias in the perception of personal risk: Patterns in schizophrenia. *American Journal of Psychiatry, 162*, 507–512.

Prochaska, J., & DiClemente, C. (1983). Stages and processes of self-change of smoking: Towards an integrated model of change. *Journal of Consulting and Clinical Psychology, 51*, 390–395.

Prochaska, J., & DiClemente, C. (1986). Toward a comprehensive model of change. In W. R. Miller & N. Heatther (Eds.), *Treating addictive behaviors: Processes of changes*. New York: Plenum.

Prochaska, J. O., & DiClemente, C. C. (1992). Stages of change in the modification of problem behaviors. *Progress in Behavior Modification, 28*, 183–218.

Rimondini, M., Del Piccolo, L., Goss, C., Mazzi, M., Paccaloni, M., & Zimmermann, C. (2006). Communication skills in psychiatry residents – How do they handle patient concerns? An application of sequence analysis to interviews with simulated patients. *Psychotherapy and Psychosomatics, 75*, 161–169.

Rimondini, M., Del Piccolo, L., Goss, C., Mazzi, M., Paccaloni, M., & Zimmermann, C. (2009). The evaluation of training in patient-centred interviewing skills for psychiatric residents. *Psychological Medicine, 23*, 1–10.

Rodriguez-Osorio, C. A., & Dominguez-Cherit, G. (2008). Medical decision making: Paternalism versus patient-centered (autonomous) care. *Current Opinion in Critical Care, 14*, 708–713.

Rollnick, S., Mason, P., & Butler, C. (1999). *Health behaviour change. A guide for practitioners*. Edinburgh, UK: Churchill Livingstone.

Rollnick, S., & Miller, W. R. (1995). What is motivational interviewing? *Behavioural and Cognitive Psychotherapy, 23*, 325–334.

Roter, D. L., Hall, J. A., & Katz, N. R. (1987). Relations between physicians' behaviors and analogue patients' satisfaction, recall, and impressions. *Medical Care, 25*, 437–451.

Safran, D. G., Taira, D. A., Rogers, W. H., Kosinski, M., Ware, J. E., & Tarlov, A. R. (1998). Linking primary care performance to outcomes of care. *Journal of Family Practice, 47*, 213–220.

Scala, D., D'Avino, M., Cozzolino, S., Mancini, A., Andria, B., Caruso, G., et al. (2008). Promotion of behavioural change in people with hypertension: An intervention study. *Pharmacy World & Science, 30*, 834–839.

Schron, E. B., Ockene, J. K., & Mc Bee, W. L. (Eds.). (1998). *The handbook of health behavior change* (2nd ed.). New York: Springer.

Shepherd, H. L., Tattersall, M. H., & Butow, P. N. (2007). The context influences doctors' support of shared decision-making in cancer care. *British Journal of Cancer, 97*, 6–13.

Slingsby, B. T. (2004). Decision-making models in Japanese psychiatry: Transitions from passive to active patterns. *Social Science and Medicine, 59*, 83–91.

Smith, R. C. (2002). *Patient-centered interviewing. An evidence-based method*. Philadelphia, PA: Lippincott Williams & Wilkins.

Stewart, M., Brown, J. B., Donner, A., McWhinney, I. R., Oates, J., Weston, W. W., et al. (2000). The impact of patient-centered care on outcomes. *Journal of Family Practice, 49*, 796–804.

Strull, W. M., Lo, B., & Charles, G. (1984). Do patients want to participate in medical decision making? *Journal of the American Medical Association, 252*, 2990–2994.

Sullivan, M. D., Leigh, J., & Gaster, B. (2006). Brief report: Training internists in shared decision making about chronic opioid treatment for non-cancer pain. *Journal of General Internal Medicine, 21*, 360–362.

Svensson, S., Kjellegren, K. I., Ahlner, J., & Säljö, R. (2000). Reasons for adherence with antihypertensive medication. *International Journal of Cardiology, 76*, 157–163.

Towle, A., Godolphin, W., Grams, G., & Lamarre, A. (2006). Putting informed and shared decision making into practice. *Health Expectations, 9*, 321–332.

Weiss, M., & Britten, N. (2003). What is concordance? *Pharmaceutical Journal, 271*, 493.

Weston, W. W., Brown, J. B., & Stewart, M. A. (1989). Patient-centred interviewing. Part I: Understanding patients' experiences. *Canadian Family Physician, 35*, 147–151.

Williams, G. C., & Deci, E. (2001). Activating patients for smoking cessation through physician autonomy support. *Medical Care, 39*, 813–823.

Williams, G. C., Freedman, Z. R., & Deci, E. (1998). Supporting autonomy to motivate patients with diabetes for glucose control. *Diabetes Care, 21*, 1644–1651.

Williams, S., Weinman, J., & Dale, J. (1998). Doctor–patient communication and patient satisfaction: A review. *Family Practice, 15*, 480–492.

Wong, J. G., Clare, I. C. H., Holland, A. J., Watson, P. C., & Gunn, M. (2000). The capacity of people with a "mental disability" to make health care decisions. *Psychological Medicine, 30*, 295–306.

Zimmermann, C., Del Piccolo, L., & Mazzi, M. (2003). Patient cues and medical interviewing in general practice. Examples of the application of sequential analysis. *Epidemiologia e Psichiatria Sociale, 12*, 115–123.

Chapter 5
Nonverbal Communication in Clinical Contexts

Arnstein Finset and Lidia Del Piccolo

5.1 Introduction

5.1.1 A Definition of Nonverbal Communication

Nonverbal communication is a basic phenomenon, an important aspect of behavior, literally from the very first day of life. Nonverbal communication can be conveyed through gesture and touch, by body movements and posture, by facial expression and eye contact, as well as by such as clothing and hairstyle. Speech contains nonverbal elements known as *paralanguage*, including voice quality, emotion, and speaking style, as well as prosodic features such as rhythm, intonation, and stress. In psychotherapy nonverbal communication represents valuable information for both the patient and the therapist, influencing the therapeutic alliance.

In order to define nonverbal communication, we need to arrive at a definition of communication in general. There are, however, many different definitions of communication. One approach is to define communication processes as "sign-mediated interactions between at least two agents which share a repertoire of signs and semiotic rules" (http://www.en.wikipedia.org/wiki/Communication). During these interaction processes, *messages* (composed of a series of signs) are transmitted from a *sender* to a *receiver*, and all agents involved are both senders and receivers of messages simultaneously. The process of sending a message is labeled *encoding*, and receiving it is referred to as *decoding*. By *signs* we mean representations of reality (objects, ideas, etc.) that carry a certain meaning for the agents involved, whereas *semiotic rules* are principles for how this meaning is organized. The repertoire of signs and semiotic rules may be *explicit* (in the sense that agents

A. Finset (✉)
Department of Behavioural Sciences in Medicine, University of Oslo,
N-0317, Norway
e-mail: arnstein.finset@basalmed.uio.no

M. Rimondini (ed.), *Communication in Cognitive Behavioral Therapy*,
DOI 10.1007/978-1-4419-6807-4_5, © Springer Science+Business Media, LLC 2011

are aware of the meaning they convey) or *implicit* (the signs or behaviors influence the agents, but senders are not necessarily conscious of the signals that they send and how their behavior may be decoded by others). Watzlawick et al., in their *Pragmatics of Human Communication*, contend that all behavior is communication (Watzlawick et al. 1967). According to this view, everything we do may carry a message, not necessarily intended, experienced as meaningful by a receiver.

Following the terminology outlined above, we may define nonverbal communication as any behavior, intentional or not, with one common characteristic: that the signs and semiotic rules involved in the decoding and encoding of the message are not verbal in nature.

5.1.2 Child Development, Implicit Communication, and Nonverbal Behavior

Developmental psychology may help to understand the distinction between explicit and implicit communication. During the first year of life all communication is implicit. A baby shows dyadic interactions with one other person at a time only or with an object, but he or she is not yet able to introduce the object into a social exchange. Shared attention, which appears at the ending of the first year, is the premise to introduce an object as a common focus of attention. At this stage communication becomes triadic (the baby, another person, and an object), and intentionality appears when the infant is aware to produce gestural (and gradually also verbal) behaviors that have an effect on another person. Gradually, communication becomes explicit. Intentional behaviors appear as signs by means of body movements and sounds. Linguistic abilities (in terms of verbal or manual form of expression, depending on hearing abilities) develop only when children are able to express communicative intentions; that is, they use language as a means to obtain the attention of others (Camaioni 1993). In this sense, language is structurally related to intentionality, and signs become a language when they are used as means to relate to another person.

Infant research has shown that as early as in the first few days after birth, a baby is able to respond selectively to social stimuli (Johnson and Morton 1991; Meltzoff 1985, 1990; Meltzoff and Gopnik 1993), mainly the human face (Simion et al. 2007) and eyes (Farroni et al. 2006), to show perceptual specificity in the processing of human voice (DeCasper and Fifer 1980; Levy et al. 2001) and to display a preference for the mother's smell. Moreover, in face-to-face interactions between a baby and the caregiver, we may observe a process of attunement characterized by synchronicity, contingency, coordination, and turn-taking (Stern 1985; Trevarthen and Aitken 2001; Jaffe et al. 2001; Beebe et al. 1988, 1992, 2000). Beebe et al. (2000) have shown that these nonverbal and temporally characterized dimensions are relevant to define the quality of the baby and his or her caregiver interaction. The authors adopted a microanalytic approach to analyze the vocal rhythm coordination between 82 dyads at 4 and 12 months. When the infants were 4 months old, face-to-face interactions between mother–infant, stranger–infant, and mother–stranger were recorded in the home.

Bidirectional contingencies of vocal rhythm were used to predict infant attachment at 12 months (Ainsworth Strange Situation). The study showed that high and low indexes of vocal rhythm coordination were associated, respectively, with insecure and avoidant attachment at one year, whereas a more secure attachment was observed at an intermediate degree of vocal rhythm coordination. To explain this phenomenon, the authors adopt a "systems model of pathology as a relative balance between simultaneous interactive regulation and self regulation" (Tronick 1989). The authors also document how the timing of preverbal dialogues (both vocal and kinetic) is remarkably similar to the timing of adult verbal dialogue and the regulation of the turn exchange by coordinating the duration of the switching pause is similar in both (Beebe et al. 1988). As the authors write, this coordination of the switching pause duration is the major way in which each partner knows when it is their turn. Too short a switching pause in adult conversation is experienced as rudeness; too long a switching pause as being "out of it." Thus, the coordination of timing in infancy is the scaffolding, the melody, on which verbal content is later superimposed: we are learning how to converse before we have words. (Bloom 1993) Learning the regulation of timing patterns constitutes learning nonverbal ways of being with the partner. The similarity of patterns of timing coordination between preverbal and verbal dialogues argues for a concept of vocal timing as a "life-span" measure (Beebe et al. 2000).

The same phenomenon may be described for inexpressive and impassive attitudes. Tronik, adopting his "still-face" paradigm (Tronick et al. 1978), in which the mother shows for two minutes an inexpressive and unresponsive face in response to her baby, proved that this condition (which is very similar to that of depressed mothers) determined the activation of "prolonged negative affective states" in the baby, either experimentally (Mesman et al. 2009) or clinically (Chon and Tronick 1983; Field et al. 2009).

All the nonverbal aspects described so far are related to preverbal competencies. They are part of an affective communication, referring to how the relation grows within the dyad, which at this stage is essential to let the baby feel secure. They convey the more immediate meaning of the state of the relation and maintain this function all along the life span.

5.1.3 The Psychophysiology of Nonverbal Behavior

Nonverbal behavior exists in the interface between nature and culture. As we have seen, the human infant displays rapid encoding and decoding capacities for nonverbal messages early, in particular, facial emotional signals (Segerstråle and Molnár 1997), and some of these signals are shared by other primates and even lower animals (Marler and Evans 1997). In any ongoing interpersonal relationship, the current behavior, in terms of talk, gestures, gaze, etc., is accompanied by psychophysiological processes and responses, for instance, heart rate and electrodermal skin responses. Similar physiological responses accompany behavior also in other species.

Compared to other species, humans are specifically sensitive to precise nonverbal social stimuli (delicate touch, calm tone of voice, positive facial expressions) that signal genuine caring and safety. Interestingly, the same nonverbal behaviors may have a positive effect on patients' feelings of confidence during psychotherapy (Gilbert 2005).

Porges (2001) postulates the existence of a "social security system" that is unique to mammals and is characterized by a myelinated vagus that can rapidly regulate cardiac output to foster engagement and disengagement with the environment. The mammalian vagus is neuroanatomically linked to the cranial nerves that regulate social engagement via facial expression and vocalization. Depue and Morrone-Strupinsky (2005) describe an appetitive and a consummatory reward process, mediated independently and respectively by the activity of the ventral tegmental area dopamine–nucleus accumbens shell pathway and the central corticolimbic projections of the u-opiate system. The first system mediates positive emotions related to gratification, and the second intervenes in positive feelings like being calm and relaxed.

A fundamental characteristic of interpersonal behavior is symmetry or synchrony in the interaction. There is ample evidence that individuals in interpersonal interactions tend to mimic and imitate one another's posture and movements in an intricate dance of mirrored actions (Sharpley et al. 2001; Bargh et al. 1996). Gallese (2001) and Kerr (2008) define this phenomenon as "embodied simulation." A few studies have analyzed something similar between doctor and patient (Levenson and Ruef 1997) or during psychotherapeutic relationship (DiMascio et al. 1957; Reidbord and Redington 1993; Marci et al. 2007). A high level of synchrony has been considered an indicator of a high degree of rapport (Levenson and Ruef 1997). There is evidence that the nonverbal, perceptual-motor imitation and mimicry characteristic of rapport facilitate the smoothness and mutual positivity in the interaction (Chartrand and Bargh 1999).

To summarize, nonverbal communication is rooted in basic behavior patterns, which may be observed in other mammals and which develop in early childhood. Nonverbal behavior is particularly important as an expression of affect. Even in the adult, the nonverbal behavior may remain implicit, although the nonverbal behavior of the adult will also include elements that are cognitively more sophisticated than that of the infant. But it is important to understand that the roots of nonverbal behavior are the preverbal communication of affect acquired at an early stage of the child's development. Therefore, the distinction between verbal and nonverbal communication becomes relevant in psychotherapy when we look at the function of explicit and implicit communication according to intentionality and relationship building.

5.1.4 Nonverbal Communication in Clinical Settings

It has been suggested that upwards of 60% (or even more) of the meaning in any social situation is communicated nonverbally (Burgoon and Bacue 2003), but the reference to research supporting this popular view seems to boil down to an unpublished master's thesis in psychology (Philipott 1983). Another source for the conception that most interpersonal information is of a nonverbal nature may be a misunderstanding of Mehrabian's famous 7-38-55 rule (Mehrabian 1972). According to Mehrabian, the verbal content, tone of voice, and body language account differently for the extent to which we like individuals who present an emotional message: Words account for 7%, tone of voice accounts for 38%, and body language accounts for 55% of the liking. However, the 7-38-55 rule applies explicitly only to liking persons as they convey an emotional message, not to the amount of meaning or information communicated in any social situation.

There is little research to guide us in evaluating the relative importance of nonverbal vs. verbal behavior in clinical communication. The nonverbal channels will often convey the emotional aspects or qualities of the messages involved in the communication process. Nonverbal messages may be conveyed by subtle signals often called cues or prompts. In a recent review, Zimmermann et al. (2007) reviewed the literature on cues and concerns in medical consultations. Surprisingly, few of the studies reviewed by Zimmermann and colleagues specified the nonverbal cues present in the consultation. In one early study, nonverbal cues were found to be quite frequent. Davenport et al. (1987) analyzed 48 audiotaped interviews from the practices of six general practitioners (three good and three bad detectors of emotional distress). They found an average of only 1.1 verbal cues per interview, but identified on average 3.2 nonverbal cues. The nonverbal cues were categorized in three main categories: movement cues (agitated, restless, demonstrative, gesticulating, immobile), vocal cues (monotonous, sighing, tense, strained, distressed, weeping, plaintive, whining, angry), and postural cues (dejected, tense, on edge, gaze avoidance). In the following a number of examples of different nonverbal behaviors will be given, but the relative importance of verbal vs. nonverbal content is hard to determine.

5.2 Assessment of Nonverbal Communication

In the research literature on social psychology, there are a number of instruments for assessment of nonverbal communication, which is very time-consuming and complex (many parameters have to be considered). Most assessment methods are limited to measure either receiving (decoding) or sending (encoding) nonverbal messages. In this section we can only present a few brief examples of different assessment approaches.

5.2.1   Assessment of Nonverbal Decoding

A well-known approach to nonverbal decoding ability is the Profile of Nonverbal Sensitivity, the PONS (Rosenthal et al. 1979). The PONS test is a 45-minute video that contains 220 auditory and visual segments that viewers are instructed to respond to. Twenty different scenes are presented in these segments, all portrayed by a white North American female. Each of the scenes is presented to the viewer and listener in 11 different channels, involving the face, the body, or both, as well as two different kinds of content-masked speech. The PONS test measures the ability to recognize affective or attitudinal states in a situational context. Research on PONS has found a number of tasks and personal characteristics that influence the accuracy of decoding nonverbal cues [for a recent review, see Knapp and Hall (2009)]. There is, for instance, a consistent finding that women and girls have better nonverbal decoding abilities than boys and men.

Ickes et al. (1997) take a somewhat different approach in their assessment of the ability to identify the emotion of another person, the capacity to be moved by the same or similar emotions in the encounter with that person, and the expression of this experience back to the other person (empathic accuracy). The authors have designed a task to assess the first element in this process of empathy, the ability to identify another person's emotions. In the accuracy task, observers are asked to view videos of episodes of interpersonal interaction and to indicate the emotions of the participants in the video. Results showed that the good perceivers were just as likely to be male as they were to be female. Moreover, there was essentially no correspondence between the perceivers' self-estimated accuracy and their actual accuracy.

The empathic accuracy paradigm has been tested in a number of different studies. For instance, Mast et al. (2008) recently found that subjects in a situation that provided an experimentally manipulated power status, in particular involving an empathic leadership style, displayed significantly higher interpersonal sensitivity than subjects with less power.

5.2.2   Assessment of Nonverbal Encoding

A number of systems have been developed for the observation of nonverbal behavior. One example is the Facial Action Coding System (FACS), with detailed categories of facial behaviors based on the muscles that produce them (http://www.face-and-emotion.com/dataface/facs/description.jsp). A shorter version of the FACS is the EMFACS (acronym for Emotion FACS), used to score only the facial actions that might be relevant to detecting emotion (Friesen and Ekman 1984).

There are also examples of questionnaire approaches to this. One example is the Affective Communication Test (ACT), which measures expressiveness by presenting self-related statements such as, "I can easily express emotions over the telephone" (Friedman et al. 1980). In general, there is little correspondence between self-reported and observed communication on emotions, but a number of studies have found that individuals who scored themselves as more expressive on the ACT also exhibited behaviors indicative of more nonverbal expressiveness.

5.2.3   Assessment of Nonverbal Communication in Clinical Settings

A few instruments have also been specifically constructed for assessment of nonverbal communication in the therapeutic relationship. In most studies researchers have counted the phenomena they study based on observation of videotapes. A typical example is eye contact. A measure quite often applied in the research on nonverbal communication is the percentage of utterances associated with eye contact between provider and patients.

A number of different coding systems have been applied in clinical research of nonverbal behavior, such as the criteria applied by Mast et al. (2008) for assessment of 21 specific nonverbal qualities of facial communication (gazing, smiling, etc.), bodily gesturing and appearance, tone of voice, and global ratings of the atmosphere in the consultation room, with inter-rater reliability from 0.71 to 0.98.

Gorawara-Bhat and colleagues have developed an assessment tool for nonverbal communication in clinical encounters, the Nonverbal Communication in Doctor–Elderly Patient Transactions (NDEPT; Gorawara-Bhat et al. 2007). The NDEPT is a coding system based on video observations. The system consists of the coding of three main elements: (1) the static attributes of the exam room (the physician's desk and chair, the patient's chair, exam table, equipment, etc.); (2) the dynamic attributes of the exam room (the interaction distance, the vertical height difference, the physical barriers, and the angle of interaction between the doctor and the patient); and finally, (3) the kinetic nonverbal communication of the physician (open or closed bodily stance, eye contact, facial expression, gesture, touch).

Gallagher et al. (2005) have applied a different approach. They constructed a 34-item rating scale of what they characterize as relational communication. The items do not exclusively measure nonverbal components of communication, but most often qualities of behavior that include both nonverbal and verbal components. The scale consists of six subscales, three of them assessing different aspects of intimacy, characterized with the word pairs immediacy/affection, similarity/depth, and receptivity/trust. The other three subscales are composure, formality, and dominance.

Recently, D'Agostino et al. developed a systematic observational system of nonverbal behavior in medical consultations, the Nonverbal Accommodation Analysis System (NAAS; D'Agostino and Bylund, in press). The NAAS is built on the basis of the conversation accommodation theory (CAT) developed by Giles and his colleagues (Giles and Powesland 1975; Giles and Coupland 1991) to explain the cognitive and affective processes underlying speech convergence and divergence, or *approximation*. Approximation concerns responses to the productive performance of the other person, as it actually is, as it is perceived, or as it is stereotyped (Gallois and Giles 1998). Jones et al. (1999) have proposed a coding system for conversation interaction, based on CAT and containing 12 variables to analyze nonverbal behavior. The NAAS builds on Jones and colleagues' work and assesses 10 aspects of the verbal and nonverbal exchanges in medical settings (talk time, pauses, simultaneous speech, speech rate, interruption frequency, smiling, laughing, gesturing, nodding, and eye contact).

5.3 Categories of Provider Nonverbal Behavior and Effect on Outcome

5.3.1 Eye Contact and Facial Expression

The type of nonverbal behavior that has been most studied in the research literature on provider–patient communication is eye contact. In a number of studies the percentage of time or the percentage of number of utterances in which the provider has eye contact with the patient has been included as a variable along with other indicators of communication. In the large Eurocommunication Study, conducted in the late 1990s, communication behavior in 2,825 general practice consultations in six different countries was reported (van Brink-Muinen et al. 2003). Interestingly, there were significant differences between the countries in terms of the percent of the total number of utterances in which eye contact was present. On one end of the scale, British and Swiss doctors had eye contact with their patients more than half of the time (55.2 and 50.4%, respectively), whereas Spanish doctors were observed to hold eye contact only during a little more than one third of the utterances (35.5%). This corresponded to some extent with how time was allotted to psychosocially oriented talk in the consultation. The positive association between eye contact and psychosocial aspects of the consultation is consistent with findings from a number of other studies. Bensing et al. (1995) found also that eye contact was associated with more successful recognition of psychological distress in patients. Zantinge et al. (2007) examined data from 2,095 videotaped consultations from 142 Dutch general practitioners. They found a mean percentage of eye contact of 41%. More eye contact was significantly associated with higher awareness of psychological problems, along with higher expression of empathy and (not surprisingly) more frequent questions about psychosocial issues. These researchers also conducted a multilevel linear regression analysis with the percentage of eye contact as dependent variable and found that more eye contact was associated with decreasing age of the doctor and increasing age of the patient as well as increasing patient distress. Neither patient nor doctor gender was associated with more eye contact.

5.3.2 Bodily Posture

A number of different studies have looked at bodily posture in therapeutic and medical consultations. In a couple of older studies, Harrigan and colleagues studied the relationship between bodily posture and rapport between physician and patient (Harrigan et al. 1985). They found significant differences between physicians characterized by high versus low rapport. High-rapport physicians tended to lean more forward, to have more symmetrical arm positions, and to spend more time in the consultation with arms and legs uncrossed. High rapport was also associated with more frequent nodding. Low-rapport physicians, on the other hand, tended to orient away from the patient and had more asymmetrical and crossed positions of arms and legs.

Street and Buller (1987) found differences in body posture related to patient characteristics. For instance, physicians tended to be more consistent in their body orientation when speaking to highly anxious patients.

Fewer studies have looked at the effect of bodily posture and satisfaction. Some studies indicate that leaning forward and maintaining a symmetrical body position are associated with higher satisfaction. In a study of 462 consultations with residents in internal medicine, DiMatteo et al. (1986) found that physicians who were more sensitive to body movement and posture to emotional cues received higher satisfaction ratings from their patients than did less sensitive physicians. On the other hand, Comstock et al. (1982) did not find physician body positioning to be associated with satisfaction in their study of 150 consultations in a university hospital.

5.3.3 Tone of Voice

Nonverbal communication also includes the nonlinguistic aspects of verbal communication, above all voice quality. Haskard et al. (2009) examined vocal affect in medical providers' and patients' content-filtered (CF) speech in two studies. A digital methodology for content-filtering and a set of reliable global affect rating scales for CF voice were developed. In Study 1, ratings of affect in physicians' CF voice correlated with patients' satisfaction, perceptions of choice/control, medication adherence, mental and physical health, and physicians' satisfaction. In Study 2, ratings of affect in the CF voices of physicians and nurses correlated with their patients' satisfaction, and the CF voices of nurses and patients reflected their satisfaction.

Hall et al. (1981) used a method in which patients listened to medical consultations in which the speech had been filtered, so that only the nonverbal tone of the talk was presented. Surprisingly, when the physicians in filtered speech sounded angry, the patients were more content. But when the physician uttered words (judged in transcripts) that were more sympathetic, patients were more content.

They interpreted the positive response to an angry voice as an indication that patients took the seemingly negative emotions as a sign of engagement on the part of the physician.

Ambady et al. (2002) studied the association between surgeons' tone of voice and their malpractice history. They found that surgeons who were judged to express more dominance and less concern in their voice were more likely to have been sued than those who were judged to be less dominant and more concerned and anxious.

5.3.4 Silence as Nonverbal Behavior

In ordinary daily life, shorter or longer moments of silence may often be experienced as difficult and provocative. In most social conversations the taking of turns goes quite fast and does not permit shorter or longer periods of silence. Different languages have diverse expressions to explain or make up for the sudden silencing of talk, such as, "An angel passed through the room." There are cultural differences between countries in terms of how much silence there is in medical consultations. For instance, in a study comparing medical consultations in the United States and Japan, Japanese doctor–patient conversations included more silence than those in the United States (Ohtaki et al. 2003).

There is a reluctance to permit silence also in therapeutic and medical consultations. However, silence on the part of the physician may be an effective way to elicit disclosure from the patient. Eide et al. (2004) studied consultations from outpatient clinics in oncology and hematology in Oslo, Norway. They applied sequence analysis to investigate what physician behaviors preceded and followed patient concerns, as defined within the RIAS coding system (Roter and Larson 2002). They found that the physician behavior that most significantly was associated with expression of patient concern was to permit a brief pause in the flow of speech.

Rowland-Morin and Carroll (1990) found that the use of silence or the reaction-time latency between speakers was associated with patient satisfaction. Silence may be applied as a way to facilitate emotion and may play an important role both in medical consultations and in psychotherapy (Lane et al. 2002).

5.3.5 Patterns of Nonverbal Behavior

So far we have discussed nonverbal behaviors as they appear in separate channels: facial expressions, tone of voice, bodily posture. But do these different behaviors form patterns of behavior, and may these patterns be identified and categorized? A Swiss study of suicidal behavior may elucidate these questions. In this study 59 patients admitted to a large university hospital after suicide attempts were video-recorded during an interview by a psychiatrist (Haynal-Reymond et al. 2005). At 24 month follow-up, 10 individuals were repeaters, that is, had made another suicide attempt.

The researchers compared the video recordings of the repeaters with recordings of matched nonrepeaters to see if specific nonverbal behavioral patterns could be identified in the repeaters. To make the comparison, specific software, THEME, was applied to identify characteristic patterns. Interestingly, by way of the THEME analysis, certain features of the doctors' behavior were identified that occurred significantly more often in interviews with repeaters than with nonrepeaters, such as more frowning and longer time spent looking into the patient's eyes. However, the objective identification of patterns provided a better prediction of who were repeaters than the predictions based on the doctors' judgment. The findings may indicate that nonverbal communication is governed by subtle cues not consciously perceived during the ongoing interaction.

5.3.6 Quality of Rapport

A concept that integrates many of the different components of nonverbal communication in a therapeutic setting is *rapport*. According to Tickle-Degnen and Rosenthal (1992), high levels of rapport are characterized by (1) high levels of mutual attentiveness or involvement, (2) high levels of positivity or warmth, and (3) high levels of behavioral coordination.

The rapport phenomenon in provider–patient relations was recently investigated in a study of interaction between medical students and standardized patients (Hall et al. 2009). Rapport was rated by trained coders and coded on a single scale from 1 (no rapport) through 9 (high rapport). Rapport was defined as a relationship that was pleasant and engaging, a high degree of liking and positive affect, mutual attention, harmonious relationship, smooth communication, and a high degree of symmetry and synchrony in the interaction. Rapport was coded in three one-minute excerpts of the consultation. Interestingly, rapport as observed in the consultations was positively associated with a number of personal characteristics of the student, such as the student's accuracy in decoding nonverbal emotions in terms of facial expressions of emotion. Rapport was also associated with higher patient satisfaction (Hall et al. 2009).

5.3.7 Context (Seating, Distance, Level)

The effect of the context on communication is obvious. Measures of context are central in Gorawara-Bhat's NDEPT measure of nonverbal communication (Gorawara-Bhat et al. 2007). Applying NDEPT in a study of 50 videotapes of consultations between physicians and elderly patients, Gorawara-Bhar and colleagues found that the context had a considerable effect on the communication process. Physicians in exam rooms with no desk in the interaction, no height difference, and optimal interaction distance were observed to have more eye contact and touching behavior than physicians in rooms with a desk and larger distance between doctor and patient.

One element in the context that has become increasingly important is the interference of physician–patient interaction with electronic record systems. McGrath et al. (2007) have studied how physicians apply computers in the consultations and conclude that taking "breaks" from the computer use and direct undivided attention to the patient would strengthen the doctor–patient relationship.

5.4 Nonverbal Communication in Psychiatric and Psychotherapy Contexts

5.4.1 A Review of the Literature

There are a large number of publications on the nonverbal behavior of patients with specific diagnoses (for example, Ellgring 1986; Berenbaum 1992; Gaebel and Wölwer 2004; Benecke and Krause 2005), but few actually investigate the interaction between patient and therapist and their reciprocal effect. Even fewer studies are experimental in nature (Sherer and Rogers 1980; Geerts et al. 1997). Many of these studies refer to psychiatric consultations (Fairbanks et al. 1982; Fisch et al. 1983; Geerts et al. 1996, 1997; Bouhuys and Van den Hoofdakker 1991; Bouhuys and Sam 2000), several adopt a psychodynamic perspective (Anstadt et al. 1997; Merten et al. 1996; Merten and Brunnhuber 2004; Merten 2005; Benecke and Krause 2005; Benecke et al. 2005; Callahan 2000), and only a few are from the area of cognitive therapy (Marcus 1985; Yarczower et al. 1991; Keijsers et al. 2000; Tracey et al. 1999). This may be due to the fact that cognitive therapy tends to emphasize explicit cognitive content in therapy, rather than more subtle subconscious processes. Historically, cognitive therapy started devoting more attention to the patient's cognitions, and any modification in the feeling state or behavior was conceptualized as a result of the reformulation of dysfunctional thoughts (Marcus 1985).

The necessity of dealing with personality disorders has determined a new interest toward the affective modulation, that is, to emotions' disclosure and affective awareness, during the psychotherapy process (Bender 2005; Herbert 2007; Fiore et al. 2008; Dimaggio et al. 2008).

In a psychiatric context, Fairbanks et al. (1982) videotaped interviews of 50 psychiatric inpatients and 25 healthy controls with five psychiatrists and analyzed the nonverbal behavior, which was coded [according to Merhabian's categories (1972)] and recorded every 10 seconds for 25-minute segments per interview. After the interview, the therapists rated the subjects on the Brief Psychiatric Rating Scale (BPRS). Results showed that the psychiatric patients displayed quite different nonverbal behaviors than the control subjects did. For instance, they shifted posture, and frowned more, smiled and looked toward the therapist less than control subjects did. Moreover, the nonverbal behavior of patients varied according to their BPRS scores.

For instance, a symptom of withdrawal was positively associated with turning the head away and negatively associated with smiling, and distress (anxiety-depression) was associated with holding the head even and with hand tapping. Also, the therapists' behavior differed in interviews with patients versus controls in terms of head orientation, smiling, hand tapping, and foot movements. They spent more time looking toward patients than toward controls, while they smiled and showed more body movement with controls. The therapists' behavior also differed according to the patients' ratings on the BPRS. As the patient's score on withdrawal increased, the therapist decreased both smiling and extraneous body movements and increased eye contact with the patient. The authors interpreted the nonverbal interaction between patients and psychiatrists in terms of therapeutic role, that is, the use of direct gaze, facial affect, and relatively constrained body movements. These attitudes express an attempt to increase contact, but in the authors' opinion, "may have the opposite effect of increasing avoidance responses in the patient," as direct gaze may be perceived as threatening to the recipient and may induce further avoidance. These results are evidence of the importance for the therapists to be aware of their own nonverbal behaviors, to help patients feel more comfortable, and to better assess their problems.

Many of the studies that analyze clinician–patient interaction in a psychiatric context report data on depressed patients (Fisch et al. 1983; Geerts et al. 1996, 1997; Bouhuys and Sam 2000; Keijsers et al. 2000). Fisch et al. (1983) adopted a time series approach to record movements of the head, trunk, shoulders, upper arms, hands, upper legs, and feet. These movements were transcribed as a series of positions over time for the first three minutes of each of 26 doctor–patient interviews. Results showed that, beneath high individual variability, the complexity of body movement strongly reflected recovery from depression, suggesting an increased effort at communication by the patient. The analysis of the interaction evidenced also a high correlation between patient movement indices and the doctor's impression of patients' recovery, reflecting some kind of adaptation in response to their depressed patients' state. The authors concluded that doctors respond very alertly to the differences in the movement complexity of patients. Geerts et al. (1996) and Bouhuys and Sam (2000) tried to identify the nonverbal patterns of depressed patients that could predict subsequent improvement or recurrence, respectively. Based on the coordination-rapport hypothesis, by which the coordination of nonverbal behavior (*attunement*) is related to the degree of therapeutic alliance, Bouhuys and Sam (2000) showed that the more attunement increased over the interview, the more favorable the subsequent course of depression was. Conversely, Geerts et al. (1996) showed that the time course of nonverbal attunement differed between interviewers and patients remitted from a recurrent episode, compared to interviewers and patients who just remitted from a first episode. The authors interpreted this result as a consequence of an accumulated deficit in controlling attunement, due to multiple negative experiences of low coordination, which in turn lead to negative reactions during interpersonal relationships. Geerts et al. (1997) studied experimentally the causal role of interviewers' nonverbal behavior on depressed patients. They showed that support-seeking behavior (gesticulating and looking at the interviewer during patients' own speech) by mildly depressed patients was higher when the interviewer showed more nonverbal support giving (nodding yes and verbal back-channel during patients' speaking), suggesting that attunement still occurs in mild depression, in spite of a reduced decoding ability.

Yarczower et al. (1991), in a study of 20 cognitive therapy sessions, found also that the nonverbal behavior of depressed patients changed within a therapeutic session. Patients displayed more prosocial behavior by looking more at and leaning more in the direction of therapists at the end than at the beginning of a session. The same pattern was observed in the therapist's nonverbal behavior with the addition of behaviors reflective of anxiety or impatience.

Bearing in mind anxious patients, Callahan (2001), in a small study on short-term dynamic psychotherapy, found fewer breaks in eye contact during anxiety from early to late therapy, whereas Benecke and Krause (2005) studied smile attitude in 20 female patients with panic disorder and compared this group to a mixed-patient group without panic disorders. The facial expressive behavior was codified using EMFACS (Friesen and Ekman 1984). Results evidenced two sub-groups of facial behavior: The first group of patients showed more anger, disgust, sadness, and surprise and a tendency for more contempt than the other group. The mixed group showed the expression of smiles and an extensive absence of displays of negative emotions, supporting the authors' hypothesis that panic patients deal with a conflict between autonomy and dependency, and express this nonverbally in the use of less distancing, emotionally negative elements (more smile and less anger) to maintain relational bonding. In a following paper Benecke et al. (2005) suggested different relational attitudes to these two groups of patients: Abstinent psychotherapeutic behavior had good prognostic value for therapeutic success in the first group of patients, whereas in the second one the frequency of the therapists' smiling contributed to treatment success.

These observations bear out the role of complementarity (the extent to which the behavior of the second interactant corresponds to the behavior desired by the first interactant) over the course of treatment. As evidenced by Tracey et al. (1999), who reported data from 20 clients seeing four experienced therapists conducting cogniti-vebehavioral therapy, more successful dyads demonstrated a pattern of initial high levels of complementarity, decreasing levels in the middle of treatment, and then increasing levels at the end, but not as high as the beginning (U-shaped pattern of complementarity). On the line of this study, there are some interesting publications on the affective relationship patterns that contribute to therapeutic change (Bänninger-Huber and Widmer 1999; Keijsers et al. 2000; Merten 2005). All underline similar relationship variables, which are support, competence, unconditional positive regard, and empathy. Finally, in an interesting experiment, Sherer and Rogers (1980) consid-ered the effect of three theoretical dimensions (Mehrabian 1972) of nonverbal behav-ior as evaluated by 118 students who were assessing immediacy (close distance and eye contact), potency or status (asymmetrical position of arms and legs, reclining position, and sideways lean), and responsivity (gesticulation and head nods) in eight audiovisual tapes of a reenactment of a client-centered therapy session. The results showed that a therapist who used high-immediacy nonverbal cues would have been rated as possessing superior interpersonal skills and also as having higher status and responsivity. That is, the immediacy dimension may be the most salient, easily noticed, and readily interpreted nonverbal dimension in therapy sessions. Therefore, liking and acceptance may be the most important feelings that a therapist may communicate nonverbally.

5.4.2 An Example of the Analysis of Nonverbal Behavior During Psychotherapy

The ability of a psychotherapist to be aware of what happens *hic et nunc* during the psychotherapeutic process is essential to make the patient aware of his or her relational style and contributes to the process of change (Stern 2004). Interaction during psychotherapy may be analyzed by means of different communication channels: verbally, by explicitly putting into words what the therapist observes in the patient's behavior orfeels while interacting with him or her; nonverbally, by the use of touch or gaze to express involvement, participation, or detachment. In addition to cited verbal and nonverbal strategies, a more technological aid could be adopted, which is the use of a video camera to record a portion of or the entire consultation. The recorded material can be watched and commented on together with the patient, during the same consultation or in the next one. This helps the patient to become more aware of his problematic attitudes, which are the nonverbal behaviors she adopts in specific and difficult moments of interaction, to compare what he thinks of himself during these moments and how this appears when looking at himself from the outside. The patient then has the opportunity to match her internal image with the external appearance, having the chance to link her internal feelings and beliefs with an outside image of these same aspects. Moreover, all this happens in relation to somebody else who is part of the process and in turn has feelings and impressions and shows some kind of reaction to the same fragment of behavior observed together. Of course, to introduce such an invasive instrument, the therapeutic alliance should have been built, and both psychotherapist and patient have to share the therapeutic project and the strategies to gain from it. Therefore, the use of a video camera should be aimed at very specific aspects of nonverbal behavior or personality attitudes, such as the tendency to move the body or the gaze away in a patient with avoidant personality, or the presence of specific expressions of discomfort, irritation, or uneasiness in patients who deny any emotion.

5.5 Conclusions

Most research on clinical communication tends to emphasize verbal communication. However, nonverbal communication processes are crucial in all interpersonal interaction. The main message in this somewhat selective review of the literature may be summarized in six conclusions:

First, nonverbal communication is deeply rooted in basic behavior patterns also seen in other mammals and in the early implicit expression of emotion in the child. The preverbal competencies of the baby are essential for regulation of emotion. Subtle cues and implicit patterns of affective communication remain throughout the life span.

Second, nonverbal communication is governed by basic principles of reciprocity. The mirroring and synchrony of nonverbal behavior that is characteristic of good rapport between patient and provider may be seen as the adult version of the attunement between caregiver and child.

Third, nonverbal communication patterns are not static, but may develop throughout sessions and over time in general. Even if Hall et al. (2009) found that the quality of rapport in the first minute of a consultation is highly predictive of rapport throughout the consultation, we have seen how nonverbal patterns may develop over time, as in the study by Yarczower et al. (1991), who found an increase in nonverbal prosocial behavior over time within sessions of therapy.

Fourth, researchers have identified certain nonverbal behaviors that consistently seem to further the therapeutic process. Hall et al. (1995) summarized these characteristics to include "a moderate amount of head nodding and smiling; frequent, but not staring, eye contact; active, but not extreme, facial responsiveness; and a warm, relaxed, interested vocal tone. Touching the client appears to have some benefit, provided the touching is brief and involves the client's more public body surfaces (hand, shoulder, upper back)."

The fifth conclusion is embedded in the quote from Hall et al. (1995) above. Even if we have identified good nonverbal communication patterns, it is important to notice that it may be too much of the good. Too much smiling may jeopardize the credibility of the person who smiles, too much eye contact may turn into an unpleasant stare, and too much touch may be considered invasive.

And, finally, good nonverbal communication along these lines is important not only because it facilitates communication during the consultation. Nonverbal communication may also be associated with outcome variables, such as patient satisfaction and adherence (Roter et al. 2006; Mast 2007). For instance, Griffith et al. (2003) studied the effect of nonverbal communication in three different clinical situations with standardized patients. Nonverbal skills were coded according to a seven-item rating scale assessing facial expressivity, frequency of smiling, eye contact and nodding, body lean and posture, and tone of voice. Nonverbal communication skills were an independent predictor of patient satisfaction, predicting up to 32% of the variance. Interestingly, a recent study of students who watched videotapes of real consultations indicated that physician gender affected how physician nonverbal behavior was related to patient satisfaction. For instance, female students were most satisfied with female doctors with a nonverbal behavior in accordance with sex-role stereotypes (Mast et al. 2008).

Knowing all this, the important question for the clinician is whether nonverbal communication may be learned or not. It is not an easy question to answer. The problem with teaching nonverbal communication skills is the fact that so much nonverbal behavior is unintended as a communication act. The sender may be unaware of what messages are conveyed. It is difficult to teach people how to change unintended behaviors.

Still, a number of studies indicate that nonverbal skills may actually be learned, at least the sensitivity to emotional messages (Ambady et al. 2000). Research on decoding skills, applying the PONS, indicates that correct identifications of emotional messages improve considerably with practice. Benefits due to practice and training are particularly striking for judgments of the body, but the same does not apply to auditory cues, for which the practice effects are reported to be smaller.

Unfortunately, there are few studies in the literature on the effects of communication skills training that explicitly document the effect of training on nonverbal encoding behavior. Short-term changes in nonverbal behavior have been seen, but in summarizing the research on improvement of nonverbal skills, Knapp and Hall (2009) conclude that we still know little about how long such improvements last and how they affect interpersonal functioning.

Nevertheless, there is enough evidence on the importance of nonverbal communication to give more emphasis to these abilities in communication skills training. However, as indicated above, more research is needed in order to test what training methods are effective in producing lasting changes in nonverbal communication behavior in clinical settings.

References

Ambady, N., Bernieri, F., & Richeson, J. A. (2000). Toward a histology of social behavior: Judgmental accuracy from thin slices of the behavioral stream. In M. Zanna (Ed.), *Advances in experimental social psychology* (Vol. 32, pp. 201–271). San Diego: Academic Press.

Ambady, N., LaPlante, D., Nguyen, T., Rosenthal, R., Chaumeton, N., & Levinson, W. (2002). Surgeons' tone of voice: A clue to malpractice history. *Surgery, 132,* 5–9.

Anstadt, T., Merten, J., Ullrich, B., & Krause, R. (1997). Affective dyadic behavior, core conflictual relationship themes, and success of treatment. *Psychotherapy Research, 7*(4), 397–417.

Bänninger-Huber, E., & Widmer, C. (1999). Affective relationship patterns and psychotherapeutic change. *Psychotherapy Research, 9*(1), 74–87.

Bargh, J. A., Chen, M., & Burrows, L. (1996). Automaticity of social behavior: Direct effects of trait construct and stereotype-activation on action. *Journal of Personality and Social Psychology, 71,* 230–244.

Beebe, B., Alson, D., Jaffe, J., Feldstein, S., & Crown, C. (1988). Vocal congruence in mother–infant play. *Journal of Psycholinguistic Research, 17,* 245–259.

Beebe, B., Jaffe, J., & Lachmann, E. (1992). A dyadic systems view of communication. In N. Skolnick & S. Warshaw (Eds.), *Relational views of psychoanalysis* (pp. 61–81). Hillsdale, NJ: Analytic Press.

Beebe, B., Jaffe, J., Lachmann, F., Feldstein, S., Crown, C., & Jasnow, M. (2000). Systems models in development and psychoanalysis: The case of vocal rhythm coordination and attachment. *Infant Mental Health Journal, 21*(1–2), 99–122.

Bender, D. S. (2005). The therapeutic alliance in the treatment of personality disorders. *Journal of Psychiatric Practice, 11*(2), 73–87.

Benecke, C., & Krause, R. (2005). Facial affective relationship offers of patients with panic disorder. *Psychotherapy Research, 15*(3), 178–187.

Benecke, C., Peham, D., & Bänninger-Huber, E. (2005). Nonverbal relationship regulation in psychotherapy. *Psychotherapy Research, 15*(1), 81–90.

Bensing, J. M., Kerssens, J. J., & van der Pasch, M. (1995). Patient-directed gaze as a tool for discovering and handling psychosocial problems in general practice. *Journal of Nonverbal Behavior, 19*, 223–242.

Berenbaum, H. (1992). Posed facial expressions of emotion in schizophrenia and depression. *Psychological Medicine, 22*, 929–937.

Bloom, L. (1993). *The transition from infancy to language.* New York: Cambridge University Press.

Bouhuys, A. L., & Sam, M. M. (2000). Lack of coordination of nonverbal behaviour between patients and interviewers as a potential risk factor to depression recurrence: Vulnerability accumulation in depression. *Journal of Affective Disorders, 57*, 189–200.

Bouhuys, A. L., & Van den Hoofdakker, R. H. (1991). The interrelatedness of observed behavior of depressed patients and of psychiatrist: An ethological study on mutual influence. *Journal of Affective Disorders, 23*, 63–74.

Burgoon, J. K., & Bacue, A. E. (2003). Nonverbal communication skills. In J. O. Greene & B. R. Burleson (Eds.), *Handbooks of communication and social interaction skills.* Mahwah, NJ: Lawrence Erlbaum.

Callahan, P. E. (2000). Indexing resistance in short-term dynamic psychotherapy (STDP): Change in breaks in eye contact during anxiety (BECAS). *Psychotherapy Research, 10*, 87–99.

Camaioni, L. (1993). The development of intentional communication. A reanalysis. In J. Nadel & L. Camaioni (Eds.), *New perspectives in early communicative development* (pp. 82–96). London: Routledge.

Chartrand, T. L., & Bargh, J. A. (1999). The chameleon effect: The perception–behavior link and social interaction. *Journal of Personality and Social Psychology, 76*, 893–910.

Chon, J. F., & Tronick, E. Z. (1983). Three month old infants' reaction to simulated maternal depression. *Child Development, 54*, 185–193.

Comstock, L. M., Hooper, E. M., Goodwin, J. M., & Goodwin, J. S. (1982). Physician behaviors that correlate with patient satisfaction. *Journal of Medical Education, 57*(2), 105–112.

D'Agostino, T, Bylund, C. (in press) the nonverbal accommodation analysis system (NAAS): Initial application and evaluation. *Patient Education and Counseling.*

Davenport, S., Goldberg, D., & Millar, T. (1987). How psychiatric disorders are missed during medical consultations. *Lancet, 2*(8556), 439–441.

DeCasper, A. J., & Fifer, W. P. (1980). On human bonding: Newborns prefer their mother's voices. *Science, 208*, 61–90.

Depue, R. A., & Morrone-Strupinsky, J. V. (2005). A neurobehavioral model of affiliative bonding: Implications for conceptualizing a human trait of affiliation. *Behavioral and Brain Sciences, 28*(3), 313–350.

Dimaggio, G., Lysaker, P. H., Carcione, A., Nicolò, G., & Semerari, A. (2008). Know yourself and you shall know the other... to a certain extent: Multiple paths of influence of self-reflection on mindreading. *Consciousness and Cognition, 17*(3), 778–789.

DiMascio, A., Boyd, R. W., & Greenblatt, M. (1957). Physiological correlates of tension and antagonism during psychotherapy: A study of "interpersonal physiology". *Psychosomatic Medicine, 19*, 99–104.

DiMatteo, M. R., Hays, R. D., & Prince, L. M. (1986). Relationship of physicians' nonverbal communication skill to patient satisfaction, appointment noncompliance, and physician workload. *Health Psychology, 5*(6), 581–594.

Eide, H., Quera, V., Graugaard, P., & Finset, A. (2004). Physician–patient dialogue surrounding patients' expression of concern: Applying sequence analysis to RIAS. *Social Science and Medicine, 59*(1), 145–155.

Ellgring, H. (1986). Nonverbal expression of psychological states in psychiatric patients. *European Archives of Psychiatric and Neurological Science, 236*, 31–34.

Fairbanks, L. A., McGuire, M. T., & Harris, C. J. (1982). Nonverbal interaction of patients and therapists during psychiatric interviews. *Journal of Abnormal Psychology, 91*(2), 109–119.

Farroni, T., Menon, E., & Johnson, M. H. (2006). Factors influencing newborns' preference for faces with eye contact. *Journal of Experimental Child Psychology, 95*(4), 298–308.

Field, T., Diego, M., & Hernandez-Reif, M. (2009). Depressed mothers' infants are less responsive to faces and voices. *Infant Behavior and Development, 32*(3), 239–244.

Fiore, D., Dimaggio, G., Nicoló, G., Semerari, A., & Carcione, A. (2008). Metacognitive interpersonal therapy in a case of obsessive-compulsive and avoidant personality disorders. *Journal of Clinical Psychology, 64*(2), 168–180.

Fisch, H. U., Frey, S., & Hirsbrunner, H. P. (1983). Analyzing nonverbal behavior in depression. *Journal of Abnormal Psychology, 92*(3), 307–318.

Friedman, H. S., Prince, L. M., Riggio, R. E., & DiMatteo, M. R. (1980). Understanding and assessing nonverbal expressiveness: The affective communication test. *Journal of Personality and Social Psychology, 39*, 333–351.

Friesen, W., & Ekman, P. (1984). *EMFACS-7: Emotional facial action coding system, version 7.* Unpublished manuscript.

Gaebel, W., & Wölwer, W. (2004). Facial expressivity in the course of schizophrenia and depression. *European Archives of Psychiatry and Clinical Neurosciences, 254*, 335–342.

Gallagher, T. J., Hartung, P. J., Gerzina, H., Gregory, S. W., Jr., & Merolla, D. (2005). Further analysis of a doctor–patient nonverbal communication instrument. *Patient Education and Counseling, 57*(3), 262–271.

Gallese, V. (2001). The "shared manifold" hypothesis: From mirror neurons to empathy. *Journal of Consciousness Studies, 8*, 33–50.

Gallois, C., & Giles, H. (1998). Accommodating mutual influence in intergroup encounters. In M. Palmer, & G. A. Barnett (Series Eds.), & G. A. Barnett (Vol. Ed.), *Mutual influence in interpersonal communication: Theory and research in cognition, affect, and behavior.* Vol. 14, Progress in communication science (pp. 135–162). Stamford, CT: Ablex.

Geerts, E., Bouhuys, A. L., & Bloem, G. M. (1997). Nonverbal support giving induces nonverbal support seeking in depressed patients. *Journal of Clinical Psychology, 53*(1), 35–39.

Geerts, E., Bouhuys, N., & Van den Hoofdakker, R. H. (1996). Nonverbal attunement between depressed patients and an interviewer predicts subsequent improvement. *Journal of Affective Disorders, 40*(1–2), 15–21.

Gilbert, P. (2005). *Compassion: Conceptualisations, research and use in psychotherapy.* London: Routledge.

Giles, H., & Coupland, N. (1991). *Language: Contexts and consequences.* Pacific Grove, CA: Brooks/Cole.

Giles, H., & Powesland, P. (1975). *Speech style and social evaluation.* London: Academic Press.

Gorawara-Bhat, R., Cook, M. A., & Sachs, G. A. (2007). Nonverbal communication in doctor–elderly patient transactions (NDEPT): Development of a tool. *Patient Education and Counseling, 66*(2), 223–234.

Griffith, C. H., III, Wilson, J. F., Langer, S., & Haist, S. A. (2003). House staff nonverbal communication skills and standardized patient satisfaction. *Journal of General Internal Medicine, 18*, 170–174.

Hall, J. A., Jinni, A. H., & Rosenthal, R. (1995). Nonverbal behavior in clinician–patient interaction. *Applied and Preventive Psychology, 4*, 21–37.

Hall, J. A., Roter, D. L., Blanch, D. C., & Frankel, R. M. (2009). Observer-rated rapport in interactions between medical students and standardized patients. *Patient Education and Counseling, 76*(3), 323–327.

Hall, J. A., Roter, D. L., & Rand, C. S. (1981). Communication of affect between patient and physician. *Journal of Health and Social Behavior, 22*(1), 18–30.

Harrigan, J. A., Oxman, T. E., & Rosenthal, R. (1985). Rapport expressed through nonverbal behavior. *Journal of Nonverbal Behavior, 9*(2), 95–110.

Haskard, K. B., DiMatteo, M. R., & Heritage, J. (2009). Affective and instrumental communication in primary care interactions: Predicting the satisfaction of nursing staff and patients. *Health Communication, 24*(1), 21–32.

Haynal-Reymond, V., Jonsson, G. K., & Magusson, M. S. (2005). Nonverbal communication in doctor–suicidal patient interview. In L. Anolli, S. Duncan, M. S. Magnusson, & G. Riva (Eds.), *The hidden structure of interaction: From neurons to culture patterns* (pp. 142–148). Amsterdam: IOS Press.

Herbert, J. D. (2007). Avoidant personality disorder. In W. O'Donohue, K. A. Fowler, & S. O. Lilienfeld (Eds.), *Personality disorders: Toward the DSM-V* (Vol. xvii, pp. 279–305). Thousand Oaks, CA: Sage Publications.

Ickes, W., Marangoni, C., & Garcia, S. (1997). Studying empathic accuracy in a clinically relevant context. In W. Ickes (Ed.), *Empathic accuracy* (pp. 282–310). New York: Guilford Press.

Jaffe, J., Beebe, B., Feldstein, S., Crown, C. L., & Jasnow, M. D. (2001). Rhythms of dialogue in infancy: Coordinated timing in development. *Monographs of the Society for Research in Child Development, 66*(2), vi-131.

Johnson, M. H., & Morton, J. (1991). *Biology and cognitive development: The case of face recognition*. Oxford, UK: Basil Blackwell.

Jones, E., Cynthia, G., Callan, V., & Barker, M. (1999). Strategies of accommodation: Development of a coding system for conversational interaction. *Journal of Language and Social Psychology, 19*(2), 123–152.

Keijsers, G. P., Schaap, C. P., & Hoogduin, C. A. (2000). The impact of interpersonal patient and therapist behavior on outcome in cognitive–behavior therapy. A review of empirical studies. *Behaviour Modification, 24*(2), 264–297.

Kerr, C. E. (2008). Dualism redux in recent neuroscience: "Theory of Mind" and "Embodied Simulation" hypotheses in light of historical debates about perception, cognition, and mind. *Review of General Psychology, 12*(2), 205–214.

Knapp, M. L., & Hall, J. A. (2009). *Nonverbal communication in human interaction*. Boston: Wadsworth.

Lane, R. C., Koetting, M. G., & Bishop, J. (2002). Silence as communication in psychodynamic psychotherapy. *Clinical Psychology Review, 22*(7), 1091–1104.

Levenson, R. W., & Ruef, A. M. (1997). Physiological aspects of emotional knowledge and rapport. In W. Ickes (Ed.), *Empathic accuracy* (pp. 44–72). New York: Guilford Press.

Levy, D., Granot, R., & Bentin, S. (2001). Processing specificity for human voice stimuli: Electrophysiological evidence. *Neuroreport, 12*(12), 2653–2657.

Marci, C. D., Ham, J., Moran, E., Orr, S. P. (2007). Physiologic Correlates of Perceived Therapist Empathy and Social-Emotional Process During Psychotheraphy. *Journal of Nervous and Mental Disease, 195*(2), 103–111.

Marcus, N. N. (1985). Utilization of nonverbal expressive behavior in cognitive therapy. *American Journal of Psychotherapy, 39*(4), 467–478.

Marler, P., & Evans, C. S. (1997). Communication signals of animals: Contribution of emotions and reference. In U. Segerstråle & P. Molnár (Eds.), *Nonverbal communication. Where nature meets culture* (pp. 151–170). Mahwah, N.J: Lawrence Erlbaum.

Mast, M. S. (2007). On the importance of nonverbal communication in the physician–patient interaction. *Patient Education and Counseling, 67*(3), 315–318.

Mast, M. S., Hall, J. A., Kockner, C., & Choi, E. (2008). Physician gender affects how physician nonverbal behavior is related to patient satisfaction. *Medical Care, 46*(12), 1212–1218.

McGrath, M. J., Arar, H. N., & Pugh, A. J. (2007). The influence of electronic medical record usage on nonverbal communication in the medical interview. *Health Informatics Journal, 13*: 105–117. Retrieved from http://www.scopus.com/authid/detail.url?authorId=16309836300.

Mehrabian, A. (1972). *Nonverbal communication*. Chicago: Aldine-Atherton.

Meltzoff, A. (1985). The roots of social and cognitive development: Models of man's original nature. In T. Field & N. Fox (Eds.), *Social perception in infants* (pp. 1–30). Norwood, NJ: Ablex.

Meltzoff, A. (1990). Foundations for developing a concept of self: The role of imitation in relating self to other and the value of social minoring, social modeling, and self practice in infancy. In D. Cicchetti & M. Beeghiy (Eds.), *The self in transition: Infancy to childhood* (pp. 139–164). Chicago: University of Chicago Press.

Meltzoff, A., & Gopnik, A. (1993). The role of imitation in understanding persons and developing a theory of mind. In S. Baron-Cohen, H. Tager-Flusberg, & D. Cohen (Eds.), *Understanding other minds* (pp. 335–366). New York: Oxford University Press.

Merten, J. (2005). Facial microbehavior and the emotional quality of the therapeutic relationship. *Psychotherapy Research, 15*(3), 325–333.

Merten, J., & Brunnhuber, S. (2004). Facial expression and experience of emotions in psychodynamic interviews with patients suffering from a pain disorder. Indicators of disorders in self- and relationship-regulation in the involuntary facial expression of emotions. *Psychopathology, 37*, 266–271.

Merten, J., Ullrich, B., Anstadt, T., Krause, R., & Buchheim, P. (1996). Emotional experiencing and facial expression in the psychotherapeutic-process and its relation to treatment outcome. A pilot-study. *Psychotherapy Research, 6*, 198–212.

Mesman, J., van Jzendoorn, M. H., & Bakermans-Kranenburg, M. J. (2009). The many faces of the still-face paradigm: A review and meta-analysis. *Developmental Review, 29*(2), 120–162.

Ohtaki, S., Ohtaki, T., & Fetters, M. D. (2003). Doctor–patient communication: A comparison of the USA and Japan. *Family Practice, 20*, 276–282.

Philipott, J. C. (1983). *The relative contribution of meaning of verbal and nonverbal chanels of communication*. Unpublished master's thesis, University of Nebraska, Lincoln, Nebraska.

Porges, S. W. (2001). The polyvagal theory: Phylogenetic substrates of a social nervous system. *International Journal of Psychophysiology, 42*(2), 123–46. Review.

Reidbord, S. P., & Redington, D. J. (1993). Nonlinear analysis of autonomic responses in a therapist during psychotherapy. *Journal of Nervous Mental Disorders, 181*, 428–435.

Rosenthal, R., Hall, J. A., DiMatteo, M. R., Rogers, P. L., & Archer, D. (1979). *Sensitivity to nonverbal communication: The PONS test*. Baltimore: Johns Hopkins University Press.

Roter, D. L., Frankel, R. M., Hall, J. A., & Sluyter, D. (2006). The expression of emotion through nonverbal behavior in medical visits. Mechanisms and outcomes. *Journal of General Internal Medicine, 21*(Suppl 1), S28–S34.

Roter, D., & Larson, S. (2002). The Roter interaction analysis system (RIAS): Utility and flexibility for analysis of medical interactions. *Patient Education and Counseling, 46*(4), 243–251.

Rowland-Morin, P. A., & Carroll, J. G. (1990). Verbal communication skills and patient satisfaction. A study of doctor–patient interviews. *Evaluation and the Health Professions, 13*(2), 168–185.

Segerstråle, U., & Molnár, P. (1997). Nonverbal communication: Crossing the boundary between culture and nature. In U. Segerstråle & P. Molnár (Eds.), *Nonverbal communication. Where nature meets culture* (pp. 1–21). Mahwah, NJ: Lawrence Erlbaum.

Sharpley, C. F., Halat, J., Rabinowicz, T., Weiland, B., & Stafford, J. (2001). Standard posture, postural mirroring and client-perceived rapport. *Counseling Psychology Quarterly, 14*, 267–280.

Sherer, M., & Rogers, R. W. (1980). Effects of therapist's nonverbal communication on rated skill and effectiveness. *Journal of Clinical Psychology, 36*(3), 696–700.

Simion, F., Leo, I., Turati, C., Valenza, E., & Dalla Barba, B. (2007). How face specialization emerges in the first months of life. *Progress in Brain Research, 164*, 169–85.

Stern, D. N. (1985). *The interpersonal world of the infant*. New York: Basic Books.

Stern, D. N. (2004). *The present moment in psychotherapy and everyday life*. New York: W.W. Norton.

Street, R. L., Jr., & Buller, D. B. (1987). Nonverbal response patterns in physician-patient interactions: A functional analysis. *Journal of Nonverbal Behavior, 11*(4), 234–253.

Tickle-Degnen, L., & Rosenthal, R. (1992). Nonverbal aspects of therapeutic rapport. In R. S. Feldman (Ed.), *Applications of nonverbal behavior theories and research* (pp. 143–164). Hillsdale, NJ: Erlbaum.

Tracey, T. J. G., Sherry, P., & Albright, J. (1999). The interpersonal process of cognitive-behavioral therapy: An examination of complementarity over the course of treatment. *Journal of Counseling Psychology, 46*(1), 80–91.

Trevarthen, C., & Aitken, K. J. (2001). Infant intersubjectivity: Research, theory, and clinical applications. *Journal of Child Psychology and Psychiatry, 42*(1), 3–48.

Tronick, E. (1989). Emotions and emotional communication in infants. *American Psychologist, 44*, 112–119.

Tronick, E. Z., Als, H., Adamson, L., Wise, S., & Brazelton, T. B. (1978). The infant's response to entrapment between contradictory messages in face-to-face interaction. *Journal of the American Academy of Child Psychiatry, 17*(1), 1–13.

van Brink-Muinen, D., Verhaak, P. F., Bensing, J. M., Bahrs, O., Deveugele, M., Gask, L., et al. (2003). Communication in general practice: Differences between European countries. *Family Practice, 20*, 478–485.

Watzlawick, P., Beavin, J. H., & Jackson, D. D. (1967). *Pragmatics of human communication.* New York: Norton.

Yarczower, M., Kilbride, J. E., & Beck, A. T. (1991). Changes in nonverbal behavior of therapists and depressed patients during cognitive therapy. *Psychological Reports, 69*(3 Pt 1), 915–919.

Zantinge, E. M., Verhaak, P. F., de Bakker, D. H., Kerssens, J. J., van der Meer, K., & Bensing, J. M. (2007). The workload of general practitioners does not affect their awareness of patients' psychological problems. *Patient Education and Counseling, 67*(1–2), 93–99.

Zimmermann, C., Del Piccolo, L., & Finset, A. (2007). Cues and concerns by patients in medical consultations. A literature review. *Psychological Bulletin, 133*, 438–463.

Chapter 6
Communication in Depressive States

Franco Baldini

6.1 Introduction

In this chapter I will describe first the cognitive-behavioral approach and refer specifically to A. T. Beck and A. Ellis. Next, I will describe the particular characteristics of the patient's and psychotherapist's communicative styles in the various phases of clinical treatment, quoting the most significant parts of some psychotherapy sessions (for a definition and description of some of the communication skills described here, see also Chapters 2–5).

6.2 Depression According to Beck and Ellis

In 1967, Beck wrote *Depression*, where he describes the depressive triad:

1. a negative concept of the world, characterized by the idea that "the world, the surrounding reality, present insurmountable difficulties and barriers that compromise the reaching of one's desired goals";
2. negative considerations about oneself: The individual has a marked tendency to see himself as inadequate, incapable, a kind of handicapped creature from a psychological point of view, so he tends to consider himself undesirable, without any value, and is convinced of being refused by the others;
3. Negative and pessimistic considerations about the future, causing the individual to have catastrophic expectations.

In 1976, Beck modified the triad, a relative change for me, and introduced the concept of underestimation (it is always a self-undervaluing concept such as, "I am not worthy of happiness") and the concept of negative consequences of present experiences. He better distinguished the two assumptions: (1) the world asks too

F. Baldini (✉)
Associazione di Psicologia Cognitiva, Via Trezza Gaetano, 12, 37100 Verona, Italy
e-mail: Francobaldini.franco@tiscali.it

M. Rimondini (ed.), *Communication in Cognitive Behavioral Therapy*,
DOI 10.1007/978-1-4419-6807-4_6, © Springer Science+Business Media, LLC 2011

much of me, and (2) I cannot manage (self-undervaluation) either today or in the future ("The present difficulties will go on forever," "It will always be the same," "I have no hope").

The point of view expressed by Ellis is like Beck's; the differences are minimal. The only real different element is that for Beck to speak of a true depression, conceptually considered, all three elements of the triad must be present; for Ellis, instead, the presence of only one element is enough. In other words, there can be an individual who gets depressed by undervaluing herself, and in this case we can maintain that it is a self-undervaluing depression, even if sometimes we can find a combination of more elements (for example, it often happens that in undervaluing herself, the individual tends to develop a sense of despair regarding the future).

This same triad, redefined by Ellis (1962), can be summed up in the following way:

- negative considerations about oneself = lack of self-acceptance;
- negative concept of the world = self-commiseration;
- negative considerations about the future = despair.

Ellis defines self-undervaluing depression as the attitude the person takes on when he tends to see himself in a negative way, to have a bad opinion of himself, to consider himself disgusting, with ideas such as, "I am worth nothing, I am a nonentity . . .," and gets depressed starting from this concept and sometimes exclusively with this.

Self-commiseration consists of a continuous tendency to lament, to consider oneself incapable, and to be angry with others, with the world, with the surrounding reality. In this case, we can speak of self-pity depression.

Hauck (1973), a collaborator of Ellis's, identified other-pity depression and added it to self-undervaluing depression and to self-pity depression. In practice, it is possible to become depressed not only from one's own problems (self-pity) but also from other people's problems, from the misfortunes of the world that we take on our shoulders (wars, massacres, etc.). For example, we watch a TV program regarding refugees and identify ourselves with these persons and feel responsible for them. It is an excessive tendency to put ourselves in other people's shoes, to the point that we tend to feel their problems as if they were our own problems. It can also be a mere ruminating over how the world is going, an existential reflection. Though other-pity depression is a rare form of depression, it can also come out alone, without any self-pity.

Ellis's dysfunctional ideas (1994) that better sum up people's tendency to get depressed are the following [the quotation is from Cesare De Silvestri's translated and adapted version (1999)]:

> I, an adult human being, absolutely need (extremely necessitate or demand) to be (always) loved, appreciated and approved (or at least not badly judged—or at the very least ignored) by all the persons (I believe) significant (important) in my life—by all those I say—otherwise it is very bad, horrible, terrible, catastrophic.

> I must always absolutely be (and/or show to be) perfectly adequate, competent and successful in all that I do and in all respects (or at least in this specific matter, or at least in one thing) otherwise I am not praiseworthy—I am worth little or nothing.

Ellis's dysfunctional ideas are tightly linked to depressive symptoms, but are less frequent. In my opinion, to have a greater conceptual clearness, it is useful to keep Beck's first classification of the depressive triad, the same we will then find in Ellis.

6.3 The Problem on the Problem

An interesting scheme, pointed out by both Beck and Ellis and of extreme strategic importance, is the vicious cycle mechanism, or secondary or circular problem, that we rather frequently find in clinical practice. It is an anxiety problem on a primary level that later turns into a problem of depression on a secondary level. It is possible to explain all this if we analyze the patient's way of thinking. The DSM IV describes a depressed mood mixed with anxiety, or depressive symptoms on which inadequate or contradictory information is available (the fact that anxiety and depression are together is an apparent contradiction). For cognitive-behavioral psychotherapists, it is not so strange because the patient's problems are considered on different levels: on a primary level and on a secondary level. De Silvestri (1999) defines the secondary problem in a very clear way: Human beings not only are able to create for themselves a psychological, emotional and behavioral disorder, but they are often able to create one more uneasiness and suffering, that is to say a new disorder, watching and judging the fact of having the initial original disorder; such secondary disorder (secondary only because it occurs later, because it is of secondary level or superior level compared with the first) is often much more serious than the first and almost always represents the most important task both in the diagnostic interview and in the intervention sessions. In many cases, panic attacks, for example, tend to become a psychological problem of the depressive type to the secondary level. We can understand that by analyzing the patient's cognitive contents. When he realizes he is having a panic attack and starts thinking, "Oh, my God, see how disgusting I am, I am worth nothing, it will be worse and worse, I will always have these troubles, I cannot manage ...," he will have more panic attacks associated with moments in which he will ruminate over his problems and get depressed. For cognitive-behavioral psychotherapists, it is a logical and simple mental process, but often other clinicians just make a diagnosis of descriptive type and the DSM IV itself defines this problem as a not-otherwise-specified depressive disorder. These mental states frequently originate from an idea of incapability, self-undervaluation, that later tends to develop in the following way: "I consider myself an incapable person and have always been like this. When I am with other people, I greatly fear their judgment and feel exposed to possible criticism. This makes me feel anxious and incapable." In other words, the initial hypothesis is confirmed and becomes a vicious cycle mechanism. In this way of thinking, we find Ellis's first two dysfunctional ideas: The first consists of the need for esteem and love, and consequently the fear of being badly judged; the second is that of perfectionism: "I must always be perfect, always up to the situation, I must consider myself praiseworthy":

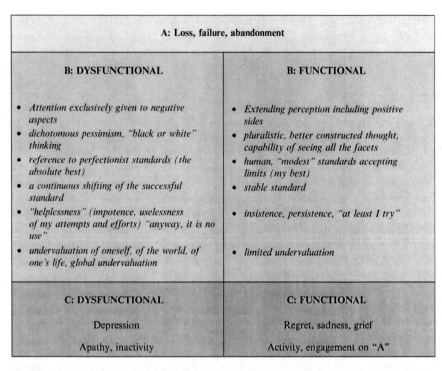

Fig. 6.1 Depression (C) development according to dysfunctional interpretations (B) of activating events (A)

I AM INCAPABLE ⇔ I AM OPEN TO OTHERS' NEGATIVE JUDGMENT.

Sometimes we can find depression overstructured on a tertiary or quaternary level. Figure 6.1 sums up how depression can develop.

At point A we find the triggering event or events: It is often a loss or a failure (an unreached goal). Usually, a person who is greatly conditioned by an idea of perfectionism increases the possibilities of a failure and consequently is more vulnerable to depression (circular mechanism). At point C we find the emotion of depression accompanied by a behavior characterized by asthenia. At point B we can notice the following line of thought: The selective attention is almost exclusively addressed to the negative aspects with the typical way of "black or white" thinking (dichotomous thought). Another characteristic is to refer to perfectionist standards ("I must always get the best" (in an absolute sense), "I must always be up to the situation," "I must always reach my goals according to my expectations"). The standard of success is moved higher and higher, with the consequence that all the efforts to reach the prearranged aims are useless. In this way depressed people tend to pave the way to their undervaluation. In the case of a loss, the mental state could be different; there is a prevailing idea of intolerability, impossibility to accept this kind of condition; it is a concept connected to a low capability to tolerate frustrations (low frustration tolerance, or L.F.T.). Thoughts might be of this kind:

"He abandoned me, I cannot manage by myself, I cannot stay alone." In mourning, when we lose a dear person we were effectively dependent on, it is possible we do not undervalue ourselves: "I didn't lose him because I am an incapable person" (even if in some cases we can find this), but we consider the loss in this way: "The world is so bad, reality so unfair because they take this person away from me and I can do nothing, my life has no sense, I cannot manage."

The functional ideas' alternative to depression must be developed considering the following criteria. At first, the aim of psychotherapy is to help the patient widen his or her perception, including also positive sides, favoring a better constructed, pluralistic way of thinking. Instead of referring to perfectionist standards, we suggest to pass to modest, human standards, accepting limits, favoring the shifting from "the absolute best" to "my best." Consequently, instead of a continuous shifting of the success standard, it is more appropriate to refer to a little more stable standard, which allows one to plan a program of work and better accept possible mistakes or upsets.

Instead of impotence, uselessness of efforts, the alternative is insistence, persistence, "at least I try," and instead of the undervaluation of oneself and of the world, it is an undervaluation limited to the context.

6.4 Communicative Styles of a Depressed Patient

Now it is useful to shortly analyze the typical styles that a depressed patient tends to show during his or her talk with the psychotherapist in the various phases of the therapy.

In the initial phase, the depressed patient tends to show and describe his emotional state with statements or descriptions of his mental states that are easily referrable to Beck's or Ellis's depressive triad.

The statements will be of the self-pity type ("I am in a bad situation indeed," "Everything happens to me," "I am really unlucky"). In some cases, helplessness ("Everything is useless," "There is nothing I can do") and despair ("It will be worse and worse," "I have no hope") are particularly clear. We frequently note in the depressed patient, especially in the first sessions, very poor speech, characterized by long silences, bare descriptions, crying, and answers in monosyllables.

Other patients express in a very evident way the typical characteristics of self-undervaluing depression ("It is all my fault," "I am a really incapable person," "I am a nonentity," "I have got it all wrong," "I am a failure").

Other-pity depression, even if more uncommon, is easily recognizable from statements of this kind: "It is not right that the world is so unfair," "If such bad things happen, it makes no sense living."

In many other cases in the communicative modality of a depressed patient, we can find statements that describe in a clear way the low frustration tolerance (L.F.T.) of the depressed patient. The typical sentences are "It is unbearable," "I will never manage," "I can't accept it."

In the intermediate phase of the therapy, we can note some significant changes in communication. The depressed patient often shows a greater ability in expressing her emotions and mental states.

If the therapeutic treatment is being efficacious, the patient will be able to identify the moments in which he is pitying or undervaluing himself. We observe a significant increase in the quantity of information from the patient, who is becoming more and more sharing and collaborative. In this phase we can find sentences that can be considered as the first statements pointing out a cognitive change: "Maybe I am not so incapable" (self-undervaluing depression); "If I say to myself that I will never get better, I will go on feeding my suffering" (self-pity depression).

In the final phase of the psychotherapy, the statements showing a good cognitive restructuring are particularly evident: "I have understood that I can accept myself with my limits and my faults," "Even if I make a mistake, it is not the end of the world," "If I work to solve this problem, I will feel better also in the future," "I can always improve myself," "If something does not go right, I will be sorry, but I can accept it."

It is clear that the patient's statements I have described represent a significant sign of therapeutic efficacy. In the case I am going to describe here, the changes I have shown above are quite evident.

6.5   The Case of Francesco

Following the above theoretical and clinical presentation, I will describe the case of Francesco, a patient I treated some years ago using standard cognitive-behavioral techniques. I chose this case because it is a clear example of a depressive problem secondary to a primary problem of obsessive-compulsive disorder. A second reason for this choice is determined by the fact that all the psychotherapy sessions were audiotaped, and on this material there was a study by a research team from the Psychology Association of Cognitive Psychotherapy of Rome on the analysis of the communicative process according to the method of Conversational Analysis (Sacks et al. 1978). Another reason regards the fact that the case of Francesco was solved with a psychotherapy strategy mainly focused on the secondary problem of depression. I presented the case of Francesco at the 2002 meeting of the SITCC (Italian Society of Cognitive and Behavioural Therapy) in Turin with the title: "The case of the happy obsessive person, an example of the therapeutic efficacy of an intervention on the secondary problem."

Francesco, 35 years old, lives alone in a small flat bought some years ago. He has a degree in engineering with a specialization in data processing and works with a banking company, where he attends to programming.

Since he was a child, he has suffered from OCPD (obsessive-compulsive personality disorder) (DSM-IV) and reveals a serious depression on a secondary level.

He contacted me by phone, and I made the first appointment for two weeks later. During the phone call, he asked me if he could send a letter to explain the problems that trouble him. I refer to the text of his letter below, because it is an exact diagnostic description:

> ... I have decided to ask for help because I want to eliminate the frequent anxiety and anguished states I have been suffering from for some time and that cause me:
>
> – Lack of concentration during work
> – Great loss of free time
> – Depression and stress
> – Loss of attention toward dear people
> – Decline in the quality of my life
>
> I think I have identified two centers of my suffering ...
>
> They are:
>
> 1. Mania or obsession for perfectionism
> 2. My house, all things in it, and all that belongs to me
>
> ... I have always been a careful person, attentive to details, and this is certainly a value in itself. But for some time, maybe one year, my tendency to do everything well, aiming at an unreachable perfection, has taken on maniacal aspects that cause me the disorders I described at the beginning. My maniacal perfectionism has to do with my house and its content, my car, and my things. On the contrary, I behave in a sound and normal way when I am at work, in other people's houses, with friends, except for the moments of absence when I think about what I must or can do in my house to arrange this or that thing.
>
> ... I am worried by the thought, which I see as abnormal, that everything in my house must be perfectly in order. And so I waste my free time to clean my house in parts that are very strange and difficult to reach, ... to check the locks of the doors, if I find a scratch on a wall, I plaster and paint it, if I am already in bed and think of something wrong I get up and control.
>
> ... The fact that somebody, a family person or a friend, enters my house or my car disturbs me because then I will have to clean where he walked or leaned. Little by little I gave up buying food for my supper (I have dinner out) so as not to create a mess while cooking my meal or dirty the fridge putting in things that come from the outside. By now, just opening a door to take out a tuna can is for me disagreeable, because I could realize the door does not open or close well, and I would be compelled to repair it. .... So I am progressively freezing, for fear of putting things in a mess, breaking or dirtying something.
>
> At night, when I get home and put the key into the lock, I am anguished. My house is bare, there is the minimum furniture. I have never bought any light fixtures because I don't know what type to choose and I fear I would not be able to assemble them well, or they could have some little defects. I would like to underline that the things I do have in my house, I repair and arrange, even if they are little, ridiculous and useless, are for me of extreme importance, because in case I did not do them, I would feel very badly. I tried to examine my obsessive pursuit of perfection and thought that, if I could have in my hands an undoubtedly and certainly perfect object and this perfection would last undamaged forever, this contact with the absence of any defect would give me confidence and peace. Obviously this is completely unreachable for anything and above all for my things and my life. Hence all my problems ...

We can briefly sum up the patient's problems in the following way:

– Vulnerability factors: The tendency since he was a child toward order and precision (counting, controlling, tidying everything up), determined by a cold and schematic

relationship with his mother, with whom he has developed a conflicting and ambivalent relationship, expressing a strong incapacity to become autonomous.
– Triggering factors: When the patient started to live alone in a small flat of his own, increasing his sense of responsibility and feeling the weight of solitude and abandonment toward the maternal figure, there was the beginning in a very serious way of the obsessive symptoms accompanied by compulsive behaviors.
– Maintenance factors: At present, the patient, aware of the serious and difficult situation he is living in (his everyday life is strongly conditioned by his continuous controls), has developed a serious depression of the self-pity type, as he sees himself stuck in a situation that has no way out and as he considers himself incapable of accepting such a highly compromised lifestyle.

As to the therapeutic strategy, after a careful assessment and the definition of the goals, we decided, together with the patient, to face the secondary problem of depression. After overcoming the secondary problem, we decided to face the obsessive-compulsive symptoms. Psychotherapy started on July 29, 1996, and finished on February 27, 1998. There were 23 sessions, with an average of one session every three weeks.

The most significant sessions, for what concerns depression on a secondary level, are the 9th, 10th, and 11th. Analyzing the dialogue between psychotherapist and patient, it is possible to identify the cognitive themes of self-pity depression. On the contrary, there is no signal of self-undervaluing depression (the patient considers himself a worthy person and declares it openly). The therapeutic strategy I used is rather clear: It is centered in a very determined way on the theme of self-acceptance. In that phase of the therapy, the main goal was to help the patient to accept himself and so not to fall into depression even if the obsessive symptoms greatly complicated his existence. In other words, it was necessary to lead him to consider himself a "happy" obsessive person instead of a depressed one (see the analysis of the communication in the final part of this chapter).

In the following sessions we tried to strengthen the change we had reached.

At the same time, his compulsive behaviors gradually reduced to 50% in terms of their frequency and length.

Anxiety decreased and the patient began to sleep and eat at home again. After 12 more sessions, in accordance with the patient, we decided to conclude the therapy.

The intensity of the anxiety and the frequency and length of the obsessive behaviors regarding tidying and cleaning at home consolidated at about 40% compared with the beginning of the therapy. The behaviors connected with the necessity of writing long lists of things to do or check completely disappeared. The patient's tendency to perfectionism is still present, considering his personality characteristics, but he has learned to accept it and consequently live with it without any big problems.

First follow-up: After two years and four months, on June 15, 2000, I received the following e-mail:

Dear Franco, you are right: my problems are still present, but the dejection I once felt is far away now. The psychotherapy, both that with Lucia and that with you, has given me fundamental moments of evolution, and continues to produce its fruits. I often remember our conversations, and I suggest this experience to my friends in difficulty. I have a chronic disease, probably caused by stress: ulcerative colitis. My doctor has suggested I change my life completely, possibly winning the state lottery. But I decided something else, a bit to seize an opportunity, and a bit because I had been thinking of it for a long time. I have decided to move to Naples, where, as you will remember, my girlfriend lives. I have made this decision not just to escape or look for miraculous remedies, but listening to your suggestions, I am making this step without expecting too much of it and ready for any type of development. In conclusion: with serenity and curiosity. I have made this decision recently, and I have already solved the problem regarding my job. My real move will occur in the course of a year, probably toward the end, in combination with some conditions. At the moment I am living the happy period that follows having made an important decision, and permits one to feel the thrill of one's power, and that comes before the engagement, with the inevitable practical troubles that accompany these big steps. But I don't think of it: I am enjoying the thrill. Let's hope everything will be okay ... Good-bye!

Second follow-up: One year and two months later, on August 2, 2001, I received a second e-mail:

Dear Franco, about two years ago, when I came to you for the first time, I thought the cost of your sessions was a bit high. Now I believe that rarely in my life have I spent my money in a better way. Do you remember me? Francesco from P., an obsessive individual, referred to you by Lucia S., with an impossible relationship with my house and my objects, and with a very desired relationship with a woman from N., older than me. In January I moved, house and work, to the province of N. I feel very well. I have a satisfying affective life, I am relaxed and light-hearted; my obsessive symptoms are limited to check if the door is closed only twice when I go out in the morning. I often smile. I live in a very old and large rented flat at T, and from its landing I can see the square, C., and a bit further C. At last with this house I have a normal and pleasant relationship, quite different from the relationship I had in P. with the other house, that I still own and to which I sometimes go back. In conclusion, it is much better than some time ago, and this is also, and above all, a consequence of a more functional way of thinking, that I have learned thanks to you and L. So I thank you once again for such an important and vital, dynamic and continually evolving progress. Last time you told me you were preparing a website. Can you give me the address? Bye and happy holidays.

From the two above-quoted mails, I received confirmation of the reinforcement of the changes made, of how efficacious the process of acceptance was for the patient and for determining the therapeutic strategy. In this case you can clearly see the efficacy of the intervention on the secondary problem of depressive type.

6.6 Conversation Analysis on the Case of Francesco: A Research Project on Linguistic Interactions in CBT

In this section I refer to research carried out in 1998 by a group of residents of the Psychology Association of Cognitive Psychotherapy of Rome on the linguistic interactions and exchanges that occurred during Francesco's psychotherapy, which were analyzed on the basis of the Conversational Analysis method.

The aims of the research were to outline the trend of the communicative process in the course of the whole therapy, using a quantitative analysis of the communicative events, and to describe, in detail, what happened within the setting, thanks to a qualitative analysis of the therapeutic talk.

6.6.1 Method

The inquiry method chosen by the group was that of the analysis of conversation developed by Sacks, Schegloff, and Jefferson (1978), which represents a successful attempt to document the verbal techniques people use in their daily interactions, through an inductive process, based on the analysis of the conversational interactions (see also Chapter 11).

6.6.1.1 Methodological Steps

1. Listen to all the audiotapes of a positively concluded therapy (Francesco).
2. Randomly choose tapes representative of the whole therapeutic process (initial, intermediate, and final).
3. Transcribe the sessions according to the procedural notes suggested by Jefferson (1974) since it allows the conversational data to be described without being interpreted.
4. Analyze the transcribed material, identifying some quantitative indicators of the communicative process.
5. Perform a detailed and deeply studied analysis of the conversation of a psychotherapy session.

6.6.2 Results

Here I will report the findings of the research group.

They will describe the results of the quantitative analysis followed by some conclusions drawn from the analysis carried out.

Table 6.1 reports the turns of the single sessions, both of the therapist (T) and the patient (P), and to these they associate a detailed analysis of the minimal turns. They have calculated the minimal turns (maximum four verbal units) to be able to infer who, either P or T, in essence spoke longer in the entire course of the therapeutic treatment. As one can observe, P produces a larger number of minimal turns compared with T (except for the last session). From this it is possible to infer that in the whole course of therapy, T produced a significantly larger number of long conversational turns (Table 6.1).

The analysis of the modalities of the turn-taking permits us to understand how the conversation goes on (if each speaker respects the other person's turn or if there is a "more intrusive" modality in the turn-taking). The turn-taking with overlapping

Table 6.1 Number of conversational turns and quantity of both the patient's (P) and the therapist's (T) minimal turns

Session	Total turns	Min. turns P	Min. turns T	Min. turns total
1°	353	64	40	104
2°	337	75	59	134
3°	341	75	28	103
4°	235	48	33	81
9°	439	103	59	162
10°	317	43	19	62
12°	182	18	12	30
20°	364	68	51	119
21°	318	39	50	89
Total	2,886	533	351	884

shows those communicative events in which, due to an overlapping of language, the speaker leaves the turn to his or her conversation partner.

On the contrary, we have the "natural" modality when the speaker has concluded his subject, or takes a pause that allows his partner to take the turn without "forcing" the times of the conversation.

The table points out some interesting data: In the general total of the turn-takings, it is appropriate to underline that those with overlapping are 4.5% of the total vs. 95.5% of the natural ones, which consequently prove to be prevailing. In the first and second sessions, it is possible to observe a total sharing of the modalities of turn-taking between P and T, both as to the natural modalities and as to those with overlapping. In the ninth session, one observes a prevalence of T as to the turn-takings with overlapping (65% vs. P's 35%), within a total incidence of such modalities, 4.5% of the total. In the 10th sitting, the trend changes in the sense that the modalities of turn-taking with overlapping are mainly carried out by P (76% vs. T's 24%), in a session in which the total of the modalities with overlapping is 7.9% of the total; such a value is the highest that has appeared until now. In this session, too, the modality of natural turn-taking is balanced between P and T. In the 20th and 21st sessions, one observes slightly more significant gaps between P and T. In this specific case, P has a larger number of turn-taking with overlapping (60% vs. T's 40%), within a total percentage of such modalities that is quite high compared to the other sittings (23%). P and T, instead, continue to be equivalent in the modalities of natural turn-taking that in any way are still prevailing.

Then they can conclude that in the space of the nine examined sessions the modalities of turn-taking with overlapping are, on average, low if compared with the natural ones, except for the 20th and 21st sittings, which, however, do not significantly weigh on the total. Moreover, there is not a constant significant difference between P and T as to the different modalities of turn-taking. The trend of the therapy, then, comes out balanced and consistent from this point of view (Table 6.2).

Changing the subject can be considered an indicator of the conduction of the conversation. The group thought to analyze this indicator to see if there was a

Table 6.2 Modality of turn taking (P vs. T): Natural or with overlapping

Sessions	With overlapping			Natural		
	P	T	Total	P	T	Total
1°	8	8	16	168	169	337
2°	8	8	16	160	161	320
3°	12	11	23	159	159	318
4°	1	3	4	112	113	225
9°	7	13	20	209	210	419
10°	19	6	25	139	153	292
12°	3	4	7	87	88	175
20°	45	30	75	100	139	239
21°	32	15	47	127	144	271
Total	*135*	*98*	*233*	*1,261*	*1,336*	*2,597*

Table 6.3 Quantity of conversational turns in which there are patient's changes of subject vs. therapist's changes of subject

Sessions	P	T	Total
1	21	29	50
2	2	8	10
3	7	3	10
4	8	7	15
9	14	11	25
10	8	5	13
12	8	5	13
21	11	11	22
22	14	13	27
Total	*91*	*90*	*181*

suggestion of subjects from T or if T's role was to accept the subjects suggested by P. It is interesting to note that in the course of the therapy, "the author" of the change of subject alternates during the various sessions; in fact, in the first sessions, it is T who changes the subject of conversation most of the time, while in the intermediate sessions (9, 10, 12), it is P as the principal author of the change. In the last two sessions, there appears to be an absolute balance between the two actors of the interaction. This could suggest an evolution in the therapeutic relationship, in which there was a continuous "negotiation" of conversation subjects (Table 6.3).

Analyzing the subjects that came out during the sessions, the group singled out some constant categories of content: obsessive rituals, autonomy, solitude, family relationships, relationship with partner, secondary problem.

As Table 6.4 shows, the most recurring themes are those connected with solitude and obsessive rituals. Solitude is the main theme, as it is present in all sessions, except for the last, while the theme of the secondary disorder is the one least discussed together, with that of autonomy and that of relationships with his family

Table 6.4 Quantitative analysis of the content macro-frames (the most recurring themes in the course of the whole therapy)

Sessions	Obsessive rituals	Autonomy separations	Solitude	Relations with family	Relation with fiancée	Secondary problem	Total
1°	1	1	1	0	1	1	5
2°	1	1	1	1	0	0	4
3°	1	0	1	0	1	0	3
4°	0	0	1	0	1	0	2
9°	1	0	1	1	1	1	5
10°	1	0	1	1	0	0	3
12°	1	0	1	0	0	0	2
20°	0	1	1	0	1	1	4
21°	1	1	0	1	1	1	5
Total	*7*	*4*	*8*	*4*	*6*	*4*	*33*

of origin. In the 4th and 12th sessions, there are only two subjects, and from this it appears clear the time devoted to them is quantitatively larger compared with that of the sessions where more subjects are dealt with. The 9th and 21st sessions are like the first, in which we dealt with almost all the analyzed subjects, as if there was cyclically, from the two "actors of the conversation," a recall to all the subjects of the therapy.

6.6.2.1 Analysis of the Conversation

The analysis of the conversation carried out on some sessions (the 9th, 10th, and 11th) highlighted a series of very interesting data. My interest focused on the modalities and characteristics of the "sharing of meanings" between P and T. After identifying some content macro-frames, we analyzed the communicative modalities through which the process of sharing was going on. From this analysis it came out that during the session, in the conversation between P and T, linguistic episodes of sharing were evident. This process developed by passing from an initial linguistic sharing (some terms used by P or T were reciprocally reused) to an actual sharing of meanings. To make the description clearer, here we report an explanatory passage.

In this passage the patient tries to lead the conversation, proposing a series of considerations he made. His intention seems to be that of presenting a list of different themes in a rather superficial way:

P: And I thought I started having my problems since I began this relationship with my girlfriend.

T: The last time you talked to me of the relationship pattern between son and mother and I thought it over a lot. . . .

P: I saw that even my relationship with my girlfriend could be considered ambivalent in an apparent and superficial way: in the sense that at times she is present and at times she is not, and maybe also for this reason there can be a connection with the fact that this relationship can somehow follow closely the relationship I had with my mother in an apparently, I repeat, negative sense.

The therapist, who up to now has followed the patient, now forces him not to abandon the theme soon, proposing once more a term used before by the patient, beginning a "long" process of sharing meanings with regard to a suggested theme:

T: It seems to me a sharp consideration

P: But it is a mere appearance because then in the end, in essence, this relation instead means a lot for me; in fact, it means almost everything. Then the second matter on which I reflected ...

T: Yes, but I was reflecting on the theme 'ambivalent,' because there is one thing that . . .

P: Yes . . .

T: Your girlfriend said it more than once, she explained it very well even when there was a prospect you had aired to move to N., that she cared for her autonomy, she told you not to rely too much on her, and, on several occasions, she declared this openly to you, didn't she?

After a series of turns in which there is a slow process of "negotiation," there is a marked shift from a sharing of terms to a deeper sharing of meanings:

T: . . . in the sense that it could become the proof of the reasoning we had last time, the style of the mother's attachment comes into play, we had supposed ...

P: Yes

T: that probably since that point, there was a proof that was likely to start, but, keep in mind that one thing is the maternal relationship, which can be ambivalent (as we had aired), another thing instead is the adult affective relationship, which has quite different assumptions, where . . .

P: Of course!

T: It could also be a proof of maturity.

P: Hmm.

T: But we must ask how much you, in the affective relationship.

P: Yes.

T: You had, maybe you superimpose, or in a certain sense . . .

P: Eeh?

T: You might mistake it for a possible maternal relationship.

P: Ah, yes, I understand what you mean, yes.

T: I don't know whether you have understood it well, eh?

From this point on, the style of the conversation changes:

P: Somehow I could . . . a behavior could be to keep the two things separated, to see the difference between the two . . .

T: . . . Exactly.

P: To see the difference clearly . . . this is what I should do.

T: . . . Yes, yes . . . because there is the risk you might mistake an adult affective relationship for the maternal relationship and even identify it with this figure of your girl or see . . .

P: Ah, yes.

T: ... As that between son and mother.

P: Sure! And so even expect too much of it.

T: That's it! You see.

P: And even senses of revenge, grudge. And this is what I would like to avoid.

T: Yes at this point, yes, yes, in this sense yes.

P: And then the second consideration I made is that ...

As the preceding passage shows, the sharing of meanings is pointed out by the fluent conversation; it seems both P and T follow the same thread of thought, the overlappings decrease, and there is a fluent and harmonious shift from one turn to the other.

When T feels there has been a sharing of meaning, he gives the patient the "power" to change the subject and suggest another theme (the same attempt made by P had not been accepted by T, who had insisted on keeping the preceding subject active). The modality with which T allows his patient to change the subject after reaching the sharing of meaning occurs also in other moments of the conversation.

In this second part, I will point out in parentheses some of the patient's typical expressive modalities for what concerns the depressive aspect. I have chosen one of the most representative moments of the psychotherapy in which both patient and therapist reach the sharing about the possibility for the patient to feel like "a happy obsessive person":

P: Yes ... now this fact, for example: I have in my mind an idea I have found in the book I am reading, actually I have realized that I am making my life bad, that's why I hate my ...

T: Yes.

P: My house, my car, and myself, I hate these three things that are my things! To the point that I would rather not have them, I would rather not have a house, a car and sometimes I would rather not even have myself! *(He smiles.)* *(self-pity depression)*

T: *(smiling)* Eh! Here you are, I was waiting for the third and last point! Because I understand the house, I understand the car, and then I have said to myself: "Wait, let's see what he tells me about himself."

In this passage there is once again an attempt from P to abandon the matter, or at least not to consider it in detail, but T, through the use of some terms used by the patient, suggests again the "key" subject associated with his secondary disorder. P appreciates this intervention and decides to follow T and accept this linguistic sharing. In fact, in the successive turn, he says

P: Yes, this is a key point because ... *(Awareness of the importance)*

T: Well, this then suggests there is, in certain moments, ... a rage, a hatred against you in this ...

P: Yes, yes, a hatred. *(Assertion of a full awareness)*

T: A nonacceptance of you with these problems!

P: I am getting rid of all my things! *(Hypothesis of a negative solution)*

T: ... I agree with all the other themes, but if we can do a little mental operation (*proposal of a cognitive restructuring*), but actually not so little, that is to eliminate this hatred toward yourself or get rid of ...

P: Not rage or hatred ... it is ... (*Becoming aware of an alternative*)

T: ... Yourself, but instead to like yourself

P: No ... it is a thing, eh yes, yes, that's then ... (*Difficulty in accepting the alternative*)

In this short passage, T looks for a sharing of meanings that the patient seems not to accept yet, as he raises his tone, overlaps, and starts his turn with a negation. The lack of sharing of meanings is clear also after a series of successive turns. Next I quote a passage in which the patient openly speaks of his incapability to accept himself and consequently his difficulty in sharing the meaning suggested by T.

P: But when I check for the thousandth time that I have lowered the blinds in my house, turned all the taps off before going out, in that moment I can't say to myself, "Well, I accept myself as I am," because it is as if a person accepted, it is as if ... it is like accepting one's torturer, isn't it: If, if you had a person that inflicted such sufferings on you, could you ever tell him, "Well, I accept you," it is not possible. (*Self-pity depression*) (*Difficulty in accepting the alternative*)

T: Hmm.

P: Accepting oneself even in the moment when one hurts himself so much! (*Awareness of an alternative*)

T: Yes, you see that as a part of an active process from an external torturer, I agree. Only one devoted to holiness (*he smiles*) can reason in this sense.

P: Yes, yes!

The patient starts (after 20 turns) to resume and use a word expressed by the therapist and from now on the process of sharing becomes deeper and deeper:

P: An advantage could be to say to myself: "Yes, I have my problems, I know they take away a lot of time from me, etc., I have two possibilities: One is not to accept even myself because of these difficulties, and so create one more problem (*Awareness of the secondary problem of depression*) because, besides what I materially have to do when I clean the house for three hours, there is then also the implication regarding a question between me and me, to get to the point of saying to myself: I would rather eliminate even myself, a kind of self-exclusion, so one more problem."

T: And what I can do in the meantime ...

P: This: then say to myself, "I do things, that are not right, etc. etc., no, but I accept myself!" (*Acceptance of the alternative*) Oh, my God! What do you expect I think just in the moment when I am fully convinced to say to myself: "I accept myself just as I am!"

T: Hmm!

P: In your opinion, can't he be an obsessive happy person? At the end, yes. (*Acceptance of the cognitive restructuring*)

T: Why not? See it is not such a foolish idea, in the sense that I know I have to do all these things and that I waste a lot of time, my life surely gets poorer because I could spend that time ... (*Confirmation of the cognitive restructuring*)

P: Yes, yes.

T: ... doing many other things, but, in the end, but worse than so, just the idea of the happy obsessive person! (*Reinforcement of the alternative*)

P: Yes, yes, it could be, at least you don't, you don't live strong states of anxiety, this could surely be one step forward, yes. (*Full acceptance of the cognitive restructuring*)

T: In fact, I am telling you it is not to underestimate ...

P: Yes, yes, and I think it is important even because the fact of having a bad relationship, a very bad relationship, with oneself is surely a heavy disadvantage that causes depressive effects too. (*His voice is apparently broken by a restrained crying.*) (*Self-undervaluing depression*)

In this passage, too, the conversation, after the sharing of meanings, takes on a fluent and regular trend, the patient and the therapist complement each other, and the patient has accepted the possibility of a cognitive change, sharing the proposal made by the therapist about 70 turns before.

When the therapist feels he has reached a sharing of meanings, he gives the patient the possibility to change subject and follows him in his initiative.

To conclude, I quote an emblematic passage that, in our opinion, contains the essence of a deep sharing between patient and therapist and that sums up the aim of the therapy.

After a series of turns, in which the margins of the sharing have been outlined, P says

P: Yes, it's a bit like this, it is frustrating that we can consider we are at the mercy of such casual events, but maybe this is another question. It would be nice to have an internal soundness, an internal mental soundness such as to resist the attacks coming from everyday life events that can take either to depression or to anxiety. (*Awareness of the possibility of a change*)

T: Yes, yes, but it is our goal. The goal of psychotherapy is to get to this point, not always of course, because we ... (*Sharing of psychotherapeutic objectives*)

In this passage both the patient and the therapist use the pronoun "we," which they had never used before, describing a sharing of both goals and meanings. This concept is taken again and widened by the therapist after a series of conversational turns:

T: We are now touching a thing in which I strongly believe from a psychotherapeutic point of view. After so many years of this job I have come to a very precise conviction, that's why I insist so much on this point of the happy obsessive person, as you have defined it in a very brilliant way. With all that meaning we are giving it, you have defined it very well. In the end I have come to a consideration I was trying to experiment and also verify in my practice: that the effort of psychotherapy and probably the true element of change passes almost inexorably through this bottleneck, through this kind of funnel that is equivalent to accepting oneself with one's own limits, which seems a paradoxical thing, because seen from another point of view, it seems a paradoxical thing (*he smiles*) or even a joke. It is like saying: I go to the psychotherapist because I have obsessive problems and so certain rituals, certain things that complicate my life very much. I work hard in psychotherapy and get to the conclusion, in inverted commas, that I have to live with these problems, that I can be happy with these problems. The patient could say, "But it is madness, seen in this sense," but if we consider it in the preceding terms, with that meaning we have somehow tried to define, I am strongly convinced that it is a key shift. (*Reinforcement and reconfirmation of the cognitive restructuring*)

In turn, too, I note that T, taking terms used earlier by P, introduces the sharing of meanings reached during the session. After this intervention, P concludes with two turns in which he underlines his cognitive change.

> P: Certainly, I am starting to have a liberating awareness that is deeply learned (*awareness of the change*), but it can always happen that the other reasoning, that vice versa takes to the other negative side, may arrive. (*Awareness of the importance of mental states*)

> P: Anyway, the well-being is already a positive fact.

The patient's last two turns highlight the importance of the process of sharing to reach a cognitive change. Additionally, it is possible to assume, as it came out from the analysis of the conversation, that there are constant modalities through which the process of the meaning of sharing develops. The elements that, in my opinion, come out with a certain cyclicity are

- The sharing of meanings occurs through an initial sharing of verbal terms.
- After the therapist perceives there has been a sharing of meanings (and this sharing can be observed from the outside, as there is an increase of approvals on P's side, decreases in overlapping, fluency in the conversation), he gives the patient the initiative to change the subject.
- If there has not been a sharing of meanings, it is T who suggests the subjects to deal with and does not give P the possibility to lead the conversation.
- From the analysis of the communication of these three sessions, it is evident that the process of acceptance is consolidated in the patient's mind in a significant way. It is not a consistent movement, as on several occasions the patient wavers from one conviction to another. At some moments, he seems convinced to be able to accept himself with all his limits and faults, while in others he openly declares he is not in a condition to accept such a faulty thing as himself. But slowly, from session to session, this idea makes its way in the patient's mind and the change occurs (on this subject the sentence "I could be a happy obsessive person" is full of meaning).

6.7   Conclusion

In this chapter I began by describing depression according to the Beck and Ellis models. In particular, I emphasized the importance of beliefs and dysfunctional cognitive patterns in the origin and maintenance of this type of disorder. Then I addressed the issue of a secondary problem and its clinical significance in terms of diagnosis and treatment strategies. An overview of some of the depressed patient's communication peculiarities was offered together with examples extracted from a clinical case. I then described the problem of a particular patient and subsequent treatment that led to a positive outcome. In the final section, I reported a study where conversation analysis was applied to a psychotherapist–patient interaction.

References

Baldini, F. (1998). *Il caso dell'ossessivo felice. Un esempio dell'efficacia terapeutica dell'intervento sul problema secondario* [In Italian]. Congresso SITCC, Torino, 2004.

Beck, A. (1967). *Depression.* New York: Hoeber-Harper.

Beck, A. (1976). *Cognitive therapy and the emotional disorders.* New York: International Universities Press.

De Silvestri, C. (1981). *I Fondamenti teorici e clinici della terapia razionale-emotiva [In Italian].* Rome: Astrolabio.

De Silvestri, C. (1999). *Il mestiere di psicoterapeuta [In Italian].* Rome: Astrolabio.

Ellis, A. (1962). *Reason and emotion in psychotherapy.* Seaucus, NJ: Lyle Stuart.

Ellis, A. (1994). *Reason and emotion in psychotherapy, revised and updated.* New York: Birch Lane Press.

Hauck, P. A. (1973). *Overcoming depression.* Philadelphia, PA: Westminster Press.

Jefferson, G. (1974). Error correction as an interactional resource. *Language in Society, 3,* 181–199.

Musso, R., Chianese, A., Coppola, B., Cordasco, G., D'angelosante, E., Lodoli, L., et al. (1998). *Una finestra sul setting.* Unpublished manuscript, Associazione Psicologia Cognitiva, Verona.

Sacks, H., Schegloff, E., & Jefferson, G. (1978). A simplest systematic for the organization of turn taking for conversation. In Schenkein (Ed.) (pp. 1–55).

Chapter 7
Interpersonal Vicious Cycles in Anxiety Disorders

Angelo Maria Saliani, Barbara Barcaccia, and Francesco Mancini

7.1 Introduction

In this chapter we intend to illustrate, on the basis of the clinical work carried out at the Outpatient Clinic of Psychotherapy APC[1]–SPC[2] in Rome, some of the most frequent interpersonal vicious cycles that occur in anxiety disorders.

Notably, those communicative cycles that so often start up between a patient and a family member—and occasionally also between patient and psychotherapist—will be presented. Such interpersonal cycles largely account for the maintenance and exacerbation of the anxiety's symptomatology, just as intrapsychic vicious cycles do (Saliani et al. 2008, 2009; Saliani and Barcaccia 2009).

Clinical observation reveals that, when a patient, in the grip of anxiety, consults other people in search of reassurance, typical communicative cycles start up that are very similar in form, content, and effects to the internal pathogenic dialogue that anxious individuals generate within themselves in an attempt to calm down.

A clinical example will make this more explicit:

Paolo is a 39-year-old man, obsessed by the fear of running over pedestrians with his car. When he is assailed by this doubt, he ruminates inwardly, trying to convince himself that there's nothing to worry about: After all, he hasn't heard any crash, hasn't seen any pedestrians crossing the road, and couldn't find any dents on his car.... After half an hour or so spent in ruminations, the doubts and anxiety have not decreased: After all, how can he be certain of not having heard any crash? And how can he be certain that there were no pedestrians, considering it was a bit misty? And who can guarantee that the car's body is necessarily dented when you run over a pedestrian? By then he would say to himself that perhaps he should go and check the very spot where he fears he has run over a pedestrian. He reaches the

---

[1] Associazione di Psicologia Cognitiva, Rome.

[2] Scuola di Psicoterapia Cognitiva, Rome.

A.M. Saliani (✉)
Associazione di Psicologia Cognitiva APC,
Viale Castro Pretorio, 116, 00185 Rome, Italy
e-mail: saliani@apc.it

M. Rimondini (ed.), *Communication in Cognitive Behavioral Therapy*,
DOI 10.1007/978-1-4419-6807-4_7, © Springer Science+Business Media, LLC 2011

controversial spot, and after having verified that there's no evidence of an accident, and being partially reassured, a new doubt crosses his mind: Might it be that having rushed to reach the spot, and in the grip of anxiety, he has driven through a red light and thus collided with a baby stroller? So his anxiety increases, and new attempts at reassuring himself and new checks follow for hours on end. At this point Paolo realizes he has wasted the whole day performing obsessive-compulsive activities, and he harshly reproaches himself, because with his behavior he's destroying his and his relatives' lives.

Paolo has been assailed by an obsessive fear, has tried to reassure himself by inwardly ruminating on the soundness of his fear, could not dispel the doubt through reasoning, and so has decided to go and check the place in which he fears he could have run someone over. Precisely because of his attempts at reassuring himself, new doubts have assailed him (the new doubt crosses his mind while he's going by car to check the "controversial" spot), and eventually he has reproached himself and felt guilty about his pathological behavior.

Let's now ask ourselves what happens when Paolo, in the grip of obsessive doubt, asks his girlfriend for reassurance:

One evening Paolo comes back home tormented by the doubt of having run someone over, and in order to reassure himself asks his girlfriend if she finds this is really possible. Francesca tries her hardest to convince him that there is nothing to worry about, since if he had run someone over, he would most certainly have realized it, he would have heard a crash and the pedestrian's screams of fright and pain.... But Paolo easily refutes every reassurance: He might not have heard the crash because the radio was playing at full volume, and the poor man, struck down, might not have had time to scream. Therefore, Francesca suggests that the only way to put a lid on his doubts is to reach the spot and check personally. Having done that, and being partially reassured, Paolo is assailed by a new doubt: Might not the poor man have been rushed away by an ambulance? Again, new doubts cross the patient's mind, and again his girlfriend tries to reassure him; eventually Francesca gives him a thorough scolding, resulting in Paolo feeling a strong sense of guilt. Indeed, he says to himself, with his absurd worries he's ruining his and her lives, and should their relationship come to an end, he would only have himself to blame!

Thus, even when an interlocutor is involved, the pathogenic cycle starts up with a fear, continues with attempts at reassuring oneself aimed at refuting the anxiety-inducing hypothesis—first through reasoning, then through empirical evidence ("*let's go to the spot and check!*")—and continues due to the persistence of the anxiety-provoking doubt and the need for reassurance. Indeed, checks and attempts at reassuring oneself are not only insufficient to shake off anxiety, but also provide the starting point for new obsessive doubts. Eventually, the cycle ends in a bitter reproach from the interlocutor and a strong sense of guilt experienced by the patient.

The difference lies in the fact that when a patient is by himself, he autonomously starts up an internal dialogue characterized by the contrast between the anxiety-provoking hypothesis and the attempt at reassuring himself, while when an interlocutor is involved, the very same contrast is played by two distinct actors, engaging in real debate, in which the patient advances the anxiety-provoking hypothesis and the interlocutor tries to reject it.

In this chapter we shall not dwell upon the intrapsychic vicious cycles in anxious patients; we will try instead to show through clinical examples and patient–therapist/relative dialogue excerpts how some interactions can specifically and pathogenically affect the structures and the processes involved in some anxiety disorders. We shall detail six typical interpersonal vicious cycles observed in clinical practice, illustrate how they appear in different disorders, and eventually suggest some strategies and techniques aimed at detecting and defusing them.

7.2   The Vicious Cycles

Before describing the six interpersonal vicious cycles that most attract our clinical attention, we shall quote a series of dialogues that are typical of anxious patients and their relatives. We shall analyze these dialogues in order to show the characteristic problematic exchanges shared by a variety of anxiety disorders, and we shall refer back to them in the second part of this chapter, when describing the releasing strategies from the above-mentioned vicious cycles.

7.2.1   Luigi

Luigi: By the way, Clara, I'm so worried about that business trip I have to make in a fortnight. . . . I fear I might have a panic attack . . . my heart sinks just at the idea of it!

Clara: Come off it! Everything will be fine, you'll see.

Luigi: But the last time I flew I didn't sleep a wink for three days in a row. Besides, throughout the flight I felt like death warmed up! I felt I was losing control and going out of my mind.

Clara: But it was a long while ago, and it's been six months now since you had the last panic attack!

Luigi: Yes, but in the last few months I haven't traveled, let alone flown!

Clara: Calm down, will you? By the way, I read in a scientific journal that if one doesn't have panic attacks for six months in a row, it means one is fully recovered and that they will never occur again.

Luigi: What nonsense! Panic attacks can occur again at any moment!

Clara: Why don't you go by train, then?

Luigi: Hmm . . . I've considered it, but you know how it is, the windows are sealed, if I choked I couldn't even get a breath of fresh air.

Clara: I'll tell you what! You could tell your boss that on the days of your supposed trip to Milan, your presence in the office is essential, to work on the taxes. Maybe Filippo, your young colleague, could go in your place?

Luigi: Hmm ... I wouldn't know, I have got to think about it ... or else you could come with me. ... I would feel much more confident.

Clara: Okay, I'll come with you, don't worry.

Luigi: Thank you my darling, I'm grateful to you, you're a wonderful wife ... I don't know what I'd do without you!

Clara: That's all right ... even though, honestly, I'm sick and tired of this and can't understand how you can have such irrational fears!

7.2.2 Federico

Federico: Mom, did you wash your hands with the disinfectant?

Mother: Come on, they're clean, don't worry.

Federico: Please, wash your hands with the disinfectant, it's very important!

Mother: It's all right, don't worry, my hands are clean. I have touched none of the "dirty things," calm down, everything will be all right.

Federico: Noooo! You're lying! You bought the newspaper, so you must have touched the money ... don't you see I can't trust you?

Mother: Believe me, I've washed them well. ... Come on, let's sit down to eat.

Federico: No, soap is ineffective, because it isn't a disinfectant; it can't eliminate germs.

Mother: Come on, that's just nuts ... nobody does it.

Federico: But they should!

Mother: Be reasonable ... everybody behaves this way, uses soap, and nothing happens. ... This proves there's no danger at all.

Federico: How do you know it for sure?

Mother: I don't, but it wouldn't be safe even if we used the disinfectant.

Federico: Hmm ... indeed, but at least one can reduce the risk by 90%, while you can't do that by using soap!

Mother: All right, let's do it like this: From now on you will eat in your bedroom, with your own personal dishes and cutlery that nobody else will use, and which will be replaced in your own kitchen cupboard; this way you'll be 100% certain that nobody is going to infect you with germs and whatnot, so all of us will rest easy on that score.

Federico: That's a thought! ... However, since now it's lunchtime, please disinfect your hands before putting the food on my dish.

Mother: Dear me! Enough is enough! Stop it, I can't stand this anymore. You have made our lives a living hell, you'll drive us crazy with all your fixations! I'll do it if it is going to shut you up!

7.2.3 Marta

Marta: Darling, I can't get to sleep.

Husband: Why, dear?

Marta: I'm not sure whether I have shut off the gas or not.

Husband: Why, of course! You definitely shut it off . . . sleep easily!

Marta: How can I sleep easily with such a terrifying thought?! We have two children, Paolo!

Husband: Didn't you get up half an hour ago to check the gas?

Marta: Yes, to be sure . . .

Husband: Then, what's the problem?

Marta: The point is that I'm not sure whether I checked it properly or not.

Husband: Listen, tonight you've already checked three times . . .

Marta: Yes, but I'm afraid that I've checked too hastily, I must have been miles away, that's why I can't remember at all the moment in which I turned the valve!

Husband: Marta, please, let's use our brains: You checked three times, so it's highly likely that everything is okay. But even supposing that the shutoff valve had been left on by mistake . . . what might happen? Lots of people leave the shutoff valve on. The main thing is that the burners aren't malfunctioning and that there are no gas leaks.

Marta: Yes, but . . . now I come to think of it, how can I be certain that there are no gas leaks?

Husband: I'm 100% certain about it, because the gas cooker is new!

Marta: Yes, but sometimes they have manufacturing defects. . . .

Husband: Let me think about it . . . Tonight, before going to bed, I had a look at the gas cooker and everything was okay.

Marta: Paolo, are you sure? You would never check the gas tap. . . . Are you telling me this just to reassure me?

Husband: No, I mean, yes! How I wish we could have one peaceful night!

Marta: I see, you're quite right, I just can't help it.

Husband: Listen, I'll tell you what: From now on, when you check something you can mark down the result of your check on a piece of paper, which you'll always bring along with you. This way if a doubt nags you, having a look at the piece of paper will suffice to reassure you. How does that idea strike you?

Marta: Yeah, it seems a good idea. I'll try.

Husband: Okay.

Marta: Yes, but, you know, the trouble is that tonight this anxiety simply won't go away. . . . I'll get up and check for the last time.

Husband: Listen Marta, I'll go with you and we'll check together, so that we'll dispel all doubt. But it's time to put an end to this; going to bed has become nightmarish. We can't go on like this any more! Besides I'm very worried for Marco. The other day, when we were walking to the park, he asked me continuously if I had really locked the door. Your behavior will make him become obsessive, just as you are. God forbid! Do you realize what might happen?!

7.2.4 Gianni

Gianni: You know, I don't think I'll go to the awards ceremony for the school basketball team.
Father: Why, Gianni? You're on the team!
Gianni: I'm overemotional. . . . My hands would shake, and my voice would falter.
Father: Come on! Everything will be fine!
Gianni: No, it won't, I'm afraid. There will be dozens of people staring at me, they will notice I'm jittery and awkward . . . they will think I'm a dummy!
Father: Why on earth?
Gianni: Because when I'm in the midst of a crowd, I start trembling, feel confused, can't utter a word, go as red as a beetroot, break out in a cold sweat. That's why!
Father: Listen, the whole team will be on the podium to be awarded the prize. . . . There will be so many of you! Who do you think will notice you're nervous?
Gianni: That only makes matters worse, because my teammates will be breezy and relaxed, while I'll be hardly able to utter my name. I'll look like a real jerk!
Father: Hmm . . . keeping your hands in your pockets to conceal the trembling, drinking a mouthful of water before speaking and learning a brief speech by heart will do the trick!
Gianni: And what about my flushing cheeks? And what if I start stuttering?
Father: Look here, Gianni, these fears of yours are really foolish. You must overcome them! It's high time you started acting like a man!

7.2.5 Brando

Brando: I've been having twitches in my legs since yesterday. I'm very worried. What do you think?
Sister: I think all's well, and you shouldn't worry. It will soon pass, believe me!
Brando: What a facile answer! Do you think it normal for the legs to shake for 24 hours at a stretch for no apparent reason?
Sister: I can't say, maybe it's just stress.
Brando: Stress! When you're stuck for an answer you come out with stress, while it could turn out to be a serious illness . . . stress my ass!
Sister: Brando, be reasonable. You're young and as fit as a fiddle! You undergo medical examinations time and again, your clinical tests have always been

negative, and less than a week ago your GP told you that you should stop worrying so much about your health!

Brando: Hmm ... you've got something there ... but you know, the thing is, if these twitches are the symptoms of a neurological condition, the check-ups I've undergone so far are pointless. ... Many severe neurological conditions have an insidious onset and symptoms at the beginning are often underestimated. ... I should see a neurologist and undergo an EMG!

Sister: Brando, you were examined by a doctor less than a week ago!

Brando: Yes, but the doctor in question wasn't a neurologist!

Sister: Look here, at least get two days of complete rest before seeing another doctor. If the twitches go away, it means it was just tiredness.

Brando: The twitches appeared after the weekend: I wasn't tired!

Sister: Then why don't you have a look at that medical website. ... You'll find a lot of useful information and advice ...

Brando: Yeah, that's an idea! I'll have a look.

– After about half an hour of surfing the Internet –

Sister: So, what did you find out on the medical website?

Brando: Twitches can depend on lots of different reasons, and they often can be wholly physiological.

Sister: There you are! Can't you see I was right?

Brando: But it also said that twitches are the symptoms of severe neurological conditions and that shouldn't be underestimated. The fact of the matter is that before I was doubtful about what to do, and now I'm sure I've no alternative but seeing a neurologist.

Sister: What can I say? Suit yourself! I can't reason with you: When it comes to health issues, you go bananas! You look ghastly, have grown too thin, and have gotten little sleep since these worries started. You'll end up being really and truly ill!

7.2.6 Valeria

Valeria: Darling, I'm so worried!

Husband: Why?

Valeria: Because it's two in the morning and Gino hasn't come back yet.

Husband: If I remember correctly, before going out tonight, while we were at dinner, he said he would get home later than usual. ...

Valeria: Tonight Gino didn't eat with us! Do you take me for a fool?

Husband: Valeria, Gino is 18 years old, it's Saturday night, and he has gone out with his friends. ... He'll stay out till all hours, like every Saturday night.

Valeria: You see things in black and white, but I'm very worried. I even heard the ambulance siren just now. ... When I'm so worried, there is always a reason; it's as if I can sense it!

Husband: Valeria, you're always worried! At any rate, just for once in a while, try to be reasonable: Gino has never gotten home before two in the morning since he was 16. He's responsible, he has never given us problems, he is good at school, if he has drunk alcohol he doesn't drive, he's never taken drugs and his friends are good kids, too. Don't you think this is enough to keep calm and sleep easily?

Valeria: Yes, you're right … but, you see, neither him nor his friends do worry me. The town is full of violent people at night. I read in the newspaper that two teenagers were beaten black and blue by two mad-men simply because they dared to smile at a girl; and a young man on his scooter was run over by a hit-and-run driver. … How can I sleep easily?

Husband: By trying not to think about it!

Valeria: I see, but what can I do? I just can't help it! How I wish I could keep calm, but at the same time I'd feel irresponsible in doing that. … Life is so full of unforeseen events; accidents of all sorts are just round the corner. … If you relax even for just a second, things get out of control, and at that very moment misfortune hits you!

Husband: At any rate, why don't you call him and stop pestering me?

Valeria: No, call him yourself. … When I do, he complains that I am overanxious, as usual.

— after a few fruitless attempts —

Husband: I think his cellphone is off.

Valeria: Off?! See if I wasn't right? Oh my God, something serious must have happened!

Husband: Maybe the battery is dead.

Valeria: And maybe he needs help and can't make a call for an ambulance. … Please, try to call Alessandro, his best friend … Gino was in his car. … Here is his number.

— after a few fruitless attempts —

Husband: Alessandro's cellphone is on, but he's not answering.

Valeria: Can't you see something dreadful has happened? Let's call the police; they must know if something serious has happened in town!

Husband: That's it! I've had enough! What nonsense! You've called the police and the hospitals a hundred times in the last year, thanks to your ludicrous fears! Enough is enough; I'm going to sleep on the sofa.

What do Luigi, Federico, Marta, Brando, Gianni, and Valeria have in common? Their fears are very different and are specific to distinct disorders:

Luigi suffers from Panic Disorder with Agoraphobia, Federico from Obsessive-Compulsive Disorder (with fears of contamination), Marta from Obsessive-Compulsive Disorder (with compulsive checkings), Gianni from Social Anxiety, Brando from hypochondriac fears, and Valeria from Generalized Anxiety Disorder. Nevertheless, all of them suffer from an anxiety disorder[3] and all of them ask for help and reassurance from their relatives. All the interlocutors try to reassure their beloved one suffering from anxiety: an attempt that eventually turns out to be unsuccessful, and often results in heated discussion. Why? Why, despite the patients' relatives trying in every conceivable way to reassure them, do their attempts at reassuring invariably miss the mark?

Which kinds of communication exchanges take place between a patient and his interlocutor, and what brings about their initialization and maintenance in time?

Analyzing the above-mentioned dialogues, within every one of them six typical communication cycles can be detected. We have labeled these cycles as follows: *pat on the back, white lie, rational debating, solution prompter, compliant rescue,* and *blame.* We will describe them in the following sections.

7.2.7 *"Pat on the Back"*

Usually, when a patient gives voice to his worries, the interlocutor tends, at least in the first instance, to reassure him rapidly and superficially, without getting to the heart of the matter, and without presenting detailed evidence of why he should calm down.

The interlocutor contents herself with giving the patient what we could metaphorically name a "pat on the back." Such an attitude is revealed by verbalisms such as, *"Everything is going to be all right," "Don't worry," "Everything is okay", "Never fear, there's nothing to worry about,"* etc. An anxious individual is hardly ever reassured by statements like these. Rather, most times answers like these leave the patient's worries untouched and reinforce his need for reassurance, as indicated in Table 7.1, showing examples drawn from the above-cited dialogues.

The "pat on the back," besides being evaluated by the patient as a superficial form of help and a feeble attempt at persuasion, is thus incapable of demolishing the anxiety-provoking hypothesis, and not infrequently rouses his anger. Actually, the patient feels that his worries are being underestimated and that he's not being helped as he should be. In these cases the pat on the back is often followed by a strong reaction: The patient reiterates the grounds for his anxiety, the interlocutor newly attempts to reassure his, and the patient again raises objections, thus establishing an outright vicious cycle.

A model is shown in Fig. 7.1.

---

[3] Although Hypochondriasis is classified as a somatoform disorder (APA 2000), many authors within the field of CBT have conceptualized it as a form of health anxiety (Salkovskis and Warwick 1986; Salkovskis 1996; Wells 1997; Mancini 1998; Salkovskis et al. 2003; Warwick 2004, 2007).

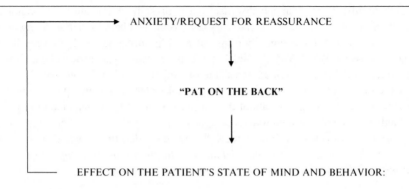

ANXIETY/REQUEST FOR REASSURANCE

↓

"PAT ON THE BACK"

↓

EFFECT ON THE PATIENT'S STATE OF MIND AND BEHAVIOR:

The patient considers the answer superficial and incapable of modifying the feared scenario. Not infrequently it rouses anger instead. Anxiety persists and the reassurance's request is strongly and insistently reasserted.

Fig. 7.1 Pat on the back

Table 7.1

Luigi and his wife	Federico and his mom	Gianni and his dad
L.: …I fear I might have a panic attack on the plane. **W.: Everything will be fine.** L.: But throughout the flight I felt like death warmed up!	F.: Mom, did you wash your hands with the disinfectant? **M.: They're clean, don't worry!** F.: They aren't clean enough. Please, wash your hands with the disinfectant!	G.: …during the awards ceremony, my hands will shake, and my voice will falter. **D.: Come on! Everything will be fine!** G.: Not a chance! I'll look a real jerk!
Marta and her husband M.: I'm not sure whether I have shut off the gas or not. I'm afraid I haven't. I must check. **H.: Why, of course! You definitely shut it off… sleep easy!** Marta: How can I sleep easily with such a terrifying thought?!	**Brando and his sister** B.: I've been having twitches in my legs since yesterday. **S.: They will soon pass away, believe me!** B.: Do you think it normal for the legs to shake for 24 hours at a stretch for no apparent reason?	**Valeria and her husband** V.: It's two in the morning and Gino hasn't come back yet. Something serious must have happened! **H.: Certainly not! He'll stay out till all hours, like every Saturday night.** V.: You see things in black and white, but I'm very worried.

7.2.8 *"White Lie"*

Another typical response to a pathologically anxious individual is lying—or omitting anxiety-provoking information—in order to reassure his. This strategy, too, just like the pat on the back, not only is ineffective, but also is detrimental, because it brings

Table 7.2

Federico and his mom	Marta and her husband	Valeria and her husband
F.: Did you wash your hands with the disinfectant?	M.: I'm not sure whether I have shut off the gas or not.	V.: . . . it's two in the morning and Gino hasn't
M.: *It's all right, don't worry, I didn't go out, I have touched none of the "dirty things."*	Shouldn't I double-check?	come back yet. I'm wrung out with worry!
	H.: *Never fear! Tonight, before going to bed, I had a look at the gas cooker and everything was ok.*	H.: *If I remember correctly, before going out tonight, while we were at dinner, he said he would get home later*
F.: Noooo! You're lying! You bought the newspaper, so you must have touched the money. . . . Don't you see I can't trust you?	M.: Paolo, are you sure? You would never check the gas tap. . . . Aren't you telling me this just to reassure me?	*than usual. . . .*
		V.: Tonight Gino didn't eat with us! Do you take me for a fool?

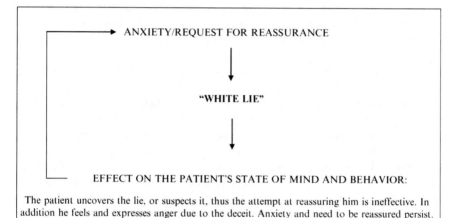

ANXIETY/REQUEST FOR REASSURANCE

"WHITE LIE"

EFFECT ON THE PATIENT'S STATE OF MIND AND BEHAVIOR:

The patient uncovers the lie, or suspects it, thus the attempt at reassuring him is ineffective. In addition he feels and expresses anger due to the deceit. Anxiety and need to be reassured persist.

Fig. 7.2 White Lie

about the reiteration of the request for reassurance and introduces embitterment into the communication.

The patient, indeed, is very often capable of seeing through the trick and therefore, besides feeling angry at the attempt at deceit, keeps his guard even further and increases her control on the interlocutor's behavior. Actually, he feels that other people underestimate his worries and believes he has to prove to them how well founded they are (Table 7.2).

Federico and Valeria soon uncover the lie of their respective interlocutors and react, bristling with indignation. Marta, instead, simply expresses a doubt, fearing her husband is lying, even though with the best intentions; unfortunately, the mere suspicion is enough to keep her fears alive.

In conclusion, even a lie told with the best of intentions (a sort of "pious fraud") can contribute to keeping the patient's fears and requests for reassurance alive, perpetuating fruitless and pathogenic communication cycles (see Figure 7.2).

7.2.9   Rational Debating

The interlocutors of anxious individuals do not content themselves with superficially reassuring or lying; instead, they often pull out all the stops to find consistent, logical, and rational arguments, capable of demolishing the patients' belief of danger.

The start of a rational debating cycle is very often revealed by verbalisms such as, *"Okay, let's try to reason," "Let's use our brains," "Listen, let's assume, for the sake of argument, that ... don't you think ...?"* Unfortunately, hardly ever do the ensuing rational arguments, brought up that way, prove themselves to be effective, even though they might be reasonable and convincing in principle. Hence, long and exhausting discussions follow, which not only leave the patient's fears utterly unaltered, but end up by embittering and keeping them alive.

These outcomes are explained, at least to some extent, by the fact that patients not only possess a logical ability every bit as good as "normal" individuals, but very often demonstrate, within their own critical domains, strategies of reasoning that are more accurate and thorough when compared to "normals" (Mancini and Gangemi 2006).

The difficulties in being reassured wouldn't seem to depend on a fault in the faculty of reason, but on a strict and hyperprudential reasoning strategy, executed in order to comply with one's own safety goals. To put it differently, anxious patients, more than holding absurd and irrational beliefs, hyperinvest in the goal of preventing a perceived catastrophic and unacceptable event—either external or internal—(e.g., cutting a poor figure, losing self-control, being guilty, etc.) and adopt very rigid and strict criteria, thus extremely difficult to meet, to rationally evaluate the soundness of the safety hypothesis.

Therefore, the attempts at reassurance, even the most sophisticated, come into collision with such criteria, and for that reason either fail, achieve poor results, or are of short duration.

Unfortunately, a large number of vicious cycles also intervene to complicate and maintain matters. Such vicious cycles are precisely determined by the unexpected effects of the attempts at solution, although both the patient and his interlocutor are completely unaware of it.

Indeed, as it has been shown in the "pat on the back" and "white lie" cases, not only are these strategies incapable of demolishing the threatening hypothesis, but they also contribute to further embitter the patient–interlocutor dialogue and to reinforce the need for new and more effective reassurances.

Even when the interlocutor drops such, so to speak, "superficial" strategies and goes into rational, thorough, and in-depth criticism of the patient's fears, similar effects are achieved. In such cases the dialogue will soon resolve itself into a thorough dialectic debate, which will very likely not end in the removal of the

Table 7.3

Marta and her husband	Brando and his sister	Valeria and her husband
M.: I'm not sure whether I have shut off the gas or not. *H.: Marta, please, let's use our brains: you checked three times, so it's highly likely that everything is okay. But even supposing that the shutoff valve had been left on by mistake... what might happen? Lots of people leave the shutoff valve on. The main thing is that the burners aren't malfunctioning and that there no gas leaks.* M.: Yes, but ... now I come to think of it, how can I be certain that there are no gas leaks? *H.: I'm 100% certain about it, because the gas cooker is new!* M.: Yes, but they some-times have manufacturing defects ...	B.: I've been having twitches in my legs since yesterday. . . . Maybe I should see a doctor. *S.: Brando, be reasonable. You're young and as fit as a fiddle! You undergo medical examinations time and again, your clinical tests have always been negative, and less than a week ago your GP told you should stop worrying so much about your health!* B.: Hmm ... you've got something there ... but you know, the thing is: if these twitches are the symptoms of a neurological condition, the check-ups I've undergone so far are pointless. . . . Many severe neurological conditions have an insidious onset. . . . I should see a neurologist and undergo an EMG!	V.: ... it's two in the morning and Gino hasn't come back yet. I'm wrung out with worry! *H.: Valeria, you're always worried! At any rate, just for once in a while, try to be reasonable: Gino has never gotten home before two in the morning since he was 16. He's responsible, he has never given us problems, he is good at school, if he has drunk alcohol he doesn't drive, has never taken drugs and his friends are good kids too. Don't you think this is enough to keep calm and sleep easy?* V.: Yes, you're right ... but, you see, neither him nor his friends do worry me. The town is full of violent people at night! How can I sleep easy?

patient's worries; he, on the contrary, endeavoring to scrupulously evaluate and rebut the safety hypotheses advanced by the interlocutor, will look out for new anxiety-provoking details and will come to new logical conclusions capable of reinforcing his perception of threat and his will to protect himself by avoidances and safety-seeking behaviors.

Table 7.3 provides some examples of this kind of problematic interaction.

In the clinical vignettes shown in Table 7.3, the attempt to rationally persuade the patient, although undermining the threatening hypothesis, has not proven effective once and for all in any of the provided examples; on the contrary, the rational debate afforded the patient the opportunity to sharpen still further his or her threatening hypothesis: Marta, who was previously worried only of not having shut off the gas valve, during the discussion starts fearing that the burners might have manufacturing defects; Brando, after an initial general form of worry about his health, realizes, while debating with his sister, that he might be affected by a neurological condition; Valeria, reacting to her husband's attempts to reassure her, realizes that the danger regarding her son Gino might arise not only from his own behavior, but also, and most of all, from other people's behavior.

In conclusion, we can maintain that the use of logical reasoning too, when performed with a goal of eliminating the threatening hypothesis, can easily contrib-ute to starting a vicious cycle (see Fig. 7.3).

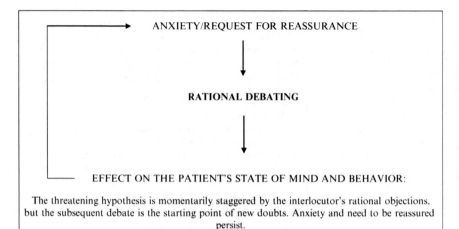

Fig. 7.3 Rational debating

7.2.10   Solution Prompter

In the difficult task of helping patients to calm themselves down, their interlocutors not only try to reassure them by "pats on the back," by long rational debates, and even by some white lies, untruths sometimes told with the best intentions, but they often inspire practical solutions, calculated to modify or eliminate the conditions that are frightening and even alarming for the patients.

As a matter of fact, patients, as in the case of the rational debate, appear to listen carefully to practical advice and, after having analyzed and judged it proper and fit, they try to put it into practice. Sometimes, when they do, both the patient and his relative initially imagine they have solved the problem, or, at any rate, that they have found a good remedy; thus, a momentary reduction of anxiety and an intermission of the problematic interaction can really follow.

However, in quite a large number of cases, the prompted solutions, even though apparently new and more effective, do not actually differ in quality from those previously and autonomously enacted by the patient: The "new solutions" end up being added to his ample store of avoidances and safety-seeking behaviors, which, as is generally known, are among the most powerful maintenance factors of anxiety disorders.

To be more specific, when a father suggests his social phobic son (scared to death at the thought of making a fool of himself by looking overemotional) should keep his hands in his pockets in order to conceal the sweat and trembling due to anxiety, since the boy is extremely ashamed of them, all this will inevitably backfire: Actually, the father is not only implicitly confirming that showing others signs of anxiety is unacceptable, but he is also preventing his son from experiencing that, if he gave up

Table 7.4

Luigi and his wife	Federico and his mom
L.: …I'm so worried about that business trip I'll have to make in a fortnight. … I fear I might have a panic attack. … My heart sinks just at the idea of it! *W.: I'll tell you what! You could tell your boss that on the days of your supposed trip to Milan, your presence in the office is essential, to work on the taxes. Maybe Filippo, your young colleague, could go in your place?* L.: Hmm … I wouldn't know. I have got to think about it. …	F.: Mom, I fear that if I sit down at the table, I could contaminate myself. *M.: Listen, from now on you will eat in your bedroom, with your own personal dishes and cutlery that nobody else will use, and which will be replaced in your own kitchen cupboard; this way you'll be 100% certain that nobody is going to infect you with germs and whatnot, so all of us will rest easy on that score. What do you say?* F.: That's a thought! … However, since now it's lunchtime, please disinfect your hands before putting the food on my dish.
Marta and her husband	Brando and his sister
M.: You know, I'm not sure whether I have shut off the gas or not, even though I've already checked three times. *H.: Listen, I'll tell you what: from now on, when you check something, you can mark down the result of your check on a piece of paper, which you'll always bring along with you. This way, if a doubt nags you, having a look at the piece of paper will suffice to reassure you. How does the idea strike you?* M.: Yeah, it seems a good idea. I'll try.	B.: Twitches appeared after the weekend: I wasn't tired! *S.: Then why don't you have a look at that medical website. … You'll find a lot of useful information and advice? Maybe it will help to calm you down …!* B.: Yeah, that's an idea! I'll have a look.

the safety-seeking behaviors, he would presumably find out that the feared scenario, however disagreeable it may be, is surmountable and not catastrophic.

In other words, when a patient's interlocutor prompts this kind of advice, much as he's doing it for the best, he'll end up unintentionally contributing to maintaining the patient's anxiety disorder.

Table 7.4 provides some examples of the solution prompter cycle.

In the dialogue excerpts cited in Table 7.4, one can see that the provided suggestions seem to be initially welcomed by the patient. But what will be the subsequent effects of these tips on the patient's state of mind and on the interaction with his interlocutor? After a momentary relief, Luigi won't accept his wife's proposal (sending his colleague to Milan in his place), but even if he complied with it, the result would be an avoidant behavior, similar to the ones he already brings about, and his fears of having panic attacks when away from home would remain unaltered. In other words, the patient would be under the impression of having dodged danger, but his fear of catching a flight would endure. Federico will take his mother's advice, but this will turn out in a series of avoidant behaviors even more exaggerated than the current ones, leaving unchanged his basic fear of contamination. Marta, too, will follow her husband's advice and will mark down the results of her checks on a piece of paper, but the chosen solution will turn out in the form of "checking of checks": So new rituals will come on top of the old ones, leaving

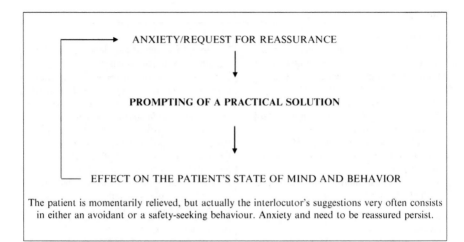

ANXIETY/REQUEST FOR REASSURANCE

PROMPTING OF A PRACTICAL SOLUTION

EFFECT ON THE PATIENT'S STATE OF MIND AND BEHAVIOR

The patient is momentarily relieved, but actually the interlocutor's suggestions very often consists in either an avoidant or a safety-seeking behaviour. Anxiety and need to be reassured persist.

Fig. 7.4 Solution prompter

unaltered her obsessive fears. Brando will accept his sister's advice and will check on the Internet: After initial relief, and precisely because of the information gathered while surfing the Internet, his fear of being affected by a neurological illness will be reinforced, as will his need to ask family members and doctors for reassurance.

In summary, even when the requests for reassurance are answered by prompting solutions in the above-mentioned ways, one most likely runs the risk of starting up a vicious cycle that will negatively affect the patient's state of mind and the quality of the ongoing interaction (see Fig. 7.4).

7.2.11 Compliant Rescue

Relatives and, in general, people surrounding an anxious patient, not infrequently, in the mistaken belief of helping him or her, comply with his requests without argument. Indeed, the patient, too, is persuaded that this is the only way to be helped, and spares no pains to persuade the interlocutor to indulge his requests.

It's very common for agoraphobics who beg to be accompanied in all their comings and goings to attain their goal, as it is for obsessive patients with fear of contamination and who ask not to be touched, or to touch, in their place, items perceived as dirty (handles, banknotes, etc.) to be indulged, just as it is for obsessive patients with checking rituals who ask to be helped in their checks (Van Noppen and Steketee 2008; Merlo et al. 2009). Relatives of individuals suffering from generalized anxiety likewise comply with the patient's requests to be constantly reachable by telephone, so that the patient can check at any time that they are well and nothing serious has happened.

Actually, quite a number of the patient's requests consist of maneuvers aimed at avoiding the exposure to the anxiety-provoking situation or at allowing his to

Table 7.5

Luigi and his wife	Marta and her husband	Valeria and her husband
L.: I'm still very worried about that business trip I'll have to make in a fortnight . . . if you came with me, I'd feel much more confident. W.: *Okay, I'll come with you, don't worry.* L.: Thank you my darling, I'm grateful to you, you're a wonderful wife. . . . I don't know what I'd do without you!	M.: . . . yes, but, you know, the trouble is that tonight this anxiety simply won't go away. . . . I'll get up and check for the last time. H.: *Listen Marta, I'll go with you and we'll check together, so that we'll dispel all doubt.* M.: Thank you, my dear, I really appreciate your help.	V.: Please call Gino, he hasn't come back yet and I'm very worried. . . . Won't you call him yourself? When I do, he complains that I am overanxious, as usual. H: *All right, I'll call him.* −*after a few fruitless attempts*− H: I think his cellphone is off. V.: Off?! See if I wasn't right? Oh my God, something serious must have happened!

confront it in a protected way. Thus, the seemingly helping behavior ends up by being a circling maneuver, which leaves unaltered the patient's underlying fears and his need to ask for new reassurance in the future.

That's why behaving in a way that is exceedingly indulging, or even anticipating the patient's requests, turns out to be a strong mechanism in the maintenance of the disorder (see Table 7.5).

Luigi's wife complies with her husband's request of being accompanied on his business trip; Marta's husband doesn't even wait for his wife to ask him and offers himself as an aid for the obsessive checks. Valeria's husband calls Gino in the dead of night, since she fears something serious might have happened to him. The effect on the patient's state of mind and on the quality of the patient–relative interaction will unfortunately be by no means positive and the taken precautions will eventually backfire.

Luigi and Marta indeed, after a momentary relief, can't be reassured once and for all about their fundamental fears: Luigi will go on fearing leaving home on his own, and Marta will go on fearing not being scrupulous enough in her checks. Valeria won't even experience a single moment of relief; on the contrary, her husband's compliant rescue will be the starting point of her worry's exacerbation.

In conclusion, in all three of them the anxiety disorder is maintained by the rescue attempts carried out by their relatives and the patients will soon feel the urge to ask them for reassurance (Fig. 7.5).

7.2.12   Blame

Sooner or later, in the interactions between anxious patients and their usual interlocutors, expressions of blame make their appearance. In this section we shall dwell upon the criticism that the relative, exasperated by the patient's symptoms and requests, levels against him; still, it is worthwhile noting that not infrequently the

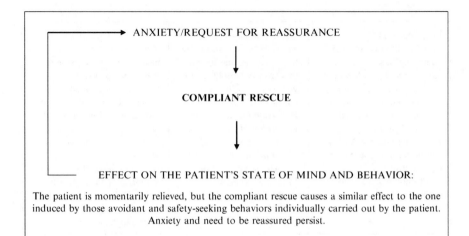

Fig. 7.5 Compliant rescue

patient as well reproaches the relative, for not being attentive enough to his or her needs, for not understanding his or her misery, or even for being the very source of it.

The negative effect of the patient's reproaches on the general relational atmosphere and on the interactions implied in the disorder is by no means marginal. Actually, the interlocutor, perceiving one moment the rebuke as fair, the next one as unfair, will swing between feelings of guilt and anger, which will drive him or her to responses that end up being fatally pathogenic for the patient.

The relative's feeling of guilt will increase the number of compliant rescue behaviors and solution promptings, which, as illustrated in the previous sections, represent a severe maintenance factor of the disorder. Differently, anger will lead to reproachful and aggressive responses, which will further embitter the relationship between the patient and the relative and sometimes (as will be shown below) will act as a specific pathogenic factor.

Reproaching, obviously, isn't brought about only by verbal expressions; there are actually many different ways of expressing criticism, disapproval, disappointment, condemnation, contempt, etc., but not infrequently the interactions between a patient and relative are characterized by explicit and outspoken assertions and exclamations, such as, "Enough of this nonsense! I cannot put up with you any longer!", "When will you bring yourself around to behaving in a mature way?", "Stop pestering me! I'll do it if it is going to shut you up!", "Do you realize you've made our lives a misery?" (see Table 7.6).

The dialogues involving Luigi, Federico, Marta, and Gianni all end in a harsh judgment expressed by their respective relatives, which will assume different meanings according to the type of interaction and, above all, according to the patient's state of mind.

In the course of psychotherapy, the clinician may learn that the criticisms leveled at the patient by others are not infrequently similar in content to their self-reproaches: When a patient reflects upon his being affected by a psychological

Table 7.6

Luigi and his wife	Federico and his mom
L.: You could come with me... I would feel much more confident.	F.: Please disinfect your hands before putting the food on my dish.
C.: *Okay, I'll come with you; don't worry.*	M: *Dear me! Enough is enough! Stop it,*
L.: Thank you my darling, I'm grateful to you.	*I can't stand this any more, you have made*
C: *That's all right ... even though, honestly,*	*our lives a living hell, you'll drive us crazy*
I'm sick and tired of this and can't understand	*with all your fixations! I'll do it if it is going*
how you can have such irrational fears!	*to shut you up!*
Marta and her husband	Gianni and his dad
M.: ... you know, the trouble is that tonight this anxiety simply won't go away. ... I'll get up and check for the last time.	G.: I don't think I'll go to the awards ceremony of the school basketball team. ... I'd start trembling and sweating. ... I'd look like a real jerk!
H.: *Listen Marta, it's time to put an end to this. Going to bed has become nightmarish. We can't go on like this anymore! Besides I'm very worried for Marco. ... Your behaviors will make him become obsessive, just as you are. God forbid! Do you realize what might happen?!*	D.: *Gianni, can't you see these fears of yours are really foolish and childish? It's high time you started acting like a man!*

problem, he would call himself, e.g., "a hopeless case," "a weakling," "irrational," "whimsical," "guilty." Therefore, patients do often develop depressive states consequent to their anxiety disorder.

However, criticism and self-reproaches can, actually, play even a more specific role in the disorder's maintenance, when they activate personal themes directly involved in the development of the anxiety's symptomatology.

Research in the field of experimental psychopathology in recent years has shown that, for example, obsessive-compulsive symptoms are probably due to a hypertrophic sense of responsibility (inflated responsibility) (Ladouceur et al. 1997; Salkovskis et al. 1999; Arntz et al. 2007; Lopatka and Rachman 1995; Mancini et al. 2004; Mancini and Gangemi 2004) and that both checking and washing rituals are aimed at preventing feelings of guilt and interpersonal expressions of anger and moral judgment (Mancini 2001, 2005; Zhong and Liljenquist 2006; Gangemi et al. 2007). Now, in the light of the aforementioned, if we consider the effect of the reproaches suffered by Federico and Marta, it can be hypothesized they will specifically reinforce exactly their deepest fear, the one closely related to the obsessive symptoms, that is, being irresponsible and morally deplorable.

Similarly, even though concerning different contents, it's easy to imagine that the accusation of irrationality leveled at Luigi will reinforce his fear of losing control, typical of individuals with Panic Disorder; and the harsh admonishment suffered by Gianni, whose father urges him to overcome his "foolish" fears and to "act like a man," will inevitably confirm his idea of being socially inadequate and a laughing stock.

In summary, the cycle of blame, often started after long, repeated, and fruitless debates aimed at reassuring the patient, can directly and specifically impact his

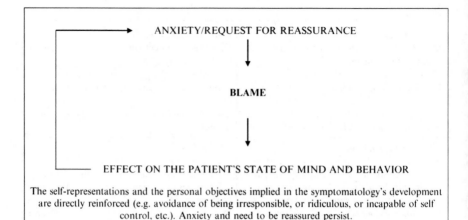

The self-representations and the personal objectives implied in the symptomatology's development are directly reinforced (e.g. avoidance of being irresponsible, or ridiculous, or incapable of self control, etc.). Anxiety and need to be reassured persist.

Fig. 7.6 Blame

self-representation, which is involved in the symptomatology's development: This process will lead the patient to apply himself even more to prevent the feared scenarios (moral unworthiness in Marta, loss of self control in Luigi, social humiliation in Gianni, etc.) (see Fig. 7.6).

7.3   Acknowledgment of the Vicious Cycles

The first stepping stone to getting out from the vicious cycles is helping the patient to detect the typical responses from relatives to his requests for reassurance; right after, he can be helped to acknowledge the consequences of these reactions on both his behaviors and state of mind.

In order to achieve this, it is useful to show in session the typical reactions between patient and family members. In addition, the therapist will ask the patient to fill out some forms (see Table 7.7) between sessions, as homework assignments.

Sometimes, when family members are heavily embroiled in the maintenance of the disorder, seeing the patient individually could be insufficient; in such cases a number of sessions involving the relatives' participation, along with the patient, can be specifically designed, and family members will be asked between sessions to fill out forms regarding the interpersonal cycles, in a similar manner to the patient's forms (Table 7.8).

Patients and relatives, once trained to acknowledge the vicious cycles with the help of the psychotherapist, will try to break them and arrange new strategies of coping with the problematic situations.

In evaluating the effects of the family member's response to the patient's state of mind and behavior (see Table 7.7), it is important to take into account their

Table 7.7 Patient's form

ANXIETY-INDUCING SITUATION Describe an event that has caused you anxiety.	PATIENT'S STATE OF MIND (BEFORE ASKING FOR REASSURANCE) Write how you were feeling right then.	PATIENT'S REQUEST TO HIS RELATIVE Write what you asked your relative.	RELATIVE'S RESPONSE Write what your relative said/did after your request for reassurance.	PATIENT'S STATE OF MIND (AFTER HAVING ASKED FOR REASSURANCE) Write what you thought of your relative's response and how you felt.	PATIENT'S REACTION Write what you did/said after your relative's response.

Table 7.8 Family member's form

ANXIETY-INDUCING SITUATION Describe a situation in which the patient asked you for reassurance.	PATIENT'S REQUEST Write what the patient's request was and how he justified it.	RELATIVE'S STATE OF MIND Write what you thought and how you felt when the patient made the request for reassurance.	RELATIVE'S RESPONSE Write what you did/said after the patient's request.	PATIENT'S REACTION Write what the patient did/said after your response.

duration: Often, indeed, either verbal reassurance or practical suggestions provided by the interlocutor can initially relieve anxiety, but in the medium and long term they become ineffective and, even worse, harmful.

7.4 The Problem of Reassurance and the Importance of Acceptance

Vicious cycles, once started, are by definition hard to break. Usually people swing from one vicious cycle to another in a toilsome attempt to stem the patient's need for reassurance.

In actual fact, both the anxious individual and his interlocutor often and instinctively believe that the problem will be solved when evidence is found that the perceived threat is either exaggerated, flimsy, or absent. The final objective of the reassurance maneuvers, both dialogical and practical, is the finding of such evidence.

Thus, since the irrefutable evidence of the threat's absence is impossible to find, there is nothing left to do but fall back on maneuvers aimed at either shifting away from the threat or at least curbing it. More specifically, avoidances and safety-seeking behaviors will be carried out, such as staying inside, or going out only if accompanied by a family member, not touching money, or touching it only after having put on one's gloves, etc. That is tantamount to saying that patients curb the symptoms by executing other symptoms.

The stepping stone to breaking the vicious cycle is acknowledging that satisfying the anxious patient's need for reassurance once and for all is herculean and counterproductive. Actually, (1) the criteria applied by patients to assess the effectiveness of the reassurance maneuver are far stricter and more rigorous than the ones followed by ordinary people; (2) generally, the patient doesn't strive for partial reassurance, but rather for conclusive reassurance: He or she would like to achieve absolute certainty that the feared event will not occur; (3) the attempts at finding the mathematical certainty bring about maintenance of the fears and even embitterment: The solution becomes the problem (vicious cycles).

Therefore, an effective intervention should be aimed not so much at eliminating conclusively the feared threat, as to accepting the possibility that the feared event could occur (Barcaccia 2007, 2008; Bach and Moran 2008; Mancini and Gragnani 2005). Once again, to explain ourselves further, we shall resort to some clinical examples, trying to imagine how the dialogues involving Federico, Luigi, and Gianni would have gone had their relatives strayed from the winding route of reassurance:

7.4.1 Federico

Federico: Mom, did you wash your hands with the disinfectant?
Mother: I won't wash my hands with the disinfectant, Federico.

Federico: Please wash your hands with the disinfectant, it's very important ... It is crucial to have one's hands perfectly clean when sitting down to eat.

Mother: I don't know what you mean by "perfectly clean," but I agree with you on washing hands before sitting down to eat ... that's why I washed them using liquid soap.

Federico: But liquid soap is ineffective, because it can't eliminate either germs or the risk of contagion!

Mother: Probably not, I grant you that, but I believe it can reduce the risk significantly. ... Anyway, I prefer running this small risk than washing my hands with the disinfectant.

Federico: But if you won't use the disinfectant, I'll be gripped by panic and won't be able to eat.

Mother: I can understand that, Federico, and I am aware that you feel anxious when I won't do what you ask me. I'm truly sorry, and I'll try to help you, but I don't think that the solution is avoiding anxiety at any cost through repeated washings or other safety-seeking behaviors.

7.4.2   Luigi

Luigi: You know, Clara, I'm so worried about that business trip I'll have to make in a fortnight.

Wife: And what are you frightened of?

Luigi: I fear I might have a panic attack and lose control ... my heart sinks just at the idea of it!

Wife: Hmm ... I see.

Luigi: You know, I was thinking that you could come with me. ... I would feel much more confident.

Wife: I know that only too well, Luigi, but I don't think I'll go with you.

Luigi: Why, are you already otherwise engaged?

Wife: I'm not, but I don't believe that the solution is sparing you the anxiety deriving from the idea of traveling by yourself.

Luigi: And what, may I ask, is the solution to my problem?

Wife: Unfortunately, I don't know; maybe an experienced psychotherapist could help you find it. At any rate, I'm certain that the solution doesn't imply either avoidances or reassurances.

7.4.3   Gianni

Gianni: You know, I don't think I'll go to the awards ceremony for the school's basketball team. ... I'm afraid I'll get into a state and will look like a real jerk.

Father: You care about that ceremony, don't you?

Gianni: Yeah, I've been waiting for it for a year. .... But I'm afraid I'd break out in a cold sweat, my hands would shake, and my voice would falter; people will notice I'm jittery and awkward ... they will think I'm a dummy!

Father: Hmm ... it's likely you could get stage fright and you know, if you're nervous you can start trembling and sweating, which is disagreeable, no doubt. But after all, I believe there's no harm in getting nervous.

Gianni: And what if I get flustered and tongue-tied?

Father: You're right, this might happen, too, even though it must be said that when we're frightened, we tend to overestimate risks. Maybe this is what it's happening to you right now. Anyway, I'm aware it might happen, and that it would be disagreeable, but I think it's a risk worth taking. What do you say?

In the above-mentioned dialogues, the interlocutors of Federico, Luigi, and Gianni haven't drawn on pats on the back, white lies, or long rational debates in order to prove to their dear one that there is no danger, neither did they comply with his request, nor did they suggest solutions involving avoidance of anxiety, let alone blame him. They contented themselves with listening and contemplating, without dramatizing, the possibility that the feared scenarios might come true.

Such an attitude naturally will not suffice to cure the anxiety disorders; on the contrary, at the beginning, the patient will doggedly persist in demanding reassurances. But by interlocutors adopting this attitude steadily in the long run, many interpersonal vicious cycles responsible for maintenance of the disorder will die away.

It is important to make it clear that the interpersonal attitude intended to help patients accept the possibility of the feared event's occurrence doesn't coincide with resignation or with pessimism.

In addition, once the acceptance of the threat is achieved, and the reassurance attempt at any cost is given up, it will be easier to bring into use programs of Exposure with Response Prevention, which remain to this day the elective treatment for anxiety disorders.

To give further details, the strategy of acceptance (Hayes et al. 2006) will imply two different levels: one of the "external" events and one of the "internal" states. This strategy will facilitate the process of giving up the avoidant and safety-seeking behaviors. For instance, when Gianni's father tells him that getting nervous isn't wrong, he is legitimating his son's feared internal events: anxiety and embarrassment; and when he says that making a fool of oneself "is just one of those things," he is defining as acceptable and surmountable another feared event, this time external and overt: not uttering a single word in front of an audience.

Similarly, when Federico's mother replies she prefers running the risk of contaminating oneself and won't wash her hands with the disinfectant, she is defining as tolerable an external event; and when she states that eliminating anxiety at any cost isn't the solution to her son's problems, she is implicitly evaluating as surmountable and acceptable an internal event, that is, the disagreeable sensations due to anxiety.

The interlocutor can motivate the patient to replace the search for absolute certainty (pursued through avoidant behaviors, reassurance requests, and other safety-seeking behaviors) with an acceptant attitude, by using three ia 2004):

1. the *ineffectiveness* of avoidant and other safety-seeking behaviors and of reassurance requests;
2. the *disadvantages* due to those behaviors;
3. the *legitimacy* of lowering one's guard, thus giving up those behaviors;

Any interlocutor, whether a family member or a psychotherapist, can help the patient to consider the above-mentioned ingredients, whose discussion will be further illustrated in the following sections (see also Chapter 3 for further clarification on *reassurance* and Chapter 6 on the theme of *acceptance*).

7.4.4 Drawing Out the Ineffectiveness of the Reassurance Attempts

In order for the patient to give up the reassurance attempts and the other safety-seeking behaviors, he should consider how ineffective they are. As long as he goes on believing that the only effective way to stem anxiety is either avoiding the feared situations or confronting them only after having taken precautions in every conceivable way, he will inevitably perpetuate those intrapsychic and interpersonal vicious cycles that maintain his disorder. That's what happens when he avoids going out or when he goes out only if accompanied by someone whom he can trust.

In the following dialogue a possible way of conducting this intervention will be illustrated. The chosen communication mode is a typical one in cognitive-behavioral therapy: guided discovery, a strategy whereby the psychotherapist uses questions, instead of statements, in order to draw out the ineffectiveness of reassurance attempts. The patient won't feel that the therapist wins his point, but she will have the chance of autonomously finding out the effects both of her own actions and of the interlocutor's responses.

Therapist: So, when you're very worried of not having properly checked the gas or the front door, you usually express your doubts to your husband, don't you?

Marta: Yes, I do.

Therapist: And may I ask you why do you talk about it with your husband?

Marta: Because he reassures me.

Therapist: Well, will you help me to get this right; how does your husband reassure you?

Marta: He tells me that it's the same old story, and that the front door is definitely closed.

Therapist: Hmm ... so, all in all, your husband tells you that you may rest easy on that score, and that there's nothing to worry about, doesn't he?

Marta: Just so.

Therapist: Well, and is that enough to reassure you?

Marta: Hardly ever ... to tell you the truth, it's an answer that tends to annoy me, because it seems as if he was making light of my worry.

Therapist: I see ... so a hasty reassurance can't calm you down, but it can annoy you, in fact.

Marta: Precisely so. Sometimes I have a sneaking suspicion he tells me lies to calm me down. And naturally, this attitude too ... I mean ... I know he does it for me, but it irritates me.

Therapist: What kind of lies?

Marta: Well, he will sometimes state he remembers having watched me close the front door, while he had already gotten into the car; thus, he couldn't have seen me.

Therapist: Hmm ... I see ... and does he do something else to reassure you?

Marta: Yeah, he's very helpful ... sometimes he will talk my worries over with me, he'll try to make me reason, he'll show me some details that I had neglected, and I often settle down.

Therapist: Hmm ... so when he gives his all, so to speak, and tries to show you by logical reasoning that everything is okay, he can reassure you, can't he?

Marta: Well, yes.

Therapist: You know, I was wondering whether this is a truly effective reassurance.

Marta: What do you mean by that?

Therapist: I mean, does your worry disappear and so you've done with it?

Marta: Sometimes it does, but other times it won't suffice, and I'll ask him for reassurance once again.

Therapist: Okay. So, in about half of the cases reassurance doesn't seem to work right away. I mean, your anxiety doesn't ease off, and you go on discussing it, don't you?

Marta: Just so.

Therapist: Well, and when it seems to work instead, do anxiety and your doubts disappear once and for all?

Marta: They do sometimes. I mean, if I discuss it with my husband, I become convinced in the end I actually closed the front door, and then I am done with it.

Therapist: So sometimes a single worry is eased off by reasoning and dialogue. But I wonder whether afterward new doubts or worries cross your mind.

Marta: Well, to be quite honest my mind is always restless. ... I may set my mind at rest about the door, and after a few minutes I'm assailed by the doubt of not having closed the gas valve. ... I can't help it.

Therapist: So what you're essentially saying is that even when reassurance seems to have worked, your basic anxiety persists, in fact, and you soon feel the urge to ask for new reassurance?

— a few seconds' pause—

Marta: I think so, unfortunately.

Therapist: I see. And is there anything else your husband does at that point to reassure you?

Marta: Yes, there is.

Therapist: Such as?

Marta: Well, I ask him to help me in my checks, so he performs them with me. You know, two heads work better than one ... so I feel safer. Or sometimes he would check in my place. In a nutshell, he accommodates my needs.

Therapist: That is to say, he accepts doing the things you ask him to do.

Marta: Precisely so.

Therapist: Hmm ... and what happens afterward?

— a few seconds' pause—

Marta: You know, I was telling you what happens: I settle down, it seems I've set my mind at rest. However, at that point, I'm assailed by new worries, actually.

Therapist: And your husband, at that point ...

Marta: You see, he would think up a dodge ...

Therapist: Such as?

Marta: Oh, well, a few months ago he advised me to mark down the result of my checks on a piece of paper, which I should always bring along with me. This way any time a doubt nags me, having a look at the piece of paper will suffice being reassured. A stroke of genius, in a sense, don't you agree?

Therapist: Well, in a way ... but did it work?

Marta: At first, yes, really, I thought that I had made it, that I had cracked the checks' problem.

Therapist: And why do you say "at first"?

Marta: Because the first times it worked exceedingly well, but then I started hoarding hundreds of paper' slips, and I was often assailed by the doubt of having checked the wrong piece of paper ... so I decided to mark down also the date, the correct time, and then the type of check: front door, gas tap, air conditioning, car door, medicine cabinet, and so forth ... an endless list! Believe me, it was sheer madness ... and it was so time-consuming! It had become a sort of job. I was so scrupulous in marking down my checks that I ended up forgetting the "real" check, then I was assailed by the doubt of having performed it badly, and at that point my notes were pointless: I had to check another time, or ask my husband for reassurance, and then write again the result of my check. I felt I was going crazy. It was a maze with no way out. Don't you think so?

Therapist: Precisely so. Sometimes your husband will answer hastily to your requests, or he will tell white lies to calm you down, but other times he will debate with you for a long time, trying to prove that your fears are ungrounded. And in other circumstances he will agree to help you in your checks or he will give you advice on how to dispel your doubt. At least initially some of these maneuvers seem to work, but sooner or later anxiety and need for reassurance will appear again. Isn't that so?

Marta: I'm afraid so.

Therapist: And what does this suggest to you?

— a few seconds' pause —

Marta: I wouldn't know; my head's a bit fuzzy. But now I'm inclined to believe that I took the wrong way. Actually, I'm in a catch-22. Yeah, maybe I need to do something different if I want to get rid of my obsessive problem.

7.4.5 Drawing Out the Disadvantages of Reassurance Attempts

The second ingredient to take into account in order for the patient to give up reassurance attempts and other safety-seeking behaviors is the inconvenience of such behaviors. The patient should consider not only how ineffective they are, but also how disadvantageous they are due to their costs.

For an exposition, we shall illustrate the continuation of the therapist–patient dialogue set up in the previous section, but it must be noted that the adopted communicative style and its objectives can be transposed and applied to the majority of anxiety disorders.

Therapist: It seems, actually, that searching for reassurance at any cost hasn't proven effective.

Marta: Hmm … no.

Therapist: Well, I wonder whether besides being ineffective, your requests for reassurance have also led to other consequences.

Marta: What do you mean by that?

Therapist: You know, I was thinking to what you said before: "a maze with no way out"…

Marta: Yes, exactly, but I don't quite follow.

Therapist: Okay, I'll try to retrace the sequence of what happens to you when you're anxious; tell me if it makes sense to you.

Marta: Okay.

Therapist: Everything starts off with a state of anxiety, a worry, for instance, the doubt of not having shut off the gas.

Marta: Yes.

Therapist: And by that point you try to reassure yourself alone or with the help of your husband, and those attempts don't work at all, or only temporarily.

Marta: I'm afraid so.

Therapist: So the anxiety won't completely vanish and sooner or later the need for reassurance will forcefully come back.

Marta: Right!

Therapist: But that's nowhere near enough, because the more you exert yourselves to solve the problem, the more the plot thickens, as in the case of the tip your husband gave you to mark down the result of your check on a piece of paper. Well, it's as if you and he had been caught in a snare, in a maze with no way out, and the more you try to escape, the more you get stuck. … Is that so?

Marta: Just so!

Therapist: Well, and what does this suggest to you?

— a few seconds' pause —

Marta: That sometimes I shoot myself in the foot . . . that in the long run asking for reassurance isn't only ineffective, but is nothing short of harmful. . . .

Therapist: That is the case.

Marta: Yeah . . .

Therapist: Do you think there are other negative effects of the requests for reassurance?

Marta: Well, actually we sometimes end up by fighting, because he loses his temper. . . . I can understand him: He's not a saint. When he gets angry, he tells me I'll pass my anxieties to our children. . . . You know, I think my ongoing requests for reassurance are wearing our marriage out and could damage my children. I'm paying a very high price for my obsessions.

Therapist: I see . . . and how do you feel when your husband reproaches you?

Marta: Terribly guilty. I believe he's right.

Therapist: And how does this affect your urge to check?

Marta: It wouldn't decrease it . . . far from it! Even though I try my hardest to restrain myself.

Therapist: I see.

Marta: And on top of it all, the arguments, the checks are dreadfully tiring and time-consuming. . . . Some days I'm exhausted and I realize I've wasted hour after hour of my husband's and my time.

Therapist: Yeah, it actually seems that the requests for reassurance are not only ineffective, but even come at a very high price.

Marta: Yes, horrific.

Therapist: To such a degree that you want to try to give them up?

Marta: I don't know, but I'd like to have a try, even though I'm afraid to fail. Can you help me with this?

Therapist: Yes, if you like, I'll help you to find other solutions.

7.4.6   Legitimizing the Relinquishment of Reassurance Attempts

Most patients believe that giving up their attempts at reassurance isn't only dangerous, but also illegitimate. In other words, they think they are not entitled to lower their guard and accept the consequences that might stem from a less "safe" behavior.

Marta, for instance, could regard it as her duty to reiterate the requests for reassurance, even after having realized and seen for herself how ineffective they are.

Gianni could think himself not entitled to get stage fright, and for this reason reiterate avoidant behaviors and requests for advice on how to conceal his anxiety, even after having realized that those behaviors are worsening his disorder.

Valeria could believe that if she stopped worrying continuously about her son, this would mean failing in her duty as a mother, even after having realized that her worries and requests can't really safeguard him against risks, and on top of that they imply a great many disadvantages.

To sum up, many patients don't only value the practical effects of their safety-seeking behaviors, but also attach much importance to the moral principle that, in their mind, prescribes these behaviors.

That's why it is important not to content oneself with drawing out the practical ineffectiveness and disadvantages of the requests for reassurance, but to carefully explore to what extent patients consider it morally legitimate to give them up.

The task of making their sense of responsibility more flexible will be particularly hard, especially with individuals who are particularly scrupulous, such as patients affected by OCD, Hypochondriasis, and GAD, as any experienced psychotherapist knows only too well.

Nevertheless, it is possible to foster the relinquishment of the requests for reassurance by taking at least two paths: The first one consists of drawing out, without blaming the patient, that rigidly sticking to a principle can make it impossible for him or her to follow other equally important principles, such as protecting one's marriage or the emotional well-being of one's children; the second one consists of helping the patient to realize that making one's safety criteria more flexible doesn't mean becoming a "base person," but simply accepting the risk of being somehow responsible for a negative event, like everybody else (Freeston et al. 1996; van Oppen and Arntz 1994; Mancini and Barcaccia 2004).

Marta: You know, I've figured out at last that continuously asking for reassurance has proven to be fruitless and even self-defeating, but I just can't help it.

Therapist: Can you tell me what you mean by that?

Marta: On those occasions I feel I really have to behave like that, I feel bound to. . .

Therapist: Bound?

Marta: Yes, if I didn't do everything in my power to make sure there are no risks, I'd feel irresponsible.

Therapist: Even though this attitude proves itself to be ineffective and detrimental?

Marta: Just so. I have to do my duty, and check. Should anything serious happen despite my checks, it would be bad, but at least I wouldn't reproach myself for not having given a hang about it.

Therapist: It seems that the object of the requests for reassurance and of the other safety-seeking behaviors isn't just preventing harm, but doing the done thing, regardless of its usefulness . . . a matter of principle, isn't that so?

Marta: I should think so . . . a matter of principle.

Therapist: And how would you feel if you failed in this principle?

Marta: Hmm . . . irresponsible. Like a very bad mother.

Therapist: I see.

Marta: Yeah, like a very bad person indeed.

Therapist: Marta, we were reflecting before upon the disadvantages arising from giving in to the need for reassurance, don't you remember?

Marta: Yes, I do.

Therapist: Does any of them pain you more than the others?

Marta: Yes . . . ruining my children's lives because of my obsessions.

— a few seconds' pause —

Marta: I have it! Now I know what you're trying to tell me.

Therapist: What do you think I'm trying to tell you?

Marta: That when I give in to the need for reassurance, I do already act like a bad person. ... Now I realize it. Do you think I'm a bad mother?

Therapist: To be honest, Marta, I don't think in the least that you're a bad mother. I do believe the reverse is true: You're a very scrupulous mother and you find yourself right in the middle of a paradox. The trouble is that by adhering all-out to your sense of responsibility, you inevitably end up unwittingly producing some harmful consequences for you and your dear ones.

— a few seconds' pause —

Marta: I should be a little less rigid ... not look for certainty at any cost of having done things perfectly ... but how do you do it? You see, I never know how it 'should' be, when it is good enough, when checking is normal and when it's pathological. It's as if I can't discriminate normal behaviors from obsessive ones. It's as if I mistrusted my own perceptions and judgment. I sometimes fear I might be suffering from a neurological condition that prevents me from discriminating.

Therapist: Marta, do you think you can discriminate between a person behaving responsibly and an irresponsible one?

Marta: Hmm ... yeah, I guess so.

Therapist: Can you think of anyone whom you believe a responsible person?

Marta: Yes, Giulia, a colleague of mine.

Therapist: Well, since Giulia is a responsible person, I suppose she too checks, sometimes.

Marta: Yes, of course.

Therapist: And Marta, can you tell me if Giulia's checks are either useful and necessary or obsessive?

Marta: Hmm ... let me think about it ... I believe she's very reliable and responsible, but I wouldn't say she's obsessive. No, I don't think she checks in an obsessive way.

Therapist: Responsible, but not obsessive ... an interesting discrimination. Doesn't this ring a bell?

Marta: Well, maybe I don't lack judgment ... at least regarding other people. ... Why on earth when it comes to me do I always feel uncertain?

Therapist: Well, do you remember when you had your last obsessive doubt?

Marta: A doubt crossed my mind while I was coming here, that I hadn't set the burglar alarm in my house, so I called my husband to ask for reassurance.

Therapist: Could you then tell if it was a necessary request or an obsessive one?

Marta: I wondered, but I couldn't tell, I remained in doubt, and being torn by it, I chose to call my husband.

Therapist: And how did you feel at that moment?

Marta: Anxious!

Therapist: And what did you exactly worry about at that moment?
Marta: Of having left my house exposed to burglars!
Therapist: And what if the burglar alarm had really been switched off, and the burglars had got in?
Marta: It would have been an unforgivable carelessness. . . . I would have never have forgiven myself!
Therapist: And what if this had happened to Giulia, what if Giulia had forgotten to set the burglar alarm? Would have you forgiven her? Would have you considered her mistake an unforgivable one?
Marta: Are you asking me if I would have considered it equally serious?
Therapist: Precisely so. Would have you considered it equally serious?
Marta: No, I'd say no.
Therapist: And what does this suggest to you?
Marta: Maybe I come down more heavily on myself . . . That's why I never know how many times I should check, when it's good enough.
Therapist: Yeah.
Marta: Maybe I have the right to stop checking even if I'm not 100% certain about it. . . .

7.5 Conclusions

To sum up, in this chapter we have presented some of the most frequent interpersonal vicious cycles that occur in anxiety disorders and which largely account for the anxiety symptomatology's maintenance and exacerbation.

It is common knowledge among psychotherapists that when a patient is in the grip of anxiety, he or she tends to consult other people in search of reassurance. Thus, some typical communicative cycles start up, very similar in form, content, and effects to the internal pathogenic dialogue that anxious individuals generate within themselves in an attempt to calm down. All this will result in more symptoms and more misery, for both the patient and his or her interlocutor.

This is the reason why it is very important, in order to treat any anxiety disorder, to detect these typical vicious cycles and figure out strategies to defuse them. And from our perspective, the acceptance of the possibility that the feared event might unfortunately occur, despite all of one's efforts, is the winning frame of reference in any form of psychotherapy.

References

American Psychiatric Association. (2000). *Diagnostic and statistical manual of mental disorders* (4, TRth ed.). Washington, DC: Author.
Arntz, A., Voncken, M., & Goosen, A. C. A. (2007). Responsibility and obsessive-compulsive disorder: An experimental test. *Behaviour Research and Therapy, 45*(3), 425–435.

Bach, P. A., & Moran, D. J. (2008). *ACT in practice: Case conceptualization in acceptance & commitment therapy*. Oakland, CA: New Harbinger.

Barcaccia, B. (2007). Aderire all'evento: attualità della proposta stoica di Seneca. *Dissertation in Philosophy*, University Roma Tre. "unpublished manuscript"

Barcaccia, B. (2008). *Accepting limitations of life: Leading our patients through a painful but healing path*. Invited lecture, June 10, 2008, Leopoldstr. 13 80802 München Department Psychologie, Ludwig-Maximilians Universität, Munich.

Freeston, M. H., Rhéaume, J., & Ladouceur, R. (1996). Correcting faulty appraisals of obsessional thoughts. *Behaviour Research and Therapy, 34*, 433–446.

Gangemi, A., Mancini, F., & van den Hout, M. (2007). Feeling guilty as a source of information about threat and performance. *Behaviour Research and Therapy, 45*(10), 2387–2396.

Hayes, S. C., Luoma, J. B., Bond, F. W., Masuda, A., & Lillis, J. (2006). Acceptance and commitment therapy: Model, processes and outcomes. *Behaviour Research and Therapy, 44*(1), 1–25.

Ladouceur, R., Rheaume, J., & Aublet, F. (1997). Excessive responsibility in obsessional concerns: A fine-grained experimental analysis. *Behaviour Research and Therapy, 35*, 423–427.

Lopatka, C., & Rachman, S. (1995). Perceived responsibility and compulsive checking: An experimental analysis. *Behaviour Research and Therapy, 33*, 673–684.

Mancini, F. (1998). La mente ipocondriaca e i suoi paradossi [In Italian]. *Sistemi Intelligenti, X*, 85–98.

Mancini, F. (2001). Un modello cognitivo del disturbo ossessivo-compulsivo [In Italian]. *Psicoterapia, 22–23*, 43–60.

Mancini, F. (2005). Il disturbo ossessivo-compulsivo [In Italian]. In B. Bara (Ed.), *Manuale di psicoterapia cognitiva*. Torino: Bollati Boringhieri.

Mancini, F. & Barcaccia, B. (2004). *The importance of acceptance in obsessive-compulsive disorder*. Presentazione all'Università Ludwig-Maximilians di Monaco di Baviera, 24 giugno 2004.

Mancini, F., D'Olimpio, F., & Cieri, L. (2004). Manipulation of responsibility in nonclinical subjects: Does expectations of failure exacerbate obsessive-compulsive behaviours? *Behaviour Research and Therapy, 42*, 449–457.

Mancini, F., & Gangemi, A. (2004). Fear of guilt from behaving irresponsibly in obsessive–compulsive disorder. *Journal of Behavior Therapy and Experimental Psychiatry, 35*, 109–120.

Mancini, F., & Gangemi, A. (2006). The role of responsibility and fear of guilt in hypothesis-testing. *Journal of Behavior Therapy and Experimental Psychiatry, 37*(4), 333–346.

Mancini, F., & Gragnani, A. (2005). L'esposizione con prevenzione della risposta come pratica dell'accettazione [In Italian]. *Cognitivismo Clinico, 2*(1), 38–58.

Merlo, L. J., Lehmkuhl, H. D., Geffken, G. R., & Storch, E. A. (2009). Decreased family accommodation associated with improved therapy outcome in pediatric obsessive-compulsive disorder. *Journal of Consulting and Clinical Psychology, 77*, 355–360.

Saliani A. M., Barcaccia B., Capo R., Cieri L., Cosentino T., Gangemi A., Gragnani A., Perdighe C., Rainone A., Romano G., Mancini F. (2008). *The role of interpersonal cycles in the treatment of OCD*. 6th World Congress of Cognitive Psychotherapy, June 19–22, 2008, Rome.

Saliani A. M., Barcaccia B. & Mancini F. (2009). *La formulazione dei circoli viziosi individuali e dei cicli dialogici di mantenimento come intervento specifico di psicoeducazione nel trattamento del disturbo ossessivo-compulsivo*, 13° Congresso nazionale della Società Italiana di Psicopatologia (SOPSI), Roma, Park Hotel Marriott, 10–14 febbraio 2009.

Saliani A. M., e Barcaccia B. (2009). *Interpersonal cycles in the treatment of OCD: Empirical data and indications for treatment*. 39° Congresso EABCT, September 16–19, 2009, Dubrovnik.

Salkovskis, P. M. (1996). The cognitive approach to anxiety: Threat beliefs, safety-seeking behavior and the special case of health anxiety and obsession. In P. M. Salkovskis (Ed.), *Frontiers of cognitive therapy* (pp. 48–74). New York: Guilford Press.

Salkovskis, P., Shafran, R., Rachman, S., & Freeston, M. H. (1999). Multiple pathways to inflated responsibility beliefs in obsessional problems: Possible origins and implications for therapy and research. *Behaviour Research and Therapy, 37*(11), 1055–1072.

Salkovskis, P. M., & Warwick, H. M. C. (1986). Morbid preoccupations, health anxiety and reassurance: A cognitive–behavioural approach to hypochondriasis. *Behaviour Research and Therapy, 24*, 597–602.

Salkovskis, P. M., Warwick, H. M. C., & Deale, A. C. (2003). Cognitive-behavioral treatment for severe and persistent health anxiety (hypochondriasis). *Brief Treatment and Crisis Intervention, 3*, 353–367.

Van Noppen, B., & Steketee, G. (2008). Testing a conceptual model of patient and family predictors of obsessive compulsive disorder (OCD) symptoms. *Behaviour Research and Therapy, 47*(1), 18–25.

Van Oppen, P., & Arntz, A. (1994). Cognitive therapy for obsessive-compulsive disorder. *Behaviour Research and Therapy, 32*, 79–87.

Warwick, H. (2004). Treatment of health anxiety. *Psychiatry, 3*(6), 80–83.

Warwick, H. (2007). Psychopathology and treatment of severe health anxiety. *Psychiatry, 6*, 240–246.

Wells, A. (1997). *Cognitive therapy of anxiety disorders: A practice manual and conceptual guide.* New York: Wiley.

Zhong, C. B., & Liljenquist, K. (2006). Washing away your sins: Threatened morality and physical cleaning. *Science, 313*, 1451–1452.

Chapter 8
Cognitive-Behavioral Family Interventions in Psychosis

Juliana Onwumere and Elizabeth Kuipers

8.1 Introduction

Neurobiological models of psychosis (Garety et al. 2007) alongside cognitive models of caregiving (Kuipers et al. 2010) postulate a key role for families in a patient's environment. Families can help us to extend our understanding of psychosis and patient outcomes. Given the complexity of psychosis, illness-related difficulties such as disorders of thought and apathy can often interrupt and adversely affect normal patterns of communication between family members. In turn, this may have a negative impact on relationships. Thus, developing optimal communication styles between family members remains an important consideration for service providers.

This chapter reviews the relationship between families and psychosis and examines the contribution of cognitive-behavioral family interventions, particularly as they relate to addressing communication difficulties that can arise in families.

8.2 Background

The burden linked to schizophrenia spectrum illnesses is well documented (Rossler et al. 2005). People with psychosis experience high levels of economic, social, and physical disadvantage (Morgan et al. 2008). Individuals with schizophrenia are at greater risk of being the victims of violent crime, including homicide, compared to those in the general population (Brekke et al. 2001; Schomerus et al. 2008). Mortality rates in this group are significantly higher compared to levels recorded within the general population (Surgeon General Report 1999; World Health Organization 2001). Likewise, suicide and suicidal ideation are elevated (Fialko et al. 2006;

J. Onwumere (✉)
Department of Psychology, King's College London, Institute of Psychiatry,
Henry Wellcome Building, De Crespigny Park, London SE5 8AF, UK
e-mail: juliana.1.onwumere@kcl.ac.uk

M. Rimondini (ed.), *Communication in Cognitive Behavioral Therapy*,
DOI 10.1007/978-1-4419-6807-4_8, © Springer Science+Business Media, LLC 2011

Nordentoft et al. 2002). In addition, higher rates of poor physical health in general (Osborn et al. 2007) and of co-morbid chronic medical disorders, including HIV and stroke, are recorded in psychosis populations (Chwastiak et al. 2006; Stoskopf et al. 2001; Lin et al. 2008).

Over the last 50 years, a program of deinstitutionalization in many western countries has led to a shift in the organization of care for service users with psychosis. Informal carers are increasingly acknowledged by service users and mental health staff to play a central role in patient care and supporting their recovery. The social networks of service users can be small, but many maintain close regular contact with their families, particularly during the earlier course of the illness (Berry et al. 2007; Fisher et al. 2008). Service users are known to obtain better outcomes when they have carers. Recent evidence, for example, indicates that service users with carers exhibit greater long-term gains from psychological therapy compared to those without (Garety et al. 2008). Carers also play a key role in facilitating service users' engagement with pharmacological treatments (Garcia et al. 2006), and identifying and responding to early signs of crisis or relapse (Bergner et al. 2008). Overall, caregivers of those with psychosis are mainly female and the parents of service users, although a sizable proportion are partners or children (Grandon et al. 2008).

8.3   The Physical and Psychological Implications of Caregiving

The caregiving role has significant implications for the health status of carers. Approximately 50 years of research confirm that caregiving can have a negative impact on a carer's psychological and physical well-being (Kuipers and Bebbington 2005; Awad and Voruganti 2008). Carers report poor physical health, including sleep difficulties (Schulz and Beach 1999; Phillips et al. 2009). The negative impact of psychosis on carers is commonly described as carer burden. Traditionally, carer burden has been measured along two dimensions: objective and subjective burden. Objective burden provides a measure of the tangible and observable effects of the patient's mental health problems on the family, such as disrupted domestic routines. In contrast, subjective burden reflects the carers' negative appraisal of their experiences and circumstances. Negative appraisals include feelings such as loss, shame, and anger (Jungbauer et al. 2003; Lauber et al. 2003). Carer burden is a universal phenomenon and has been documented in carers from diverse regions, including the Middle East, Asia, Europe, Africa, and America (Ostman and Hansson 2004; Ukpong 2006; Grandon et al. 2008; Karanci and Inandilar 2002; Tang et al. 2008). It has also been reported in different types of carers such as spouses and siblings (Friedrich et al. 2008; Jungbauer and Angermeyer 2002).

Significantly higher rates of carer distress and mood disturbance are found in carers (Singleton et al. 2002), and levels of distress vary over the course of the illness and can extend beyond the end of the caregiving relationship (Brown and Birtwistle 1998). Higher levels have been found among carers of recent-onset patients and those recently admitted to the hospital (Martens and Addington 2001; Boye and Malt 2002).

Psychosis is a stigmatized condition where many carers, similarly to the patients they care for, report feelings of social isolation and stigma (Kuipers and Raune 2000; Lee and Gramotnev 2007). It is not uncommon for carers to have found themselves victims of verbal and physical violence from patients (Kjellin and Ostman 2005; Vaddadi et al. 2002). Moreover, recent evidence suggests as many as one third of carers of patients with psychosis meet criteria for posttraumatic stress (Barton and Jackson 2008). Carers will often take on their new role with little warning or choice, and in the absence of specialist mental health knowledge and skills. Caregiving duties will often be subsumed into existing duties and roles, which is likely to have a negative impact on their time and well-being. Dual caregiving roles are increasingly common among mental health caregivers. The illness course in psychosis, and the inability of treatments, including pharmacology, to provide a "cure," ensures that carers are often faced with a patient's residual symptoms and will experience the stress of patients going through episodes of relapse (Karp and Tanarugsachock 2000).

8.4 The Relationship Between Carer Burden and Patient Functioning

There has been continued interest in exploring the links between carer burden and patient clinical characteristics. Researchers are keen to determine whether specific patient symptoms and profiles are linked to carer burden and distress. Thus far, these findings remain inconclusive. Negative symptoms (e.g., social withdrawal) have been directly associated with levels of carer burden and distress (Dyck et al. 1999; Ukpong 2006). Likewise, positive symptoms (e.g., auditory verbal hallucinations) have been linked with significantly higher rates of carer distress and burden (Wolthaus et al. 2002). Some studies have also reported links with positive and negative symptoms (Addington et al. 2003). It does appear, however, that carer burden tends to be associated with patient difficulties that are not readily perceived as being directly linked to symptoms or illness. Thus, carers are more inclined to report higher levels of distress and burden when patients exhibit difficult disruptive behaviors and when they have marked impairments in their social and role functioning. Moller-Leimkuhler and Obermeier (2008), as part of a two-year follow-up of patients admitted for their first time, reported significant reductions in carer burden were associated with improvements in the psychosocial functioning of patients.

8.4.1 Carer Burden and Coping Styles

The coping literature has drawn distinctions between "emotion-" and "problem-" focused coping (Folkman and Lazarus 1980). Emotion-focused coping reflects behavior designed to diminish the negative emotional impact of the stressor using strategies such as avoidance and denial. Problem-focused coping describes the direct action an individual adopts to change the situation, such as seeking social support and problem solving.

Negative caregiving experiences in terms of burden and distress have also been closely linked with their style of coping. Although carers are known to employ a broad range of coping strategies (e.g., ignoring, coercion, humor, acceptance) (Birchwood and Cochrane 1990), there is consistent evidence that attests to a positive relationship between negative caregiving experiences and emotion-focused avoidant coping styles. For example, Scazufca and Kuipers (1999) reported that higher rates of carer burden were observed in the period prior to and post inpatient admission for carers who used more avoidant styles of coping. Magliano et al. (2000) investigated 159 caregivers of patients with psychosis who were recruited from five European countries. During a 12-month follow-up, carers who employed less emotion-focused coping strategies (e.g., avoidance of patient) and had higher levels of practical support from their social network also recorded lower levels of objective and subjective burden.

8.5 Expressed Emotion and Families with Psychosis

The caregiving environment and the relationship between psychosis and carers have been traditionally studied through the expressed emotion (EE) concept. EE has been defined in many ways and is said to reflect a carer's evaluation of his or her relationship quality with the patient (Scazufca and Kuipers 1996). Studies of EE date back to the late 1950s and the seminal work of George Brown and colleagues, who investigated outcomes of patients with psychosis following community discharge (e.g., Brown 1959; Brown et al. 1958, 1962, 1972). The main findings from their series of studies indicated higher levels of relapse and readmissions for those patients who returned to live with parents or spouses or in large hostels (Brown 1959; Brown et al. 1958). There were also higher levels of relapse for patients who returned to households with carers with "high emotional involvement" rather than "low emotional involvement." The results showed that relapse rates were independently predicted by high levels of carer emotional involvement. It was during their later studies that the term "EE" was coined and the specific dimensions developed (Brown et al. 1972).

EE is measured across five separate subscales. *Criticism* refers to unfavorable remarks about the patient's behavior or personality. *Hostility* reflects extreme aspects of criticism that are often communicated as a rejecting remark or global negative expression about the patient. *Emotional overinvolvement* (*EOI*) reflects a range of carer behaviors, including overprotection and self-sacrifice. *Positive remarks* are unambiguous positive statements about the patient's personality, skills, and attributes. *Warmth* reflects carer expressions of empathy, sympathy, and concern toward the patient. Ratings of EE are based on both the content and prosodic aspects of speech; thus, tone and emphasis are important. Of the five subscales, criticism, hostility, and EOI are the only ones found to be predictive of patient outcomes (Bebbington and Kuipers 1994; Butzlaff and Hooley 1998) and critical comments are the most predictive of the three (e.g., "It really irritates me how we can never have friends around without Sarah talking to those voices"). Carers can obtain a high EE rating when they have scored above-threshold levels of criticism and/or hostility and/or EOI.

Investigations of patterns of language and communication have a long history in psychosis and as part of studies on EE (Goldstein and Strachan 1987; Strachan et al. 1986). Individuals with psychosis are known to exhibit higher levels of referential-type communication disturbances (e.g., where the speaker generates unclear communication that comprises vague, ambiguous, missing, and idiosyncratic referents) when compared to control groups, including their nonaffected parents, siblings, and offspring (Docherty et al. 1996, 1998a, 2004; Harvey et al. 1982). Communication difficulties appear to be more evident in response to emotionally negative versus positive material (Docherty and Herbert 1997; Docherty et al. 1998b) and is argued to indicate a genetic vulnerability to developing a schizophrenia spectrum disorder (Docherty et al. 2004; Subotnik et al. 2002).

Ratings of expressed emotion are reported to reflect the "usual" communication and behavior of caregivers toward individuals with psychosis in the home environment, particularly with regard to critical comments (Miklowitz et al. 1984). Overall, the evidence suggests that high-EE caregivers tend to display poorer communication patterns with individuals with psychosis; they are more likely to talk more, talk in a more rigid fashion, and are less effective listeners [Kuipers et al. 1983 (E. Kuipers published as L. Kuipers until 1996); Wuerker et al. 2001]. High-EE (criticism) caregivers are also known to have difficulties with conveying their thoughts in a clear, supportive, and coherent manner (Kymalainen et al. 2006). In contrast, low-EE carers appear more comfortable in and adept at taking a step back and being silent; a style that lends itself to being a good listener (Berkowitz et al. 1981). There is a tendency for high-EE caregivers to find themselves entangled in a sequence of negative interactions with individuals with psychosis, unlike their low-EE counterparts, who are more likely to withdraw from difficult situations with patients *before* they escalate or are able to defuse them (Rosenfarb et al. 1995; Simoneau et al. 1998). Results from a novel study of adults with a history of unipolar depression in remission and healthy controls undergoing brain scans while negative comments from their mothers were relayed via audiotape indicated an increase in negative mood and failure to activate the dorsolateral prefrontal cortex (DLPFC) after hearing negative comments (Hooley et al. 2005, 2009). Interestingly, activation of the DLPFC is associated with effective antidepressant treatments (Kennedy et al. 2001).

Further studies from health psychology have also highlighted that impact of negative communication between family members on patient and family functioning. Kiecolt-Glaser et al. (2005) examined approximately 40 healthy married couples who, as part of the study procedure, were purposely admitted to a hospital unit for two 24-hour periods. On each admission (as part of the study) couples were administered a blister wound and subsequently asked to complete an interaction task. The first task required participants to engage in a positive and supportive discussion. In contrast, the second task asked couples to discuss a marital disagreement. Overall, the results confirmed slower and incomplete wound healing following a marital conflict task, when compared to the pattern of healing following the supportive and positive interaction task. It appears that promoting constructivecommunication and positive interactions between family members may have a role to play in adaptive functioning.

Many researchers have examined the relationship between EE and carer factors, particularly carer attributions about the patient's illness and difficulties. The evidence suggests that high-EE (critical and/or hostile) compared to low-EE/EOI carers tend to perceive patients as having greater control for their symptoms and link the illness to factors internal and specific to the patient (e.g., their personality) (Barrowclough and Hooley 2003; Barrowclough et al. 1994; Hooley and Campbell 2002; McNab et al. 2007). Carers are more likely to make these attributions for negative symptoms rather than positive symptoms (Harrison and Dadds 1992; Weisman and Lopez 1997). In contrast, high EOI has been associated with attributions to factors that are external, uncontrollable, and universal (Barrowclough et al. 1994; Yang et al. 2004). However, the finding that high-EOI and low-EE attributions were not distinguishable has been disproved recently by a study that looked at positive attributions (Grice et al. 2009).

More recently, attention has also been given to a broader range of illness beliefs in addition to those of causality and controllability (Barrowclough et al. 2001; Kuipers et al. 2007). For example, Lobban et al. (2005) reported that higher levels of carer criticism were associated with caregivers perceiving more negative consequences of psychosis for themselves. Finally, it is important to note that high carer EE has been positively linked with less adaptive (avoidant) coping and higher levels of burden (Raune et al. 2004; Shimodera et al. 2000).

EE continues to remain of interest to clinicians and researchers due to its ability to predict patient outcomes. High carer EE is a significant predictor of patient relapse (Bebbington and Kuipers 1994). In one of their earlier studies, Brown and colleagues recorded a 58% relapse rate in patients with psychosis living with a high-EE relative compared to only 16% for patients with low-EE carers (Brown et al. 1972). Similar findings have been reported. Bebbington and Kuipers (1994) undertook an aggregate analysis of actual data and published results from 25 worldwide EE outcome studies. Based on data from 1,346 cases, the authors observed a 50.1% relapse rate for patients living in high-EE households compared to 21.1% for patients in low-EE households. The results were not significantly affected by the location of the sample or by patient gender. Likewise, the links between high EE and poor patient outcomes remained irrespective of whether patients received regular medication or not. Interestingly, the authors observed that while high levels of face-to-face contact between high-EE carers and patients increased the risk of relapse, high levels of contact with a low-EE carer were protective. Similar predictive links between high EE and patient relapse were reported by Butzlaff and Hooley (1998) as part of their meta-analyses of 27 EE–outcome studies. Overall, the authors observed levels of relapse in high-EE households of 65% compared to 35% in the low-EE group. The predictive relationship was stronger for patients with a longer duration of illness, whereas the findings from patients during the early course of the illness were equivocal (Butzlaff and Hooley 1998).

Although contrary results have been reported (Kopelowicz et al. 2002; Lopez et al. 2004), the predictive link between high EE and poorer patient outcomes has been reported in diverse cultural groups (Kopelowicz et al. 2006; Marom et al. 2002). Bebbington and Kuipers (1994) reported that stronger links exist between high EE and poor patient outcomes in North America and Southern and Northern Europe. The predictive links between high EE and poor patient outcomes have also been observed in a range of mental health conditions, including depression (Hooley et al. 1986), borderline personality disorder (Hooley and Hoffman 1999), posttraumatic stress disorder (Barrowclough et al. 2008), and autism (Greenberg et al. 2006).

In any discussion of EE, it is important to note the contribution of the warmth subscale. Although it has received significantly less attention, Brown and colleagues recognized the importance of carer warmth in patient outcomes (Brown et al. 1972). Their results suggested that higher levels of warmth, in the absence of criticism, hostility, and emotional overinvolvement, were associated with lower relapse rates (Brown et al. 1972). As part of their review of EE studies, Bebbington and Kuipers (1994) observed that carer warmth and positive comments predicted good patient outcomes. Bertrando et al. (1992) recorded significantly fewer readmissions among individuals with psychosis from "high-warmth" compared to "low-warmth" households. Carer warmth appears to provide protection against relapse; however, this may not apply equally to all cultural groups (Lopez et al. 2004).

8.6 Patient Appraisals of Caregiving Relationships

In recognition of the relational aspect of caregiving relationships, the literature has witnessed a growing number of studies investigating patients' appraisal of their carer's attitude toward them and how this overlaps with the carers' reported attitudes (Cutting et al. 2006). Scazufca et al. (2001) observed a significant relationship between caregiver EE status and a patient's perception of caregiver criticism at admission; patients from high-EE households perceived higher levels of caregiver criticism than low-EE patients. A patient's perception of caregiver criticism was not associated with his or her symptom severity. Onwumere et al. (2009) examined recently relapsed patients with psychosis and found that patient perceptions of carer criticism were positively linked with carer ratings of criticism, hostility, and high EE. These links were not explained by the patient's mood or symptoms of psychosis. Further, a patient's negative perception of his or her carer was significantly predicted by carer high EE.

Patient outcomes can also be influenced by their perceptions of carer attitudes (Lebell et al. 1993). Tompson et al. (1995) observed that perceived carer criticism, particularly in black and minority ethnic groups, rather than carer EE, predicted relapse over a 12-month follow-up in patients with psychosis. It is the view of some researchers that patients' perceptions of their caregivers' attitudes provides unique information about the caregiving relationship (Bachmann et al. 2006) and might reflect how much high-EE behavior is "getting through" to patients (Hooley and Teasdale 1989).

The links between patient outcome and carer functioning have meant that EE has played an instrumental role in the development of cognitive-behavioral family treatments in psychosis.

8.7 Cognitive-Behavioral Family Interventions with Patients with Psychosis and Their Families

As part of a long history of research dating back 30 years and with more than 40 clinical trials, there are robust findings that confirm cognitive-behaviorally based family interventions, when delivered as an adjunct to medication, are efficacious in significantly reducing relapse rates and levels of high EE and carer burden. Their positive impact on improving social functioning in patients and adherence with medications are also well documented (Pilling et al. 2002; Pharoah et al. 2006; Pfammatter et al. 2006; Stam and Cuijpers 2001). Family interventions can provide a cost-effective alternative to inpatient admission (Falloon 2003). The UK evidence-based treatment guidelines for schizophrenia continue to recommend family interventions for patients with carers (National Institute for Clinical Excellence updated guidelines 2009). Similar recommendations are observed in the United States (American Psychiatric Association 2006) and in the PORT study (Lehman et al. 2004). There is also strong evidence to support the effectiveness of family interventions in routine services (Barrowclough et al. 1999; Magliano et al. 2006).

There are a small number of evidence-based manuals for family interventions (e.g., Barrowclough and Tarrier 1992; Falloon et al. 1984; Kuipers et al. 2002; McFarlane et al. 1995). Over the years, these have developed to suit the needs and clinical presentation of a broad range of families. For example, there are manuals suited to the needs of families during early illness phases (Addington and Burnett 2004) and for families seen in large groups (McFarlane 2002). Although there are some differences between the manuals, for example, whether patients are routinely included in sessions or whether sessions are offered in the family home, the manuals continue to share a number of core features. Overall, interventions are designed to minimize the risk of patient relapse and reduce the negative sequelae of the illness on family members. Further, they are focused on current problems and difficulties.

Key therapeutic activities of family interventions advocate information sharing (psychoeducation) as a first step, in order to help change unhelpful carer attributions such as blaming the patient for poor social functioning. For example, some of the primary objectives of the intervention will be met, initially, through active and focused attempts by the therapists to facilitate the carer's understanding about psychosis, and to be able to discuss distressing experiences reported by the patient with the family. This work is mainly achieved through information sharing with the whole family, eliciting and exploring meanings, and helping carers to reappraise their beliefs about the illness (see also Chapter 4 on information-sharing skills).

Facilitating positive and constructive communication between family members and positive interactions also forms an essential feature of the intervention for families and can improve warmth (e.g., Kuipers et al. 2002). In FI sessions, three main communication strategies are usually prioritized. First, family members are asked to talk *directly* to each other rather than *about* one another. This helps to diminish the use of negative and critical comments between family members. Clinical experience suggests that it is easier to make negative comments when you are referring to someone in the second or third person (e.g., "He is lazy"; "She does not try at all"; "She is messy") compared to speaking directly to the person. Further, we also know that referring to patients in the second person, particularly when reporting negative comments, can, for some patients, mirror the experience of auditory verbal hallucinations. Thus, direct speech requires that family members display greater thought and sensitivity both to *what* they say and to *how* they say it. Second, within sessions the therapists seek to ensure that only *one* family member talks at any given time. This strategy helps to control the session and ensure that the therapists and each family member are able to hear what is being said, and do not miss important information. Third, given the impact that psychosis can often have on patient communication styles (e.g., poverty of speech), the final guideline proposes that each family member be given *equal* talking time within the session. This prevents the session from being dominated by any one member, but it also allows *all* members to feel they have something important to contribute while encouraging listening skills. It is the role of the FI therapists to ensure that family members remain aware of, and make continued attempts to adhere to, the communication guidelines. Further, FI therapists are also expected to take a lead role in modeling optimal communication to family members (Kuipers et al. 2002). Anecdotal evidence suggests that promoting optimal styles of communication usually continues throughout the course of the intervention. Additional key features of the evidence-based manuals include problem solving, relapse prevention, and emotional processing (Kuipers et al. 2007). Improved communication between family members can obviate difficulties associated with implementing other areas of the intervention, such as emotional processing.

Despite the strong evidence base of family interventions, their successful application in routine settings, and national treatment guidance, the number of families receiving the interventions in clinical services remains low (Fadden 2006). This is not an isolated picture since similar difficulties have been reported within the United States (Dixon et al. 2001). The levels of contact between professionals and families are minimal and are often limited to telephone calls during crisis periods (Kim and Salyers 2008). This pattern of service provision is disappointing given the negative impact of psychosis on carers and the links between carer functioning and patient outcome. Further, recent cognitive models of caregiving highlight an important role for family work (Kuipers et al. 2010). In addition, family interventions are acceptable to carers and patients. The low provision of family interventions has been attributed to various factors, including organizational barriers (e.g., heavy staff workload), a lack of suitably trained staff with a focus on family work as part of their job, limited access to training, and negative attitudes toward families (Fadden 2006; Kim and Salyers 2008).

8.8   Conclusion

Psychosis is a complex condition, and communication difficulties between family members can be common. Patients can be sensitive to negative comments and those that are perceived as negative. Patients are also sensitive to stressful environments and remain vulnerable to the type of care they receive (Oyebode 2003). Being a carer can be challenging. Carers who are highly distressed and negatively affected by their role are likely to struggle to cope and become unable to provide care (Moller-Leimkuhler 2005; Quinn et al. 2003). Carers are active participants in the provision of patient care and patient outcomes; they often want to be more involved and work in close partnership with patients and services (Askey et al. 2009). When a carer's health is negatively affected by his or her role and caregiving duties and the carer lacks support, patient outcomes are likely to suffer.

Cognitive-behavioral family interventions for psychosis have a long and strong evidence base, and they have an important role to play in improving the caregiving environment for both patients and carers, and in facilitating positive and adaptive styles of communication between family members. Warm and positive communication styles between family members are linked with indices of improved functioning in patients. Unfortunately, the provision of family interventions remains limited across services. Greater efforts are required to address the obstacles to implementing family interventions in health services. These are likely to include widening access to specialist training in family intervention for psychosis, a focus on workers providing support to carers and their families as their main job of work, as well as revisions to organizational infrastructures to support such developments.

8.9   Key Resources

1. Kuipers E., Leff J. & Lam D. (2002). *Family Work for Schizophrenia. A Practical Guide,* 2nd ed. London: Gaskell Press.
2. Kuipers E. & Bebbington P. (2005). *Living with Mental Illness: A Book for Relatives and Friends,* 3rd ed. London: Souvenir Press.
3. Jones S. & Hayward P. (2004). *Coping with Schizophrenia: A Guide for Patients, Families and Caregivers.* Oxford: Oneworld Publications.
4. http://www.rethink.org
5. http://www.mentalhealthcare.org.uk

References

Addington, J., & Burnett, P. (2004). Working with families in the early stages of psychosis. In J. F. M. Gleeson & P. D. McGorry (Eds.), *Psychological interventions for early psychosis*. Chichester, UK: Wiley and Sons.

Addington, J., Coldham, E. L., Jones, B., Ko, T., & Addington, D. (2003). The first episode of psychosis: The experience of relatives. *Acta Psychiatrica Scandinavica, 108*(4), 285–289.

American Psychiatric Association (2004), "Practice guideline for the treatment of patients with schizophrenia" *American Journal of Psychiatry 161(2suppl)* pp. 1–56.

Askey, R., Holmshaw, J., Gamble, C., & Gray, R. (2009). What do carers of people with psychosis need from mental health services? Exploring the views of carers, service users and professionals. *Journal of Family Therapy, 31*, 310–331.

Awad, A. G., & Voruganti, L. N. P. (2008). The burden of schizophrenia on caregivers – A review. *Pharmacoeconomics, 26*(2), 149–162.

Bachmann, S., Bottmer, C., Jacob, S., & Schroder, J. (2006). Perceived criticism in schizophrenia: A comparison of instruments for the assessment of the patient's perspective and its relation to relatives' expressed emotion. *Psychiatry Research, 142*(2–3), 167–175.

Barrowclough, C., Gregg, L., & Tarrier, N. (2008). Expressed emotion and causal attributions in relatives of post-traumatic stress disorder patients. *Behaviour Research and Therapy, 46*(2), 207–218.

Barrowclough, C., & Hooley, J. M. (2003). Attributions and expressed emotion: A review. *Clinical Psychology Review, 23*(6), 849–880.

Barrowclough, C., Johnston, M., & Tarrier, N. (1994). Attributions, expressed emotion, and patient relapse – An attributional model of relatives' response to schizophrenic illness. *Behavior Therapy, 25*(1), 67–88.

Barrowclough, C., Lobban, F., Hatton, C., & Quinn, J. (2001). An investigation of models of illness in carers of schizophrenia patients using the Illness Perception Questionnaire. *British Journal of Clinical Psychology, 40*, 371–385.

Barrowclough, C., & Tarrier, N. (1992). *Families of schizophrenic patients: Cognitive behavioural intervention*. London: Chapman and Hall.

Barrowclough, C., Tarrier, N., Lewis, S., Sellwood, W., Mainwaring, J., Quinn, J., et al. (1999). Randomised controlled effectiveness trial of a needs-based psychosocial intervention service for carers of people with schizophrenia. *British Journal of Psychiatry, 174*, 505–511.

Barton, K., & Jackson, C. (2008). Reducing symptoms of trauma among carers of people with psychosis: Pilot study examining the impact of writing about caregiving experiences. *Australian and New Zealand Journal of Psychiatry, 42*(8), 693–701.

Bebbington, P., & Kuipers, L. (1994). The predictive utility of expressed emotion in schizophrenia – An aggregate analysis. *Psychological Medicine, 24*(3), 707–718.

Bergner, E., Leiner, A. S., Carter, T., Franz, L., Thompson, N. J., & Compton, M. T. (2008). The period of untreated psychosis before treatment initiation: A qualitative study of family members' perspectives. *Comprehensive Psychiatry, 49*(6), 530–536.

Berkowitz, R., Kuipers, L., Eberlein-Vries, R., & Leff, J. (1981). Lowering expressed emotion in relatives of schizophrenics. In M. J. Goldstein (Ed.), *New developments in interventions with families of schizophrenics* (pp. 27–48). San Francisco: Jossey-Bass.

Berry, K., Wearden, A., & Barrowclough, C. (2007). Adult attachment styles and psychosis: An investigation of associations between general attachment styles and attachment relationships with specific others. *Social Psychiatry and Psychiatric Epidemiology, 42*, 972–976.

Bertrando, P., Beltz, J., Bressi, C., Clerici, M., Farma, T., Invernizzi, G., et al. (1992). Expressed emotion and schizophrenia in Italy – A study of an urban-population. *British Journal of Psychiatry, 161*, 223–229.

Birchwood, M., & Cochrane, R. (1990). Families coping with schizophrenia – Coping styles, their origins and correlates. *Psychological Medicine, 20*(4), 857–865.

Boye, B., & Malt, U. F. (2002). Stress response symptoms in relatives of acutely admitted psychotic patients: A pilot study. *Nordic Journal of Psychiatry, 56*, 253–260.

Brekke, J. S., Prindle, C., Bae, S. W., & Long, J. D. (2001). Risks for individuals with schizophrenia who are living in the community. *Psychiatric Services, 52*(10), 1358–1366.

Brown, G. W. (1959). Experiences of discharged chronic schizophrenic mental hospital patients in various types of living group. *Milbank Q, 37*, 105–131.

Brown, G. W., Birley, J. L. T., & Wing, J. K. (1972). Influence of family life on the course of schizophrenic disorders: A replication. *British Journal of Psychiatry, 121*(3), 241–258.

Brown, S., & Birtwistle, J. (1998). People with schizophrenia and their families – Fifteen-year outcome. *British Journal of Psychiatry, 173*, 139–144.

Brown, G. W., Carstairs, G. M., & Topping, G. (1958). Post-hospital adjustment of chronic mental patients. *Lancet, 272*(7048), 685–689.

Brown, G. W., Monck, E. M., Carstairs, G. M., & Wing, J. K. (1962). The influence of family life on the course of schizophrenic illness. *British Journal of Preventive Social Medicine, 16*(2), 55–68.

Butzlaff, R. L., & Hooley, J. M. (1998). Expressed emotion and psychiatric relapse – A meta-analysis. *Archives of General Psychiatry, 55*(6), 547–552.

Chwastiak, L. A., Rosenheck, R. A., Mcevoy, J. P., Keefe, R. S., Swartz, M. S., & Lieberman, J. A. (2006). Interrelationships of psychiatric symptom severity, medical comorbidity, and functioning in schizophrenia. *Psychiatric Services, 57*(8), 1102–1109.

Cutting, L. P., Aakre, J., & Docherty, N. M. (2006). Schizophrenia patients' perceptions of stress, expressed emotion attitudes, and sensitivity to criticism. *Schizophrenia Bulletin, 32*, 743–750.

Dixon, L., McFarlane, W.R., Lefley, H., Lucksted, A., Cohen, M., Falloon, I., Mueser, K., Miklowitz, D., Solomon, P., & Sondheimer, D. (2001). Evidence-based practices for services to families of people with psychiatric disabilities. *Psychiatric Services 52*(7), 903–910.

Docherty, N. M., De Rosa, M., & Andreasen, N. C. (1996). Communication disturbances in schizophrenia and mania. *Archives of General of Psychiatry, 53*, 358–364.

Docherty, N.M. & Hebert A.S. (1997). Comparative affective reactivity of different types of communication disturbances in schizophrenia. *Journal of Abnormal Psychology, 106*, 325–330.

Docherty, N. M., Hall, M. J., & Gordinier, S. W. (1998). Affective reactivity of speech in schizophrenia patients and their nonschizophrenic relatives. *Journal of Abnormal Psychology, 107*, 461–467.

Docherty, N.M., Rhinewine, J.P., Labhart, R.P., & Gordinier, S.W. (1998a). Communication disturbances and family psychiatric history in parents of schizophrenic patients. *Journal of Nervous and Mental Disease, 186*(12), 761–768.

Docherty, N. M., Hall, M. J., & Gordinier, S. W. (1998b). Affective reactivity of speech in schizophrenia patients and their nonschizophrenic relatives. *Journal of Abnormal Psychology, 107*, 461–467.

Docherty, N. M., Gordinier, S. W., Hall, M. J., & Dombrowski, M. E. (2004). Referential communication disturbances in the speech of nonschizophrenic siblings of schizophrenia patients. *Journal of Abnormal Psychology, 113*(3), 399–405.

Docherty, N. M., Rhinewine, J. P., Labhart, R. P., & Gordinier, S. W. (1998). Communication disturbances and family psychiatric history in parents of schizophrenic patients. *Journal of Nervous and Mental Disease, 186*(12), 761–768.

Dyck, D. G., Short, R., & Vitaliano, P. P. (1999). Predictors of burden and infectious illness in schizophrenia caregivers. *Psychosomatic Medicine, 61*, 411–419.

Fadden, G. (2006). Training and disseminating family interventions for schizophrenia: Developing family intervention skills with multi-disciplinary groups. *Journal of Family Therapy, 28*(1), 23–38.

Falloon, I.R.H. (2003). Family interventions for mental disorders: efficacy and effectiveness. *World Psychiatry 2*(1).

Falloon, I. R. H., Boyd, J. L., & McGill, C. W. (1984). *Family care of schizophrenia.* New York: Guildford Press.

Fialko, L., Freeman, D., Bebbington, P. E., Kuipers, E., Garety, P. A., Dunn, G., et al. (2006). Understanding suicidal ideation in psychosis: Findings from the Psychological Prevention of Relapse in Psychosis (PRP) trial. *Acta Psychiatrica Scandinavica, 114*(3), 177–186.

Fisher, H., Theodore, K., Power, P., Chisholm, B., Fuller, J., Marlowe, K., Aitchison, K. J., Tanna, R., Joyce, J., Sacks, M., Craig, T., & Johnson, S. (2008), "Routine evaluation in first episode psychosis services: feasibility and results from the MiData project", *Social Psychiatry and Psychiatric Epidemiology*, vol. 43, no.12, pp. 960–967.

Folkman, S., & Lazarus, R. S. (1980). An analysis of coping in a middle-aged community sample. *Journal of Health and Social Behavior, 21*(3), 219–239.

Friedrich, R. M., Lively, S., & Rubenstein, L. M. (2008). Siblings' coping strategies and mental health services: A national study of siblings of persons with schizophrenia. *Psychiatric Services, 59*(3), 261–267.

Garcia, J.I.R., Chang, C.L., Young, J.S., Lopez, S.R., & Jenkins, J.H. (2006), "Family support predicts psychiatric medication usage among Mexican American individuals with schizophrenia" *Social Psychiatry and Psychiatric Epidemiology, 41*(8), pp. 624–631.

Garety, P. A., Bebbington, P., Fowler, D., Freeman, D., & Kuipers, E. (2007). Implications for neurobiological research of cognitive models of psychosis: A theoretical paper. *Psychological Medicine, 37*(10), 1377–1391.

Garety, P. A., Fowler, D. G., Freeman, D., Bebbington, P., Dunn, G., & Kuipers, E. (2008). Cognitive behavioural therapy and family intervention for relapse prevention and symptom reduction in psychosis: Randomised controlled trial. *British Journal of Psychiatry, 192*, 412–423.

Goldstein, M. J., & Strachan, A. M. (1987). The family and schizophrenia. In T. Jacob (Ed.), *Family interaction and psychopathology: Theories, methods and findings* (pp. 481–508). New York: Plenum Press.

Grandon, P., Jenaro, C., & Lemos, S. (2008). Primary caregivers of schizophrenia outpatients: Burden and predictor variables. *Psychiatry Research, 158*(3), 335–343.

Greenberg, J. S., Seltzer, M. M., Hong, J., & Orsmond, G. I. (2006). Bidirectional effects of expressed emotion and behaviour problems and symptoms in adolescents and adults with autism. *American Journal on Mental Retardation, 11*(4), 229–249.

Grice, S. J., Kuipers, E., Bebbington, P., Dunn, G., Fowler, D., Freeman, D., et al. (2009). Carers' attributions about positive events in psychosis relate to expressed emotion. *Behaviour Research and Therapy, 47*(9), 783–789.

Harrison, C. A., & Dadds, M. R. (1992). Attributions of symptomatology – An exploration of family factors associated with expressed emotion. *Australian and New Zealand Journal of Psychiatry, 26*(3), 408–416.

Harvey, P. D., Weintraub, S., & Neale, J. M. (1982). Speech competence of children vulnerable to psychopathology. *Journal of Abnormal Child Psychology, 10*, 373–388.

Hooley, J. M., & Campbell, C. (2002). Control and controllability: Beliefs and behaviour in high and low expressed emotion relatives. *Psychological Medicine, 32*(6), 1091–1099.

Hooley, J.M., Gruber, S.A., Parker, H.A., Guillaumot, J., Rogowska, J., & Yurgelun-Todd, D.A. (2009). Cortico-limbic response to personally challenging emotional stimuli after complete recovery from depression (vol 171, pg 106, 2009). *Psychiatry Research-Neuroimaging 172*(1), 82–91.

Hooley, J. M., Gruber, S. A., Scott, L. A., Hiller, J. B., & Yurgelun-Todd, D. A. (2005). Activation in dorsolateral prefrontal cortex in response to maternal criticism and praise in recovered depressed and healthy control participants. *Biological Psychiatry, 57*(7), 809–812.

Hooley, J. M., & Hoffman, P. D. (1999). Expressed emotion and clinical outcome in borderline personality disorder. *American Journal of Psychiatry, 156*(10), 1557–1562.

Hooley, J. M., Orley, J., & Teasdale, J. D. (1986). Levels of expressed emotion and relapse in depressed-patients. *British Journal of Psychiatry, 148*, 642–647.

Hooley, J. M., & Teasdale, J. D. (1989). Predictors of relapse in unipolar depressives – Expressed emotion, marital distress, and perceived criticism. *Journal of Abnormal Psychology, 98*(3), 229–235.

Jungbauer, J., & Angermeyer, M. C. (2002). Living with a schizophrenic patient: A comparative study of burden as it affects parents and spouses. *Psychiatry, 65*(2), 110–123.

Jungbauer, J., Wittmund, B., Dietrich, S., & Angermeyer, M. C. (2003). Subjective burden over 12 months in parents of patients with schizophrenia. *Archives of Psychiatric Nursing, 17*(3), 126–134.

Karanci, A. N., & Inandilar, H. (2002). Predictors of components of expressed emotion in major caregivers of Turkish patients with schizophrenia. *Social Psychiatry and Psychiatric Epidemiology, 37*(2), 80–88.

Karp, D. A., & Tanarugsachock, V. (2000). Mental illness, caregiving, and emotion management. *Qualitative Health Research, 10*(1), 6–25.

Kennedy, S. H., Evans, K. R., Kruger, S., Mayberg, H. S., Meyer, J. H., McCann, S., et al. (2001). Changes in regional brain glucose metabolism measured with positron emission tomography after paroxetine treatment of major depression. *American Journal of Psychiatry, 158*(6), 899–905.

Kiecolt-Glaser, J. K., Loving, T. J., Stowell, J. R., Malarkey, W. B., Lemeshow, S., Dickinson, S. L., et al. (2005). Hostile marital interactions, proinflammatory cytokine production, and wound healing. *Archives of General Psychiatry, 62*(12), 1377–1384.

Kim, H. W., & Salyers, M. P. (2008). Attiudes and perceived barriers to working with families of persons with severe mental illness: Mental health professionals' perspectives. *Community Mental Health Journal, 44*, 337–345. doi:10.1007/s10597-008-9135-x.

Kjellin, L., & Ostman, M. (2005). Relatives of psychiatric inpatients – Do physical violence and suicide attempts of patients influence family burden and participation in care? *Nordic Journal of Psychiatry, 59*(1), 7–11.

Kopelowicz, A., Lopez, S. R., Zarate, R., O'Brien, M., Gordon, J., Chang, C., et al. (2006). Expressed emotion and family interactions in Mexican Americans with schizophrenia. *Journal of Nervous and Mental Disease, 194*(5), 330–334.

Kopelowicz, A., Zarate, R., Gonzalez, V., Lopez, S. R., Ortega, P., Obregon, N., et al. (2002). Evaluation of expressed emotion in schizophrenia: A comparison of Caucasians and Mexican-Americans. *Schizophrenia Research, 55*(1–2), 179–186.

Kuipers, E., & Bebbington, P. (2005). Research on burden and coping strategies in families of people with mental disorders: Problems and perspectives. In N. Sartorius, J. Leff, & J. J. Lopez (Eds.), *Families and mental disorder: From burden to empowerment* (pp. 217–234). Chichester, UK: Wiley.

Kuipers, E., Leff, J., & Lam, D. (2002). *Family work for schizophrenia: A practical guide.* London: Gaskell Press.

Kuipers, E., Onwumere, J., & Bebbington, P. (2010). A cognitive model of caregiving in psychosis. *British Journal of Psychiatry, 196*, 259–265.

Kuipers, E., & Raune, D. (2000). The early development of expressed emotion and burden in the families of first onset psychosis. In M. Birchwood, D. Fowler, & C. Jackson (Eds.), *Early intervention in psychosis* (pp. 128–140). Chichester, UK: John Wiley & Sons.

Kuipers, L., Sturgeon, D., Berkowitz, R., & Leff, J. (1983). Characteristics of expressed emotion – Its relationship to speech and looking in schizophrenic-patients and their relatives. *British Journal of Clinical Psychology, 22*, 257–264.

Kuipers, E., Watson, P., Onwumere, J., Bebbington, P., Dunn, G., Weinman, J., et al. (2007). Discrepant illness perceptions, affect and expressed emotion: In people with psychosis and their carers. *Social Psychiatry and Psychiatric Epidemiology, 42*, 277–283.

Kymalainen, J. A., Weisman, A. G., Rosales, G. A., & Armesto, J. C. (2006). Ethnicity, expressed emotion, and communication deviance in family members of patients with schizophrenia. *Journal of Nervous and Mental Disease, 194*(6), 391–396.

Lauber, C., Eichenberger, A., Luginbuhl, P., Keller, C., & Rossler, W. (2003). Determinants of burden in caregivers of patients with exacerbating schizophrenia. *European Psychiatry, 18*(6), 285–289.

Lebell, M. B., Marder, S. R., Mintz, J., Mintz, L. I., Tompson, M., Wirshing, W., et al. (1993). Patients' perceptions of family emotional climate and outcome in schizophrenia. *British Journal of Psychiatry, 162*, 751–754.

Lee, C., & Gramotnev, H. (2007). Transitions into and out of caregiving: Health and social characteristics of mid-age Australian women. *Psychology and Health, 22*, 193–209.

Lehman, A. F., Kreyenbuhl, J., Buchanan, R. W., Dickerson, F. B., Dixon, L. B., Goldberg, R., et al. (2004). The Schizophrenia Patient Outcomes Research Team (PORT): Updated treatment recommendations 2003. *Schizophrenia Bulletin, 30*(2), 193–217.

Lin, H. C., Hsiao, F. H., Pfeiffer, S., Hwang, Y. T., & Lee, H. C. (2008). An increased risk of stroke among young schizophrenia patients. *Schizophrenia Research, 101*(1–3), 234–241.

Lobban, F., Barrowclough, C., & Jones, S. (2005). Assessing cognitive representations of mental health problems. II. The illness perception questionnaire for schizophrenia: Relatives' version. *British Journal of Clinical Psychology, 44*, 163–179.

Lopez, S. R., Hipke, K. N., Polo, A. J., Jenkins, J. H., Karno, M., & Vaughn, C. (2004). Ethnicity, expressed emotion, attributions, and course of schizophrenia: Family warmth matters. *Journal of Abnormal Psychology, 113*(3), 428–439.

Magliano, L., Fadden, G., Economou, M., Held, T., Xavier, M., Guarneri, M., et al. (2000). Family burden and coping strategies in schizophrenia: One-year follow-up data from the BIOMED I study. *Social Psychiatry and Psychiatric Epidemiology, 35*(3), 109–115.

Magliano, L., Fiorillo, A., Malangone, C., De Rosa, C., & Maj, M. (2006). Patient functioning and family burden in a controlled, real-world trial of family psychoeducation for schizophrenia. *Psychiatric Services, 57*(12), 1784–1791.

Marom, S., Munitz, H., Jones, P. B., Weizman, A., & Hermesh, H. (2002). Familial expressed emotion: Outcome and course of Israeli patients with schizophrenia. *Schizophrenia Bulletin, 28*(4), 731–743.

Martens, L., & Addington, J. (2001). The psychological well-being of family members of individuals with schizophrenia. *Social Psychiatry and Psychiatric Epidemiology, 36*(3), 128–133.

McFarlane, W. R. (2002). *Multifamily groups in the treatment of severe psychiatric disorders.* New York: Guilford Press.

McFarlane, W. R., Lukens, E., Link, B., Dushay, R., Deakins, S. A., Newmark, M., et al. (1995). Multiple-family groups and psychoeducation in the treatment of schizophrenia. *Archives of General Psychiatry, 52*(8), 679–687.

McNab, C., Haslam, N., & Burnett, P. (2007). Expressed emotion, attributions, utility beliefs, and distress in parents of young people with first episode psychosis. *Psychiatry Research, 151*(1–2), 97–106.

Miklowitz, D.J., Goldstein, M.J., Falloon, I.R.H., & Doane, J.A. (1984). Interactional Correlates of Expressed Emotion in the Families of Schizophrenics. *British Journal of Psychiatry 144*(MAY), 482–487.

Moller-Leimkuhler, A. M. (2005). Burden of relatives and predictors of burden. Baseline results from the Munich 5-year-follow-up study on relatives of first hospitalized patients with schizophrenia or depression. *European Archives of Psychiatry and Clinical Neuroscience, 255*(4), 223–231.

Moller-Leimkuhler, A. M., & Obermeier, M. (2008). Predicting caregiver burden in first admission psychiatric patients. Two-year follow-up results. *European Archives of Psychiatry and Clinical Neuroscience, 258*, 406–413.

Morgan, C., Kirkbride, J., Hutchinson, G., Craig, T., Morgan, K., Dazzan, P., Boydell, J., Doody, G.A., Jones, P.B., Murray, R.M., Leff, J., & Fearon, P. (2008). Cumulative social disadvantage, ethnicity and first-episode psychosis: a case-control study. *Psychological Medicine 38*(12), 1701–1715.

NICE Schizophrenia Guideline (Update, 2009) www.nice.org.uk/guidance/index.jsp?action=byId&o=11786

Nordentoft, M., Jeppesen, P., Abel, M., Kassow, P., Petersen, L., Thorup, A., et al. (2002). OPUS study: Suicidal behaviour, suicidal ideation and hopelessness among patients with first-episode psychosis: One-year follow-up of a randomised controlled trial. *British Journal of Psychiatry, 181*(43), s98–s106.

Onwumere, J., Kuipers, E., Bebbington, P., Dunn, G., Freeman, D., Fowler, D., et al. (2009). Patient perceptions of caregiver criticism in psychosis: Links with patient and caregiver functioning. *Journal of Nervous and Mental Disease, 197*(2), 85–91.

Osborn, D. P. J., Levy, G., Nazareth, I., Petersen, I., Islam, A., & King, M. B. (2007). Relative risk of cardiovascular and cancer mortality in people with severe mental illness from the United Kingdom's General Practice Research Database. *Archives of General Psychiatry, 64*(2), 242–249.

Ostman, M., & Hansson, L. (2004). Appraisal of caregiving, burden and psychological distress in relatives of psychiatric inpatients. *European Psychiatry, 19*(7), 402–407.

Oyebode, J. (2003). Assessment of carers' psychological needs. *Advances in Psychiatric Treatment, 9*, 45–53.

Pfammatter, M., Junghan, U. M., & Brenner, H. D. (2006). Efficacy of psychological therapy in schizophrenia: Conclusions from meta-analyses. *Schizophrenia Bulletin, 32*(Suppl 1), S64–S80.

Pharoah, F., Mari, J., Rathbone, J., & Wong, W. (2006). Family intervention for schizophrenia. *Cochrane Database of Systematic Reviews, 4*(4), CD000088. 10.1002/14651858.CD000088. pub2.

Phillips, A. C., Gallagher, S., Hunt, K., Der, G., & Carroll, D. (2009). Symptoms of depression in non-routine caregivers: The role of caregiver strain and burden. *British Journal of Clinical Psychology, 48*, 335–346.

Pilling, S., Bebbington, P., Garety, P., Kuipers, E., Geddes, J., & Martindale, B. (2002). Meta-analysis of psychological treatment in psychosis I: Family work and individual CBT. *Psychological Medicine, 32*, 763–782.

Quinn, J., Barrowclough, C., & Tarrier, N. (2003). The Family Questionnaire (FQ): a scale for measuring symptom appraisal in relatives of schizophrenic patients. *Acta Psychiatrica Scandinavica, 108*(4), 290–296.

Raune, D., Kuipers, E., & Bebbington, P. E. (2004). Expressed emotion at first-episode psychosis: Investigating a carer appraisal model. *British Journal of Psychiatry, 184*(4), 321–326.

Rosenfarb, I. S., Goldstein, M. J., Mintz, J., & Nuechterlein, K. H. (1995). Expressed emotion and subclinical psychopathology observable within the transactions between schizophrenic-patients and their family members. *Journal of Abnormal Psychology, 104*(2), 259–267.

Rossler, W., Salize, H. J., van Os, J., & Riecher-Rossler, A. (2005). Size of burden of schizophrenia and psychotic disorders. *European Neuropsychopharmacology, 15*(4), 399–409.

Scazufca, M., & Kuipers, E. (1996). Links between expressed emotion and burden of care in relatives of patients with schizophrenia. *British Journal of Psychiatry, 168*(5), 580–587.

Scazufca, M., & Kuipers, E. (1999). Coping strategies in relatives of people with schizophrenia before and after psychiatric admission. *British Journal of Psychiatry, 174*(2), 154–158.

Scazufca, M., Kuipers, E., & Menezes, P. R. (2001). Perception of negative emotions in close relatives by patients with schizophrenia. *British Journal of Clinical Psychology, 40*, 167–175.

Schomerus, G., Heider, D., Angermeyer, M. C., Bebbington, P. E., Azorin, J. M., Brugha, T., et al. (2008). Urban residence, victimhood and the appraisal of personal safety in people with schizophrenia: Results from the European Schizophrenia Cohort (EuroSC). *Psychological Medicine, 38*, 591–597.

Schulz, R., & Beach, S. R. (1999). Caregiving as a risk factor for mortality: The caregiver health effects study. *Journal of the American Medical Association, 282*, 2215–2219.

Shimodera, S., Mino, Y., Inoue, S., Izumoto, Y., Fujita, H., & Ujihara, H. (2000). Expressed emotion and family distress in relatives of patients with schizophrenia in Japan. *Comprehensive Psychiatry, 41*(5), 392–397.

Simoneau, T. L., Miklowitz, D. J., & Saleem, R. (1998). Expressed emotion and interactional patterns in the families of bipolar patients. *Journal of Abnormal Psychology, 107*(3), 497–507.

Singleton, N., Maung, N., Cowie, A., Sparks, J., Bumpstead, R., & Meltzer, H. (2002). *Mental health of carers*. London: Office for National Statistics.

Stam, H., & Cuijpers, P. (2001). Effects on family interventions on burden of relatives of psychiatric patients in the Netherlands: A pilot study. *Community Mental Health Journal, 37*, 179–187.

Stoskopf, C. H., Kim, Y. K., & Glover, S. H. (2001). Dual diagnosis: HIV and mental illness, a population-based study. *Community Mental Health Journal, 37*(6), 469–479.

Strachan, M., Leff, J. P., Goldstein, J., Doane, J. A., & Burtt, C. (1986). Emotional attitudes and direct communication in the families of schizophrenics: A cross-national replication. *British Journal of Psychiatry, 149*, 279–287.

Subotnik, K. L., Goldstein, M. J., Nuechterlein, K. H., Woo, S. M., & Mintz, J. (2002). Are communication deviance and expressed emotion related to family history of psychiatric disorders in schizophrenia? *Schizophrenia Bulletin, 28*(4), 719–729.

Tang, V., Leung, S., & Lam, L. (2008). Clinical correlates of the caregiving experience for Chinese caregivers of patients with schizophrenia. *Social Psychiatry and Psychiatric Epidemiology, 43*(9), 720–726. DOI 10.1007/s00127-008-0357-6.

Tompson, M. C., Goldstein, M. J., Lebell, M. B., Mintz, L. I., Marder, S. R., & Mintz, J. (1995). Schizophrenic-patients perceptions of their relatives' attitudes. *Psychiatry Research, 57*(2), 155–167.

Ukpong, D. I. (2006). Demographic factors and clinical correlates of burden and distress in relatives of services users experiencing schizophrenia: A study from south-western Nigeria. *International Journal of Mental Health Nursing, 15*, 54–59.

US Surgeon General (1999) *A report of the Surgeon General*. Rockville: Department of Health and Human Services, Substance Abuse and Mental Health Services Administration, National Institutes of Health.

Vaddadi, K., Gilleard, C., & Fryer, H. (2002). Abuse of carers by relatives with severe mental illness. *International Journal of Social Psychiatry, 48*(2), 149.

Weisman, A. G., & Lopez, S. R. (1997). An attributional analysis of emotional reactions to schizophrenia in Mexican and Anglo cultures. *Journal of Applied Social Psychology, 27*, 224–245.

Wolthaus, J. E. D., Dingemans, P. M. A. J., Schene, A. H., Linszen, D. H., Wiersma, D., Van den Bosch, R. J., et al. (2002). Caregiver burden in recent-onset schizophrenia and spectrum disorders: The influence of symptoms and personality traits. *Journal of Nervous and Mental Disease, 190*, 241–247.

World Health Organisation (2001). *World Health Report*. Mental Health: New understanding, New Hope. Geneva, World Health Organisation.

Wuerker, A. K., Haas, G. L., & Bellack, A. S. (2001). Interpersonal control and expressed emotion in families of persons with schizophrenia: Change over time. *Schizophrenia Bulletin, 27*(4), 671–685.

Yang, L. H., Phillips, M. R., Licht, D. M., & Hooley, J. M. (2004). Causal attributions about schizophrenia in families in China: Expressed emotion and patient relapse. *Journal of Abnormal Psychology, 113*, 592–602.

Chapter 9
Learner-Centered Interactive Methods for Improving Communication Skills

Jonathan Silverman and Michela Rimondini

9.1 Introduction

In the Outcomes Project, the *Accreditation Council for Graduate Medical Education* (ACGME) mandated that all medical specialties ensure that its residents develop competency in different areas, including "interpersonal and communication skills." The Psychiatry Residency Review Committee of the ACGME fixed additional requirements for psychiatrists, who also need to demonstrate competency in CBT and four other different kinds of psychotherapy (ACGME 2000). This implies that communication and CBT are considered core skills in the curriculum of mental health providers (see Chapter 1). How then are communication and interpersonal skills best learned?

The photograph in Fig. 9.1 shows a typical example of communication skills teaching in action. A facilitator and an actor work with a small group of learners using video recording and instantly available playback. This experiential learning approach is the mainstay of communication skills teaching.

But why? It is clearly a resource-intensive and expensive approach to teaching. Are such interactive methods really necessary? Why not teach this by lecture, by reading, or by e-learning? Do we know that traditional apprenticeship or didactic teaching methods by themselves won't bring about the same changes in behaviors and skills? Why, when experiential methods are potentially more challenging and threatening to the learner, do we insist on their use?

In this chapter, we explore how learners can improve their communication skills, the evidence behind the necessity for using experiential interactive learning, and the different approaches that can lead to behavioral change in communication skills.

J. Silverman (✉)
School of Clinical Medicine, Addenbrooke's Hospital,
Hills Road, Box 111, Cambridge CB2 0SP, UK
e-mail: js355@medschl.cam.ac.uk

M. Rimondini (ed.), *Communication in Cognitive Behavioral Therapy*,
DOI 10.1007/978-1-4419-6807-4_9, © Springer Science+Business Media, LLC 2011

Fig. 9.1 This photograph shows a typical example of communication skills teaching in action

9.2   Can You Teach and Learn Communication
Skills in Psychotherapy?

Before we explore which methods to use, we need to answer a more fundamental question: can communication skills really be taught and learned? Could it be simply personality—that some people can do it and others will never be able to? And if they can be learned, perhaps it is merely a matter of learning by experience or osmosis. Maybe we learn best just by watching our superiors do it. After all, for many years psychotherapy training traditionally followed an apprenticeship model where students learned how to interact with patients by watching seniors conducting interviews and by students undertaking their own psychotherapy. During the last few decades, this trend has seemed to change, and now evidence-based methods for assessing compe-tence and for teaching psychotherapy are available and could be advocated in the future (Weerasekera et al. 2010).

Much of the evidence that can guide us here comes from the world of medical education, where there is an extensive research literature on teaching communica-tion skills that goes back 30 years. Communication is clearly a core clinical skill in medicine. Unfortunately, communication skills do not necessarily improve with time alone, and experience may well be a poor teacher (Association of American Medical Colleges Panel on the General Professional Education of the Physician and College Preparation for Medicine 1984; Byrne and Long 1976; Maguire et al. 1986; Ridsdale et al. 1992).

Fortunately, medical education research has shown us conclusively that communication skills can be taught (Aspergren 1999; Duffy 1998; Fallowfield et al. 2002; Kurtz et al. 1999, 2005; Smith et al. 2007; Wilkinson et al. 2008). From undergraduate to postgraduate medicine and from primary to specialist care, including psychotherapy, a large body of literature demonstrates substantial changes in learners' behavior from effective communication skills training.

But we also need to question whether such changes in behavior are long-standing. If learning is not retained and only gives short-term benefit, embarking on communication skills training for professionals would be a waste of precious resources. Gratifyingly, changes in learners' communication skills have been shown to be long-lasting, with follow-up periods of as long as five years post-training (Fallowfield et al. 2003; Laidlaw et al. 2004; Maguire et al. 1986; Oh et al. 2001; Stillman et al. 1977).

9.3   Why Use Experiential Learning Methods?

So what teaching methods have the research demonstrated to be required for effective communication skills learning? The evidence serves to underline the significant difference between knowing about the skills and behaviors that comprise effective communication and being able to put these skills into practice. Knowledge does not translate directly to performance: a further step of specific experiential work is required to acquire new skills and change learners' behavior.

Research has demonstrated the deficiencies of the traditional apprenticeship model of learning communication skills and also that didactic methods by them-selves are not sufficient to achieve change in learners' behavior. Observation, supervision, feedback, and video or audio recording of performance are required to effect improvement in learners' skills (Aspergren 1999; Kurtz et al. 2005; Simpson et al. 1991; Sholomskas et al. 2005). These training methods are also perceived by learners to be differentially effective. Bennett-Levy et al. (2009) have shown that experienced CBT therapists found traditional methods such as lectures/talks and modeling more useful for the acquisition of declarative knowledge, while interactive learning strategies, like role-play, were perceived to be most effective in enhancing procedural skills. Experiential work and reflective practice were seen as particularly helpful in improving reflective capability and interpersonal skills.

It is not that the traditional apprenticeship model does not have anything to offer learners in developing their communication skills. All practitioners observed by learners are modeling skills, behaviors, and attitudes (Bandura 1988; Ficklin 1988; Kurtz 1990). However, while modeling may change attitudes, neither modeling nor appropriate attitudes are sufficient to ensure that learners can identify the skills that they see, much less develop and use them appropriately in practice (Kurtz 1990). Often learners comment on a mentor as being particularly skilled at communicating with patients, but when asked what makes the mentor so good, they cannot identify exactly what he does.

What then are the essential ingredients of experiential communication skills learning?

9.3.1   Systematic Delineation and Definition of Essential Skills

It is important to delineate the specific communication process skills that form the curriculum of communication in the professional–client relationship under consideration. Without inclusion of this element, experiential learning is unlikely to be successful (Association of American Medical Colleges 1999; Cegala and Lenzmeier Broz 2002; Kurtz et al. 2003; Participants in the Bayer-Fetzer Conference on Physician–Patient Communication in Medical Education 2001; Silverman et al. 2005).

9.3.2   Observation

Direct observation of learners interviewing is the key element of effective communication training. It should not be surprising that observation has been shown to be of central importance: Observation is vital in learning any skill. Ask any group of learners about their experience of observation in learning and they will immediately come up with examples from their sports experiences, from learning musical instruments, from becoming skilled in practical procedures such as painting or driving. Of course, you can learn from trial and error, by practice alone, but it is much more efficient to be observed and receive feedback on your work.

Without direct observation, the teacher only gets a filtered version of what actually happened in an interview. Self-reporting is often not detailed enough to allow the teacher to understand the problem. It is very difficult for learners to remember what happened in the heat of the moment, to be specific rather than vague. It is, of course, impossible by definition to comment on one's own blind spots. The feedback offered in response is then of little value, as it may well not address the difficulties that actually occurred. Feedback without observation is like therapy without diagnosis.

9.3.3   Well-Intentioned, Detailed, and Descriptive Feedback

It is commonplace for learners to have had experiences of feedback following observation that were highly negative. Teachers may have appeared unsupportive and the feedback learners received judgmental and without useful suggestions for change. To benefit from communication skills teaching, learners need to experience observation where they are supported by a well-motivated teacher, able to give non-judgmental yet constructive criticism (Westberg and Jason 1993). They need to be able to deliberately and willingly expose their difficulties without fear of being marked down. Observation and feedback need careful handling if their full potential for learning is to be realized. In psychotherapy, this aspect is crucial because during the feedback sessions, the trainer is not just commenting on learner performances; he is also, within his facilitation, modeling the psychotherapeutic style he wishes to teach. In the eyes of the learner, the credibility of the teacher as clinician, and consequently of the clinical model she proposes, starts from this interaction. As stated by Fleming (1967) in the interpersonal relationship between a supervisor–teacher and a student–therapist, the experience of communicating with each other closely approximates and serves as a model for the exchanges that occur in psychotherapy. For example, the opportunity to learn experientially the positive impact of a facilitating atmosphere on one's own sense of self-efficacy and global wellness is a powerful way for teaching empathy and motivational interviewing.

For learners to benefit from observation, feedback needs to be specific, detailed, nonjudgmental, and well intentioned (Silverman et al. 1997, 1996). The tennis coach never just observes; he provides a supportive environment and gives positive encouragement that highlights the learner's accomplishments. At the same time, he provides useful, practical, and well-intentioned feedback on areas that would benefit from change. Feedback is constructive: It is specific and detailed enough for learners to see how to alter their behavior and develop their skills. Feedback is well intentioned and is provided for the benefit of the learner: the coach is there to help and encourage learners, not to demonstrate either how unskilled the learner is or how skilled the teacher is.

9.3.4   Video and Audio Playback

It is not surprising that research highlights the importance of video and audio recordings in communication skills teaching. Learning any skill is greatly helped by self-observation, by being able to see for ourselves what exactly we are doing and where improvements might be made. In sports coaching, it is now common-place to use video recording to enable learners as well as coaches to gain insight and to learn from observation.

Moreover, in CBT the use of these methods (especially audiotaping) is widely applied with patients as homework or as a method for keeping track of the internal changes occurring during therapy; so it is essential that clinicians are familiar with and comfortable in using these recording approaches.

The use of video or audio recording to guide feedback offers many advantages over the provision of feedback from observation of the live interaction alone (Beckman et al. 1994; Hargie and Morrow 1986; Silverman et al. 1997, 1996; Westberg and Jason 1994):

- Learners who can observe or listen to themselves understand their own strengths and weaknesses much more readily than if they rely on reflection alone.
- Recordings encourage a learner-centered approach with the learner being more centrally and actively involved in the analysis of the interview.
- Recordings help prevent misconceptions and disagreements over what actually occurred from getting in the way of learning.
- Recordings allow feedback to be much more specific, as there is always an exact referent for any particular item of discussion.
- Recordings help feedback to focus on description rather than evaluation, an essential aspect of constructive feedback.
- Recordings allow areas to be reviewed on several occasions and enable the learner to revisit feedback and learning at a later date.

Video recording has advantages over audio recording that offset the disparity in ease of use. Video makes it possible to focus feedback and self-assessment on a much broader range of nonverbal as well as verbal behaviors that could otherwise be lost to learning.

9.3.5 Repeated Practice and Rehearsal

Practice and rehearsal are often neglected aspects of communication skills teaching and learning. Returning to our tennis analogy, good coaches do not simply make recommendations and suggest that you go away and try them out during your next competitive match. They ask you to try out new moves away from the hurly burly of a real match and practice them repeatedly in a safe situation until you feel comfortable. They observe you as you practice new skills and give further feedback, which allows you to refine your technique as you proceed. Rehearsal with coaching is equally necessary in learning communication skills. What does rehearsal offer learners?

9.3.5.1 Practicing Skills in Safety

When talking with patients during a psychotherapeutic session, it is quite difficult to understand and control the emotional process produced by the interaction. One of the core competencies of a therapist is to recognize the origin of his or her own emotions, establishing if they are patient- or self-generated. Of course, the more intense and involving these feelings are, the harder this becomes. It is asking too much of learners to expect them to experiment with this juxtaposition of feelings and new skills for the first time in real consultations. The great selling point of experiential learning is that it can provide opportunities to practice skills in safety. Safe for the learner means that the emotional arousal is tailored to his or her own needs and when it becomes too high, it can be easily reduced by interrupting the simulation or changing the level of difficulty. Safety also means that the setting is supportive, attempts at using skills are not subject to put-downs and risk-taking, and experimentation is valued. Safe for the patient means he or she is not at risk of damage, as the learner's experimentation has been done first in simulation. The key to rehearsal is to provide safe learning opportunities that are as near as possible to real-life situations while still allowing multiple opportunities for trial and error plus feedback.

9.3.5.2 Enabling Ongoing Feedback and Rehearsal

Rehearsal leads to further observation, self- and peer assessment, and feedback. Feedback then leads to yet further rehearsal, which enables the learner to gradually refine and master skills. It is in fact this helical, repetitive observation and feedback that so often pushes the learning process forward.

9.3.5.3 Developing an Individual Approach

Each psychotherapist needs to develop his or her own method of accomplishing a skill so that it can become incorporated into his or her own personality and style. One criticism of skills-based communication skills teaching and CBT is that they are a cookbook approach that says prescriptively, "Here are the skills to be learned; this is how you should do it." How do we reconcile the need for flexibility, individuality, and personal style with the skills-based approach in which the skills of the curriculum are clearly defined and delineated?

The answer lies in how learners and facilitators approach these skills. Each skill is only a clue that this is an area where specific behaviors and phrases need to be worked on and developed experientially. The list by itself is not enough; each learner has to discover his own way to put each skill into practice. The challenge during the teaching session is to generate alternatives and give participants the opportunity to try out and refine various phrases and behaviors without reducing flexibility or negating the influence of individual personalities. In fact, communication training should increase rather than reduce flexibility by providing an expanded repertoire of skills that clinicians can adeptly and intentionally choose to use as they require. Following the parallel between teaching and the healing process, going beyond specific skills into individuality with learners indirectly teaches a central aspect of CBT. In this approach, patients learn more functional strategies in order to increase the chances of achieving their personal goals, without necessarily changing their basic personality in the attempt to reach an ideal, stereotypical model of being or behaving.

9.3.6 Active Small Group or One-to-One Learning

Experiential learning through observation, recording, feedback, and rehearsal is clearly not suited to the familiar and comfortable large group and independent-study contexts used so extensively for more traditional cognitive learning. Communication skills training requires one-to-one or small group learning in which the numbers are small enough to allow each learner frequent opportunity for practice, participation, and individualized coaching.

This approach requires learners to take a more active role, to learn by doing rather than by listening or reading. This is not the world of listening to expert lectures, making notes, participating in large group discussions, studying written material, and writing essays and examinations. Experiential study shifts the primary focus away from the lecture and the book to one's own behavior. Experiential learning is more learner- and less teacher-centered. It is more active and less passive for learners with more time spent practicing, observing, and giving and receiving feedback.

9.4 Why Use a Learner-Centered Approach to Communication Skills Teaching?

So we know that learning communication skills requires specific experiential methods. But where do we start? What do we observe and why? The answer lies in a learner-centered approach in which the learners' own perceived difficulties provide the focus for observation and learning.

In recent years, problem-based and other experiential learning approaches have gained increasing popularity in education. Historically, Knowles' principles of adult learning (Knowles 1984) were one of the major influences in promoting this shift. Knowles examined what motivates adults to learn and how to capitalize on this in teaching. He suggested that adult learners are motivated to learn when they perceive learning to be relevant to their current situation and when it enables them to acquire skills and knowledge that they can use in immediate and practical ways. The more relevant the learning is to the real world of their immediate experience, the more quickly and effectively adults learn. Learners are therefore motivated by a problem-based (rather than a subject-based) approach where the practical difficulties that they themselves are experiencing act as the stimulus for learning.

Building upon learners' past experiences also motivates adults to learn. Adult learners have considerable experience of the world and a great deal to offer: if their contributions are valued, accepted, and used, learning will flourish.

The principles of adult learning contrast with traditional teacher-centered or didactic learning, which is concerned with the direct transmission of content by the teacher to a passive learner. In problem-based learning, facilitators encourage learners to be actively involved. Not only do learners acquire knowledge, but they also develop the understanding and skills to apply that knowledge in practice.

The following list characterizes what motivates adults to learn. Adults are motivated by learning that is

- relevant to the learners' present situation,
- practical rather than just theoretical,

- problem- rather than subject-centered,
- built on learners' previous experience,
- directed toward learners' perceived needs,
- planned in terms of negotiated and emergent objectives,
- participatory, actively involving learners,
- geared to the learners' own pace,
- primarily self-directed,
- designed so that learners can take responsibility for their own learning,
- designed to promote more equal relationship with teachers,
- evaluated through self- and peer assessment.

This description of what motivates learners to learn is particularly relevant to communication skills teaching in psychotherapy. Taking a problem-based approach eases the defensiveness that can accompany experiential learning. We have to remember that considerable discomfort may well ensue from entering a program that requires you to examine and possibly change something that seems so closely bound to your personality and self-concept as communication behavior. Experiential methods are potentially more challenging and threatening and less safe for the learner than more traditional forms of learning. It can feel uncomfortable to perform interviews while others assess your skills and, at the same time, a camera records your performance. Following the principles of adult learning can help reduce learners' defensiveness and enable them to benefit from communication training.

9.5 Why Use a Problem-Based Approach in Practice?

So, to maximize learning, we not only have to use specific experiential methods, in which skills can be actively tried out and practiced in a supportive environment, but also have to encourage a problem-based approach (Kurtz et al. 2005). Starting from where learners are, we attempt to address their needs, make learning and teaching relevant to their current situation, and build on their existing knowledge, skills, and experience. To prevent defensiveness, communication skills teaching must seem relevant and not simply like "this is what you need because we're telling you so."

9.5.1 Discovering Learners' Perceived Needs

A starting point for any experiential learning is to discover needs that learners bring with them from their work or experience. What problems and difficulties are they experiencing and what areas would they like help with? What is their previous experience and their present level of knowledge and skill? Begin with learners' starting points (where they are), their current problems and needs (their agenda), and where they would like to go (their objectives). For example, if we want to teach which kind of open questions or comments can be used during the functional analysis of a patient maladaptive behavior, we should tailor our intervention according to the learner's level of knowledge and expertise in order to effectively fulfill his agenda. Indeed, proposing to an inexperienced therapist a too complex clinical case (i.e., personality disorder) may create in the learner an internal conflict between paying attention to the communication process or putting all her efforts in trying to identify what creates and what maintains the described symptoms.

9.5.2   Creating a Supportive Climate

Experiential, problem-based approaches to learning communication skills necessitate the development and maintenance of a supportive climate where learners collaborate rather than compete, where they can gain confidence in themselves, their peers, and their facilitators, and where they are encouraged to voice their difficulties in a safe and supportive setting.

9.5.3   Developing Appropriate Experiential Material

The material for analysis may be developed by facilitators and course directors (for instance, though simulation or inviting specific patients to participate) or brought by the learners themselves (e.g., in the form of videotapes of their interactions with patients that they bring to the session). When facilitators or course directors are responsible for developing the material, it is important that the setting and case are as close as possible to those that learners will encounter in real life.

9.5.4   Taking a Problem-Based Approach
to Analyzing the Consultation

Whether the consultation is live or on videotape, with real or simulated patients, the problem-based approach starts by asking the learner who has been observed for her agenda: what problems she experienced and what help she would like from the rest of the group. Once this is determined and if time permits, ask other members of the group if the consultation raised additional issues they would like to discuss, and only then add your own ideas to the agenda if they have not already been raised, especially if they fit in with issues that learners have already identified.

9.6   What Place Is There for More Didactic Teaching Methods?

We have discussed the evidence that experiential methods of learning are necessary to effect a change in learners' communication skills. This does not mean, however, that *only* experiential methods are of any value and that there is no place for didactic methods in communication skills courses. So what are the advantages of including didactic teaching in the communication skills program?

Knowledge is important. There is a need to make available to learners the concepts, principles, and research evidence that can illuminate experiential learning. Such knowledge allows learners to understand more fully the issues behind communication skills training and the evidence for the value of each skill. Although by themselves, cognitive approaches such as reading, analyzing, hypothesizing, and classifying do not generate skills, intellectual understanding can augment and guide our use of skills and aid our exploration of attitudes and issues.

Knowledge of the integral relationships between various communication skills is also extremely important. Understanding the logical connection between various skills and how they can be used together in different parts of the consultation can both enhance learning and enable the skills to be used more constructively in the interview. Providing schema that group skills into categories and define their interrelationship enables learners to piece together their learning into a form that they can remember and then use at will. Learners need to understand the structure and conceptual framework of the consultation to make sense of their learning and to retain it over time.

Possible didactic approaches include

- didactic lecture presentations,
- assigned literature study,
- critical reading of research evidence,
- tutorial and discussion groups,
- project work,
- demonstrations (live or videotaped),
- seminars and panels,
- "e"-learning.

9.7   What Experiential Approaches Are Available?

A variety of experiential methods are available that make it possible to observe learners interacting with patients:

- audio and video recordings,
- real patients,
- simulated patients,
- role-play.

What are the relative merits of each of these methods?

9.7.1   Audio and Video Feedback

Research into communication skills teaching has clearly demonstrated the central importance of the recording and playback of interviews. There is no doubt that video recording represents the gold standard of communication teaching. Although potentially more obtrusive and threatening to learners and patients than audiotape, videotape holds the attention of reviewers far better and enables a more detailed analysis of the interview (Westberg and Jason 1994). Moreover, it permits a focus on visual aspects of nonverbal behavior, so crucial in psychotherapy for patient assessment and in the decoding of the message produced during the interaction.

9.7.1.1   Practical Issues in the Use of Video Recording

But what are the practical issues involved in using videotape in communication programs?

Expense

It is an expensive medium. There is considerable capital outlay required to equip a program with the hardware for both recording and playback. Equipment needs to be serviced, maintained, and eventually replaced as the march of technology renders the original machinery obsolete. Fortunately, modern unobtrusive camcorders have become considerably cheaper and more available over recent years.

Technology

Video technology can interfere with the process of training. Cameras need to be set up, microphones checked, and sound levels confirmed prior to recording sessions. Playback equipment needs to be connected and compatible with the recording hardware. Failure of sound or vision in recording or playback can sabotage a session and undermine the confidence of learners and facilitator. To overcome these problems, every effort should be made to simplify the setting up of equipment. The recording equipment should be readily available, preferably permanently in situ. In clinical situations or teaching rooms regularly used for video recording, permanently installed cameras and hard-wired microphones help to facilitate recording.

Setting

The setting of experiential learning requires consideration. Some teaching institutions provide the setting of paired observation rooms with one-way mirrors between them.

The consultation takes place in one room with a built-in camera and microphone. The small learning group observes, records, and sometimes briefly discusses the interview in progress in the second room. Alternatively, movable dividers can be used to separate observers from practitioner and patient or silent observers can sit at some remove and watch the encounter as it is being recorded (the "fishbowl" technique), or the videotape can be recorded privately for use later without others observing the live interview.

Time

Using video and audio during teaching sessions takes time. Replaying the whole tape or even sections of the recording adds considerably to the length of the teaching session. Handling video efficiently requires expertise on the part of the facilitator, particularly if selected skills and behaviors are searched for as the session progresses. It is helpful if group members note specific tape times or counter numbers as they watch interviews so that short sections can be found and replayed during feedback or so that learners can refer to those specific moments when reviewing the tape later.

Apprehension

The use of videotape can add to the fear and apprehension of observation (Hargie and Morrow 1986). If being observed and receiving feedback is unsettling, it can be even worse enduring a live camera in the corner of a room and being forced to watch your behavior. In CBT, talking with patients can become very involving, and sometimes a therapeutic choice can lead to a personal self-disclosure by the clinician. The experience of rewatching the video of these interactions with other colleagues may become emotionally overwhelming and frustrating. Therefore, it is necessary to expend a lot of effort to protect learners from potentially uncomfortable experiences.

The very advantages of using recording and playback (self-assessment, learner involvement, objectivity, accuracy, specificity of feedback, description and microanalysis of behavior) can all cause discomfiture to learners (Beckman and Frankel 1994).

Patients' Diagnoses

The presence of a video camera can be very threatening for some patients. In a social phobia, for example, the idea of being observed by other people later on may activate worries of judgment or confirm the sense of inadequacy/indignity characteristic of this disorder. In other cases, the presence of a video camera can compromise patients' disclosure with the therapist, because it is perceived as an objective and real threat to the basis of a preexisting delusion of self-reference. Therefore, some psychiatric disorders like paranoid personality disorder or some types of psychosis may represent a serious obstacle for videotaping. It is very important to carefully consider the pros and cons for both the learner and the patient before proposing this method.

Despite these potential difficulties, video recording remains a most valuable tool for communication skills programs. Rather than holding back the use of video work, these issues need overcoming, as the benefits to learners and teachers are so significant. The immediate benefits to learners are clear from the research. But longer-term benefits also accrue. Learners can keep a record of the encounter and can review the teaching session later to reinforce learning. The program director can also keep a record, perhaps developing a bank of interviews to assist in future teaching or for use in preparing "trigger tapes."

9.7.2 Real Patients

The use of real patients in the communication skills curriculum can take several forms.

9.7.2.1 Prerecorded Videotapes of Real Consultations

A common experiential method used is the video recording of real consultations that have taken place within the learner's own practice. Participants can bring interviews that they have found to be difficult and can ask the group for help with specific issues. Bringing prerecorded videos to the communication course in this way has its drawbacks. The patient cannot personally provide feedback on the performance and is also not available for further rehearsal: alternative methods using role-play have to be employed. We know that recording and observation is not enough by itself: further rehearsal is also necessary for new behaviors to be incorporated into the learner's repertoire. We therefore need to engineer rehearsal in all experiential sessions that employ recordings. This is relatively easy with simulated patients—the group can watch the interaction between "patient" and practitioner as it occurs, the video record can be used immediately afterward during feedback, and further rehearsal with the actor can take place. Rehearsal can, however, be more difficult when using prerecorded videos of real patients who are not present at the time of the teaching session. Here it is important for one member of the group to watch the recording from the patient's perspective and be prepared to role-play the patient during feedback and rehearsal.

9.7.2.2 Live Interviews of Patients Brought to the Communication Unit

An alternative way of using real patients is to bring them to the communication course to be interviewed expressly for the purpose of helping learners. Patients can be involved in the learning process with different goals, which range from helping students to practice with new skills in a simulated interview, to offering them the chance to listen to histories of illnesses, told by the real protagonists. The observation of patients' personal narratives provides the opportunity to identify and recognize psychological or psychiatric symptoms until then read only in manuals. Discovering how, in "real life," functional and dysfunctional beliefs are mixed together or how adaptive emotions become destructive is the first step in understanding one of the core assumptions of psychotherapy: the continuity between health and disease. Especially at the beginning of a curriculum, using real patients in this way can be of considerable value.

As we have said, real patients can be also used for role-playing. Here it is important to remember that many psychiatric patients may not be suitable for this task or it could be too stressful for them. However, when clinical and personality variables do make this possible, we gain the considerable advantage of reducing the lack of spontaneity, often lamented by learners during simulation. Indeed learners are eager to see real patients talking about real symptoms and value the opportunity to practice with them in the safety of the communication unit. Immediate feedback from the patient can be extremely valuable to learners—they can discover if a line of questioning was sensitively handled from the patient's perspective or if the patient wanted more information than the learner had assumed. Unfortunately, patients are sometimes so supportive to learners that they find it difficult to make constructive criticisms.

Using real patients poses other difficulties, only some of which can be ameliorated through well-developed volunteer or community patient programs.

Rehearsal Limitations

Although trying out alternatives is possible, repeated rehearsal can be difficult for real patients. Real patients often have trouble both picking up the thread of the consultation at the point where a particular problem appeared and behaving differently in each rehearsal: they are not actors. In other cases, talking about their concerns over and over could reduce their emotional involvement or conversely make them feel emotionally overwhelmed. In order to protect patients' comfort and well-being, a careful selection of those suitable for this experience is not enough; we should also pay considerable attention to monitoring their emotional changes during the learning session, remembering that they might be unpredictable. Other ways of reducing patients' arousal include limiting sessions to a maximum of two hours and reducing as much as possible the number of role-plays (no more than four for each patient).

Restricted Types of Patients

Whether you use patients to bring their own experiences or to role-play, you may find some difficulties in selection. Sometimes this may be due to sociological characteristics; for example, retired people who are free during the day and poorer people wishing to obtain money are easier to recruit. In other cases, the diagnosis or the severity of the disorder may represent an exclusion criterion. For instance, psychotic patients or some personality disorders (such as borderline, antisocial, narcissistic, dependent) may not strictly respect rules during the simulation or give reliable feedback on communication skills afterward.

Realism

The medium itself greatly influences the interviews that are observed. Much of the realism of a true interview is negated by the way in which the interview has to be engineered. Because it is a repeat interview, most patients will not present the symptoms or their concerns in the same way as when they saw the therapist initially. Much of the emotional climate will have been ameliorated by what has happened to them since their initial interview.

Consent

Consent is, of course, a major issue in any situation in education where real patients are invited to help learners. This is particularly true when recordings are made. Truly informed consent is necessary, and patients must be given a genuine opportunity both to refuse to participate and also to change their minds after the consultation (Southgate 1993). The patient must sign before and after the consultation to give fully informed consent.

9.7.3 Simulated Patients

Simulated patients have been used successfully in communication teaching, evaluation, and research since their first introduction in the 1960s (Anderson et al. 1994; Barrows and Abrahamson 1964; Kaufman et al. 2000; Kurtz and Heaton 1995). Simulated patients portray live interactive simulations of specific problems and communication challenges to order. Initially, real patients were used to produce standardized presentations of illnesses they themselves had previously experienced. Simulated patients are now more commonly either professional or amateur actors or trained members of the community without formal acting background who portray roles from outside their own experience.

Simulated patients provide opportunities for learners to experiment and learn in a safe environment, without the possibility of harming real patients, yet in as close an approximation to reality as possible. The use of simulated patients has been shown to be acceptable to learners and faculty and to be effective, reliable, and valid as a method of instruction and evaluation (Bingham et al. 1996; Hoppe 1995; Vu and Barrows 1994).

The use of simulated patients in psychiatry and psychotherapy is controversial, mainly for two reasons; the first is that portraying psychological symptoms is harder than simulating a physical problem, which means that there is an intrinsic risk of lack of credibility in the patient's performance. Some studies disconfirmed this critique, showing that, when properly trained, simulated patients can perform reliable psychiatric scripts (Maguire et al. 1984; Rimondini et al. 2010) and prove to be a valuable alternative to real patients (Wündrich et al. 2008).

The second challenge is that engaging in a psychotherapeutic relationship with a person who is not really grieving can compromise the spontaneity of the interaction. Brenner (2009) suggests that standardized patients are most appropriate for exposing trainees to a variety of psychopathologies and testing very discrete skills, while their use is most problematic for teaching psychotherapy and assessing complex interpersonal skills, such as empathic responsiveness. In medical settings, this seems not to be true, as indicated by studies where students interviewing real and simulated patients were unable to discriminate between the two groups and no significant differences were found in their levels of empathy (Sanson-Fisher and Poole 1980; Maguire et al. 1986).

In cognitive-behavioral therapy (CBT), the healing process goes, of course, through complex dynamics between the therapist and the client, but the intervention is also based on structured and standardized protocols that require the use of specific, discrete communication skills. For this last aspect, CBT, compared to other approaches in psychotherapy, fits better with the requirements mentioned above for using simulated patients.

9.7.3.1 Advantages of Simulated Patients

Rehearsal

Simulated patients provide ideal opportunities for rehearsal during feedback sessions. Here is the ultimate offer to learners: feel free to experiment and to rehearse skills over and over again—do what you can hardly ever do with real patients in the outside world: Say out loud, "That didn't seem to work very well; let me try it again differently"! Simulated patients are willing for learners to make mistakes and to provide multiple opportunities for trial and error so that learners can practice skills in safety without any adverse consequences of "botching" an attempt at a new skill. Of course, this is only possible if the actor is present at the time of the group's discussion of the consultation. It is not available if the interview is recorded before the group meets and the simulated patient is not present when the tape is reviewed.

Improvisation

Simulated patients are able to replay parts of an interview, to reenter the consultation at any point, reacting appropriately and differently each time as participants try varying approaches. Simulated patients can adapt flexibly to learners' different approaches. For example, with a learner who is unskilled at using rapport-building skills, the simulated patient can look anxious or become quiet as a real patient would; on the other hand, the simulated patient can divulge his ideas or concerns in response to the more skilled learner who is able to pick up cues.

These improvisational qualities are very important because they enable the value of different behaviors to be seen in action. They also enable the learner to stop the consultation at any point to discuss what is happening: The actor can remain in suspended animation and can then pick up the consultation whenever the learner or another member of the group is ready to continue. As we have described, it is unfair to expect real patients to repeatedly rehearse complex or difficult situations and be able to change their behavior in relation to the learner's skills. In contrast, actors have the great advantage of being trained to immediately reenter situations as if they had never been there before and give a fresh performance each time. Their skillful flexibility is invaluable.

Standardization

Simulated patients also provide standardization, that is, reproducibility of roles. The level of standardization required varies depending on how the simulation is used. Teaching situations require presentation of the same case or situation in a reasonably consistent manner. Different learners can face the same challenge on different days. Learners will benefit from seeing how their peers cope with identical situations. Facilitators and program directors can work out criteria for evaluation and feedback in advance and even try out communication challenges for themselves. In the case of high-stakes examinations, standardization has to be at a higher level with totally consistent presentation of the case, so that candidates face identical challenges in their assessments. Standardization of simulated patient roles has enabled great strides to be made in the assessment of clinical competence and in the research of communication skills. An example of a possible standardized script is in Fig. 9.2.

Customization

The use of simulated patients allows the interview to be customized to a particular learner's level and tailored to her needs. Simulated patient cases can be varied so that the degree of challenge is increased as basic skills are mastered. Preceptors and program directors need to work closely with actors regarding such decisions: it would be inappropriate for actors to change the role on their own or have license to do whatever they wish.

Socio demographic data
- Your name is Elena Palombelli
- You was born in Verona on the ...., you are 53 years old.
- You have a degree in Philosophy. You work as a teacher at the .... School.
- You live with your husband, your 2 sons and your mother.

Main complain (reason for the consultation)
- You feel tired, with no energy

Other symptoms

- You have lost your appetite, and actually you have probably lost a few kilos.
- You often have gastritis and for this reason you try to eat less.
- Often now you start crying suddenly without any reason and in these moments you feel stupid.

Past symptoms
- Tiredness: you have never felt like this, you know that you are getting on in years but recently this has been really bad.
- Appetite/weight: you have never e eaten loads, but now you eat almost nothing.
- Gastritis: you have been suffering from this problem since you were young.
- Crying: In the past you cried just for sad events like everyone else.

Onset of symptoms

- Tiredness: you don't remember exactly
- Appetite/weight: you don't remember exactly
- Gastritis: since you were young
- Crying: you don't know.

Course of symptoms

- Tiredness: you don't remember exactly, you impression is that you felt more and more tired day after day.
- Appetite/weight: you have lost more or less 5/6 kilos during the last 5 months.
- Gastritis: twice in a month.
- Crying: in the last few weeks it happens more often.

Coping strategies

- Tiredness: you have taken ginseng, but it doesn't work.
- Appetite/weight: nothing.
- Gastritis: when you have stomach-ache you take a Buscopan tablet.
- Crying: nothing

Symptoms interference on quality of life and global functioning
- Tiredness: you are not doing your housework and you feel that you should help your son more in this important time in his life
- Appetite/weight: nothing.
- Gastritis: nothing in particular.
- Crying: Recently you are scared you will burst into tears while you are talking with another person, for this reason you try to avoid any kind of discussion or conversation with your family and also with friends or colleagues.

Why now
- Your family is worried for you, they see you are thin, tired and without energy. They all think that is not just a physical problem.

Your theory
- You don't know why this is happening to you especially because you should be particularly happy in a moment like this.

Your Expectations

- You don't know what you want from the doctor and what could help you in this moment.

Social context and life events
- Your son will get married in two months. After that they will move to Padova, since your daughter –in-low lives there.
- Your mother two years ago got Alzheimer 's and she is living with all of you since last year.

Supporting network

Fig. 9.2 Example of SP' script (portraying a mood disorder)

Specific Issues and Difficult Situations

Simulated patients are able to portray cases that demonstrate particularly difficult situations and are therefore ideal for helping with dedicated sessions on specific issues. Program directors can plan ahead and guarantee that the curriculum will cover situations such as breaking bad news, cultural issues, addiction, or anger that might well not arise opportunistically if we rely solely on situations that learners experience during the time span of the communication course. Asking real rather than simulated patients to come to the communication unit to replay their own difficult or emotionally charged experiences repeatedly is clearly inappropriate. Using simulated patients overcomes such problems.

Availability

Simulated patients can be available whenever required without disturbing real patients. A bank of specific cases can be developed and made available to communication or other faculty at a moment's notice. Being freed from the constraints of patient availability allows the communication program much greater choice as to when sessions can take place.

Time Efficiency

The use of simulated patients is time-efficient: particular skills can be isolated and practiced without observing an entire interview. It is possible to run through many stages of the progression of an illness in quick succession so that learners can follow through the consequences of communication skills in action. In one day, students can experience the events that in real life might take several weeks.

Feedback

An important advantage of involving simulated patients in communication skills training lies in their ability to provide feedback to learners and give insights from the lay perspective. A group of learners and facilitators can so easily forget to include the patient's perspective in their discussion. Simulated patients, however, can explain how they feel as the patient, providing feedback that would otherwise remain unavailable. Like facilitators and the learners themselves, simulated patients benefit from training regarding how to give detailed, descriptive feedback effectively.

9.7.3.2   Challenges in the Use of Simulated Patients

Part of the potential obstacles or disadvantages of using simulated patients in psychotherapy have already been discussed; here we discuss other practical issues.

Expense

Simulated patients are expensive. Unlike the capital costs involved in purchasing video equipment, this cost is recurring. Actors rightly require payment for both acting and preparation time, and we should not undervalue their time financially.

Selection

The selection process for simulated patients is important, both before and during training. Simulated patients may be either professional or amateur actors, drama students, or trained members of the community without a formal acting background. Simulators must come across as having a genuine desire to help rather than just a propensity for putting professionals or learners down. Useful attributes to look for are an interest in helping practitioners to learn, an ability not just to memorize a role but to adapt flexibly to different interviewer styles, the ability to express emotions verbally and nonverbally, physical stamina, and emotional stability (Pololi 1995).

Hidden Agendas

Although most learners comment on how realistic and useful simulated patients are, learners occasionally feel that they are being "set up" by the facilitator and actor. Learners sometimes think there are hidden aspects of the role that they are being asked to discover, akin to peeling away the layers of an onion until the real flesh is found. As only the actor and facilitator know the details of the patient's story in advance, it can appear that they are deliberately planning to trip up the learner. This suspicion can be reduced by introducing the actor to the group early on. Of course, some aspects of the case are there to challenge the learner's communication skills, but it is important that learners see this as a chance to practice skills rather than as a "setup." Using real cases with events that happened in actual practice as the basis for the simulation rather than making cases up also helps to resolve this problem.

Administrative Time

Another practical issue to consider is the time it takes to write up new simulated patient cases and periodically update those already on file; develop patient roles; recruit, train, and follow up simulated patients; and organize them to be available at appropriate times.

Training

Simulated patients require training (King et al. 1994). It is vital for the success of the program that simulators are trained to accurately depict the behavior of patients in various settings, to portray specific roles, and to give well-intentioned and constructive feedback. Before moving on to train for a particular role, simulated patients require a general orientation to the communication program, to the ethos and teaching methods of the unit, and to any responsibilities they may have in teaching or evaluating learners. Simulators need to be in tune with the objectives and methods of the communication skills program: they need to understand what communication training is hoping to achieve and to comprehend the difficulties that learners might have in buying into a program that is attempting to change their behavior.

When simulated patients are lay people, or people that have no experience of psychiatric/psychological disorders, there might be the tendency to overemphasize some emotions or behaviors on the basis of stereotypes or biases. In order to preserve performance reliability, we recommend the inclusion in simulated patients training of role-plays with clinicians giving feedback and sessions in which they observe videos of real patient interviews.

9.7.4 Role-Play

Role-play is another valuable method that can be used to advantage in the communication curriculum (Cohen-Cole et al. 1995), with several research *examples coming from psychiatry and psychotherapy settings* (McNaughton et al. 2008; Rimondini et al. 2006). In CBT, role-play is a therapeutic tool as well as, for example, in social skills training; therefore, therapists, before suggesting it to patients, are encouraged to experience it themselves. We have already discussed how role-play is an integral part of all experiential methods involving rehearsal. Group members are encouraged to adopt the practitioner's role during the analysis of the consultation to practice and rehearse skills. We have also seen how, in consultations that have been recorded earlier and other situations where the real or simulated patient is not available to take part in the discussion of the interview, a participant can adopt the role of the patient to facilitate feedback and rehearsal.

Here we discuss a specific form of role-play where one learner becomes the patient for an entire interview. The learner role-playing the patient may be given a particular role to play (e.g., through a printed "script" that describes the details) or alternatively "creates" the role herself based on a problem she has experienced personally or seen as a practitioner. A second learner (who does not know the case) plays the practitioner. Afterwards the group analyzes the interview as usual.

There are clear advantages to role-play:

- It is cheap—in fact, free.

- Little if any training is required.
- It is always available—it can be done whenever the program director wishes without planning and without much organization. Tapes do not have to be prepared in advance or actors trained and booked.
- It allows some learners to adopt the patient role, a significant learning experience in itself since it permits identification with patients' feelings but also enables verification of the positive or negative impact of some interventions made by the therapist.
- It can be used during any teaching session both inside and outside the communication curriculum whenever facilitators or learners wish to practice communication skills relevant to a specific topic. A group that is familiar with role-play can slip in and out of this method with ease.

Role-play is useful in various circumstances.

9.7.4.1 Difficult Cases

Role-play can be used in an impromptu fashion to illustrate difficult cases that learners have experienced in their work and that they bring to the learning group. Reverse role-play is particularly valuable here: the practitioner who has experienced a difficulty takes the part of a patient with whom he had a problem while another participant plays the practitioner. Alternative skills can be demonstrated while at the same time the initial practitioner can gain valuable insights by experiencing the patient's feelings at first hand.

9.7.4.2 Problem Scenarios

Learners can be asked to develop their own role-plays to demonstrate the specific problem or area of the interview that is the focus of the current teaching session. These role-plays can be based on scenarios that they themselves have experienced in real life as students, practitioners, or patients. The technique of the critical incident, widely applied in medical education (Flanagan 1954; Dunn and Hamilton 1986; Bradley 1992), may help in the definition of the key elements to portray in the role-play. Figure 9.3 demonstrates an example of a possible application.

9.7.4.3 Specific Issues

Scripts of patient and practitioner roles can be developed by the facilitators prior to the session so that a particular issue can be explored and discussed in detail. One approach here is for two participants to portray the patient and the practitioner and for the subsequent interview to be videotaped and analyzed in the same way as it would be with a simulated patient. Alternatively, role-plays can be performed simultaneously by dividing the group into pairs of practitioner and patient or trios of practitioner, patient, and observer. Each unit performs and analyzes the interview without videotape.

9.7.4.4 Disadvantages of Role-Play

The disadvantages of using role-play relate to the degree of difficulty participants may have in adopting roles. Participants are not actors and can find it difficult at first to role-play without self-consciousness, especially if they already have a relationship with the other participant. In particular, they may find it difficult to shed their knowledge and react as if they were a patient without the background, expertise, and experience that in real life the learners have. It is easier for learners to role-play a problem they have experienced themselves (with enough personal details changed to protect privacy) or to portray real people such as a patient the role-player has seen in real life or on video. It is much more difficult for learners to adopt a role from scratch: most learners find it difficult to improvise a history as they go unless a reasonably detailed background is provided. It can often feel artificial to both "practitioner" and "patient" if the "patient" is not able to sink herself into the proposed role. This artificiality is the most common criticism of role-play. Care is

---

Critical Incidence Form
Initials of participant_____   Date ____.____.____
Patient characteristics:
Age: ...34..........   Gender : male....................
Known for: ...1 day............................ (days, months or years)
Main diagnosis:
Schizophrenia, compulsory admission to hospital ward.
....

Reason of contact:
Mental state examination

If you should describe with no more than two sentences the reason why the encounter with this patient was particularly difficult for you, how would you complete the following sentences:

The communication with this patient is particularly difficult *because the patient was hostile and uncollaborative...*

The communication with this patient particularly difficult *because I felt angry, frustrated and helpless..*

Could you now try to reconstruct with the exact words the phase of the encounter in which this difficulty became most evident?

Resident-Patient Sequence:
Resident: Hi, Mr. Johns, how are you today?

Patient: I will not tell you

Resident: ok, we will go on later. However, it is important that I get to know how you feel today, given that you are admitted here to improve and to be helped

Fig. 9.3 Example of a critical incident that may be used as a script for a role-play

therefore necessary in preparing learners for role-play, especially for the "patient," who may need help entering the role-play situation and debriefing afterward.

9.8 Planning a Curriculum

As well as considering how to organize and run individual learning sessions, it is important to turn our attention to how to organize an ongoing curriculum. There is clear research evidence as to how to organize an ongoing curriculum to enable learners to maintain and advanced communication skills learning.

9.8.1 A Curriculum Rather Than a Course

Many of the problems of past approaches to communication teaching stem from the tendency to structure communication training into a single self-contained course, offered near the beginning of the overall program. Commonly, this course concludes with a single assessment of students' communication learning in isolation from the rest of the curriculum. Yet to achieve a significant lasting impact on learners' communication skills, we need more than a one-off course. Learners' communication needs change in tandem with their increasing levels of intellectual and clinical sophistication and develop as they progress though training. Our teaching interventions therefore need to be appropriately timed and spread over the curriculum.

9.8.2 A Helical Rather Than Linear Curriculum

Just as a one-off module is not enough, neither are sequential modules that do not allow the learner to revisit areas previously covered. Communication skills learning must be reiterated throughout learners' training or else it will diminish (Razavi et al. 2003; van Dalen et al. 2002). The curriculum needs to provide opportunities for learners to review, refine, and build on existing skills while at the same time adding in new skills and increasing complexity.

9.8.3 Integrated Not Separated from, the Rest of the Medical Curriculum

Without integrating communication back into the larger medical curriculum, communication will be perceived as a separate entity—an inessential frill rather than a basic skill relevant to all encounters with patients (Silverman 2009). What does the research about curriculum design tell us about the need for integration? We know that without training, medical students' communication skills deteriorate as the curriculum progresses. We also know that without reinforcement, learning from one-off courses deteriorates over time. We know that residents graduating from schools with more comprehensive sustained communication courses have better interpersonal skills. But perhaps the most important research is that of van Dalen et al. (2002), who demonstrated that integrated longitudinal programs achieve a more effective sustained increase in skills.

9.9   Conclusion

In this chapter, we have seen that communication skills can be both taught and retained but that to do so requires specific educational approaches that have been well proven by research. Interactive learner-centered experiential learning in small groups is essential to achieve behavioral change rather than just increased knowledge. Skilled facilitation, the use of expertly trained simulated patients, and the use of video and audio recording and playback are all required to turn good intentions in communication skills teaching into effective programs. These programs need to be ongoing longitudinal curricula that are integrated into students' overall learning.

This approach to learning does not come cheap, and considerable investment in resources is required to achieve high-quality communication skills teaching. However, the prize offered in improving the effectiveness of clinical practice makes the investment well worth the reward.

References

ACGME: *ACGME: Outcome project. ACGME General Competencies Version 1.3*, 2000, 28 September 1999.

Anderson, M. B., Stillman, P. L., & Wang, Y. (1994). Growing use of standardised patients in teaching and evaluation in clinical medicine. *Teaching and Learning in Medicine, 6*, 15–22.

Aspergren, K. (1999). Teaching and learning communication skills in medicine: A review with quality grading of articles. *Medical Teacher, 21*(6), 563–570.

Association of American Medical Colleges Panel on the General Professional Education of the Physician and College Preparation for Medicine. (1984). *Physicians for the Twenty-First Century: The GPEP report*. Washington, DC: Association of American Medical Colleges.

Association of American Medical Colleges. (1999). *Report 3: Contemporary issues in medicine: Communication in medicine*. Washington, DC: AAMC. Intro, 8.3: overview and assess.

Bandura, A. (1988). *Principles of Behavior Modification*. New York: Holt, Rinehart and Winston.

Barrows, H. S., & Abrahamson, S. (1964). The programmed patient: A technique for appraising clinical performance in clinical neurology. *Journal of Medical Education, 39*, 802–805.

Beckman, H. B., & Frankel, R. M. (1994). The use of videotape in internal medicine training. *Journal of General Internal Medicine, 9,* 517–521.

Beckman, H. B., Markakis, K. M., Suchman, A. L., & Frankel, R. M. (1994). The doctor–patient relationship and malpractice. *Archives of Internal Medicine, 154,* 1365–1370.

Bennett-Levy, J., McManus, F., Westling, B. E., & Fennell, M. (2009). Acquiring and refining CBT skills and competencies: Which training methods are perceived to be most effective? *Behavioral and Cognitive Psychotherapy, 37,* 571–583.

Bingham, L., Burrows, P., Caird, R., Holsgrove, G., & Jackson, N. (1996). Simulated surgery – Using standardized patients to assess clinical competence of GP registrars – A potential clinical component of the MRCGP examination. *Education for General Practice, 7,* 102–111.

Bradley, C. P. (1992). Turning anecdotes into data. The critical incident technique. *Family Practice, 9,* 98–103.

Brenner, A. M. (2009). Uses and limitations of simulated patients in psychiatric education. *Academic Psychiatry, 33,* 112–119.

Byrne, P. S., & Long, B. E. L. (1976). *Doctors talking to patients.* London: Her Majesty's Stationery Office.

Cegala, D. J., & Lenzmeier Broz, S. (2002). Physician communication skills training: A review of theoretical backgrounds, objectives and skills. *Medical Education, 36*(11), 1004–1016.

Cohen-Cole, S. A., Bird, J., & Mance, R. (1995). Teaching with roleplay – a structured approach. In M. Lipkin Jr., S. M. Putnam, & A. Lazare (Eds.), *The medical interview.* New York: Springer.

Duffy, F. D. (1998). Dialogue: The core clinical skill. *Annals of Internal Medicine, 128*(2), 139–141.

Dunn, W. R., & Hamilton, D. D. (1986). The critical incident technique – A brief guide. *Medical Teacher, 8,* 207–215.

Fallowfield, L., Jenkins, V., Farewell, V., Saul, J., Duffy, A., & Eves, R. (2002). Efficacy of a Cancer Research UK communication skills training model for oncologists: A randomised controlled trial. *Lancet, 359*(9307), 650–656.

Fallowfield, L., Jenkins, V., Farewell, V., & Solis-Trapala, I. (2003). Enduring impact of communication skills training: Results of a 12-month follow-up. *British Journal of Cancer, 89*(8), 1445–1449.

Ficklin, F. L. (1988). Faculty and house staff members as role models. *Journal of Medical Education, 63,* 392–396.

Flanagan, J. C. (1954). The critical incident technique. *Psychological Bulletin, 51,* 327–358.

Fleming, J. (1967). Teaching the basic skills of psychotherapy. *Archives of General Psychiatry, 16,* 416–426.

Hargie, O. D. W., & Morrow, N. C. (1986). Using videotape in communication skills training: A critical review of the process of self-viewing. *Medical Teacher, 8,* 359–365.

Hoppe, R. B. (1995). Standardized (simulated) patients and the medical interview. In M. Lipkin Jr., S. M. Putnam, & A. Lazare (Eds.), *The medical interview.* New York: Springer.

Kaufman, D. M., Laidlaw, T. A., & Macleod, H. (2000). Communication skills in medical school: Exposure, confidence, and performance. *Academic Medicine, 75*(Suppl 10), S90–S92.

King, A. M., Prkowski-Rogers, L. C., & Pohl, H. S. (1994). Planning standardised patient programmes: Case development, patient training, and costs. *Teaching and Learning in Medicine, 6,* 6–14.

Knowles, M. S. (1984). *The adult learner – A neglected species.* Houston, TX: Gulf.

Kurtz, S. M. (1990). *Attending rounds: A format and techniques for improving teaching and learning.* Paper presented at the 3rd International Conference on Teaching and Assessing Clinical Competence, Groningen, the Netherlands.

Kurtz, S. M. & Heaton, C. J. (1995). *Teaching and assessing information giving skills in the communication curriculum.* Paper presented at the 6th Ottawa Conference on Medical Education, University of Toronto.

Kurtz, S. M., Laidlaw, T., Makoul, G., & Schnabl, G. (1999). Medical education initiatives in communication skills. *Cancer Prevention and Control, 3*(1), 37–45.

Kurtz, S., Silverman, J., Benson, J., & Draper, J. (2003). Marrying content and process in clinical method teaching: enhancing the Calgary-Cambridge guides. *Academic Medicine, 78*(8), 802–809.

Kurtz, S. M., Silverman, J., & Draper, J. (2005). *Teaching and learning communication skills in medicine* (2nd ed.). Oxford: Radcliffe Medical.

Laidlaw, T., Kaufman, D. M., MacLeod, H., Wrixon, W., van Zanten, S., & Simpson, D. (2004). *Relationship of communication skills assessment by experts, standardized patients and self-raters.* Paper presented at the Association of Canadian Medical Colleges Annual Meeting, Halifax.

Maguire, P., Fairbairn, S., & Fletcher, C. (1986). Consultation skills of young doctors: 1 – Benefits of feedback training in interviewing as students persists. *BMJ, 292*, 1573–1576.

Maguire, G. P., Goldberg, D. P., Hobson, R. F., Margison, F., Moss, S., & O'Dowd, T. (1984). Evaluating the teaching of a method of psychotherapy. *British Journal of Psychiatry, 144*, 575–580.

McNaughton, N., Ravitz, P., Wadell, A., & Hodges, B. D. (2008). Psychiatric education and simulation: A review of the literature. *Canadian Journal of Psychiatry, 53*, 85–93.

Oh, J., Segal, R., Gordon, J., Boal, J., & Jotkowitz, A. (2001). Retention and use of patient-centered interviewing skills after intensive training. *Academic Medicine, 76*(6), 647–650.

Participants in the Bayer-Fetzer Conference on Physician–Patient Communication in Medical Education. (2001). Essential elements of communication in medical encounters: The Kalamazoo consensus statement. *Academic Medicine, 76*(4), 390–393.

Pololi, L. H. (1995). Standardised patients: As we evaluate so shall we reap. *Lancet, 345*, 966–968.

Razavi, D., Merckaert, I., Marchal, S., Libert, Y., Conradt, S., Boniver, J., et al. (2003). How to optimize physicians' communication skills in cancer care: Results of a randomized study assessing the usefulness of posttraining consolidation workshops. *Journal of Clinical Oncology, 21*(16), 3141–3149.

Ridsdale, L., Morgan, M., & Morris, R. (1992). Doctors' interviewing technique and its response to different booking time. *Family Practice, 9*, 57–60.

Rimondini, M., Del Piccolo, L., Goss, C., Mazzi, M., Paccaloni, M., & Zimmermann, C. (2006). Communication skills in psychiatry residents – How do they handle patient concerns? An application of sequence analysis to interviews with simulated patients. *Psychotherapy and Psychosomatics, 75*, 161–169.

Rimondini, M., Del Piccolo, L., Goss, C., Mazzi, M., Paccaloni, M., & Zimmermann, C. (2010). The evaluation of training in patient-centred interviewing skills for psychiatric residents. *Psychological Medicine, 40*, 467–476.

Sanson-Fisher, R. W., & Poole, A. D. (1980). Simulated patients and the assessment of medical students' interpersonal skills. *Medical Education, 14*, 249–253.

Sholomskas, D. E., Syracuse-Siewert, G., Rounsaville, B. J., Ball, S. A., Nuro, K. F., & Carroll, K. M. (2005). We don't train in vain: A dissemination trial of three strategies of training clinicians in cognitive-behavioral therapy. *Journal of Consulting and Clinical Psychology, 73*, 106–115.

Silverman, J. (2009). Teaching clinical communication: A mainstream activity or just a minority sport? *Patient Education and Counseling, 76*(3), 361–367.

Silverman, J. D., Draper, J., & Kurtz, S. M. (1997). The Calgary-Cambridge approach to communication skills teaching 2: The Set–Go method of descriptive feedback. *Education for General Practice, 8*, 16–23.

Silverman, J. D., Kurtz, S. M., & Draper, J. (1996). The Calgary-Cambridge approach to communication skills teaching 1: Agenda led outcome based analysis of the consultation. *Education for General Practice, 7*, 288–299.

Silverman, J., Kurtz, S. M., & Draper, J. (2005). *Skills for communicating with patients* (2nd ed.). Oxford: Radcliffe.

Simpson, M., Buckman, R., Stewart, M., Maguire, P., Lipkin, M., Novack, D., et al. (1991). Doctor–patient communication: The Toronto consensus statement. *BMJ, 303,* 1385–1387.

Smith, S., Hanson, J. L., Tewksbury, L., et al. (2007). Teaching patient communication skills to medical students: A review of randomised controlled trials. *Evaluation and the Health Professions, 30*(1), 3–21.

Southgate, L. (1993). *Statement on the use of video-recording of general practice consultations for teaching, learning and assessment: The importance of ethical considerations.* London: RCGP.

Stillman, P. L., Sabars, D. L., & Redfield, D. L. (1977). Use of trained mothers to teach interviewing skills to first year medical students: A follow up study. *Pediatrics, 60,* 165–169.

van Dalen, J., Kerkhofs, E., van Knippenberg-Van Den Berg, B. W., van Den Hout, H. A., Scherpbier, A. J., & van der Vleuten, C. P. (2002). Longitudinal and concentrated communication skills programmes: Two Dutch medical schools compared. *Advances in Health Sciences Education Theory and Practice, 7*(1), 29–40.

Vu, N. V., & Barrows, H. (1994). Use of standardised patients in clinical assessments: Recent developments and measurement findings. *Educational Researcher, 23,* 23–30.

Weerasekera, P., Manring, J., & Lynn, D. J. (2010). Psychotherapy training for residents: Reconciling requirements with evidence-based, competency-focused practice. *Academic Psychiatry, 34,* 5–12.

Westberg, J., & Jason, H. (1993). *Collaborative clinical education: The foundation of effective health care.* New York: Springer.

Westberg, J., & Jason, H. (1994). *Teaching creatively with video – Fostering reflection, communication and other clinical skills.* New York: Springer.

Wilkinson, S., Perry, R., Blanchard, K., & Linsell, L. (2008). Effectiveness of a three-day communication skills course in changing nurses' communication skills with cancer/palliative care patients: A randomised controlled trial. *Palliative Medicine, 22*(4), 365–375.

Wündrich, M., Peters, J., Philipsen, A., Kopasz, M., Berger, M., & Voderholzer, U. (2008). Clinical teaching with simulated patients in psychiatry and psychotherapy. A controlled pilot study. *Nervenarzt, 79,* 1273–1274.

Chapter 10
Quantitative Methods for the Analysis of Verbal Interactions in Psychotherapy

Maria Angela Mazzi

10.1 Introduction

When psychotherapy is viewed as an interpersonal and interactive process, sequential methods for analyzing the intersubjective dimension of the psychotherapeutic dialogue become a strategic tool. In the first section, this chapter shows a short overview of the currently used methods in the quantitative approach to verbal interactions, and particularly those statistical tools able to handle information collected as a sequence of countable events. Then in the second section, we propose a process to move from recorded interviews to a statistically summarized result (see Fig. 10.1). The sequential steps identified in this process aim to codify the interviews, transferring them into a stream of units, classified by a nominal scale. Since every unit can be univocally assigned to a specific category, observations become countable. Despite the limitations of a nominal scale, this information may be quantitatively summarized by using appropriate statistical techniques based on frequency counts.

10.2 Quantitative Approach to a Verbal Interaction: An Overview

In recent decades, considerable progress has been made in the development of new statistical techniques aimed at investigating the dyadic interaction between doctor and patient and describing the relationship of the occurrences of verbal behaviors over time (Hoff 2005; Chiu and Khoo 2005; Kenny et al. 2006; Tschacher and Ramseyer 2009; Tasca and Gallop 2009).

Regarding the psychotherapeutic setting in particular, the literature shows many applications of sequential techniques, but they have been mainly focused on

M.A. Mazzi (✉)
Department of Public Health and Community Medicine, University of Verona, Policlinico G.B. Rossi, Piazzale L.A. Scuro 10, 37134 Verona, Italy
e-mail: mariangela.mazzi@univr.it

M. Rimondini (ed.), *Communication in Cognitive Behavioral Therapy*,
DOI 10.1007/978-1-4419-6807-4_10, © Springer Science+Business Media, LLC 2011

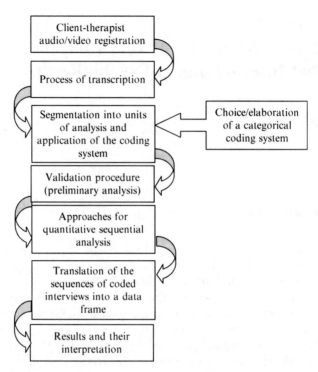

Fig. 10.1 Flowchart of quantitative analysis of psychotherapeutic dialogue

investigating the efficacy of the therapeutic treatment by monitoring the presence of specific outcomes and their developments. For example, Gaston and Marmar (1989) proposed a time-series multiple-regression analysis to explore the relationship between the therapeutic process and treatment efficacy in reducing the symptoms of psoriasis. Specifically, both patients and therapists were asked to complete a questionnaire in order to individualize the specific "points" of change that occurred within the therapeutic session. Results were aimed at generating a hypothesis on which therapeutic factors could be significantly involved in determining the expected outcome (the therapeutic change).

Another example is offered by Bockenholt (1999), who investigated the relationship between everyday emotional experiences and personality traits, by using an autoregressive negative multinomial regression model. This recent technique allows one to simultaneously analyze several outcomes/emotions (multivariate approach) and to handle the complex structures of observed data (e.g., events observed repeatedly over many individuals).

The first attempts to explore communication in psychotherapy were undertaken in the early 19th century. These early studies are worth citing because they underline the importance of exploring the communicative interaction between the therapist and the client; however, they did not employ techniques capable takeoff taking into account the sequential perspective of the interaction (Putnam and Stiles 1993; Stiles and Shapiro 1995; Hardy et al. 1998).

A further step in the sequential analysis of therapeutic conversation was due to Viney (1994), who applied a log-linear analysis on sequences of client–therapist verbal turns. In order to explore the influence of the therapeutic interaction on clients' emotional expression, she focused attention on pairs of adjacent speech turns and their relationship. This work represents an interesting improvement in conversation quantitative analysis because it performed a detailed micro-level analysis, explored how the verbal therapist–client interaction may produce changes, and led to the formulation of a model on the mechanisms through which treatments operate.

Another interesting application was due to Wiseman and Rice (1989). They analyzed moment by moment the whole transcript of a set of interviews in order to describe the effects of therapist behavior on the client productive process during the problematic reaction point (PRP).

Moving from semantic text analysis to yield content analysis, a different approach was developed by Gottschalk et al. (1993), who explored how patients choose words to describe their feelings (such as hostility, depression, hope), and used these statements as a measure of emotional states. Their contribution is also important because they expended quite an effort to support and implement the developed instruments by using specific software (Gottschalk 1994, 2000).

This short overview of the literature shows that, up to now, few studies have explored the sequential events occurring within therapeutic conversation (micro-area events) using a quantitative approach, while a lot has been written on measuring the improvement in symptoms (Margison et al. 2000; Turkington and Kingdon 2000) or on qualitative exploration (Frank and Sweetland 1962; Morberg Pain et al. 2008; Reyes et al. 2008).

However, in recent years, quantitative conversational analysis seems to have been extensively applied to study communication in the field of general medicine (Connor et al. 2009; Finset 2008; Eide et al. 2004; Langewitz et al. 2003; Zimmerman et al. 2003: Del Piccolo et al. 2007).

10.3 Moving from Recorded Interviews to Statistical Results

Figure 10.1 shows a flowchart of the sequential steps that can be followed for an adequate sequential analysis procedure. The steps entail (1) transcription of the audio/video registration, (2) segmentation into units of analysis, (3) application of the coding system, (4) assessment of inter-rater agreement, (5) choice of the appropriate approach of quantitative analysis, (6) planning of the data-frame, and (7) elaboration and interpretation of the results. All of these steps will be briefly explained next.

Box 10.1 Content Analysis: A Brief Summary

The literature shows two approaches to content analysis: qualitative and quantitative. The qualitative one is more employed in psycho-social fields and can be categorized into three types: conventional, directed, and summative (Hsieh and Shannon 2005), as a function of the source of code. The last one is widely used in information and library sciences to count manifest textual elements and to test hypotheses on them (Rourke and Anderson 2004). More generally, content analysis can be defined as an empirical method used in the social sciences primarily for analyzing recorded human communication in a quantitative, systematic, and intersubjective way. It facilitates contextual meanings in text through the development of emergent themes, both manifest contents (directly from expressed words) and latent ones (from the interpretations of observed expressions or sentences). Two definitions of the qualitative approach seem to describe it better: "an approach of empirical, methodological controlled analysis of texts within their context of communication, following content analytical rules and step by step models, without rash quantification" (Mayring 2000, p. 2) and "any qualitative data reduction and sense making effort that takes a volume of qualitative material and attempts to identify core consistencies and meanings" (Patton 2002, p. 453).

While Hsieh et al.'s paper (2005) is recommended for an exhaustive explanation, here the proposed seven steps are succinctly listed in order to perform a qualitative content analysis:

- identifying the purpose of the coding system or the research questions to be answered;
- selecting the sample to be analyzed;
- highlighting behaviors that represent the construct and then reducing the material by deleting the words that are not necessary and maintaining the basic content;
- defining the categories and subcategories to be applied and outlining the coding process;
- training the coders and holding preliminary tryouts, eventually refining the coding process;
- determining trustworthiness (reliability, validity, generalizability, replicability);
- developing guidelines for the administration, scoring, and interpretation of the coding scheme.

10.3.1   How to Turn a Psychotherapeutic Interview from a Taped Dyadic Conversation into a Systematic Observation of Coded Behavioral Sequences

The taped client–therapist conversations were transcribed and analyzed using content analysis according to a set of defined categories. Such a statement usually appears in the methodological section of an empirical search paper. This process— converting the observed information from a qualitative into a quantitative data set—is really very complex, and it is often referred to as the *tape-transcribe-code-interpret* (TTCI) cycle (Lapadat and Lindsay 1999). Here we will describe each step of the analysis protocol (transcription process, choosing or creating an appropriate coding scheme, counting frequencies, and sequence analysis), suggesting rules in the field of quantitative research using language as the data.

The first step is to transcribe verbatim the audio- or videotaped therapeutic session. The role of transcription shouldn't be underestimated in the TTCI cycle. Lapadat and Lindsay (1999) and Schilling (2006) both contain a detailed and clear exposition of the methodological and theoretical issues of the transcript process. In the last 25 years, particular attention was spent creating a standardized procedure and conventional rules for handling language data to better represent records in text format (Edwards and Lamperts 1993). Researchers had to solve some strategic questions such as whether the whole record or only the main parts should be transcribed. Should the slips of tongue be reported or corrected? Should nonverbal but audible observations during conversations (e.g., sounds, crying, and pauses) be transferred, and how?

A second step is to define what the unit of analysis is. This is a strategic decision related to what a meaningful unit is according to the coding system that has to be applied in the following step. There are many possibilities: utterance, paragraph, verbal turn, thematic level, a specific keyword from a fixed set. Schilling (2006, p. 31) stated that a "meaningful unit would mean a segment of text that is comprehensible by itself and contains one idea, episode, or piece of information." Consequently, a segmentation procedure is applied to the transcript, by identifying the unit of analysis, thereby transforming the client–therapist conversation into a sequence of distinct text-blocks, usually called "raw data." Each block has "contextual" information (about timing, duration, and position) and is usually uniquely identified by a progressive number. Last, but not least, the transcript should be made anonymous by deleting or replacing names of people with pseudonyms or identifying codes in order to protect patient privacy and at the same time maintain the link to other information sources (as patient socio-demographical and clinical characteristics).

Obviously, these two steps will direct the subsequent quantitative analysis later. The whole procedure subsumes that the translation of spoken discourse into a written text is not a merely "mechanical activity" without problems, but rather is a way to represent the observations and thus becomes a proper research method with explicit and rigorous rules. Several computer programs have recently been developed to support this step of qualitative analysis, including ATLAS/ti (Scientific Software Development), win/MAX, The Observer XT, and INTERACT.

The third step is the so-called data reduction because it is characterized by the process of coding. The reduction means a procedure of condensing, or in some way organizing, large quantities of text into many fewer standardized content categories. Through a line-by-line analysis of the transcript, an expert coder assigns to each raw unit a specific category label, selected from a fixed set of categories. In order to capture the whole message in terms of both content and context, it is recommended that the coder read the transcript several times before starting the coding procedure. According to the goals of research, a coding tool must be chosen among those offered in the literature (using a deductive or theory-driven approach) or intentionally developed for the specific research (inductive or data-driven approach, for example, by using qualitative content analysis; see Box 10.1). A good coding tool should have a user-friendly manual with detailed category definitions (which have to be exhaustive and mutually exclusive) and brief rules of application. See Chapter 1 for some examples of coding systems in psychotherapy.

10.3.2 Quality Standards in the Quantitative Approach to Qualitative Research: Validity and Reliability of the Coding System

The evaluation of the quality of the nominal data and its measurement tool allows the data collection to be statistically treated and so quantitatively synthesized.

A more detailed description of different sources of variability that may influence the validity of psychotherapy process measures can be found in Wasserman et al. (2009) and Eid et al. (2009), highlighting the multitrait–multimethod approach for test validation, while Doucette and Wolf (2009) present an overview of item-response theory. This chapter focuses on intercoder reliability (in content analysis, more specifically termed "intercoder agreement"), which represents good practice whenever a coding system is applied (Lombard et al. 2002).

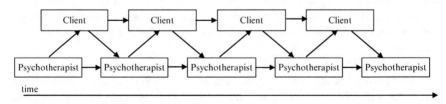

Fig. 10.2 State-space diagram for dyadic dependence structure within a psychotherapeutic conversation

In the psychometric approach, a measurement tool can be defined as reliable if it carries out the same results when it is applied by different analysts (agreement among coders) or by the same analyst at different times (agreement within coder). The high-reliability assessment is a practical way for quality research assurance, because it enhances the credibility of the analysis, above all when large samples are explored, different coders are involved, and results are derived using complex statistical techniques.

In qualitative analysis, good reliability can be practically quantified by counting the homogeneous labels repeated two or more times on the same unit of analysis. Methodologists recently have developed a robust set of techniques for estimating the reliability (e.g., percent agreement, Cohen's kappa, Scott's π, Holsti's CR, Bennett's S, Krippendorff's α) and have also widely discussed the strengths and limitations of each of these indicators (Leiva et al. 2006). They also have given some indications on how to choose the most appropriate agreement index, suggesting that this choice should be guided by the following crucial aspects: the type of measurement scale (nominal, ordinal, or numeric), the number of categories, the sensitivity to errors of systematic coding, the ability to take into account chance agreement (i.e., the agreement due to random responses), and the ability to support multiple coders.

Among these indicators, the approach proposed by Krippendorff (2004) deserves special attention since it jointly considers agreements on the categories (the content of the unit of analysis) and on the specific part of the text to which the category refers (the partition into units of analysis). On the other hand, the calculation does not look trivial, particularly on sizable samples, and the use of text analysis software combined with statistical software applications becomes a valuable aid in calculating the location and length of the coded units by comparison (Hayes and Krippendorff 2007; Quera et al. 2007).

Finally, it is good practice to provide an adequate set of information on reliability, coding instrument, and procedures in the search report in order to verify the use of a standardized protocol.

10.3.3   Some Statistical Approaches to Analyze Conversation Sequences

After the translation of the client–therapist interview into a stream of coded events, the interaction may be analyzed from different points of views. In any case, a correct perspective regards the dyadic nature of data that cannot be left since the observations have to be analyzed with respect to the sequential structure of interpersonal relations. In statistical terms, this means that the observations are dependent.

The concept of dependence in behavioral processes was well explained by Dumas (1986) and Van-Beek et al. (1992), who divided it into two components:

serial dependence and *interdependence* (see Fig. 10.2). Serial dependence is also called *autodependence* or *autocontingency* (Altham 1979; Tavaré and Altham 1983), or *dependence within subject,* and accounts for the fact that a subject may influence herself. When the client (or therapist) says something, it may be influenced by what he has said before (horizontal arrows in Fig. 10.2). The dependence within subject is an important element in the basic statistical assumptions underlying sequential analysis, because it is a nonrandom aspect of a behavioral sequence. Interdependence refers to the *dependence between subjects,* which occurs when two subjects influence each other. It is also called *cross-contingency* or *joint dependence*, which is derived from the interaction of two distinct sources (either client or therapist; oblique arrows in Fig. 10.2).

The choice of the statistical technique has to take into account this complexity of the units of analysis (code categories of speech) together with the aims of the search project (Mazzi et al. 2003). The literature offers four different approaches, and within them a set of statistical techniques more or less complex according to both the sampling design and the involved information. These techniques are the recognition of the occurrence of defined sequences (pattern recognition), Markov chain models, lag-sequential analysis, and, partially, event-history analysis.

The *pattern recognition* approach is an appropriate methodology to discover regularities in the temporal evolution of the conversation. Pattern research is based on the count of frequencies of matched specific units of analysis (more frequently couples, but also triplets or longer sequences of events) and on conditional probability theory. Prior knowledge in the field, the theoretical approach, or evidence from the literature plays an important role in determining the choice of the sequence pattern under study. Conversely, it might also happen that, without specific hypotheses (empirically driven), associations between parts of sequences are explored. The aim is to test whether the expected pattern occurs among the observed patterns more often than by chance in terms of its conditional probability distribution. The conditional probability of a sequence is estimated by dividing the number of times it occurred by the number of times it could have occurred in the observational records (the numbers of occurrences plus the number of nonoccurrences). An example of this application can be seen in Zimmermann et al. (2003), who tested the hypothesis that in a medical interview when the exploration of an issue starts with a closed question, then the physician will tend to repeat this close-ended questioning style. In their study, Tasca and Mc Mullen (1992) drew profiles of short-term psychotherapy, selecting and coding segments of therapist–client paired-speech units from audio recordings; in this way they represented the therapeutic relationship as a dyadic interaction and tested their hypothesis on dyads in successful cases versus dyads in unsuccessful cases, by a repeated ANOVA. Another interesting application was due to Yoder et al. (2001). They presented an application of sampled permutation tests to examine whether one sequential association is greater than another within a single dyad.

This simple approach to describe sequences (namely, *manifest behavioral patterns*), however, is not exhaustive, because patterns easily become invisible to the naked eye when other behaviors occur in between. The so-called hidden behavioral pattern (Magnusson 2000) approach helps to find some nested relationships among complex sequences of events and to distinguish which pattern is relevant (signal) and which is irrelevant (noise), by reducing the extraneous sources of variability (e.g., by increasing the signal-to-noise ratio).

Markov chains are defined as a collection of random variables with a specific dependency structure, called a Markov property. This theory assumes that to make predictions about "future" behaviors, it is sufficient to consider only its present state and not its past history (memory effect of one-order). The applicability of this technique to the study of behavioral sequences was due to Faraone and Dorfman (1987), who widely discussed the underlying strong assumptions (stationarity, ergodicity, and order of dependency) and their validity. Their contribution helped to illuminate the correct way to approach the sequential analysis, which most recently was studied by Dagne et al. (2002, 2007), Dagne and Snyder (2010), and Howe et al. (2005), who opened new avenues to sequential analysis by applying multilevel techniques and frailty models to calculate unbiased and robust estimates.

The *lag-sequential approach* was introduced by Sackett (1979) in order to analyze complex interactions between mother and infant. Then it was adopted by Gottman and Roy (1990) and Bakeman and Quera (1992, 1995a, b), who applied the lag-sequential analysis to study the association among categories in a two-way contingency table. The aim was to use relatively simple summary statistics on rather complex data. The information related to the sequence of codes is structured by using a transitional contingency table, which is the basis for any sequence analysis, borrowed from Markov chains. This table usually represents coded events in terms of their displacement in time (lag). Rows represent the first, or given, event (for example, therapist utterance) and columns the following, or target, event (what the patient says subsequently, that is, at lag 1 or greater than 1). The lag is the distance, in terms of subsequent code units or events, between the given event and the target event considered. Each cell represents the frequency of chains that begin with the given event and end with the target event. The advantage of transition probabilities is that "they 'correct' for differences in base rates for the 'given' behavioral states ... [and] easily show the most likely ways of 'moving' from one state to another" (Bakeman and Gottman 1997, p. 104). However, the disadvantages, according to the authors, are the great variability among subjects in transition probabilities and their questionable use for comparing groups. The sequential techniques can be distinguished into those that restrict the analyses to immediately following (lag-1) behaviors and those that refer to a multivariate contest, considering more than lag-1 sequences. The assumption underlying lag-1 sequence analysis is the presence of a short-term memory effect in the sequences (as in the "first-order Markov chain"), namely, that each behavior is influenced by the immediately preceding behavior. It would therefore be more correct to call lag-1 sequential analysis "contiguity analysis."

Finally, the *event-history approach* (in an epidemiological context, namely survival analysis, duration analysis, or transition analysis) allows one to study the

PrgNum	Subject	Text	Code Label	Value label
1	Therapist A	Ok ... tell me what is your problem.	QUOND	−45
2	Client 1	pragmatically... I think it is a type of anxiety	EO/PS	30
3	Client 1	because when I go to parties or unknown places yet and even with know people or with unknown ones, I feel...agitation and anxiety and I cannot free me from it in reality.	SPSY/EMO	20
4	Client 1	The effect is that the first thing I do in new places, since past time, I search the bathroom because I think I feel the urge... it gives me incentive to go to the bathroom and instead I have nothing to do	SQL/INT	16
5	Client 1	but I always feel the urge and I cannot feel comfortable. Here is the problem concretely	SIM/MED	13
6	Therapist A	Ok! The last time that is it happened?	DIR/PSY/EMO	−42
7	Client 1	Yesterday ... Today is Friday ... Wednesday night at a dinner.	SPSY/EMO	20
8	Therapist A	Maybe could you describe me what happened before, maybe what his first thoughts, his fears, however, perhaps ...	QUOND	−45
9	Client 1	I don't have many thoughts ...I mean for example I had to go to take some girls in order to go to this dinner, but the thought of arriving in time to take one and the other one...I hadn't unusual thoughts on dinner	SPSY/COG	20
10	Client 1	When I got out the car, I am ... I was restless and thought of looking for the bathroom concretely...	SPSY/EMO	20
...	...	....	...	...

Fig. 10.3 An example of raw data encoded using the VR_PICS/P and VR_PICS/D coding system

IDinterview	lag0 code	lag1 code	frequencies
1	DIR/PSY/EMO	SPSY/EMO	1
1	EO/PS	SPSY/EMO	1
1	QUOND	EO/PS	2
1	QUOND	SPSY/COG	2
1	SIM/MED	DIR/PSY/EMO	1
1	SPSY/COG	SPSY/EMO	4
1	SPSY/EMO	SQL/INT	1
1	SPSY/EMO	QUOND	1
1	SQL/INT	SIM/MED	2
...	...	...	...

Fig. 10.4 An example of an organized database to process sequences of events surrounding lag-1 analysis

relationship between a specific event that happens during the interview and a set of previews occurrences, taking into account the temporal distance among them (Singer and Willett 2003). In the same way as in survival analysis, the target variable is the presence or absence of a chosen behavior and is modeled as a "hazard rate" in a function of time (usually expressed as a duration, i.e., the distance from the beginning of exposition to the risk), and other explicative variables that inform of related behaviors across the observed interviews as well as characteristics of participants (Griffin and Gardner 1989).

10.3.4   How You Can Organize the Coded Text Sequences into a Database to Be Statistically Processed?

The following section briefly describes different ways in which the raw data (i.e., labels of coded data) can be stored in a two-dimensional array, namely, a data-frame, suitable for statistical analysis based on textual data. Strictly speaking, we will describe what the columns (variables) and rows (units of analysis) of the database should contain in order to apply a statistical technique accounting for time information.

Traditionally, text analysis methods were merely based on counting occurrences, without preserving any time location. The stream of coded events was implemented as count-data aggregated within each sampling unit, which was defined according to the aims of research.

In recent years, the development of a longitudinal approach (such as time-series panel data and multilevel regression models) and its software production has totally changed the architecture of databases, since the concept of multiple levels of measurement has been introduced. When the study design is hierarchical (Hox 2002; Tasca and Gallop 2009; Gallop and Tasca 2009), the units are nested in clusters; some information is measured on each unit of analysis (e.g., level 1, the observed speech turn) and other information on each cluster (e.g., level 2, the patient's characteristic-specific interview), which is the same for all units belonging to the same cluster. So variables can be distinguished within and between clusters, relating their nature, and can be correctly pasted in the statistical model to be identified.

For example, moving from an interview classified using the VR-PICS coding system (for a description of this instrument, see Chapter 1) is depicted in Figs. 10.3 and 10.4. In Fig. 10.3, a block of raw data can be observed; here only the text-related variables[1] are listed, which are a progressive number of verbal units (PrgNum; a level-1 variable) that inform of the location of the event; the source of the event (Subject: client or therapist; a level-2 variable) detailing the actor; the transcript of the target event (Text; a level-1 variable); and its coding, both in string format (Code label) and in number format (Value label). Other information can be added to the main database by using the patient's or therapist's identifier number as a link in order to take over the database on that information (level-2 variables). This is a basic database, useful when applying multilevel regression models.

In Fig. 10.4, the previous database has been modified to obtain a typical database useful in the pattern recognition or lag-1 sequential approach. In order to obtain sequences of codes (which are chains of two or more neighbors), the same

---

[1] In statistical language, the variables are often distinguished between those informing about the spoken language (what was said, who said it, when, where, and how it was said), which are usually called *text-related variables* (coded text-blocks, location, author), and *contextual variables*, which inform about the setting and the participants and are linked to each unit of analysis, in a repeated and equal way within each interview (socio-demographical and clinical characteristics of sources such as gender, diagnosis, age).

information is arranged by counting the number of couples of two adjacent events with the same behavior (see columns 2 and 3, respectively, for antecedent and consequent behavior, usually called "given" and "target" in the probabilistic approach) and pasting the resulting frequency in the fourth column (frequencies counter). To properly analyze this type of database, statistical software should perform weighted calculations (taking into account the pasted frequencies). Sequences are not limited to two adjacent events; they can cover several actions (more than one lag) and go in both forward and backward directions; an example of bidirectional lag-analysis, which also explores lag-2 sequences, is showed by Goss et al. (2005).

10.4 Conclusions

This chapter has outlined the main steps that a researcher should follow when analyzing therapist–patient interaction according to a quantitative approach. New statistical methods such as lag-sequential analysis allow one to partially overcome the limits of previous systems that assessed communication by considering it a juxtaposition of elements instead of a sequential process. The literature offers several examples of the application of these methods in psychotherapy; a growing tendency in this field is also to mix together quantitative and qualitative analyses in order to gain a broader picture of the phenomenon (see Chapter 11).

References

Altham, P. M. (1979). Detecting relationships between categorical variables observed over time: A problem of deflating a chi-squared statistic. *Applied Statistics, 28*, 2115–2125.

Bakeman, R., & Gottman, J. M. (1997). *Observing interaction: An introduction to sequential analysis.* Cambridge, UK: Cambridge University Press.

Bakeman, R., & Quera, V. (1992). SDIS: A sequential data interchange standard. *Behavioral Research. Methods, Instruments and Computers, 24*, 554–559.

Bakeman, R., & Quera, V. (1995a). Log-linear approaches to lag-sequential analysis when consecutive codes may and cannot repeat. *Psychological Bulletin, 118*, 2272–2284.

Bakeman, R., & Quera, V. (1995b). *Analysing interaction. Sequential analysis with SDIS and GSEQ.* Cambridge, UK: Cambridge University Press.

Bockenholt, U. (1999). Analyzing multiple emotions over time by autoregressive negative multi-nomial regression models. *Journal of the American Statistical Association, 94*, 757–765.

Chiu, M. M., & Khoo, L. (2005). A new method for analyzing sequential process: Dynamic multilevel analysis. *Small Group Research, 36*, 600–631.

Connor, M., Fletcher, I., & Salmon, P. (2009). The analysis of verbal interaction sequences in dyadic clinical communication: A review of methods. *Patient Education and Counseling, 75*, 169–177.

Dagne, G. A., Brown, C. H., & Howe, G. W. (2007). Hierarchical modeling of sequential behavioral data: Examining complex association patterns in mediation models. *Psychological Methods, 12*, 298–316.

Dagne, G. A., Howe, G. W., Brown, C. H., & Muthén, B. O. (2002). Hierarchical modeling of sequential behavioral data: An empirical Bayesian approach. *Psychological Methods, 7*, 262–280.

Dagne, G. A., & Snyder, J. (2010). Bayesian analysis of the repeated events using event-dependent frailty models: An application to behavioral observation data. *Communication in Statistics: Theory and Methods, 39*, 293–310.

Del Piccolo, L., Mazzi, M. A., Dunn, G., Sandri, M., & Zimmermann, C. (2007). Sequence analysis in multilevel models. A study on different sources of patient cues in medical consultations. *Social Science and Medicine, 65*, 2357–2370.

Doucette, A., & Wolf, A. W. (2009). Questioning the measurement precision of psychotherapy research. *Psychotherapy Research, 19*, 374–389.

Dumas, J. E. (1986). Controlling for autocorrelation in social interaction analysis. *Psychological Bulletin, 100*, 1125–1127.

Edwards, J. A., & Lamperts, M. D. (1993). *Talking data: Transcription and coding in discourse research.* Hillsdale, NJ: Lawrence Erlbaum.

Eid, M., Geiser, C., & Nussbeck, F. W. (2009). Multitrait–multimethod analysis in psychotherapy research: New methodological approaches. *Psychotherapy Research, 19*, 390–396.

Eide, H., Quera, V., Graugaard, P., & Finset, A. (2004). Physician–patient dialogue surrounding patients' expression of concern: Applying sequence analysis to RIAS. *Social Science and Medicine, 59*, 145–155.

Faraone, S. V., & Dorfman, D. D. (1987). Lag sequential analysis: Robust statistical methods. *Psychological Bulletin, 101*, 2312–2323.

Finset, A. (2008). New developments in analysis of turns and sequences in clinical communication research. *Patient Education and Counseling, 71*, 1–2.

Frank, G. H., & Sweetland, A. A. (1962). Study of the process of psychotherapy: The verbal interaction. *Journal of Consulting Psychology, 26*, 135–138.

Gallop, R., & Tasca, G. A. (2009). Multilevel modelling of longitudinal data for psychotherapy researchers: II. The complexities. *Psychotherapy Research, 19*, 438–452.

Gaston, L., & Marmar, C. R. (1989). Quantitative and qualitative analyses for psychotherapy research: Integration through time-series designs. *Psychotherapy, 26*, 169–176.

Goss, C., Mazzi, M. A., Del Piccolo, L., Rimondini, M., & Zimmermann, C. (2005). Information-giving sequences in general practice consultations. *Journal of Evaluation in Clinical Practice, 11*, 339–349.

Gottman, J. M., & Roy, A. K. (1990). *Sequential analysis: A guide for behavioral researchers.* Cambridge, UK: Cambridge University Press.

Gottschalk, L. A. (1994). The development, validation, and applications of a computerized measurement of cognitive impairment from the content analysis of verbal behaviour. *Journal of Clinical Psychology, 50*, 349–361.

Gottschalk, L. A. (2000). The application of computerized content analysis of natural language in psychotherapy research now and in future. *American Journal of Psychotherapy, 54*, 305–311.

Gottschalk, L. A., Fronczek, J., & Abel, L. (1993). Emotions, defences, coping mechanisms, and symptoms. *Psychoanalytic Psychology, 10*, 237–260.

Griffin, W. A., & Gardner, W. (1989). Analysis of behavioral durations in observational studies of social interaction. *Psychological Bulletin, 106*, 497–502.

Hardy, G. E., Stiles, W. B., Barkham, M., & Startup, M. (1998). Therapist responsiveness to client interpersonal styles during time-limited treatments for depression. *Journal of Consulting and Clinical Psychology, 66*, 304–312.

Hayes, A. F., & Krippendorff, K. (2007). Answering the call for a standard reliability measure for coding data. *Communication Methods and Measures, 1*, 77–89.

Hoff, P. D. (2005). Bilinear mixed-effects models for dyadic data. *Journal of the American Statistical Association, 100*, 286–295.

Howe, G. W., Dagne, G., & Brown, C. H. (2005). Multilevel methods for modeling observed sequences of family interaction. *Journal of Family Psychology, 19*, 72–85.

Hox, J. J. (2002). *Multilevel analysis: Techniques and applications.* Mahwah, NJ: Lawrence Erlbaum.

Hsieh, H. F., & Shannon, S. E. (2005). Three approaches to qualitative content analysis. *Qualitative Health Research, 15,* 1277–1288.

Kenny, D. A., Kashy, D. A., & Cook, W. L. (2006). *Dyadic data analysis.* New York: Guilford Press.

Krippendorff, K. (2004). Measuring the reliability of qualitative text analysis data. *Quality and Quantity, 38,* 787–800.

Langewitz, W., Nübling, M., & Weber, H. (2003). A theory-based approach to analysing conversation sequences. *Epidemiologia e Psichiatria Sociale, 12,* 103–108.

Lapadat, J. C., & Lindsay, A. C. (1999). Transcription in research and practice: From standardization of technique to interpretative positioning. *Qualitative Inquiry, 5,* 64–86.

Leiva, F. M., Montori, F. J., & Martinez, T. L. (2006). Assessment of interjudge reliability in the open-ended questions coding process. *Quality and Quantity, 40,* 519–537.

Lombard, M., Snyder-Duch, J., & Bracken, C. C. (2002). Content analysis in mass communication: Assessment and reporting of intercoder reliability. *Human Communication Research, 28,* 587–604.

Magnusson, M. S. (2000). Discovering hidden time patterns in behavior: T-patterns and their detection. *Behavioral Research. Methods, Instruments and Computers, 32,* 93–110.

Margison, F. R., Barkham, M., Evans, C., McGrath, G., Clark, J. M., Audin, K., et al. (2000). Measurement and psychotherapy. Evidence-based practice and practice-based evidence. *British Journal of Psychiatry, 177,* 123–130.

Mayring, P. (2000). Qualitative content analysis [28 paragraphs]. *Forum Qualitative Sozialforschung/Forum: Qualitative Social Research* [On-line Journal], 1(2). Retrieved January 25, 2010 from http://qualitative-research.net/fqs/fqs-e/2-00inhalt-e.htm

Mazzi, M., Del Piccolo, L., & Zimmermann, C. (2003). Event-based categorical sequential analyses of the medical interview. A review. *Epidemiologia e Psichiatria Sociale, 12,* 81–85.

Morberg Pain, C., Chadwick, P., & Abba, N. (2008). Clients' experience of case formulation in cognitive behaviour therapy for psychosis. *British Journal of Clinical Psychology, 47,* 127–138.

Patton, M. Q. (2002). *Qualitative research and evaluation methods.* Thousand Oaks, CA: Sage Publications.

Putnam, S. M., & Stiles, W. B. (1993). Verbal exchange in medical interviews: Implications and innovation. *Social Science and Medicine, 36,* 1597–1604.

Quera, V., Bakeman, R., & Gnisci, A. (2007). Observer agreement for even sequences: Methods and software for sequences alignment and reliability estimates. *Behavior Research Methods, 39,* 39–49.

Reyes, L., Aristegui, R., Krause, M., Strasser, K., Tomicic, A., Valdes, N., et al. (2008). Language and therapeutic change: A speech acts analysis. *Psychotherapy Research, 18,* 355–362.

Rourke, L., & Anderson, T. (2004). Validity in the quantitative content analysis. *Educational Technology Research and Development, 52,* 5–18.

Sackett, G. P. (1979). The lag sequential analysis of contingency and cyclicity in behavioral interaction research. In J. D. Osofsky (Ed.), *Handbook of infant development.* Wiley: New York.

Schilling, J. (2006). On the pragmatics of qualitative assessments. Designing the process for content analysis. *European Journal of Psychological Assessment, 22,* 28–37.

Singer, J. B., & Willett, J. D. (2003). *Applied longitudinal data analysis: Modeling change and event occurrence.* New York: Oxford University Press.

Stiles, W. B., & Shapiro, D. A. (1995). Verbal exchange structure of brief psychodynamic–interpersonal and cognitive-behavioral psychotherapy. *Journal of Consulting and Clinical Psychology, 63,* 15–27.

Tasca, G. A., & Gallop, R. (2009). Multilevel modelling of longitudinal data for psychotherapy researchers: I. The basics. *Psychotherapy Research, 19,* 429–437.

Tasca, G. A., & Mc Mullen, L. (1992). Interpersonal complementarity and antithesis within a stage model of psychotherapy. *Psychotherapy, 29*, 515–523.

Tavaré, S., & Altham, P. M. (1983). Serial dependence of observations leading to contingency tables, and corrections to chi-squared statistics. *Biometrika, 70*, 1139–1144.

Tschacher, W., & Ramseyer, F. (2009). Modeling psychotherapy process by time-series panel analysis (TSPA). *Psychotherapy Research, 19*, 469–481.

Turkington, D., & Kingdon, D. (2000). Cognitive-behavioural techniques for general psychiatrists in the management of patients with psychoses. *British Journal of Psychiatry, 177*, 101–106.

Van-Beek, Y., de-Roos, B., Hoeksma, J. B., & Hopkins, B. (1992). Sequential analysis of nominal data in mother–infant communication: Quantifying dominance and bidirectionality. *Behaviour, 122*, 306–328.

Viney, L. L. (1994). Sequences of emotional distress expressed by clients and acknowledged by therapists: Are they associated more with some therapists than others? *British Journal of Clinical Psychology, 33*, 469–481.

Wasserman, R. H., Levy, K. N., & Loken, E. (2009). Generalizability theory in psychotherapy research: The impact of multiple sources of variances on the dependability of psychotherapy process ratings. *Psychotherapy Research, 19*, 397–408.

Wiseman, H., & Rice, L. N. (1989). Sequential analyses of therapist–client interaction during change events: A task-focused approach. *Journal of Consulting and Clinical Psychology, 57*, 281–286.

Yoder, P. J., Bruce, P., & Tapp, J. (2001). Comparing sequential associations within a single dyad. *Behavioral Research. Methods, Instruments and Computers, 33*, 331–338.

Zimmermann, C., Del Piccolo, L., & Mazzi, M. A. (2003). Patient cues and medical interviewing in general practice. Examples of the application of sequential analysis. *Epidemiologia e Psichiatria Sociale, 12*, 115–123.

Chapter 11
Qualitative Methods for the Analysis of Verbal Interactions in Psychotherapy

Rolf Wynn and Svein Bergvik

11.1 Overview of Chapter

In this chapter, we will discuss qualitative research methodology and qualitative research in general and present some examples of how different qualitative methods play a part in research on psychotherapy. Furthermore, we will discuss how one method—Conversation Analysis—can fruitfully be used to study verbal interactions in psychotherapy.

11.2 Introduction

11.2.1 Qualitative Studies of Psychotherapy

While qualitative research has its strongest position within the social sciences and humanistic fields of research, there is also a long-standing tradition of qualitative research within psychology and psychiatry. For instance, Freud developed many of his theories drawing from clinical cases with just a few patients (Jones 1961). Lately, qualitative research methods have strengthened their position also within medicine, psychology, and psychiatry (Malterud 2001a; Quirk and Lelliot 2001; Baier 1995; Schulze and Angermeyer 2003).

Research on various aspects of provider–patient interactions is a large and growing field (Wynn 1995; McLeod 2001). A range of different methods and approaches have been used. Some focus on describing the interactions, while other studies result in suggestions about how to improve interactional strategies, the content of interactions, or training procedures. While most studies on this topic have probably been quantitative, quite a few have been qualitative or mixed. It is possible to distinguish between studies that focus on the content of the

R. Wynn (✉)
Institute of Clinical Medicine (FT), University of Tromsø, Tromsø, Norway
e-mail: rolf.wynn@gmail.com

M. Rimondini (ed.), *Communication in Cognitive Behavioral Therapy*,
DOI 10.1007/978-1-4419-6807-4_11, © Springer Science+Business Media, LLC 2011

interaction itself, such as how questions are posed or how information is conveyed, and studies that are concerned with how aspects of the interactions may be related to the outcome of the interactions, such as satisfaction or improvements in treatment outcomes. Many different topics lend themselves to research on psychotherapeutic interactions. The choice of topic and variables reflect the researcher's theoretical position (Roter et al. 1995; Wynn 1995). While clinicians may be concerned with which interactional techniques may function and which may not, linguists may be more concerned about linguistic phenomena, and sociologists about the distribution of interactional power (Palmer 2000). We will discuss a small selection of qualitative studies on psychotherapeutic interactions ahead.

It has been suggested that qualitative research is particularly well suited for studying clinical practice. Silverstein et al. (2006) point out that qualitative research methods have a strong focus on language and provide rich descriptions of subjective experience, and thus have some important similarities to clinical interviews or psychotherapy sessions. Drawing on a combination of inductive and deductive interpretations illuminates the complexity of psychological phenomena with multiple interrelated variables. Both the qualitative researcher and the psychotherapist typically take an exploratory approach to phenomena as they are expressed by the research subject or patient. Moreover, the qualitative paradigm requires that the researcher adopt a self-reflective attitude, comparable to how therapists often attend to transference and countertransference phenomena in clinical practice (cf. Silverstein et al. 2006).

Malterud (2001a) takes this notion a step further, arguing that qualitative research is particularly useful for investigating and communicating clinical knowledge and experience. She refers to studies showing that even though evidence-based medicine is widely accepted, clinical decisions are rarely based solely on randomized controlled experiments. This can hardly be explained just as a result of neglect or unprofessional behavior by clinicians. Rather, it may reflect what often is referred to as tacit knowledge or clinical intuition, which is a valuable form of clinical knowledge held and applied by proficient practitioners, acquired through experience, but difficult to study by quantitative methods. If we acknowledge that phenomena such as clinicians' tacit knowledge are important factors in therapy, they should indeed be investigated, shared, and contested. Malterud (2001a) and Silverstein et al. (2006) hold that a qualitative research approach is particularly useful for studying such phenomena in clinical practice. Silverstein et al. (2006) argue that qualitative research has the potential to strengthen clinical practice by describing and explaining such experience-based knowledge and how it is acted out in provider–patient interactions in clinical practice.

11.2.2   Qualitative vs. Quantitative Methodology

Although there clearly are quite a few differences between qualitative and quantitative methodologies, a qualitative researcher working on a project must deal with similar phases in his or her research as does a quantitative researcher: defining a research question and a theoretical frame of reference, selecting the study's design and method, finding an appropriate sample, collecting the data, analyzing the data, and writing up and publishing the study (see also Chapter 10).

What is qualitative research and how is it different from quantitative research? Qualitative research may be used to generate new ideas, new knowledge, new understandings, or new theories. The description and analysis of characteristics of phenomena are the central tasks of qualitative research. While quantitative research methods are used to test hypotheses, qualitative methods are used to explore the details of a phenomenon or to paint a broader picture. In fact, qualitative methods are particularly well suited for the description of psychological and interactional phenomena, including the description and analysis of perceptions, experiences, and values (Smith 2008; Malterud 2001a, b; McLeod 2001).

Thus, there are both similarities and differences between qualitative and quantitative approaches. For instance, while a quantitative study demands a random sample in order to fulfill one of the criteria for statistical representativity (external validity), qualitative studies typically have strategic and nonrandom samples. In a qualitative study, the sample is selected by the researcher with the purpose of obtaining the data that he or she deems useful. Quantitative studies follow specific designs and procedures for analysis, as is the case for qualitative studies. For instance, qualitative studies of psychotherapeutic interactions can be based on in-depth interviews of the participants, focusing on particular aspects that are not so easily observed in the interactions, such as intentions, feelings, and interpretations. The interviews follow a preplanned procedure and the analysis may follow one of a range of different methods, including grounded theory and phenomenological analysis (Kvale 1996; Knox and Burkard 2009). Although both quantitative and qualitative researchers have their specific procedures, it is also possible to mix quantitative and qualitative methods in one study, in order to approach the data from different perspectives and gain a fuller understanding of the phenomena being studied (Wynn et al. 2008). In the following, we will give examples of qualitative methods that have been used and results from some relevant studies.

11.3   Examples of Qualitative Methods Used to Analyze Psychotherapeutic Interactions

11.3.1   Clinical Case Studies

Clinical case studies have been widely used in medicine and perhaps particularly so in psychiatry. The many classical patient stories in Freud's writing follow this long tradition (Jones 1961). Clinical case studies typically present the case of a single patient, provide information about the patient's medical history, and describe the treatment and how the healing process has evolved. Even though clinical case studies may have a strong focus on medical aspects, such as symptom descriptions and treatment procedures, they often include psychosocial dimensions and the implications of the illness and treatment on the patient's everyday life. Some clinical case studies also describe and reflect on details of the relational aspects of the treatment, such as the verbal interaction between the provider and the patient.

In her work on clinical case studies as a literature genre, Wells (2003) describes how Freud used the case study method in his many patient stories. For instance, in "Notes upon a case of obsessional neurosis" (the "Rat Man" case) from 1909, Freud gives a detailed account of the first treatment session with the patient, articulating the wording of both the patient and the therapist. Although it has been argued that the therapist–patient dialogues in Freud's classical case studies should be perceived primarily as a genre technique to illustrate his theoretical ideas (Wells 2003), Freud's writing provides examples of a qualitative approach to clinical phenomena, including the dynamics of provider–patient relationships and interactions. Importantly, central aspects of his theories such as transference and countertransference are described and explained using case stories from his patients (Jones 1961).

A thorough study of the verbal interactions occurring in one or a few cases may provide an opportunity to relate details or patterns of how the provider–patient interaction evolves with the individual and contextual aspects relevant to this particular patient and this provider. Thus, case studies may profitably combine the analysis of excerpts of provider–patient dialogues with a more general case study approach.

11.3.2 Qualitative Interviews

The qualitative interview is one of the most central methods for data collection in qualitative research. Qualitative interviews typically differ from more structured interviews in that the researcher does not have a detailed guide for the interview, but he or she, when necessary, draws on a few key questions that were prepared before the interview (Kvale 1996; Smith 2008; Knox and Burkard 2009). Interviews are typically used to draw attention to the informant's experiences with a specific topic. Interviews can be with one informant or with a group of informants.

The qualitative interview is a well-known and widely used method in studies of health and medicine (Kvale 1996; Malterud 2001a, b; Smith 2008). Patients' experiences, emotional reactions, knowledge, understanding of illness and treatment, and satisfaction with treatment are among the topics studied through qualitative interviews. Qualitative interviews are also used to study patients' and providers' experiences with communication in healthcare settings in general as well as in psychotherapy (Wynn et al. 2009b; Littauer et al. 2005).

For instance, Messari and Hallam (2003) used a qualitative approach in their study of patient experiences with cognitive-behavioral therapy for psychosis. They used a discourse-analytic framework to explore how patients represented what happened in therapy. In the interviews, patients were asked about their meetings with the therapist and asked to reflect on the process of their therapy both from their own and from the therapist's viewpoint. The interviews were audiotaped and transcribed. The results provided interesting insights into how the patients perceived therapy and their own and their therapist's role. Messari and Hallam (2003) also described how patients felt that the therapeutic processes and relationships affected their own perceptions of their psychotic experiences.

At the University Hospital of Northern Norway, we have used qualitative interviews to study coronary disease patients' experiences of their hospital treatment. In one study, patients were interviewed while they were hospitalized (Bergvik et al. 2010), while in another study they were interviewed 12 months following discharge (Bäckström et al. 2006). The patients' perceptions and experiences related to their interactions with the health providers at the hospital were among the main topics in these studies. While the patients in both studies felt that the surgeons made it a priority to provide detailed information about the illness and to explain treatment procedures prior to surgery, many expressed dissatisfaction with the lack of information given by the surgeons after their surgery. Thus, the studies provided knowledge about how to improve patient information in the various stages of hospitalization.

In a different project, concerning video-mediated psychotherapy supervision (Bergvik 1997; Gammon et al. 1998; Sørlie et al. 1999), we applied both quantitative and qualitative methods. The purpose was to get a better understanding of how communication and interaction in psychotherapy supervision were affected by being mediated through videoconferencing technology. Data included video recordings of the supervision sessions, questionnaires, as well as qualitative interviews with participants. Although the questionnaire study (Sørlie et al. 1999) suggested that the quality of the supervision could be satisfactorily maintained through videoconferencing, the three studies combined provided some interesting results. The quantitative analysis of the frequency and duration of verbal and nonverbal behavior observed in the video recordings revealed a lower frequency of back-channeling (listener activity), with the risk of disrupting the flow of communication. Furthermore, the qualitative interviews revealed that the participants had some concerns related to reduced nonverbal cues, resulting in reduced spontaneity, reduced social and emotional presence, and reluctance in the expression of personal emotional material. The use of multiple research methods in this project may serve as an example of how different methods may be combined beneficially.

Participant observation (ethnographic method) is a method typically associated with social anthropology, but the method may also be used by other qualitative researchers. Its strength is that it gives an insider perspective of the phenomena being studied (Drennan and Swartz 2002). Observational studies are another important area of qualitative studies. These are often based on recordings (audio or video) of interactions or the phenomena that are being studied. In these approaches, the researcher has—more or less—an outsider's perspective to the phenomena being analyzed. A range of more or less related methods can be used to analyze observational data. In the next section, we will discuss in more detail one method for conducting observational studies, namely, Conversation Analysis.

11.4 Conversation Analysis

11.4.1 The Method of Conversation Analysis

Conversation Analysis (CA) is one type of method used for the detailed analysis of interactions in general and, in this context, for the analysis of psychotherapeutic sessions. CA is used to qualitatively and systematically approach and analyze talk that occurs in different types of interactions. Conversation analysts assume that specific conventions or rules help people in organizing talk and in securing efficient communication. People who communicate in different settings may not be able to verbalize the rules that apply to the context, but they nevertheless make full use of these rules in order to produce their own interactional contributions and in order to understand how other people communicate in that particular setting (Sacks et al. 1974; Hutchby and Woofitt 1998). Conversation analysts attempt to describe and understand the rules that apply in different interactional circumstances (Heritage 1984). Interactions may be broken down into different types of sequences, which follow specific rules and by which specific types of communication are accomplished. Examples of different types of sequences are greetings, telling a story, introducing a difficult topic, giving an explanation, and delivering bad news (Heritage 1988; Maynard 1989; Hutchby and Woofitt 1998). In addition to more general conversational sequences, specific types of sequences are likely to occur in psychotherapeutic interactions. The characterization of such sequences and the conventions or rules that govern them is an important goal for conversation analysts working to understand communication in this setting. As will be discussed further, the analysis is based on relatively detailed transcriptions of interactions. Of particular interest is how the interactants react and respond to each other's talk, as these reactions reflect their understanding of the meaning of the preceding talk. It is exactly this interplay between the interactants that allows conversation analysts to observe and characterize the conventions or rules that apply (Heritage 1988; Hutchby and Drew 1995; Peräkylä 1997).

11.4.2 CA and the Analysis of Consultations and Psychotherapy

In the last two decades, the number of studies using CA that have been carried out on provider–patient consultations has increased (West and Frankel 1991; Beach 1995; Wynn 1995, 1999; Drew et al. 2001; Drew and Heritage 1992; Heritage and Maynard 2006; Peräkylä 1995, 1997). Many studies using CA of interactions occurring within the realms of mental health services and with respect to different practices within psychotherapy and counseling have also been carried out (Barnes and Moss 2007; Forrester and Reason 2006; Wynn 2000; Wynn and Wynn 2006; Peräkylä 2005; McCabe et al. 2002, 2004; Peräkylä et al. 2008; Madill et al. 2001;

Bergmann 1992; Palmer 2000; Antaki et al. 2004, 2005; Leudar et al. 2006; Wynn et al. 2009a).

Topics that have been addressed with the method of CA are, among others, how to communicate a feeling (Barnes and Moss 2007), how empathy is conveyed in eclectic psychotherapy (Wynn and Wynn 2006), patients' responses to psychoanalytic interpretations (Peräkylä 2005), the engagement of patients suffering from psychosis in the consultation (McCabe et al. 2002), discretion in psychiatric interactions (Bergmann 1992), how symptoms can be identified as psychotic (Palmer 2000), functions of exaggerations in psychotherapy (Wynn et al. 2009a), whether patients with schizophrenia display Theory of Mind skills in CBT consultations (McCabe et al. 2004), diagnostic formulation and negotiation in CBT (Antaki et al. 2004, 2005), and therapists' self-disclosure in psychotherapy sessions (Leudar et al. 2006).

11.4.3 Research Procedures in CA

Although CA is primarily a method for the qualitative analysis of interactions, it is possible to adapt the method for quantitative analysis or use CA in a mixed-methods approach (Wynn et al. 2008; Wynn 1995, 1999). However, in the following, we will consider CA only as a qualitative method.

Typically, in CA, data sampling is strategic. Although it is, of course, possible to use data that are sampled statistically (e.g., consultations), there is usually little point in carrying out statistical sampling when the other parts of the research are qualitative and when it is difficult to make statistical claims based on CA research procedures as they are usually carried out.

Most CA studies are done with relatively small samples, ranging from a few interactions to around 50. When studying psychotherapy consultations, a sample of 20–40 interactions should be sufficient in order to identify recurring phenomena as well as phenomena that are more unique (West 1984; Wynn 1999; McCabe et al. 2002).

Recruitment can be practically carried out by having therapists record their own interactions with patients. Thus, the researcher must initially recruit therapists. Those who are willing to participate ask a selection of their own patients if they want to participate. If the aim is 30 consultations, six therapists can recruit five patients each, for example.

For studies based on CA, there is a choice between recording data (consultations) on video or on audio only. Video is often used, as it gives more contextual information, including nonverbal communication. Many therapists are already acquainted with video recording and have recorded many of their sessions for training purposes. However, if the researcher does not plan to use the visual information in the analysis (i.e., systematically analyze nonverbal elements of the interactions), it may be just as well to rely on audio recordings.

Table 11.1 Example of transcription system in CA

Utterance ends with question mark.	Question-like intonation of an utterance (usually, but not always, a rising intonation)
(Ha-ha)	Laughing.
(4)	Pauses lasting 1 s or more are denoted by numbers in parentheses.
P: He T: Really	Turn shifts are marked by line shifts.
[	Simultaneous talk begins.
]	Simultaneous talk stops.
(anonymous)	Sensitive information should be deleted.
. . .	Untimed pause, less than 1 s.
<u>Why</u>	Emphasis is marked by the underlining of words.
HELLO	Loudness is signaled with capital letters.
(text omitted)	Text may be omitted to save place, if of less relevance to present discussion.
Italics	Italics are used to mark text of central relevance.

In CA, the audio and video recordings are transcribed in detail. This may be done with the entirety of the interactions or with selected segments. Typically, a transcriptional system based on that of Jefferson (Jefferson 1984; Wynn 1999) is used. A detailed transcription allows for the rendering of important elements of the interactions, such as pauses, overlaps, intonation, and tempo (Sacks et al. 1974) (Table 11.1).

11.4.4 Data Analysis in CA

A central point in CA is to examine how people interact through the production and coordination of their interactional contributions (Sacks et al. 1974; Ten Have 1999). CA may be used to study "larger" interactional phenomena as well as "smaller" interactional phenomena. By "larger," we are referring to complex phenomena that involve a range of subelements, such as power, interactional asymmetry, patient-centeredness, and sensitivity. By "smaller," we are referring to more delineated interactional phenomena, such as how to convey bad news, how to convey a feeling, and how to communicate empathy. Next, we will give some examples of how a researcher can proceed in order to study certain of the phenomena mentioned here.

First, let us look at patient-centeredness. Studies have shown that ordinary doctor–patient consultations are organized in phases (Byrne and Long 1976) and typically follow a pattern where the doctor poses questions and the patient responds (West 1984; Frankel 1990; Beach 1995). When the patient, on his or her own initiative, deviates from this pattern, interactional problems may occur (West 1984; West and Frankel 1991; Wynn 1999). Surprisingly, despite studies that have shown that both patients and doctors benefit from conducting patient-centered consultations, many consultations are not patient-centered (Wynn 1999; Little et al. 2001). Although most studies of patient-centeredness have been carried out in general practice, the topic is also relevant for the analysis of psychotherapy sessions. For instance, we do not know how patient-centered CBT sessions with different patient groups tend to be and what the consequences of a possible lack of patient-centeredness are in these types of consultations. Are sessions with seriously ill patients more doctor-centered than other sessions? Through a detailed analysis of the interactants' contributions, for instance, the choice of topics, questions, responses, and interruptions, one may study in more detail phenomena such as interactional control and patient-centeredness (Frankel 1990; Wynn 1995; Drew et al. 2001). In order to study these issues, questions that can be asked are, for instance,

- Who controls the interaction?
- To what degree is the interaction based on the patient's expressed needs?
- To what degree do the therapists succeed in including the patients' own topics and views in the session and in the decision making?
- How do they accomplish this in practice?

(cf. Antaki et al. 2004, 2005). These questions can be operationalized, for instance, by studying who initiates the topics of the sessions, who changes the topics, who poses the questions, what types of questions are posed, whether the therapists respond to the patients' questions, and whether interruptions occur.

Another "larger" topic is that of sensitivity. Prior research of doctor–patient interactions has shown that certain topics in consultations are sensitive. That is, when these topics come up in the interactions, interactional problems may occur, often in the shape of stuttering, lengthy pauses, laughter, and a rapid change of topic (Jefferson 1984; Wynn 1999; Haakana 2001; Silverman and Peräkylä 1990). Sensitive topics are often not given the attention they deserve in the interactions. Examples of sensitive topics in somatic consultations are talk about venereal disease, HIV/AIDS, and smoking (Silverman and Peräkylä 1990; Larsson et al. 1994; Wynn 1999). One study has shown that disagreement about the meaning of delusions can be one sensitive topic in psychiatrist–patient interactions (McCabe et al. 2002), and it is not unlikely that there are other sensitive topics, especially in this type of interaction. One topic of particular interest is if the alliance is considered so important in therapeutic interactions that disagreement, conflict, and confrontation are avoided as much as possible. When studying the issue of sensitivity in therapeutic interactions, the researcher can focus on whether certain topics are marked as sensitive by stuttering, lengthy pauses, laughter, and rapid topic shifts.

When the researcher has decided what to look for in the consultations, the next step is to review all the transcriptions and recordings in detail, in order to identify the sequences where the elements being studied are a direct or indirect issue. These sequences are then compared and contrasted to each other in order to describe similarities and differences. In the next section, we will present an example of how a "smaller" interactional phenomenon occurring in psychotherapeutic interactions can be analyzed.

11.4.5   Example of Analysis in CA

Drawing inspiration from clinical observations of patients who tended to exaggerate in various manners, we decided to look at the function of patients' exaggerations in psychotherapeutic sessions (Wynn et al. 2009a). Following a purposive sampling of 15 consultations between patients suffering from psychotic disorders and their therapists, all the interactions were transcribed in detail according to a simplified version of Jefferson's system (Jefferson 1984). For the purpose of comparison, we also collected exaggerations from ordinary, everyday conversations. In a next step, we screened all the transcriptions in order to identify instances of exaggerations. We then compared and contrasted the exaggerations to each other in order to identify common features and differences; see Excerpts 1 and 2 below.

Excerpt 1

1. A: I'm so hungry I could eat a horse.
2. B: Me too.

Excerpt 2 (From Wynn et al. 2009a)

1. Patient: He is responsible for the 40 properties I am redoing downtown.
2. Psychiatrist: I think it would be a good thing if you could sort of leave some tasks ...

Excerpt 1 is hyperbole (deliberate exaggeration for emphasis or effect) from ordinary conversation, while Excerpt 2 is an exaggeration from a consultation between a patient suffering from psychosis and a psychiatrist. By looking at these two examples, we see that the exaggerations function differently in the two excerpts. The hyperbole in Excerpt 1 is received by B as an unproblematic exaggeration used as a figure of speech (signaled through his response to A), while the exaggeration by the patient in Excerpt 2 appears to be taken more literally. The psychiatrist does not display an understanding of the patient's exaggeration as a figure of speech, and responds to the exaggeration by signaling that the exaggeration is problematic. In our analysis, following a process where the various instances of exaggerations were compared, we tried to describe how the exaggerations used in ordinary conversation and those used in the consultations differed. We found that they could not be distinguished by the likelihood of the exaggerations' claims. It is quite unlikely that the patient is redoing 40 properties (Excerpt 2), just as it is quite unlikely that A (Excerpt 1) will eat a horse. Drawing on our observations, we arrived at the hypothesis that the difference between the exaggerations in the two types of interactions may be characterized by examining how the exaggerations are received. While exaggerations from ordinary conversation (i.e., hyperbole) are seen as figures of speech and responded to accordingly, exaggerations from consultations are responded to in such a way that we are led to think that psychiatrists think the patients actually believe in the content of the exaggerations (Wynn et al. 2009a). In CA studies, as in many other types of qualitative studies, the findings are presented and discussed by depicting examples or quotations, as we have shown above. Chapter 6 also offers an example of CA's application in psychotherapy.

11.4.6   Some Limitations of CA

CA has a range of limitations. It is clearly difficult to make sustainable claims about how elements in the interactions are related to specific outcomes of the interactions, such as therapeutic success and patient satisfaction. Moreover, CA is well suited for studying larger or smaller conversational phenomena, but the focus on detail makes the method less suited for giving a global analysis of interactions. CA analyses are usually based on transcriptions, and although these may be quite detailed, they necessarily constitute a simplification of the complex processes that occur in the interactions. While different methods of data gathering, such as questionnaires and interviews, may give access to the interactants' intentions, in CA, the intentions of the interactants are only evident as revealed through verbal and nonverbal behavior.

11.5   Quality Standards in Qualitative Research

In an editorial in the journal *Patient Education and Counseling*, Finset (2008) argues that studies on clinical communication based on qualitative methods provide important knowledge to the field. Finset (2008) addresses the issue of general criteria for manuscripts using qualitative research methods. In particular, he believes it is important that the procedures for data collection and data analysis are specified in detail, that data collection should reach the criterion of saturation of themes (a stage in data collection where no additional themes appear), and "thick" data (rich and detailed descriptions) should be provided within the limited space of the publication. Thus, the editorial addresses the common misunderstanding that qualitative research has less rigorous standards than quantitative methods.

Giacomini and Cook (2000a, b) have provided some guidance for how to assess and ensure scientific quality in research based on qualitative methods. They hold validity and relevance to be critical for research quality. As an alternative to the term "validity," which has specific definitions within the realm of quantitative research, qualitative researchers have suggested alternative terms such as "credibility." Judgment of the credibility of qualitative research studies involves a critical appraisal of the studies' design and analysis. Important questions to be asked include the following two: Was the study designed to address its research questions and objectives appropriately? Was it conducted rigorously enough to achieve its empirical aims? As with quantitative research, a precondition for critical judgment of a study's quality is a sufficiently detailed description of all the steps of the research process, including the aims of the study, the selection of subjects, the data collection procedures, and the analysis of the data (Giacomini and Cook 2000a). The question of "relevance" relates to how well the results of the study provide knowledge the readers can apply in their own settings. This depends partly on the quality of the data collection (e.g., the quality of the interview, the observations) and partly on how well the results are communicated to the reader. Examples of questions to be asked by a reader concerning the relevance of a study of clinical interaction include how do the results of this study help me care for my patients? Does it help me to understand the context of my practice, or my relationship with my patients? (Giacomini and Cook 2000b).

Malterud (2001a, b) addresses the topic of qualitative research in two articles in *The Lancet*. She argues that qualitative and quantitative methods should be seen as complementary rather than incompatible methods. Furthermore, although the procedures for data analysis are different, the underlying principles are comparable, and both quantitative and qualitative methods should be guided by quality standards. Malterud (2001a, b) agrees with Giacomini et al. (2000a,b) but suggests "reflexivity" as an equally important criterion in an overall standard for qualitative studies. Malterud (2001a) argues that contemporary knowledge disputes the positivistic ideal of the objective and neutral researcher, and instead acknowledges the importance of the researcher's position and perspective. Rather than striving for objectivity, the researcher should focus on, assess, and discuss the effects the researcher's position and perspective may have had on the results. Thus, discussing the researcher's impact on the construction of knowledge at every step of the research process may be considered a central criterion for ensuring quality in (qualitative) research.

In sum, we have argued against the often-held misconception that qualitative methods are less systematic and rigorous than quantitative methods (cf. Patton 1980). Although the nature of the scientific approach and the techniques and procedures of qualitative methods typically differ from those of quantitative methods, qualitative methods represent systematic scientific inquiries that should follow specific guidelines and standards. Furthermore, we have argued that qualitative methods are particularly well suited for the study of clinical interactions and may provide knowledge about aspects of clinical interactions that are not available through quantitative methods.

11.6   Conclusions

Qualitative studies are particularly well suited for the in-depth study of phenomena that have been less studied and are well suited to generate new ideas and new hypotheses about phenomena. For the investigation of psychotherapeutic interactions, qualitative methods that have been used include case studies, i.e., therapist's rendering of the interactions, qualitative interviews of patients and therapists, and different methods for the analysis of observed or recorded interactions, such as Conversation Analysis. All these methods are well suited for different purposes and goals. Case studies can be used to offer the therapist's observations and point of view relating to one interaction or the comprehensive treatment of one particular patient. Interviews may shed light on elements of the interactions that do not necessarily lend themselves to direct observation, such as the participants' feelings and intentions, while observational methods such as CA may be used to study smaller or larger recurring interactional phenomena in detail. Qualitative methods play an increasingly important part in research on communication between providers and patients. Also, with regard to the analysis of psychotherapeutic interactions, more studies are being conducted that draw on qualitative methods. Qualitative methods supplement and complement quantitative methods and can play an even more important part in efforts to characterize and understand communication in psychotherapy.

References

Antaki, C., Barnes, R., & Leudar, I. (2004). Trouble in agreeing on a client's problem in a cognitive-behavioural therapy session. *Rivista di Psicolinguistica Applicata, 4*, 127–138.

Antaki, C., Barnes, R., & Leudar, I. (2005). Diagnostic formulations in psychotherapy. *Discourse Studies, 7*, 627–647.

Bäckström, S., Wynn, R., & Sorlie, T. (2006). Coronary bypass surgery patients' experiences with treatment and perioperative care – A qualitative interview-based study. *Journal of Nursing Management, 14*, 140–147.

Baier, M. (1995). Uncertainty of illness for persons with schizophrenia. *Issues in Mental Health Nursing, 16*, 201–212.

Barnes, R., & Moss, D. (2007). Communicating a feeling. *Discourse Studies, 9*, 123–148.

Beach, W. A. (1995). Preserving and constraining options: "Okays" and "official" priorities in medical interviews. In G. H. Morris & R. J. Chenail (Eds.), *The talk of the clinic* (pp. 259–289). Hillsdale, NJ: Lawrence Erlbaum Associates.

Bergmann, J. (1992). Veiled morality: Notes on discretion in psychiatry. In P. Drew & J. Heritage (Eds.), *Talk at work* (pp. 137–162). Cambridge: Cambridge University Press.

Bergvik, S. (1997). *Communicative behavior in video mediated communication. A descriptive field study comparing video mediated and face-to-face communication on turn-taking, listener response and gestures in dyadic psychotherapy supervision.* Thesis for the professional degree of psychology. Tromsø, Norway: University of Tromsø.

Bergvik, S., Sørlie, T. & Wynn, R. (2010). Approach and avoidance coping and regulatory focus in patients having coronary artery bypass surgery. *Journal of Health Psychology, 15*, 915–924.

Byrne, P. S., & Long, B. E. L. (1976). *Doctors talking to patients.* London: HMSO.

Drennan, G., & Swartz, L. (2002). The paradoxical use of interpreting in psychiatry. *Social Science and Medicine, 54*, 1853–1866.

Drew, P., Chatwin, J., & Collins, S. (2001). Conversation analysis: A method for research into interactions between patients and healthcare professionals. *Health Expectations, 4*, 58–70.

Drew, P., & Heritage, J. (1992). Analyzing talk at work: An introduction. In P. Drew & J. Heritage (Eds.), *Talk at work: Interaction in institutional settings* (pp. 3–65). Cambridge: Cambridge University Press.

Finset, A. (2008). Qualitative methods in communication and patient education research. *Patient Education and Counseling, 73*, 1–2.

Forrester, M., & Reason, D. (2006). Conversation analysis and psychoanalytic psychotherapy research: Questions, issues, problems and challenges. *Psychoanalytic Psychotherapy, 20*, 40–64.

Frankel, R. M. (1990). Talking in interviews: A dispreference for patient-initiated questions in physician–patient encounters. In G. Psathas (Ed.), *Interaction competence* (pp. 231–262). Washington, DC: University Press of America.

Gammon, D., Sørlie, T., Bergvik, S., & Høifødt, T. S. (1998). Psychotherapy supervision conducted via videoconferencing. A qualitative study of user experiences. *Nordic Journal of Psychiatry, 52*, 411–421.

Giacomini, M. K., & Cook, D. J. (2000a). User's guide to the medical literature. XXIII. Qualitative research in health care A. Are the results of the study valid? *Journal of the American Medical Association, 284*, 357–362.

Giacomini, M. K., & Cook, D. J. (2000b). User's guide to the medical literature. XXIII. Qualitative research in health care B. What are the results and how do they help me care for my patients? *Journal of the American Medical Association, 284*, 478–482.

Haakana, M. (2001). Laughter as a patient's resource: Dealing with delicate aspects of medical interaction. *Text, 21*, 187–219.

Heritage, J. (1984). *Garfinkel and ethnomethodology*. Cambridge: Cambridge University Press.

Heritage, J. (1988). Explanations as accounts: A conversation analytic approach. In C. Antaki (Ed.), *Analysing everyday explanation: A casebook of methods* (pp. 127–144). London: Sage Publications.

Heritage, J., & Maynard, D. (2006). *Communication in medical care*. Cambridge: Cambridge University Press.

Hutchby, I., & Drew, P. (1995). Conversation analysis. In J. Verschueren, J. O. Östman, & J. Blommaert (Eds.), *Handbook of pragmatics (manual)* (pp. 182–189). Amsterdam/Philadelphia: John Benjamins.

Hutchby, I., & Woofitt, R. (1998). *Conversation analysis. Principles, practices and applications*. Cambridge: Polity Press.

Jefferson, G. (1984). On the organization of laughter in talk about troubles. In J. M. Atkinson & J. Heritage (Eds.), *Structures of social action*. Cambridge: Cambridge University Press.

Jones, E. (1961). *The life and work of Sigmund Freud*. Oxford: Basic Books.

Knox, S., & Burkard, A. W. (2009). Qualitative research interviews. *Psychotherapy Research, 19*(4–5), 566–575.

Kvale, S. (1996). *Interviews: An introduction to qualitative research*. London: Sage Publications.

Larsson, U. S., Johanson, M., & Svärdsudd, K. (1994). Sensitive patient–doctor communications relating to the breasts and prostate. *Journal of Cancer Education, 9*, 19–25.

Leudar, I., Antaki, C., & Barnes, R. K. (2006). When psychotherapists disclose personal information to their clients. *Communication & Medicine, 3*, 27–41.

Littauer, H., Sexton, H., & Wynn, R. (2005). Qualities patients wish for in their therapists. *Scandinavian Journal of Caring Sciences, 19*, 28–31.

Little, P., Everitt, H., Williamson, I., Warner, G., Moore, M., Gould, C., et al. (2001). Observational study of effect of patient centeredness and positive approach on outcomes of general practice consultation. *British Medical Journal, 323*, 908–911.

Madill, A., Widdicombe, S., & Barkham, M. (2001). The potential of conversation analysis for psychotherapy research. *Counseling Psychologist, 29*, 413–434.

Malterud, K. (2001a). The art and science of clinical knowledge: Evidence beyond measures and numbers. *Lancet, 358*, 397–400.

Malterud, K. (2001b). Qualitative research: Standards, challenges and guidelines. *Lancet, 358*, 483–488.

Maynard, D. W. (1989). Notes on the delivery and reception of diagnostic news regarding mental disabilities. In D. Helm, A. J. M. Anderson, & A. Rawells (Eds.), *The interactional order* (pp. 54–67). New York: Irvington.

McCabe, R., Heath, C., Burns, T., & Priebe, S. (2002). Engagement of patients with psychosis in the consultation: Conversation analytic study. *British Medical Journal, 325*, 1148–1151.

McCabe, R., Leudar, I., & Antaki, C. (2004). Do people with schizophrenia display theory of mind deficits in clinical interactions? *Psychological Medicine, 34*, 401–412.

McLeod, J. (2001). *Qualitative research in counselling and psychotherapy*. London: Sage Publications.

Messari, S., & Hallam, R. (2003). CBT for psychosis: A qualitative analysis of clients' experiences. *British Journal of Clinical Psychology, 42*, 171–188.

Palmer, D. (2000). Identifying delusional discourse: Issues of rationality, reality and power. *Sociology of Health and Illness, 22*, 661–678.

Patton, M. Q. (1980). *Qualitative evaluation methods*. Beverly Hills, CA: Sage Publications.

Peräkylä, A. (1995). *Institutional interaction and clinical practice*. Cambridge: Cambridge University Press.

Peräkylä, A. (1997). Reliability and validity in research based on tapes and transcriptions. In D. Silverman (Ed.), *Qualitative research* (pp. 201–220). London: Sage Publications.

Peräkylä, A. (2005). Patients' responses to interpretations: A dialogue between conversation analysis and psychoanalytic theory. *Communication & Medicine, 2*, 163–176.

Peräkylä, A., Antaki, C., Vehviläinen, S., & Leudar, I. (Eds.). (2008). *Conversation analysis and psychotherapy*. Cambridge: Cambridge University Press.

Quirk, A., & Lelliot, P. (2001). What do we know about life on acute psychiatric wards in the UK? *Social Science and Medicine, 53*, 1565–1574.

Roter, D. L., Hall, J. A., Kern, D. E., Barker, R., Cole, K. A., & Roca, R. P. (1995). Improving physicians' interviewing skills and reducing patients' emotional distress: A randomized clinical trial. *Archives of Internal Medicine, 155*, 1877–1884.

Sacks, H., Schegloff, E., & Jefferson, G. (1974). A simplest systematics for the organisation of turn-taking in conversation. *Language, 50*, 696–735.

Schulze, B., & Angermeyer, M. C. (2003). Subjective experiences of stigma. *Social Science and Medicine, 56*, 299–312.

Silverman, D., & Peräkylä, A. (1990). AIDS counselling: The interactional organisation of talk about "delicate" issues. *Sociology of Health and Illness, 12*, 293–318.

Silverstein, L. B., Auerbach, C. F., & Levant, R. F. (2006). Using qualitative research to strengthen clinical practice. *Professional Psychology, Research and Practice, 37*, 351–358.

Smith, J. A. (Ed.). (2008). *Qualitative psychology: A practical guide to research methods*. London: Sage Publications.

Sørlie, T., Gammon, D., Bergvik, S., & Sexton, H. (1999). Psychotherapy supervision face-to-face and by videoconferencing: A comparative study. *British Journal of Psychotherapy, 15*, 452–462.

Ten Have, P. (1999). *Doing conversation analysis: A practical guide*. London: Sage Publications.

Wells, S. (2003). Freud's Rat Man and the case study: Genre in three keys. *New Literary History, 34*, 353–366.

West, C. (1984). *Routine complications*. Bloomington, IN: Indiana University Press.

West, C., & Frankel, R. M. (1991). Miscommunication in medicine. In N. Coupland, H. Giles, & J. M. Wieman (Eds.), *"Miscommunication" and problematic talk* (pp. 166–194). Newbury Park, CA: Sage Publications.

Wynn, R. (1995). *The linguistics of doctor–patient interaction*. Oslo: Novus Press.

Wynn, R. (1999). *Provider–patient interaction*. Kristiansand, Norway: Norwegian Academic Press.

Wynn, R. (2000). *Incomprehensible language in psychiatric doctor-patient interaction*. Published abstract. 7th International Pragmatics Conference, Budapest, July 9–14, 2000.

Wynn, R., Bergvik, S., & Elvevåg, B. (2009a). Exaggerations in consultations between psychiatrists and patients suffering from psychotic disorders. *Communication & Medicine, 6*, 95–105.

Wynn, R., Karlsen, K., Lorntzsen, B., Bjerke, T., & Bergvik, S. H. (2009b). Users' and GPs causal attributions of illegal substance use: An explorative interview study. *Patient Education and Counseling, 76*, 227–232.

Wynn, R., Rimondini, M., & Bergvik, S. (2008). *Mixed methods in the analysis of therapist-patient interaction*. Presentation at the International Conference for Communication in Healthcare, Oslo, September 2–5, 2008.

Wynn, R., & Wynn, M. (2006). Empathy as an interactionally achieved phenomenon in psychiatric interactions. Some conversational resources. *Journal of Pragmatics, 38*, 1385–1397.

Index

A
Abel, L., 235
Ackerman, S.J., 9, 62, 67
Active listening, 35
Affective communication test (ACT), 112–113
Agras, W.S., 57
Albright, J., 120
Alliance ruptures
  communication failures, 64–65
  definition, 63–64
  patient-centered skills, 65–66
  patient-reported rupture, 64
  qualitative analysis, unrepaired
    rupture, 65
  repair interventions, 64
Ambady, N., 116
Anxiety disorders
  blame, 166–170
  compliant rescue, 164–166
  intrapsychic vicious cycles, 151
  patient–relative interaction, 165–166
  pat on the back, 157–158
  rational debating cycle, 160–162
  reassurance and acceptance
    clinical examples, 171–172
    disadvantages, 176–178
    ineffectiveness of, 173–176
    relinquishment attempts, 178–181
    strategy of, 173
  solution prompter, 162–164
  threat acceptance, 173
  vicious cycles, 151–157
  white lie, 158–160
Arar, H.N., 118
Argyle, M., 2
Arnow, B.A., 57

Assessment stage
data-gathering process
  aims and contents, 30–33
  communication skills, 33–41
  setting and barriers, 30
doctor–patient communication
  research findings, 28–29
  theoretical background, 26–28
structuring the interview
  assessment phase, 41–42
  communication skills, 44–47
  goals, 43–44
Atwell, C., 77
Auerbach, C.F., 250

B
Bachelor, A., 60
Bahrs, O., 27
Bakeman, R., 241
Baldini, F., 129
Baldwin, S.A., 57
Bänninger-Huber, E., 120
Bara, B., 2
Barber, J.P., 57
Barcaccia, B., 149
Barker, M., 114
Barrowclough, C., 190
Bebbington, P., 191
Beck, A.T., 17, 65, 120, 130
Beck, S., 9
Beebe, B., 108
Beltz, J., 191
Benecke, C., 120
Bennett-Levy, J., 205
Bensing, J.M., 114
Berger, C., 3

M. Rimondini (ed.), *Communication in Cognitive Behavioral Therapy*,
DOI 10.1007/978-1-4419-6807-4, © Springer Science+Business Media, LLC 2011